*Untersuchungen
zur deutschen
Literaturgeschichte
Band 117*

Jeffrey L. Sammons

Friedrich Spielhagen

Novelist of Germany's False Dawn

Max Niemeyer Verlag
Tübingen 2004

Bibliografische Information der Deutschen Bibliothek

Die Deutsche Bibliothek verzeichnet diese Publikation in der Deutschen National-
bibliografie; detaillierte bibliografische Daten sind im Internet über *http://dnb.ddb.de*
abrufbar.

ISBN 3-484-32117-2 ISSN 0083-4564

Satz: Johanna Boy, Brennberg
Druck: Gulde-Druck, Tübingen
Einband: Industriebuchbinderei Nädele, Nehren

Contents

III After the Dawn: Spielhagen in the Reich

Fabrice essayait en vain de lui suggérer que l'art ne consiste nullement à copier la nature, laquelle est par elle-même inerte et stupide, mais à refléter sur elle l'idée qu'elle dégage dans notre intelligence, et à lui prêter un peu de l'âme que nous avons et qu'elle n'a pas.

Octave Feuillet, *Honneur d'artiste*

Mais c'est là un rêve du poëte, une de ces rencontres comme la vie n'en sait pas inventer. Elle est bien trop cruelle, la dure vie! et quand pour sauver une existence il faudrait quelquefois si peu de chose, elle se garde bien de fournir ce peu de chose-là. Voilà pourquoi les romans vrais sont toujours si tristes.

Alphonse Daudet, *Fromont jeune et Risler aîné*

Denn es möchte dann wohl geschehen, daß besonders ästhetisch-kritisch gestimmte Geister, die der Autor etwa vielfach im einzelnen durch nicht völlig durchgebildete Form abgestoßen hat oder die wohl gar ein ganzes Werk künstlerisch verfehlt erachten, zuletzt doch von der Harmonie erfüllt werden, zu welcher sich der Mann in Geist und Gemüth durchgerungen und in der jene einzelnen Mißklänge wie Tropfen am Eimer sind. Und ebenso, daß Leser, die in erster Linie ihr Gemüth angeregt und befriedigt sehen wollen und hier und da mit dem Autor nicht fühlen konnten, ihn hier zu hart, dort zu weich und ein anderes Mal verschwommen fanden, allmählich doch dahinter kommen, welch ein reiches, großes Herz in der Brust des Mannes schlug, und sich nicht entbrechen können, ihn zu lieben, der die Menschen so sehr geliebt.

Friedrich Spielhagen, »Berthold Auerbach«

And we have to remind ourselves that it is necessary to approach every writer differently in order to get from him all he can give us.

Virginia Woolf, »How Should One Read a Book?«

Acknowledgments

Among those who have been helpful to me I should like to thank particularly Professor Dirk Göttsche, University of Nottingham; Professor Hartmut Steinecke, University of Paderborn; Professor Hartmut Keil and his assistant Anja Becker of the Department of American Studies, University of Leipzig; Professors John M. Merriman and Henry A. Turner, Department of History, and Paul Fry, Department of English, Yale University; Patricia Willis, Curator of the American Literature Collection, Beinecke Rare Book and Manuscript Library, and the staff of the Interlibrary Loan Department, Sterling Memorial Library, Yale; N. Sue Hanson, Head of Special Collections, Case-Western Reserve University Library; and Professor Katherine Roper, Department of History, Saint Mary's College of California, one of the few people in the world today who can be deemed a Spielhagen scholar.

Special thanks are owing to my colleague and friend, Professor Duncan Smith, Department of German Studies, Brown University, who generously passed on to me the editions and other materials from the library of his father, Hedley Smith, a genuine Spielhagen enthusiast, without which my project would have been very much more difficult. Thus to the numerous Smiths, Schmidts, and Schmitzes that have been observed in Spielhagen's fiction, two more have accrued in the reception history. To these may be added my wife, Christa (née Smith), Curator of the German Literature Collection at the Beinecke Library, who now rightly calls herself an information specialist and whose superior skills with the Internet have been of inestimable value to me.

Introduction

This is the final installment of my four-volume inquiry into the nineteenth-century German novel. The first volume, a period study, *Six Essays on the Young German Novel*, appeared with the University of North Carolina Press in 1972; the second, an author study, *Wilhelm Raabe: The Fiction of the Alternative Community*, with Princeton University Press in 1987; the third, a thematic study, *Ideology, Mimesis, Fantasy: Charles Sealsfield, Friedrich Gerstäcker, Karl May, and Other German Novelists of America*, again with North Carolina in 1998. I had intended to conclude the series with a genre study of the sociopolitical novel. I proposed, while avoiding the fabled »poetic realism« and canonically established writers such as Keller, Raabe, and Fontane, to begin with Ludwig Tieck's late realism and Willibald Alexis; to open up the topic of what I called the »old Young Germans,« that is, the writing of Heinrich Laube, Theodor Mundt, and especially Karl Gutzkow after the Young German episode had dissipated; to consider some women writers such as Fanny Lewald and Louise von François; to touch upon the mid-century authors Berthold Auerbach, Gustav Freytag, and Hermann Kurz; perhaps to venture into Austria with Marie von Ebner-Eschenbach and Ferdinand von Saar. But, as my mother used to say, my eyes were bigger than my stomach. The topic, widely thought among literary generalists to be barely existent, was simply too large. Furthermore, it has recently been on the rise; there are increasing numbers of studies. But they often do not have the time or space to focus on detail, while novels, after all, are complicated contraptions. I had always intended to conclude my generic study with Friedrich Spielhagen, but he has come to absorb my attention.

As unseemly as it may be for the author of a literary monograph to complain about difficulties, I cannot help remarking that the preparation and composition of this study have been more arduous than of any of the others. Spielhagen's case is a conspicuous exhibit of the obliterative effect of the canonization process in German literary history. All canonization involves discriminatory selection and is necessary, for there is a great deal more literature in the world than can be stored in the cultural memory, but the efficiency with which German canonization can turn once prominent writers into nonpersons is particularly startling. Spielhagen at one time had a claim to be regarded as a major novelist in the German language, with not only a national but also an international reputation. Over a period of forty-six years, from 1857 to 1903, he published thirty-eight novels and stories, along with six dramas, two volumes of poetry, several translations from English and French, autobiographical memoirs, and a vast amount of confrontational and controversial literary theory and criticism. He was also a prominent figure in literary life, serving as editor or co-editor of *Westermanns Monatshefte* from 1878 to 1884, among other public tasks. How this achievement and prominence fell into oblivion will be recounted in due course. But the difficulties his fate creates for the researcher, especially one working from a foreign country, are considerable.

The problem is easily illustrated by contrasting my experience with my earlier topic of Wilhelm Raabe. There I was able to employ a modern critical edition of his works and several sources of edited correspondence, a tradition of biography, and an extensive history of critical reception. I was given access to an archive in Braunschweig, where I was able to read his unpublished diary (thankfully accompanied by an informal typed transcript) and other sources unpublished or difficult of access, such as British dissertations; at every step I benefited from the ready and friendly assistance of archivists and librarians as well as, in the course of time, personal acquaintance with Raabe scholars. The student of Spielhagen has few such advantages. There is no modern edition;[1] bits and pieces of his correspondence are scattered in old, sometimes obscure periodicals. There is no modern biography, only Spielhagen's own memoirs, which extend, however, no further than the publication of his first novel, and the biography of Hans Henning in 1910, most of which seems to have been obtained from Spielhagen himself and thus may be thought of as a kind of third-person, in a sense, ghost-written autobiography.[2] There is no center of research, and although he is addressed

---

[1] Thomas Tyrell, »Theodor Fontanes ›Effi Briest‹ und Friedrich Spielhagens ›Zum Zeitvertreib‹: Zwei Dichtungen zu einer Wirklichkeit« (Diss. Rice U, 1986), 3–4, writes: »Ein vor wenigen Jahren geplanter Nachdruck dieser Ausgabe [of 1909] mußte wegen mangelnden Interesses vom Verlagsprogramm wieder abgesetzt werden.« This is the only indication I have ever encountered of such a project. Although the collected editions in Spielhagen's time vary some in format and volume numbering, the page numbering seems always the same, indicating that the same plates were used. Thus page references can be verified in any edition.

[2] Hans Henning, *Friedrich Spielhagen* (Leipzig, 1910). Motivated quite likely by a spirit of competition, Victor Klemperer, *Die Zeitromane Friedrich Spielhagens und ihre Wurzeln* (Weimar, 1913), 2, dismisses Henning as lacking »alle ernstliche Bearbeitung und Verknüpfung des Materials, alle Begründung einzelner Urteile und Meinungen,« but his work is valuable because he had complete access to

from time to time, especially in studies of the realist novel or of the history of novel theory, today there are vanishingly few »Spielhagen scholars.« There is a thin tradition of dissertations, but some of them make a disconcerting impression. Spielhagen, a writer of the profoundest philanthropic motivations, seems to have had a remarkable capacity for generating annoyance in readers, not only in the public of his own time, but also in later literary historians and critics. The authors of dissertations, starting with the first German one, Victor Klemperer, frequently seem to get irritated or impatient with him. In some cases I get a sense that the dissertation topics were assigned by professors who wanted to learn something about Spielhagen without going to the trouble themselves, thus generating resentment in their minions. It is now customary to speak of Spielhagen with condescension or disdain, even by those who betray no evidence of much or even any experience with his writing.

Might this not be just? It is not so much that he is uneven, as many prolific writers are, but that his faults and his strengths are inextricably bound together in an œuvre consistently troubling to evaluation. As a novelist and especially as a theorist he was his own worst enemy, tying his own hands, as I shall try to show, as obsessively as any writer known to history. It is not so much from incapacity as from perverse purposiveness that he lacks the finesse of Fontane, the experimentalism of Raabe, or, at least until quite late in his career, the edgy humor of Keller. Some observers have found Spielhagen's theory more worthy of attention than his fiction, but I am not among them. My view is that his theory of the novel and his practice of literary criticism constitute a disaster area; it is hard to believe that anyone committed to the principles insisted upon in the theoretical and critical writings ever could write a novel, and so it appears to me that the novels are created in spite of the theory and from a deeper place in the imagination.

However, my motivation for redirecting attention to them is not to rescue them for the evaluative canon. Rather, it seems to me that we do not yet fully understand how and why so prominent a public author fell into disrepute in the literary community and therefore have not clearly seen how his career was evolving and what its ultimate shape turned out to be. It will be my thesis that he was an idealistic and patriotic national liberal who

family materials. The best modern account is contained in the thirteen pages by Katherine Roper, »Friedrich Spielhagen,« *Dictionary of Literary Biography*, vol. 129, *Nineteenth-Century German Writers, 1841–1900*, ed. James Hardin and Siegfried Mews (Detroit and London, 1993), 348–60.

could not adapt his moral and political instincts to the Wilhelminian Reich. I shall argue that the turning point is found in his postunification novel, *Allzeit voran*, which, as far as I can see, no one has had the patience to try to understand until quite recently.[3] Thereafter his commitments to a Germany of culture and democracy came to appear increasingly obsolete to the aggressive, pragmatic, and posturing nationalists of the Reich, causing him to lose the support, if not immediately of the public, then of its ideological gatekeepers, but in historical retrospect his troubled, restless allegiance to his commitments may look more perceptive and appealing to us than Wilhelminian grandiosity. I shall argue further that he eventually lost faith in his mission, causing him to turn to satire and travesties of poetic justice, and that this turn brought him under literary influences that he had always combatted, making him towards the end less German but more international. Nor was he alone with »an ominous cultural anxiety in Germany after unification in 1871, when, inevitably, the actual political institutions of a united modern industrial state, however great a source of national pride, could not satisfy the spiritual hunger for transcendence and regeneration.«[4] Therefore I shall give more attention than has been customary to the later phases of his career rather than to those works that grounded his reputation, all of which, with the exception of *Sturmflut*, antedated the founding of the Reich, are better known to literary history, and will be more summarized than analyzed here.

There is another consideration that may bear upon Spielhagen's fate. One of my hopes for my original plan was to show that the sociopolitical realist novel was a major genre in Germany as it was in other countries, to build upon the researches demonstrating that German literary life, far from being encapsulated in a national *Sonderweg*, was in close contact with international writing, especially English and French, which circulated widely in Germany both in translation and the original languages,[5] and that reading

---

3 Dirk Göttsche, *Zeit im Roman. Literarische Zeitreflexion und die Geschichte des Zeitromans im späten 18. und im 19. Jahrhundert* (Munich, 2001), 718–21, devotes several pages to it and rightly, in my view, calls it »den Umschlagpunkt von dem liberalen Optimismus der sechziger Jahre zu jener zunehmenden Enttäuschung über die Entwicklung der Gesellschaft und ihrer Mentalität im Deutschen Reich« (721).

4 J. W. Burrow, *The Crisis of Reason: European Thought, 1848–1914* (New Haven and London, 2000), 211. Burrow is speaking of Wagner here, who, of course, became more German rather than less. Spielhagen seems to have taken the road less traveled.

5 See especially Norbert Bachleitner, *Der englische und französische Sozialroman des 19. Jahrhunderts und seine Rezeption in Deutschland* (Amsterdam and Atlanta,

experience was not restricted to an introverted, depressive »poetic realism,« which, as we have learned, was itself imported from Scandinavia.[6] The conviction that Germany did not produce a realism like that of other countries, that with its idealistic and Romantic traditions it was peculiarly situated between the materialist West and the mystical East, an idea of which writers like Thomas Mann and Hermann Hesse were particularly fond, is a deduction drawn from an unusually constrictive, academic and elitist, to some extent nationalist canonization process. In German literary study this conviction is beginning to dissolve under the influence of current researches. But it continues to thrive among comparatists, who, in this country, at any rate, are relatively uninterested in the details of German literary history except for several privileged precincts such as Romantic theory, Nietzsche, Walter Benjamin, and perhaps certain phenomena of German and Austrian modernism.

Still prestigious in this matter is Erich Auerbach's justly revered book, *Mimesis*, first published in 1946. Auerbach was a Romanist, medievalist, and Renaissance scholar by training, as we can see in his brilliant chapters on such topics as Petronius, Dante, or Cervantes, but his sense of German literary history was defined by the constricted academic canon of his time, which identified for him as »the most important works« those that »remained in the genres of semi-fantasy or of idyl or at least in the narrow realm of the local. They portray the economic, the social, and the political as in a state of quiescence.«[7] He knows that there was »the development of something like a modern novel of manners whose most popular representative at the time and on to the nineties was the now totally forgotten Friedrich Spielhagen«;[8] but indicates no awareness that his forgottenness was the consequence of a canonization process. Auerbach half apologized for his limited scholarly resources in his Istanbul exile,[9] but it is the lack not of secondary but of primary literature that restricts the scope of his observations on German realism. He simply had not read enough. In order to begin to understand German literary life in the second half of the nine-

---

  1993), and his edited volume, *Quellen zur Rezeption des englischen und französischen Romans in Deutschland und Österreich im 19. Jahrhundert* (Tübingen, 1990).

[6] Clifford Albrecht Bernd, *Poetic Realism in Scandinavia and Central Europe 1820–1895* (Columbia, SC, 1995).

[7] Erich Auerbach, *Mimesis: The Representation of Reality in Western Literature*, tr. Willard Trask (Garden City, NY, 1953), 399.

[8] Auerbach, *Mimesis*, 456.

[9] Auerbach, *Mimesis*, 492.

teenth century, it is essential to release the topic from Auerbach's prestigious grasp. I am hoping that, by taking a closer look at Spielhagen, I can make a contribution to this process, to situate him in a development of the novel that exhibits from the 1860s to the 1890s

> die Reflexion der langfristigen gesellschaftlichen Veränderungen im Zeichen des »Modernisierungssprungs,« der sozialen Mobilität und der »Beschleunigung aller Lebensverhältnisse,« die zumeist moralische Kritik am Kapitalismus der Gründerzeit und später an den illiberalen, autoritären und nationalistischen Tendenzen im Deutschen Reich, vorsichtige Wiederannäherungen an die »soziale Frage« und die sich formierende Sozialdemokratie sowie die Auseinandersetzung mit dem Selbstverständnis, der Sozialkultur und den mentalen Prägungen insbesondere der bürgerlich-adeligen Führungsschichten einer Gesellschaft, die durch eine spannungsvolle Gleichzeitigkeit von Tradition und Wandel, von Kontinuitäten und tiefgreifenden Veränderungen gekennzeichnet ist.[10]

It is, in any case, possible that his decline of reputation was associated with an early stage of the canonization process determined to erase from the cultural memory this program of a realism of European dimensions, the description of which fits Spielhagen's career perfectly.

New Haven, Connecticut
Winter 2003

---

[10] Göttsche, *Zeit im Roman*, 575.

Abbreviations

For the editions of Spielhagen's works employed here the following abbreviations will be used throughout:

AmSk = *Aus meinem Skizzenbuche* (Leipzig: Staackmann, 1874).

AmSt = *Aus meiner Studienmappe* (Berlin: Allgemeiner Verein für Deutsche Literatur, 1891).

AR = *Ausgewählte Romane* (Leipzig: Staackmann, 1889–93), published in three series of nine, eight, and five volumes respectively, of which the third series also bears the volume numbers of the *Sämmtliche Werke*, 19–23 inclusively. Cited by series, volume, and page number.

AW = *Am Wege. Vermischte Schriften* (Leipzig: Staackmann, 1903).

BT = *Beiträge zur Theorie und Technik des Romans* (Leipzig: Staackmann, 1883), reprinted with an afterword by Hellmuth Himmel (Göttingen: Vandenhoeck & Ruprecht, 1967).

FuE = *Finder und Erfinder. Erinnerungen aus meinem Leben* (Leipzig: Staackmann, 1890), two volumes. Cited by volume and page number.

G = *Gedichte* (Leipzig: Staackmann, 1892).

MAF = *Mesmerismus. Alles fließt* (Leipzig: Staackmann, 1897).

NB = *Neue Beiträge zur Theorie und Technik der Epik und Dramatik* (Leipzig: Staackmann, 1898).

NF = *Romane. Neue Folge* (Leipzig: Staackmann, 1906). Seven volumes, also bearing the volume numbers of *Sämtliche Romane*, 23–29 inclusively. Cited by volume and page number.

NG = *Neue Gedichte* (Leipzig: Staackmann, 1899).

VNbS = *Von Neapel bis Syrakus. Reiseskizzen* (Leipzig: Staackmann, 1878).

VS = *Vermischte Schriften. Neue, vom Verfasser revidirte Ausgabe. Sämtliche Werke*, vol. 7 (Berlin: Janke, [1870].[1]

When numbers alone appear in parentheses, they refer to the previous abbreviation.

For dates of book publication I have decided to follow those given in the *Gesamtverzeichnis deutschsprachigen Schrifttums*, which agree generally with those in Henning's list of works.[2] Once in a while Henning's dates indicate a discrepancy of one year from *GV*, which may be owing to the practice of postdating books appearing late in the year in order to preserve their newness. In one case there seems to be a mistake; Henning dates *Noblesse oblige* to 1888, while *GV* reports a first edition of 1882. Many of Spielhagen's works will have initially appeared in periodicals, the novels serialized. We do not have control over the bibliography of these items, or, for that matter, of his total body of journalistic criticism, and are not likely to have until the contents of the important German periodicals of the second half of the nineteenth century are calendared, which may be accomplished sometime in the future. Earlier dates given for some of the shorter works in *AR* appear to be dates of composition or first publication.

In each section full references will be given for first citations, short titles thereafter. All works cited are listed in the bibliography. The titles of unpublished dissertations appear in quotation marks, of printed dissertations in italics.

---

[1] This edition differs from the original one, *Vermischte Schriften*, 2 vols. (Berlin: Janke, 1864–68) by an altered order of the essays and the addition of 118 pages of »Amerikanische Gedichte,« which replace short essays with translated examples on William Cullen Bryant and Edgar Allan Poe in the first edition. The first volume of the first edition was reprinted in a »Zweite Auflage« in 1868 to go with the revised edition.

[2] Henning, *Friedrich Spielhagen*, 239–40.

I.
BEFORE THE DAWN: SPIELHAGEN TO 1870

1. Origins

One reason for the dearth of biographical writing about Spielhagen may be that his life was not very interesting. His youth was rather restless and diffuse, but not to a degree remarkable in the lives of writers, nor were a venture into political journalism or its melancholy conclusion untypical for the frustrating oppressiveness of public life in the German states. After he settled into his vocation as a professional writer, nothing much, as far as we know, seems to have happened to him in the way of adventure or deviance. However, we have little insight, apart from a few hints and observations, into his inner psychological constitution; the evidence is that it was labile and tense, which would be in no way surprising. A man of static inner equilibrium does not, it seems to me, write novels such as Spielhagen's or doggedly pursue idiosyncratic theoretical and critical fixations in the face of increasing hostility.

Spielhagen was born on February 24, 1829, in Magdeburg, but his real home town was Stralsund, where the family moved when he was six. He felt abandoned by his ailing and often absent mother, who, »von einer geradezu krankhaften Leidenschaft für Ruhe,« »entfremdete ... sich in seltsam bizarrer Laune ihrem Gatten, ihrem Hause, ihren Kindern« (*AmSk*, 37). His father, a self-taught and self-made man, began as a forester but eventually became an inspector of waterworks; in Magdeburg he had founded the first indoor swimming pool in Germany.[1] Spielhagen's relations with him, »ein geselliger Mann, der in keiner Weise sehr an seinen Kindern hing« (*AmSk*, 38), were compounded of respect and rebellion and would fit into any textbook of filial psychology. Although Friedrich was critical of his father's bureaucratic authoritarianism and his insensitivity to literature, he seems to have sensed that a potential for creativity in him had been thwarted by the oppressiveness of the times (*FuE*, 1: 107–30). Fathers whose lives and possibilities have been blighted in the social and political environment occur in a number of places in Spielhagen's fiction, as do breaches of the son with

---

[1]   Hans Henning, *Friedrich Spielhagen* (Leipzig, 1910), 2.

the father,[2] though in the cases of positive characters these are not usually bitter or irreparable and often retain a bond of love.

A good deal of Spielhagen's fiction is set, with greater or lesser transformations, on the Baltic coast around Stralsund or on the island of Rügen, so much so that critics complained of repetition of setting. In no way, however, was this writing a form of nostalgic *Heimatdichtung*. Of Stralsund he said that it was »sicher nicht meine Vaterstadt; aber meine Heimath ist sie eben so wenig« (*AmSk*, 4). Though he often describes the natural environment as moving and exhilarating, he recalled the town as culturally impoverished and politically backward, »die äußerste Peripherie der geistigen Bewegung« (*AmSk*, 19). Both his mother, then his father were to die of cholera, which Spielhagen blamed on the watery cellars of the unhealthy city (*FuE*, 1: 340). Rügen in particular was occupied by ignorant and arrogant Pomeranian *Junker* who regularly appear very much to their disadvantage in the novels. He declares that as a schoolboy he was as lonely as Heine's *Fichtenbaum* (100).[3] One member of the family who may have been more of a model was Ferdinand August Mons, a stepchild of an aunt and foster son of Spielhagen's father, who was twenty years older and became a railroad-building pioneer. Spielhagen had a high opinion of Mons's character; he may have been an inspiration for Spielhagen's pronounced interest in industry and technology, of which there will be more to say in connection with *Hammer und Amboß*. On the whole, however, his origins were not of a nature to inspire an intense commitment to local *Heimat* as an aspect of nationalism. He was emotionally and experientially attached to his Baltic homeland, but not in a way that ascribed political and social values to it. I think this may be important, because his critical view of his origins ambiguated the conservatism that seems to characterize his aesthetics, so that the seed of his inner contrariety was planted at the creation of his consciousness.

A bookish, directionless young man, a reader of Homer and Shakespeare as well as Heine's poetry, he began to study medicine at the University of Berlin, but immediately switched to law, thinking of a possible career in

---

[2] Alexander Robinson Anderson, »Spielhagen's Problematical Heroes« (Diss. Brown University, 1962), 147.

[3] Among the many clear echoes of Heine in his poems, there is a sonnet in a sequence »Entsagung« that explicitly replicates the imagery of Heine's »Ein Fichtenbaum steht einsam,« but places the lonely palm in Palermo (*G*, 6). Spielhagen often employs Heine's trochaic tetrameter, and sometimes makes clear allusions, such as »Lieblich waren Sie, Madame, / Als Sie Liebe mir geschworen« or rhyming »ästhetisch« with »Theetisch« (*NG*, 100, 141). Henning, *Friedrich Spielhagen*, 8, states that he knew Heine's *Buch der Lieder* by heart.

the civil service. He left Berlin on March 16, 1848, two days before the outbreak of the Revolution. That a man of his origins and age should have had no involvement in the 1848 Revolution, indeed, paid little attention to it except as a mildly interested observer, is rather remarkable, and seemed so to Spielhagen himself, who took his absence from the defining event of his generation as an indication of how unformed he was politically (246–55). It is not uninteresting that he made no retrospective claims for valor as a forty-eighter, as another writer might have. Later in 1848 he went to Bonn, where he remained for five semesters, making the acquaintance of Adolf Strodtmann, who was to be the editor of the first effort at a complete edition of Heine's works, and Carl Schurz, who was soon to contribute to Spielhagen's political education with his revolutionary adventures.[4] The celebrated charms of the Rhineland were lost on him; he never cared for the environment and his short novel set around Bonn, *In der zwölften Stunde* (1862), is exceptionally dark and, in its climactic moment, violent. The Baltic coast and the Thuringia of his father's origins and his foster brother Mons's home were his landscapes, although in the course of time he increasingly set his fiction in Berlin.

He found student life sad, nothing like in the songs, he remarks; he had no sense of fun and had difficulty maintaining friendships (212, 233, 264). He joined the fraternity Frankonia in order to make friends – Strodtmann and Schurz were members – but otherwise avoided the fabled *Burschenherr-lichkeit*.[5] Strodtmann describes him as a pale, long-haired, shy, unyouthful youth, a sarcastic outsider always quoting Goethe, Shakespeare, Homer, and Sophocles; one would not have known, Strodtmann observes in retrospect, »daß aus der grauen Puppe dieser mit sich und der Welt zerfallenen ›problematischen Natur‹ zehn Jahre später der bunte Falter der Dichtung so herrlich emporschwingen würde.«[6] From such a description we get the silhouette of a type familiar to us all: the bookish, studious boy, taking pride in an inchoate erudition, a relative nonparticipant in the interests and pastimes of the conventional and ordinary; what might today be called

---

4 Schurz was almost the same age as Spielhagen, who wrote a sonnet, »An Karl Schurz. Zu seinem siebzigsten Geburtstag (2. März 1899)« (*NG*, 224). Eleven years later, Spielhagen told a German-American readership that Schurz, especially when secretary of the interior (1877–81), had often urged him to visit America: »Friedrich Spielhagen's Gruß an die ›New Yorker Staats-Zeitung,‹« *New Yorker Staats-Zeitung*, Sunday supplement of April 24, 1910, 3.

5 Henning, *Friedrich Spielhagen*, 32.

6 Adolf Strodtmann, *Dichterprofile. Literaturbilder aus dem neunzehnten Jahrhundert* (Stuttgart, 1879), 198. Spielhagen quotes this passage in *FuE*, 1: 255–56, not,

a nerd. In middle age he was able to make a similar impression: Georg Brandes found him small and nervous when he visited him at age forty-four.[7] But he may have taken himself in hand, modeling himself according to the military ideal he admired. When he was around sixty, he was described in an American magazine as »a strong man, almost five feet four in height, with a long body and short muscular legs, broad back, sinewy arms, and a spacious chest, with firm ribs that spread to give ample room to the lungs without the least regard to the fashion of slender waists.«[8] When he was seventy-one, Hermann Bahr found that »[s]traff und stramm, knapp und regsam, gerade und scharf ist seine Art. Man möchte ihn für einen höheren Offizier oder etwa für einen preußischen Richter nehmen.... Es wundert mich, den mutigen Kämpfer für die Freiheit so soldatisch, fast sagte ich, polizeilich zu finden«; he was not soft and sentimental like his books, but displayed »[e]in hartes, starres Profil«; his eyes gazed not like those of a *Dichter* but »eher wie ein Staatsanwalt und Inquisator [sic] blickt.«[9] However, this should not be understood as an inner adaptation to the Wilhelminian tone. Rather, he asserted that he had to struggle with his own soul that was »von Haus aus gut und weich« in order to cope with the Reich and find models, among them Social Democracy, for a resistant stance (*NB*, 8). Furthermore, his firm bearing may have been a self-imposed discipline; late in life he spoke of himself as having been »nicht gar gesund und nervös überreizt, ungleichmäßig in meiner Stimmung und nicht selten in schweren Launen heimgesucht.«[10]

In Bonn he switched to philology and philosophy in order to prepare for a literary career; he studied Greek and Latin classics, Goethe, and besides Heine, recent writers such as Immermann, Platen, and Börne. He

---

he says, because he regards it as completely accurate, but because he is insecure about his own account of this period of his life.

[7] Bertil Nolin, *Den gode Europén. Studier i Georg Brandes' idéutveckling 1871–1893 med speciell hänsyn till hans förhållende till tysk, engelsk, slavisk och fransk litteratur* ([Stockholm], 1965), 67.

[8] Anonymous, [review of *FuE*, vol. 2], *Atlantic Monthly* 70 (September, 1892): 404. This gives every indication of a personal acquaintance. The anonymous items on Spielhagen in American periodicals look as though they may have been written by German-Americans or, perhaps, German correspondents.

[9] Hermann Bahr, »Friedrich Spielhagen,« Bahr, *Der Antisemitismus. Ein internationales Interview*, ed. Hermann Greive (Königstein, 1979), 17.

[10] To Peter Rosegger, January 6, 1897, »Briefe von Friedrich Spielhagen an den alten Heimgärtner,« *Roseggers Heimgarten* 35 (1911): 609. The letters are included also in Rosegger, *Mein Weltleben. Neue Folge. Erinnerungen eines siebzigjährigen* (Leipzig, 1914), 307–20.

was doubtless self-educated in modern literature. Georg Hartwig in *Hammer und Amboß*, some fifteen years older than Spielhagen, as a nineteen-year-old schoolboy labors over Sophocles in Greek but has never heard of Eichendorff and fails to pick up an allusion to *Werther* (*AR*, 1, 3: 64, 82). In what turned out to be an important move, he learned English. According to his own account, he traded English lessons for German with two unteachable Englishmen who lived in his building; he practiced whenever he could and began reading, »wie sich gebührt,« one of the best-loved English works among Germans, *The Vicar of Wakefield* (*FuE*, 1: 335). Although Henning says he spoke like an Englishman,[11] I rather doubt it, as he never visited England, but his reading knowledge opened to him a world that was coming to be of increasing importance for German literary life. From beginning to end his writings are speckled with English words and phrases; in one verse he rhymed »keiner« with »*penny-a-liner*« (*NG*, 158). A ballad of Tennyson was to be the impetus for his fictionalization of an early love affair in his first novella, *Clara Vere* (1857), and over the years he was to read extensively in the English novel. Interesting, however, is his early turn to American literature. When a German-American publisher in 1855 wanted some German folk songs translated into English, Spielhagen let himself, with misgivings, be talked into the attempt, even though, as he tells us, he had to adapt texts in a foreign language to the tunes despite knowing nothing about music. He set no great value on this achievement, wisely, as appears from the one example he cites (*FuE*, 2: 285–87),[12] but it led to a more substantial and appropriate publication, his translations of *Amerikanische Gedichte*, which appeared in 1859 and about which there will be more to say in Chapter 9.

At his worried father's urging he continued his studies in Berlin and briefly in Greifswald, but broke them off in 1851 in order to discharge his year of military service. When he had completed it, he achieved his first publication, a lecture on Homer in Karl Gutzkow's periodical, *Unterhaltungen am häuslichen Herde*, later included in *VS*, 3–28. It was the only publication his father was to see, giving some hope he might succeed as a

---

[11] Henning, *Friedrich Spielhagen*, 41.
[12] Henning, *Friedrich Spielhagen*, 41–42, repeats this tale, together with the translation example, although neither he nor anyone else has told us where this effort was published. It seems to have been printed, however, as Spielhagen claims that the publisher, several years later, in order to protect against pirating, had its authorship certified by the American consul in Hanover (*FuE*, 2: 287).

writer.[13] Gutzkow was, for better or worse, an influential figure on the literary scene; his encouraging response understandably raised Spielhagen's spirits (*FuE*, 2: 276). For a time he served as a tutor on a Pomeranian estate, an activity with a long tradition in the lives of educated young Germans. There followed an episode when he tried to be an actor in an amateur company. Here one may think that his personal *Bildungsroman* is coming to be amalgamated with *Wilhelm Meister*, and in fact, like Goethe, he had a toy theater as a child and composed plays (1: 55–58). He comments that in the provinces there was no less a general prejudice against the acting profession than had been portrayed in Goethe's novel, and he realizes that his father is horrified (2: 174); in a corresponding episode in *Was will das werden?*, the protagonist is told that real actors are just like those in *Wilhelm Meister* (*AR*, 3, 4: 244–45). Though a wise actor discouraged him, he made an attempt on the professional stage in Magdeburg. This turned out, not surprisingly, to be a fiasco, the sort of experience that is more comic to read about in someone else's life than to live through in one's own; his rueful recollections of the experience were called upon many years later for the protagonist's equally futile though more persistent attempt at an acting career in *Was will das werden?*

From 1854 to 1860 he imagined himself to be a student in Leipzig, though constantly beset by misgivings that he had no scholarly vocation. He finally obtained a position as a teacher of English in a progressive school in Leipzig which he held until the enlightened and admired director could no longer manage financially and was replaced by a clergyman who seems not to have been a bad sort, but Spielhagen, who was militantly antireligious, could not abide pastors, so that a separation was inevitable (*FuE*, 2: 382–83). Among the young teachers was Alfred Brehm, exactly the same age as Spielhagen, who was later to become famous for his *Illustriertes Tierleben*, found in nearly every German middle-class home and translated into many languages. Spielhagen's first experiments in fiction, the novellas *Clara Vere* (1857) and *Auf der Düne* (1858), both based on failed love affairs about which we know almost nothing, date from this period, as do several published essays and translations from French and English. For several years he had difficulty placing *Clara Vere* until it was accepted by a publisher in Hanover, though without an honorarium (121–22, 297–98). There it caught the attention of the editor of the liberal *Zeitung für Norddeutschland*, Ehren-

---

[13] Henning, *Friedrich Spielhagen*, 65.

reich Eichholz, who invited Spielhagen to further contributions; though Eichholz worried about the realism of *Auf der Düne*, he published it, and then offered the position of feuilleton editor, which Spielhagen assumed in 1860. In the following year he felt secure enough to marry a young widow, Therese Wittich, née Boûtin, whom he had met in the home of his foster brother. We know almost nothing about her; she was of French, possibly noble descent.[14] We do know that when she died in 1900, Spielhagen was devastated with grief, an emotion that seems to have deepened his depression and accelerated the decline of his last decade. He wrote to Peter Rosegger that his only purpose in working had been to provide her with modest luxury; now, disgusted by literature, he can see no more value in work.[15] He adopted his wife's son, who died in childhood, and her daughter, Jenny, and had another daughter with her, Toni, born in 1865, who attempted to make a literary career for herself under the name of »Paul Robran« but found herself nursing her father in his old age; she was to predecease him in October 1910, a victim of influenza. She was a significant source for Klemperer's dissertation.[16]

Since the accession of Queen Victoria in 1837, which terminated the personal union of the Kingdom of Hanover with the British Crown because a woman could not rule in the German states, Hanover had been one of the most misgoverned of them. The succession fell to Ernst August, the last surviving son of George III, an arrogant blowhard of whom the English were glad to be rid. Immediately he caused a national scandal by arbitrarily abrogating the constitution of 1830, then summarily dismissing from the University of Göttingen seven professors who protested this action, including the Brothers Grimm, the historian Friedrich Christoph Dahlmann, and the literary historian Georg Gervinus. Ernst August was succeeded in 1851 by his blind son, Georg V, who was similarly reactionary and choleric, and for his part abrogated a constitution of 1848. Some of the observations Spielhagen

---

14 Henning, *Friedrich Spielhagen*, 101–02, 229–30.
15 To Rosegger, February 20, 1900, »Briefe an den alten Heimgärtner,« 613.
16 Victor Klemperer, *Curriculum Vitae. Jugend um 1900* (Berlin, 1989), 1: 473–74. On Toni Spielhagen's career and her nursing of her embittered, regretful father, see Ella Mensch, »Erinnerungen an Friedrich Spielhagen,« *Westermanns Monatshefte* 110 (1911): 358. For a comment on Toni's writing see Heinrich Spiero, *Geschichte des deutschen Romans* (Berlin, 1950), 342, where, however, her pen name is misspelled »Kobran.« »Robrahn,« incidentally, was her paternal grandmother's maiden name (Henning, *Friedrich Spielhagen*, 1), and »Robran« the name her father gave to the lovely Sophie, bride of Dr. Braun, and her humane father in *Problematische Naturen.*

made of the, as he put it, reaction under the blind king (*AW*, 9–10) came to affect, though much altered, his novel *Allzeit voran*. As a newspaperman he did not suppose himself a great public force; he remarked deprecatingly that the *Zeitung für Norddeutschland* did not move North Germany much with its two thousand subscribers in Hanover only, where the members of the *Nationalverein* never exceeded thirty (10). However, even in the 1860s, disseminating liberal opinion was no laughing matter; Eichholz was eventually arrested and died shortly after having been released from months of interrogation in a cold fortress prison (*FuE*, 2: 312–13). Spielhagen's experiences in Hanover began to politicize him and to motivate his evolution to what he understood as a democrat. The nationalist spirit was an intermediate step, however; he took the opportunity of a visit to Norderney in 1866 to joke about the discomfiture of the »Welfen« at the absorption of the island by Prussia (*AmSk*, 255–93).

As he entered his thirties, he realized that he needed to define his vocation. In 1858 he had begun an ambitious novel, *Problematische Naturen*. He made a rather daring wager with himself that if he could not achieve success with this work, he would give up literary authorship. Fortunately the novel, published in 1861, was a splendid success. He followed it with a sequel, *Durch Nacht zum Licht,* in 1863; since then these have been seen as two parts of the same work and are published under the first title. Spielhagen's success with this book was, in fact, of uncommon dimensions. We are so accustomed to German authors scraping along at a subsistence level that his prosperity may seem disconcerting; perhaps it even contributed to the disregard in which he came to be held, for in the eyes of German intellectuals and academics, with their savage scorn for »the market,« a commercially successful writer, at least before the great public-relations machine of the *Gruppe 47* after World War II, could not be of any literary merit. In any case, there can be no doubt that Spielhagen's initial successes established a more than adequate prosperity. Despite his problems with the literary community, he was a writer of endurance. *Problematische Naturen* went through seventy-eight editions, *Hammer und Amboß* thirty-seven, *Sturmflut* forty-five. For six editions of *Sturmflut* in eight years he earned 80,000 marks.[17] Sums

---

[17] Rosa-Maria Zinken, *Der Roman als Zeitdokument. Bürgerliche Liberalismus in Friedrich Spielhagens »Die von Hohenstein« (1863/64)* (Frankfurt am Main and Bern, 1991), 43, 18–19. See also Hans-Ulrich Wehler, *Deutsche Gesellschaftsgeschichte*, vol. 3, *Von der deutschen »Doppelrevolution« bis zum Beginn des Ersten Weltkrieges 1849–1914* (Munich, 1995), 444.

like this are unheard of in the lives of the canonical German authors of the nineteenth century.

The success of his novel debut enabled him to leave his provincial newspaper and move with his family to Berlin, where, except for travels, he was to remain and where he »führte ein angesehenes Haus.«[18] By 1894 he had come to live in the elegant western part of the city, on the boundary to Charlottenburg, then an area of gardens, but by the turn of the century, he tells us, built over like America (*AW*, 240–42). Henning reports, along with lecture tours in Germany and Austria, three foreign journeys: to Paris (undated), with his wife to Italy (1873), and alone to Russia (1884).[19] Apart from diary notes of a vacation in Switzerland in 1862 (*AmSk*, 49–96), only his Italian journey yielded a publication (*VNbS*). Although it contains lively descriptions and penetrating introspections, along with the expected shadow of Goethe and historical reflections on Homer and Thucydides, in content it is no more than an account of touristing. From the time of his settlement in Berlin he seems to have made no news except in the literary world; since he was such a prominent public figure, it seems we would know about any remarkable events. His life appears to be a succession of publications, increasingly dogged by critical disapproval. It has been remarked that Spielhagen himself looked upon the early years from 1847 to 1861 as the »only really interesting ones and as if they revealed all that is essential for an understanding of his life and works.«[20]

He published his last novels in 1900; thereafter his only new work was his final biographical memoir, *Am Wege* (1903). He clearly deteriorated, mentally and physically, during his last years. An American obituary reported that he had grown »silent ... in the last decade, through domestic sorrow and physical affliction.«[21] Under the depression intensified by the death of his wife, he announced the defeat of his lifelong effort to maintain the relevance of an idealistic aesthetic to the real world. Whoever has learned how bitter and brutal real life can be, he wrote to Rosegger,

[18] Henrike Lamers, *Held oder Welt? Zum Romanwerk Friedrich Spielhagens* (Bonn, 1991), 7.

[19] Henning, *Friedrich Spielhagen*, 144. His daughter reports that on the visit to Paris he was also accompanied by his wife, along with his friends, the literary critic Karl Frenzel and his wife: Antonie Spielhagen, »Zum 80. Geburtstag Friedrich Spielhagens,« *Gartenlaube* [57] (1909): 166.

[20] Anderson, »Spielhagen's Problematic Heroes,« 21.

[21] Anonymous, »Friedrich Spielhagen, a Mirror of German Life,« *American Review of Reviews* 43 (1911): 622.

dem kommt seine sogenannte Poesie, von der man glaubte, daß sie, alles in allem, doch ein Spiegelbild der Realität sei, vor wie ein an der Wand verhuschende Schattenspiel. Und, endlich wissend, was das Leben wirklich ist, das Schattenspielerkunststück weiter treiben – es erscheint mir lächerlich, unwürdig, blasphemisch.[22]

A few years later, he described his life as lonely and aged; he rarely went out except for annual visits to a sanatorium in the Harz Mountains; his children took care of him; »das Schaffenstrieb ist völlig verschollen,« for we cannot all age like Goethe; he takes some comfort in his five grandchildren.[23] In a rhymed aphorism he mused:

> Kennt ihr den Abgrund der Melancholie?
> Ein Künstler, der im Anschauen seiner Werke,
> Die einst er schuf mit glüher Phantasie,
> Sich sagen muß: dahin ist deine Stärke. (*NG*, 151)

Spielhagen died on February 25, 1911, one day after his eighty-second birthday. We shall see that, as often happens, by dying he recalled himself to public memory and, at least briefly, improved his reputation.

---

22 To Rosegger, February 2, 1900, »Briefe an den alten Heimgärtner,« 613–14.
23 To Rosegger, April 27, June 4, 1906, »Briefe an den alten Heimgärtner,« 614, 615.

2. The Rise to Fame

a: The First Novellas

Spielhagen opened his fiction-writing career with two novellas that have
come to be of antiquarian interest only, if that. It is a received opinion
that his novellas are less accomplished than his novels, just fill-ins »turned
out between novels,«[1] and I would agree for the early part of his career,
although some of them achieved a considerable popularity. *Röschen vom
Hofe* (1864) and *Die Dorfcoquette* (1869) were reprinted numerous times,
the latter in Reclam's *Universalbibliothek*, which eventually also took up the
short novel, *Was die Schwalbe sang* (1873), an English translation of which
appeared within a year and now sits on my shelf.[2] A turning point may
have come with *Das Skelet im Hause* (1878), a humorous mystery concerning
a gentleman who has married a girl of noble descent but is afraid to admit
to her and her haughty mother that his manor house is obliged by entail
to maintain a commercial establishment; with its secret passageways and
murder victim who turns out to be perfectly safe, it reads like a parody of
the Gothic mode. It is the only Spielhagen work ever edited for American
student use.[3] It, too, was translated promptly into English.[4] In my view, the

---

[1] Anderson, »Spielhagen's Problematical Heroes,« 5; see also Christa Müller-Donges,
    *Das Novellenwerk Friedrich Spielhagens in seiner Entwicklung zwischen 1851 und
    1899* (Marburg, 1970), 15.
[2] *What the Swallow Sang*, tr. by MS., in the »Leisure Hour Series« (New York,
    1873). The generic distinction between novella and novel, which in my days as
    a student of German literature absorbed a vast amount of time and effort, no
    longer interests me at all, but was of fanatic concern to Spielhagen, so will have
    to be touched upon in another place.
[3] Friedrich Spielhagen, *Das Skelett* [sic] *im Hause*, ed. M. M. Skinner (Boston,
    1913). The pedagogues responsible for shielding schoolchildren from impurity and
    subversiveness in German texts devoted considerable attention to the Spielhagen
    problem, regularly concluding that he was too socialist and irreligious to be set
    before American pupils. See John Hargrove Tatum, *The Reception of German
    Literature in U.S. German Texts 1864–1918* (New York and Bern, 1988), 130–33.
[4] Friedrich Spielhagen, *The Skeleton in the House*, tr. M. J. Safford (New York,
    1881).

turn to a lighter tone, eventually to subversive satire, improved the quality of the shorter prose beyond what came to be its reputation.

The first novella, *Clara Vere*, was said to have been drawn from personal experience but was also modelled on Tennyson's ballad of 1842, »Lady Clara Vere de Vere,« in which a young man of plain origins declares to an aristocratic *femme fatale* that she will not drive him to cut his throat as she has another lad, yet seems a bit obsessed by her all the same. The poem has put several Familiar Quotations into the English language, among them the line »Kind hearts are more than coronets«;[5] Spielhagen, however, knew the poem from the great mediator of English poetry into German, Ferdinand Freiligrath (*FuE*, 1: 402).[6] Spielhagen fills out the pattern by relating the temporary beguilement of a young man, George Allen, foster son of a murdered forester, by the stunningly beautiful but vain and selfish Clara, until he comes to his senses and joins himself to his true love, the forester's daughter, whose brother has killed himself out of passion for Clara. Behind this story is that of the old generous, enterprising Lord Vere, revered by George, who has died in a riding accident and turns out to be George's true father. Although Clara attempts to seduce George by means of a performance of the balcony scene of *Romeo and Juliet*, he renounces his noble title and leaves her to marriage to a doltish duke.

Here we can recognize two long-lived themes: that of the beautiful *femme fatale* who is tragically split in herself and the hero's secret aristocratic heritage. But although Friedrich Hebbel found the story interesting enough to consider dramatizing it,[7] the novella is not especially promising and it is unsurprising that it was difficult to publish. It is not dexterously formed and there is an anachronistic touch of Gothic. The narrator constantly explains characters and motives, as though for an incompetent reader. Spielhagen is not at home on the foreign ground; he calls his siren »Lady Vere,« as though she were the mistress of the house; as the daughter she

---

5   Alfred, Lord Tennyson, *The Poems of Tennyson*, ed. Christopher Ricks (London and New York, 1969), 638. The title of the English translation, *Lady Clara Vere de Vere: A Story* (New York, 1881), clearly seeks to signal the connection to Tennyson.

6   Freiligrath's translation had appeared in *Englische Dichter aus neuerer Zeit* (Stuttgart and Tübingen, 1846), 358–61. See Ernst Fleischhack, *Bibliographie Ferdinand Freiligrath 1829–1990* (Bielefeld, 1993), 114. Late in life, however, Spielhagen published his own translations of several Tennyson poems (*NG*, 229–36).

7   As appears in a note he wrote to himself, Friedrich Hebbel, *Sämtliche Werke*, ed. Richard Maria Werner (Berlin, 1901–07), 1, 5: 314–15. See Henning, *Friedrich Spielhagen*, 62.

14

should be »Lady Clara.« He was soon to be convinced that a realistic writer should stay within the boundaries of his own experience. In retrospect he observed that all first novels are »verschämte Ich-Romane« but that he had had nothing to say (2: 121–23).

He felt that his second effort, *Auf der Düne*, originally a part of *Problematische Naturen* (*NB*, 198), was an improvement, not without reason; it was more exactly drawn from experience, described to us in some detail in his memoir. It is located in a familiar island locale (*FuE*, 2: 121–51), and the narration focuses less on a hackneyed plot line than on character. Hebbel, one of the most capable literary critics of the time, spoke well of it, though found its tragic turn unnecessary.[8] Alternating between a first-person, epistolary mode and third-person narration, the story tells of Paul, a young poet of sorts, who visits his friend Gustav, an inspector of dredging craft, on the island of »Nedur« (the little island of Ruden off the Baltic coast spelled backwards). A decent but undemonstrative man, Gustav married Clementine when she was young and inexperienced; she is now vaguely dissatisfied with Gustav's inattention to her emotional needs so that her erotic potential is aroused by the courting of a Lieutenant von Elze, a suave but indolent tax official who is in a kind of exile from personal miseries in his past and argues vigorously against the artificiality of marriage, at the same time impregnating a local girl. Paul, meanwhile, imagines himself in love with the intelligent, sensitive Hedda, daughter of the chief pilot, who is, as emerges gradually, more or less promised to a merchant marine officer, Gerhardt, who turns out to be not only handsome but astute and perceptive. Paul realizes he must renounce Hedda, while Gustav, unobservant but unnecessarily jealous, challenges the lieutenant to a duel in which, as a civilian inferior with weapons, he is mortally wounded. There is a great deal more in the long, wordy novella, including crises and rescues at sea and much dialectical conversation, riddled with literary allusions, especially to Heine, but turning on the contradiction between the poetic and the practical sensibilities. It ends with Paul trying to shore up poetic justice against the evidence of reality, which turned out to be a Sisyphean

---

[8] In the *Leipziger Illustrirten Zeitung*, November 27, 1858. The review is very short but has a passage, characteristic of Hebbel's acid pen, worth citing: »unsere Berliner Scheherezade, Luise Mühlbach, hat das Recht, Duelle mit blutigem Ausgang zu bringen ... der Verf. der ersten zwei Dritttheile dieser Novelle ist als Talent zu bedeutend, um in dem letzten von einem ähnlichen Privilegium Gebrauch machen zu dürfen.« Hebbel, *Sämtliche Werke*, 1, 12: 212.

task of many years: »möchte ich sagen: das Leben ist eine schale Komödie, wo die Guten und Edlen verhöhnt werden, und die Narren und Schurken frei ausgehen; und doch wieder, wenn ich es recht bedenke, beuge ich mich in Demuth vor der hohen Majestät der Gesetze, die das Menschenleben beherrschen« (*AR*, 2, 1: 348–49).

Spielhagen had found his way to one of his characteristic landscapes and one of his typical character types, the self-willed, morally careless aristocrat. In retrospect he thought that he had lacked the artistic acumen to solve both of the crucial relationships in the story (*FuE*, 2: 155). In fact, he could have composed such reasonably well-written and thoughtful novellas as an avocation all his life, for there was a tremendous demand for fiction by the periodicals and feuilletons of the time, but he would have gained no standing as a *Dichter*. He needed the space of a big novel and realized that only an ambitious work would open the way to his still inchoate calling.

b: *Problematische Naturen*

Spielhagen tells us with precision that the novel takes place from the summer of 1847 until the Revolution in March 1848 (*FuE*, 2: 444–45). It follows the convoluted affairs of a young man, Oswald Stein, beginning with his arrival at a baronial mansion to tutor the spoiled son of the house, Malte von Grenwitz, and an ill-bred orphaned relative, Bruno von Löwen, with whom Oswald is to form an affectionate relationship. He has been helped to this position by the demonic, eccentric Professor Berger, who has written an unpublishable book against the nobility. Bruno introduces Oswald to a woman he admires, the beautiful Melitta von Berkow, whose husband, to whom she was sold by her father to cover his debts, is now confined in an insane asylum; she and Oswald embrace in the forest under a statue of Venus. From a pastor, a toady of the Grenwitzes, Oswald learns of a secret bequest of the previous baron to an illegitimate child whose identity is unknown. After some experience of reading Spielhagen one will have no doubt as to who this may be; the unfolding of Oswald's secret identity is a recurrent plot element. At this point a character appears of whom we have already heard, a rough-hewn Baron Oldenburg, who has been linked to Melitta and is pejoratively characterized by Baroness von Grenwitz as one of Gutzkow's »Ritter[ ] vom Geist« (*AR*, 1, 1: 261). He admires Oswald for humbugging a stupid Baron Cloten (possibly named for the doltish royal offspring in Shakespeare's *Cymbeline*, »a fool, an empty purse,« 4, 2: 113); in what was to be a notorious scene, Oldenburg comforts Cloten, who is worried that the Bible was authored by a bourgeois because it appears that all men come from the same couple, by declaring that he has found a manuscript proving that there were two original couples, one noble and one bourgeois; he offers Cloten a copy and encourages him to claim the idea as his own.

Oswald comes to feel a link with Oldenburg's restless, labile personality, and forms a friendship with a vagabond geometer named Timm who is surveying the estate and emerges as an unreliable chatterbox who researches Oswald's parentage in the hope of an opportunity for blackmail. After a quarrel with Melitta, Oswald flirts with a young girl, Emilie von Breesen, who, to his embarrassment, falls passionately in love with him; she decides to marry the imbecile Cloten when Oswald rejects her. Concerning Melitta he is uncomfortable because, as a married woman, she is not untouched. Another friend, Dr. Braun, induces Oswald to try to prevent the beautiful, proud Helene von Grenwitz's forced marriage to her vain, stupid, and lascivious cousin Felix; Bruno is in love with her but Oswald gradually develops a passion for her, while in her interest for him she begins to overcome her class prejudices. She flatly refuses Felix, whereupon her mother expels her. At the asylum Oldenburg tries to make love to Melitta and displace Oswald; delivered to the same asylum is Professor Berger who, to Oswald's shock, has gone mad in the middle of a lecture; the odious pastor obtains Berger's position. During a party, where Felix insults Oswald, who throws him to the floor, and Oldenburg challenges everyone in Oswald's name, Bruno dies unattended. Oldenburg, departing, advises Melitta to give up Oswald because he will never be satisfied with his search for the idea; Oswald, who has invalided Felix for life in a duel, departs with Dr. Braun. Thus ends the original novel.

The second part, originally titled *Durch Nacht zum Licht*, recapitulates some of the contents of the first volume. Oswald, on a journey with Dr. Braun to visit Berger in his Thuringian asylum, is given an opportunity for a belated exposition of his own past life, of his lack of love for his (apparent) father and the aristocratic instincts alienating him from bourgeois life that led him to flee into poetry; he became »ein Jüngling an Jahren mit der Lebensmüdigkeit eines Greises« (*AR*, 1, 5: 12). Dr. Braun advises him to become socialized, to live for others rather than himself. Oswald is to enter upon a provisional year as a schoolteacher, a role he comes to scorn. A rather Schopenhauerian Berger says he meant to teach Oswald to abandon hope and despair of life; he tells of his own rather lurid past, involving a scandalous love affair and a jail sentence for patriotic activity, managing, as he intends, quite to depress Oswald, who thinks of turning himself in to the asylum. The Grenwitzes and Timm, in their town house in Grünwald (= Greifswald, decayed from its Hanseatic glory), plot against Oswald. A whole chapter (19) is given over to an awful literary reading of Schiller's *Wallenstein* in which the pastor's wife attempts unsuccessfully to be the prima donna – the first satire of the bourgeois milieu in the novel. Oswald makes love to the highborn but ostracized Helene. Prince Waldernberg appears, a dashing, class-proud Russian who beguiles Helene into an engagement, but he turns out to be the son of a circus director.

Oldenburg, while attempting to drive Oswald out of Melitta's heart, begins to sense the possibility of revolution; this is the first mention of it in the novel, two-thirds of the way through the second part (1, 5: 258), though the dating in the first sentence of the first part, »an einem warmen Juniabend des Jahres 1847« (1, 1: 1) generates an underlying tension and expectation. Oswald melodramatically flees to Paris with Emilie, who has been recently married to Cloten, just in time to encounter the Revolution, along with the released Berger, Oldenburg, and the now radical Timm. Everyone gets back to Berlin, where the various dénouements, narrative surprises, and crackups of the noble families dovetail with the outbreak of the Revolution there, which levers Oswald out of his self-centered funk; he learns of his noble heritage but refuses to make his claim, renouncing his one-and-only beloved of the moment, Helene. In a very unusual moment of narrative irony, Spielhagen has Berger say with a bitter smile: »Der Proletarier eines Fürsten Vater, der Fürst eines Proletariers Sohn – das gäbe einen hübschen Stoff zu einem modernen Romane,« and he goes on to say it is too bad the people of the world do not know of it: »Sie würden dann vielleicht dahinter kommen, was es mit dem Unterschiede von adeligem und bürgerlichen Blut auf sich hat!« (1, 5: 543). On the barricades Timm, Waldernberg, and Berger are killed, Oswald mortally wounded. Oldenburg regards the people's victory celebration as illusory, easy for the retrospective author to say, but nevertheless, at the funeral of the victims, he has the last word about the labor needed to emerge from the night that was so poor in healthy men and so full of »problematische Naturen«: »die lange schmachvolle Nacht, aus welcher nur der Donnersturm der Revolution durch blutige Morgenröthe hinüberführt zur Freiheit und zum Licht« (564).

One sees from this account how inconvenient such a novel, so packed with event, makes even abstract description, not to speak of analysis. In fact, my summary has left out a good deal, for example, among numerous encapsulated detailed stories of characters, a subplot concerning Oldenburg's connection to a gypsy family, which allows Spielhagen, like so many other novelists in succession to *Wilhelm Meister*, to introduce a Mignon figure; the involvement of a poor, decent, struggling young man, Bemperlein, whose instinctive honesty comes to contrast with Oswald's confused deviousness; the effort of Dr. Braun to relieve his father-in-law's debts, incurred when helping the poor, by sacrificing his scientific career, which his father-in-law does not allow; Timm's betrayal of a Swiss domestic, Marguerite, whom Bemperlein rescues and marries; or Timm's complicated plot to blackmail the Grenwitz family with his knowledge that Oswald is a potential heir of the entailed estate. The length and complexity caused a complaint in England that the two parts »contain as much matter as half-a-dozen English three-volume romances. They are oppressively long, and require real leisure on the reader's part.«[9] This not really fair; for example, the two parts are no more than three-quarters the length of Thackeray's *Henry Esmond* and *The Virginians*, which can be taken as a continuous narrative. Whoever does not like reading long Victorian novels will simply have to do without Spielhagen. To be sure, he himself acknowledged that there was too much »Fülle des Stoffes,« in fact, more than he could get in (*FuE*, 2: 443). It is true that he insisted of the genre of the novel »daß er lang sei, damit er breit sei,« that it must have a »beträchtlichen Umfang« (*AmSt*, 314; *BT*, 264). In part the demand for bulk and comprehensiveness is motivated by the desperate hope that the modern novel be some sort of successor to the ancient epic, but it is also motivated by the futile wish that the realistic novel be fully congruent with reality itself.

Spielhagen was more voluble about the genesis of *Problematische Naturen* than of any other of his works except for *Sturmflut*, apparently because he regarded his first novel as the climactic moment (in his early thirties!) of his personal biography. One of these retrospective accounts, »Wie die ›Problematischen Naturen‹ entstanden« (*NB*, 191–207), was composed for an ingenious collection of authors' accounts of their first works compiled by Karl Emil Franzos.[10] However, much of Spielhagen's commentary concerns the modelling of characters and settings on real people and places and the changes made in fictionalizing them. The insistence on modelling is another way of certifying realism, but, in my opinion, it is one of the several self-deceptions of the theoretical demands Spielhagen imposed upon himself; I shall come back to it. Of greater literary-historical interest would be an effort to

---

[9] Helen and Alice Zimmern, *Half-Hours with Foreign Novelists* (London, 1880), 190.

[10] Karl Emil Franzos, ed., *Die Geschichte des Erstlingswerks. Selbstbiographische Aufsätze* (Berlin, [1894]), 33–50. On its genesis, see Carl Steiner, *Karl Emil Franzos 1848–1904: Emancipator and Assimilationist* (New York and Bern, 1990), 41.

account for the novel's success, for its reception as a defining fiction of its times that impressed even Nietzsche.[11] Spielhagen's own account presents it as a kind of *succès de scandale*, at least with the deeply offended Baltic locals; the nobles, Spielhagen tells us, wanted to buy up the edition and destroy it (*FuE*, 2: 428–29). Perhaps the somewhat risqué elements of romance, such as Oswald's adultery with Emilie von Cloten in Paris (where else?), that form much of the armature of the plot were attractive to women readers, even though the reiterated attractiveness of the somewhat feckless Oswald to women may be a little puzzling to the reader. It was widely believed in the nineteenth century that women, because of their greater leisure, formed a large part, perhaps the majority of the readership of literature, especially of novels. So far as I know, much of the evidence for this is circumstantial, but it is so widespread as to be persuasive; Spielhagen complained about it at an early stage in his career (*VS*, 246) and by 1887 doubted that there were any male readers any more (*AmSt*, 351). While conservatives deplored the habit for alienating the female imagination from its true sphere, writers sometimes found the female readers constrictive on the demand side.[12] It has been said that girls born at the time all over Germany were named Melitta for the first of Spielhagen's many beautiful and intelligent women who attempt to achieve a self-defining dignity within imposed gender limitations;[13] this might be an indication of an extensive female readership. But novels that depend upon such effects are not usually long-lived.

It seems to me more likely that the novel contributed to articulating a self-definition in the *Nachmärz* readership. It is often remarked that a kind of collective depression befell the bourgeois liberals after the failures, tragedies, and farces of the 1848 Revolution. In fact, the »poetic realism,« domesticated in Germany in the gloomy aftermath of 1848, had its origin in Denmark's fall from a golden age to post-Napoleonic depression and deprivation and is thus from the outset a symptom of collective depression.[14]

---

11 Henning, *Friedrich Spielhagen*, 111.
12 Examples of Kleist, the Brothers Hart, and Raabe himself in Jeffrey L. Sammons, *Wilhelm Raabe: The Fiction of the Alternative Community* (Princeton, 1987), 40–41. See Erich Schön, »Geschichte des Lesens,« *Handbuch Lesen*, ed. Bodo Franzmann et al. (Munich, 1999), 34–35, 46–47. The distress was not only German; the Norwegian-American writer Hjalmar Hjorth Boyesen, in whom Spielhagen took a lively interest, complained in an essay of 1887 of the American girl, the »Iron Madonna, who strangles in her fond embrace the American novelist.« Cited by Clarence A. Glasrud, *Hjalmar Hjorth Boyesen* (Northfield, MN, 1963), 126.
13 Henning, *Friedrich Spielhagen*, 110.
14 Clifford Albrecht Bernd, *Poetic Realism in Scandinavia and Central Europe 1820–1895* (Columbia, SC, 1995). See my review in *South Atlantic Review* 61, no. 3 (Summer 1996): 159–61.

Spielhagen's novel is an elaborate account of personal and public failure; its autobiographical element, claimed by him as well as by others,[15] lies, it seems to me, in his rueful recognition of his own slowness to come to political consciousness and insight. It has been suggested that he underwent a political transformation as he wrote the sequel, though the account of the Revolution fills only thirty-five pages.[16] Retrospectively Spielhagen claimed a soul bond with Oswald, hating »alles, was in Staat und Gesellschaft sich übermütig spreizt und bläht und gierig von dem Schweiß der vielen mästet, deren Nähe es doch, wie die Pest, flieht, und Sonderrechte arrogiert, die ihm die Gnade eines Gottes zugeteilt haben soll, den er sich nach seinem schnöden Ebenbilde machte« (*NB*, 206), but this formulation is colored by the greater radicalism of Spielhagen's later years; in *FuE*, 1: 271–72, he remarks that he did not feel like an activist until he was working on the next novel, *Die von Hohenstein*.

Problematische Naturen itself, in its apocalypse on the barricades, seems designed more to name depression than to heal it, a feeling that may have induced the publisher to propose what Spielhagen regarded as the banal title of the second part, *Durch Nacht zum Licht* (2: 393). The original of the first part had a happier conclusion;[17] little in the final version of the novel supports this hopeful prospect other than Baron Oldenburg's tacked-on oration at the funeral of the Berlin martyrs but clearly addressed to the reader of Spielhagen's time. In it we see that the »problematic nature« is an explanatory condition but also one to be overcome. As we know, the title is taken from one of Goethe's »Maximen und Reflexionen«: »Es gibt problematische Naturen, die keiner Lage gewachsen sind, in der sie sich binden, und denen keine genugtut. Daraus entsteht der ungeheure Wider-

---

[15] Spielhagen called it a first-person novel in its inner essence (*FuE*, 2: 394); the »Stempel der Ichheit« was important, he claimed for a first work, though he was not really in it himself. Still, he called it an eight-volume confession containing ten years of his life (*NB*, 193, 201). See Victor Klemperer, *Die Zeitromane Friedrich Spielhagens und ihre Wurzeln* (Weimar, 1913), 70.

[16] Roper, »1848 in the Early Novels,« 430, 433. See also Roger Hillman, *Zeitroman: The Novel and Society in Germany 1830–1900* (Bern and Frankfurt am Main, 1983), 51: at the conclusion »a historical event is seemingly pasted together as a tableau-type backdrop to the resolution of individuals' fates.« Hillman just does not like the novel and, as so often, his objections are to its ideological-critical elements. In the first version, the critique of the brutal actions of the military was balanced with one of the violence of the mob, but the latter was deleted in the revised version. For a detailed account of the changes from the original version, see Dirk Göttsche, *Zeit im Roman. Literarische Zeitreflexion und die Geschichte des Zeitromans im späten 18. und im 19. Jahrhundert* (Munich), 687–89 and nn. 242–44.

[17] Müller-Donges, *Das Novellenwerk*, 61–62.

streit, der das Leben ohne Genuß verzehrt.«[18] Oldenburg cites this passage verbatim immediately upon making Oswald's acquaintance (*AR*, 1, 1: 344), an example of the way Spielhagen often employs his titles as leitmotifs in the texts. There has been excessive fussing, it seems to me, as to whether Spielhagen's use of the term »really« corresponds to Goethe's.[19] Such details are less important than Spielhagen's linking himself to Goethe as a claim of succession. Although the critics were more likely to put the novel's characters into succession to Young Germany,[20] Spielhagen, in his often self-important manner when defending himself, went out of his way to assert that his attention was riveted only on the »classics«:

> Ich habe nur zu konstatieren, daß, wenn ich einmal von dem Manuskript der »Problematische Naturen« die Augen hob, ich nicht Heine und Börne, nicht Karl Gutzkow und Gustav Freytag, nicht Heinrich Laube und Theodor Mundt sah – nicht den blassesten Schatten von ihnen – sondern in unerreichbarer Höhe über mir, ewigen blühenden Lebens voll, die mächtigen Gestalten, zu denen der Knabe anbetend aufgeblickt hatte, und die dem Jüngling-Mann, wenn nicht Gegenstände der Anbetung mehr, so doch der tiefsten Verehrung waren, der einzigen, die er im innersten Herzen spürte, und zu der er sich freudig vor aller Welt bekannte. (*FuE*, 2: 343)

This is especially important since there is, beyond Goethean »classicism,« no religious authority that can be acknowledged. Thus Oswald, in a particularly confused moment, sighs: »Heiliger Goethe, bitt' für mich!« (*AR*, 1, 1: 237).

Dr. Braun's father-in-law (a *Geheimrat*) makes a speech in which he defines the men of the nineteenth century as having been born without furlough (*sine missione nascitur*); like Roman proletarians, they must use all their strength in the service of a privileged class, yet they bring forth feats of science and technology. Power lies potentially with the mass of people;

---

[18] Johann Wolfgang von Goethe, *Werke* (Hamburger Ausgabe), vol. 12, *Schriften zur Kunst, Schriften zur Literatur, Maximen und Reflexionen*, ed. Herbert von Einem and Hans Joachim Schrimpf, 3rd edn. (Hamburg, 1958), 540. In the first version of the novel Spielhagen misattributed the passage to *Dichtung und Wahrheit*; see Göttsche, *Zeit im Roman*, 681, 225. According to Henning, *Friedrich Spielhagen*, 70–71, Goethe was probably thinking of Karl Philipp Moritz.

[19] See, for example, an early American review, Wm. Hand Browne, »Spielhagen's Novels,« *New Eclectic Magazine* 7 (1870): 213. To be sure, Spielhagen himself was unsure and asked his friends whether it had been mistaken to take over Goethe's concept (*FuE*, 2: 230).

[20] Especially emphasized by Gustav Karpeles, *Friedrich Spielhagen. Ein literarischer Essay* (Leipzig, 1889), 29–30. Strodtmann, *Dichterprofile*, 202, called Oswald »ein Nachzügler der jungdeutschen Anläufe, ein verkümmerter Wilhelm Meister der vierziger Jahre.«

progress will overrun the upper class. Alluding to Heine, he continues: »Mit dem todesmuthigen Instinct der Wanderratte ausgerüstet, marschirt die Fortschrittsarmee in langer, unabsehbarer Linie heran, Schulter an Schulter, der Hintermann in den Fußstapfen des Vordermanns, und wenn hier oder da eine Lücke entsteht, so schließt sie sich auch in demselben Momente.« He concludes by citing Freiligrath's radical poem sequence »Glaubensbekenntnis« of 1844 (I, 5: 324–26). Readers and critics have chronically objected to this kind of speech-making in Spielhagen's novels. But for the historian of literature and culture these set pieces are not uninteresting. They come to be increasingly differentiated as Spielhagen grows less sure of his commitments and to express the dialectic of opinion among differing views of the German situation. A little more patience in listening to their variety and nuance might be of some use. While the problematic state is a condition to be collectively overcome, it is also a badge of knowing. In a highly emotional letter, we see Helene von Grenwitz, distraught in a conflict between love and power, becoming a problematic personality; that is, she is *progressing* from aristocratic class identity to bourgeois alienation (273–84). The reader who took all this seriously could feel sorry for himself, proud of himself, and perhaps a little hopeful for the future, all at the same time.

c: *Die von Hohenstein*

The aspect of *Problematische Naturen* that probably attracted the most attention and made some readers and critics uncomfortable is its depiction of the class conflict between the aristocracy and the cultivated bourgeoisie, the longest-lived theme in Spielhagen's œuvre. He was to engage it still more directly in his second novel, *Die von Hohenstein*, originally published in the *Deutsche Wochenschrift* in 1863 and in book form in the following year (on its genesis, see *AW*, 31). We find ourselves in the immediate aftermath of the Revolution in the spring of 1848. The Hohensteins, ill-mannered, greedy, and shallow, lacking enough money to live up to their pretensions, are initially introduced as the former beauty Clotilde and her squabbling daughters, sensual Aurelie and sulky Camilla, who are trying to beat their uncle Arthur out of the will of their great-uncle, General von Rheinfelden. Clotilde's husband, Philipp, is an elegant council president; his brother, a colonel, a crude brute who rages against democrats and communists. Philipp has been trying to cope with a dismissed schoolteacher, Dr. Münzer, who is a candidate for election and defeats him; another brother, Arthur, is a black sheep, blocked in his career because he has married a bourgeoise, whom their son Wolfgang, a student, adores. He in turn is scorned by the bourgeois boys as a noble and by the nobles because his father is a speculator; the class conflict makes him desirous of justice on earth and a follower of Münzer. Wolfgang is also acquainted with a shabby schoolteacher, label-named Schmalhans, who works in a very dilapidated schoolroom in a poverty-stricken village; he keeps a secret chamber, hidden from the priest and superstitious persons, where he pursues scientific studies of things he is not supposed to know; he is in danger because he does not believe in God or the afterlife.

Wolfgang courts his cousin Camilla, a relationship her mother will support only if it appears that he is the general's heir. Now introduced is the printer Peter Schmitz and his crotchety sister Bella, »wie schon der Namen zeigte, bürgerlich, sehr bürgerlich« (*AR*, 1, 2: 83);[21] his liberal paper is failing because of the weak support for democratic ideas. It is his sister Margarethe who has formed the now regretted *mésalliance* with Arthur von Hohenstein to relieve his debts. The liberal Münzer has a wife lacking *Bildung*, the plain and unloved but loyal and undervalued Clärchen; he is indifferent to his two children, one of whom nearly drowns from his inattention. From this constellation of characters the complicated plot of the long novel unrolls. Münzer conspires to lead an uprising of workers and proletarians, but they are recalcitrant and unreliable, as well as susceptible to a vicious demagogue, Cajus, who has returned from hunting buffalo and Indians in America, where he had become a citizen, fleeing from being viciously tyrannized by

---

[21] It has been pointed out that Spielhagen's positive bourgeois figures, independently forging their own happiness, often bear the name of Schmitz, Schmidt, or, as in the case of the forty-eighter returned from America in *Ein neuer Pharao*, »Smith«; the smithy, the place of the hammer and anvil, also recurs: Katherine Roper, *German Encounters with Modernity: Novels of Imperial Berlin* (Atlantic Highlands, NJ, and London, 1991), 60, 70, n. 28. However, the Smiths (as is the case with Peter Schmitz here, Ernst Schmidt in *Sturmflut*, and »Smith«) are sometimes rigid in their confining bourgeois ideology; furthermore, some of them are negative characters, such as a sentimental usurer and snob of a landlady in *In der zwölften Stunde*, a smuggler and traitor in *Hammer und Amboß*, and a disrespectful inspector in *Herrin*. A disguised Russian nihilist in *Was will das werden?* is introduced as Captain Edgar Smith. On the other hand, Reinhold Schmidt in *Sturmflut* is one of Spielhagen's most perfect heroes: »Klassischer Name, murmelte der Präsident« (*AR*, 1, 8: 27). Else von Werben, who will eventually marry him, at first thinks: »Schmidt ist auch kein schöner Name: Frau Schmidt!« (*AR*, 1, 8: 29), and others in the novel pick up on its plebeian implications. Whether something is to be made of this is unclear to me, but the recurrence of the very common name, which another writer might avoid for just that reason, is striking, though one might think of the liberal professor Wilibald Schmitt and his bright daughter Corinna in Fontane's *Frau Jenny Treibel*.

Colonel von Hohenstein. Taking advantage of a moment of public confusion, the nearly ruined Arthur von Hohenstein steals the paper money of the town government, while his son Wolfgang, also in need of money, reluctantly joins the military, acquiring a progressive-minded superior, Major Degenfeld, who hopes to groom Wolfgang as the Napoleonic leader of an eventual people's army and is cashiered for writing a critical pamphlet. Now Wolfgang realizes he is on the wrong side and is eventually arrested for his democratic beliefs, occupying the same cell as Schmitz before him. Münzer has fallen in love with the rebellious widow Antonie von Hohenstein, the Melitta of this novel (though more of an intentional *femme fatale*), who imagines him as president of a republic, but he abandons liberalism for suicidal radical activism, causing the obstinate liberal Schmitz to break with him. Schmitz opposes the uprising now – why should the people fight for a new Kaiser? (565).

The old general, it gradually emerges, has committed a murder in his past and is being blackmailed by his housekeeper/mistress Brigitte, the schoolteacher's estranged wife; the general is arrested but, despite discovery of his victim's remains, is released through the influence of the government and the clergy.[22] The radicals plan an attack on his estate to obtain weapons; Wolfgang, who has escaped incarceration and joined the insurrection, is pained to discover this; they are defeated by soldiers but Wolfgang is saved by the schoolteacher through secret passageways. There follows a ragtag withdrawal of the rebels, disunited among themselves; it is now the summer of 1849. Münzer is charged with a capital offense; Antonie seeks a way to free him, forming an alliance with Clärchen, from whom she begs forgiveness. Wolfgang is sentenced to death in absentia. In a spectacular trial, Münzer confesses his error for deviating from liberal principles, agrees that the time is not right for change, assigns blame to the lukewarm bourgeois and intellectual evaders, and argues for class peace and a social republic by admitting the lower classes into the constitutional order. During an elaborate wedding celebration, in which Camilla and Aurelie are to be sold to unloved husbands but are already planning their infidelities, Brigitte and the servant Jean murder the old general, but he has frustrated their robbery and his scheming heirs by burning his money. At the same time, Antonie helps Münzer to flee, but Colonel von Hohenstein kills him; she stabs the colonel and Cajus strangles him. The last scene is in Switzerland,

---

[22] An original introductory chapter, comically depicting the roughhousing between Brigitte and the old man, was left out of the book version; it is reprinted by Zinken, *Der Roman als Zeitdokument*, 286–93.

two summers later. Wolfgang, associated with Schmitz in building a spa and a credit union owned by a twin brother of Major von Degenfeld, is married to Bella's daughter Ottilie, thus joining the bourgeoisie, for Bella has said long before, warning him off marriage to Camilla, »daß Du – und wenn Dein Vater zehnmal ein Hohenstein ist – ein Schmitz'sches Herz hat« (494–95), as though class identity were virtually a biological category (early she had spoken of »Schmitz'sches Blut« (194). Antonie has died, leaving her wealth to Clärchen, while Cajus has returned to America, where such a fiend doubtless belongs. Schmitz announces that the dream of freedom is immortal; the sun may go out for an individual, but not for mankind.

Here, too, much has been left out: the sometimes comic intrigues of the Hohensteins with and against one another; Clärchen's uncle, a priest who is one of Spielhagen's very few favorably drawn clergymen, who loved a married woman in his youth, whose good qualities result in his being disliked by his parishioners and superiors, and whom the general vainly begs to convert him out of fear of the state of his soul; and a great amount of political debate tending to the defense of bourgeois liberal views against both the despotic claims of the aristocracy and the untimely revolt of the uneducated and therefore unhumanized mob. I have not been able wholly to suppress the tendency to melodrama and rhetorical overkill that has persistently annoyed readers and critics. It is not unusual for a novelist who has opened his career with a success to fail with a second effort. Wilhelm Raabe, for example, followed the *succès d'estime* of *Die Chronik der Sperlingsgasse* with *Ein Frühling*, which no one has liked, including Raabe himself. Similarly, no one seems to have liked *Die von Hohenstein*, complaining regularly of its lack of verisimilitude and especially of its tendentious treatment of the class conflict.[23] Still, not long ago a whole monograph was written about it, perhaps another of those professorial assigned topics.[24]

---

[23] That Spielhagen was unfair to all three classes is a claim made in the first German dissertation written about him and in one of the most recent: Klemperer, *Die Zeitromane Friedrich Spielhagens*, 81; Alfred F. Goessl, »Die Darstellung des Adels in Prosaschriften Friedrich Spielhagens« (Diss. Tulane University, 1966), 65, citing Klemperer, as well as by Fritz Martini, *Deutsche Literatur im bürgerlichen Realismus 1848–1898*, 2nd ed. (Stuttgart, 1964), 428–29. Only rarely does one find a good word for the novel; an exception is Franz Rhöse, »Versöhnende Weltanschauung und gesellschaftliche Konflikte – Zur Theorie des Romans bei Friedrich Spielhagen,« *Konflikt und Versöhnung. Untersuchungen zur Theorie des Romans von Hegel bis zum Naturalismus* (Stuttgart, 1978), 196, who comments that it was too radical for a public already accommodating to the dominance of the Junkers.

[24] Zinken, *Der Roman als Zeitdokument.*

But it seems« to me that, if one can get over one's solicitude for the maligned aristocrats, it is in some respects better than its reputation. Like a reader of Eugène Sue, one may find oneself captivated by the plot against one's better judgment. While the murder in the general's background and his gory comeuppance seem to have been imported from Sue, the way in which shame eats away at the inner constitution of Arthur von Hohenstein, a nobleman reduced to common thievery, driving him to desperate devices that postpone the inevitable reckoning, is not without a certain narrative fascination. Furthermore, the novel grapples courageously with political issues still somewhat rare in literature. It is an early work to contain so much discourse about socialism and communism; the latter term had only begun to become current in Germany at the time in which the novel is set. Before we inquire whether Spielhagen's treatment of these matters meets our historically informed standards, we might grant him credit for taking them up at all. The aspect of this complex that has attracted the most interpretive attention has been the characterization of Münzer and its connection to the model figure of Ferdinand Lassalle, founder of the German working-class movement, whose famous courtroom defense in 1848 in Cologne had been witnessed by Spielhagen when a student in Bonn (*FuE*, 1: 276–81), and who was to die in what was widely regarded as a foolish duel in the year the book version of the novel appeared. A fair amount has been written in a positivistic vein about the parallels from Lassalle's personality and career appearing in Spielhagen's novels.[25] But Münzer, clearly named for the radical revolutionary of the time of the Reformation – he actually refers to the Peasant's War in his courtroom oration (*AR*, 1, 2: 733; Wolfgang had made the connection in his thoughts, 44) – is no more a portrait of Lassalle than any other of Spielhagen's characterizations resemble their putative models from life and experience.[26] For one thing, Spielhagen at this time did not

---

[25] Adolf Schumacher, *Ferdinand Lassalle as a Novelistic Subject of Friedrich Spielhagen* (Diss. University of Pennsylvania, 1910). See also Harvey W. Hewett-Thayer, »Ferdinand Lassalle in the Novels of Spielhagen and Meredith,« *Germanic Review* 19 (1944): 186–96.

[26] The Marxist critic Franz Mehring referred to him as »ein zu neun Zehnteln verkinkelter Marx,« »Friedrich Spielhagen,« *Beiträge zur Literaturgeschichte*, ed. Walter Heist (Berlin, 1948), 216), a reference to Gottfried Kinkel, sprung from prison in 1850 in a jailbreak organized by Spielhagen's friend Carl Schurz. He was the sort of »bourgeois radical« Marx and Marxists always enjoyed scorning; Mehring's jibe is witty but not, I think, on the mark. Zinken identifies Münzer with Kinkel rather than with Lassalle and reprints Kinkel's defense speech, *Der Roman als Zeitdokument*, 210, 294–95.

want to complicate the matter by making his figure Jewish as Lassalle was.[27] What the novel does capture with some success is the complex of issues that has constantly fascinated and also troubled observers of Lassalle: along with his charisma, energy, intelligence, and courage, his tendency to dictatorial vanity, his employment of his working-class followers as means rather than ends, his sometimes overly clever negotiations with those in power, and a susceptibility to elegance and the aristocratic – Münzer's liaison with Antonie von Hohenstein necessarily calls to mind Lassalle's with Countess Hatzfeldt.[28] In retrospect, Spielhagen fully shared the ambivalence about him, calling him »ein überaus geschickter Komödiant« and yet declaring his admiration with the observation that the genius of mankind is not always found in the purest of vessels (*FuE*, 1: 277, 280–81). As has been said, he was »the only real revolutionary among socialists in Germany during this period.«[29] These are not trivial matters, and Spielhagen was to take them on again in his next novel.

d: *In Reih' und Glied*

which first appeared in the *Deutsche Romanzeitung* in 1866 and in book form in the following year, has been rather better thought of. It is the novel that attracted Georg Brandes's admiration for Spielhagen when he read it several years later.[30] It is even by Spielhagen's standards an immensely complicated, event-filled novel that can only be abstracted here, though many of its details and subplots are not without interest. It tells of Leo Gutmann, who is seventeen when the story begins in 1847, thus about the same age as Spielhagen himself.[31] He is the son of a peasant incompetent despite his

---

27 Hewett-Thayer, »Ferdinand Lassalle,« 188.

28 For a modern assessment of his character, see Edmund Wilson, »Historical Actor: Lassalle,« *To the Finland Station: A Study in the Writing and Acting of History* (New York, 1972 [originally 1940]), 268–304.

29 Andrew Lees, *Revolution and Reflection: Intellectual Change in Germany during the 1850's* (The Hague, 1974), 182.

30 Nolin, *Den gode Europén*, 66. A Soviet diplomat is reported to have said that it impressed him as a schoolboy but, as a mature Marxist, he was disgusted by its petty-bourgeois spirit: Jürgen Kuczynski, *Gestalten und Werke. Soziologische Studien zur deutschen Literatur* (Berlin and Weimar, 1969), 1: 194.

31 This date is established when Leo's uncle Fritz muses about his role of protecting his masters in 1813 »vor vierunddreißig Jahren« (*AR*, 1, 6: 16). For some reason Schumacher, *Ferdinand Lassalle*, 89, gets this wrong, dating the first scene of the novel in 1843, thus making Leo the same age as Lassalle.

inchoate talents, but his uncle Fritz, a capable and intelligent forester on the estate of a Baron von Tuchheim, takes him in. Fritz has been in love for thirty years with the Baron's kind, wise sister Charlotte, with whom marriage was impossible because of the class difference; loyally, she remains unmarried. His son Walter becomes a liberal writer who is later persecuted and jailed; he may be thought of as the author's alter ego in the novel.[32] Fritz's daughter Silvia is a high-minded, yearning visionary who long believes that Leo incarnates her ideal of heroism. Leo loves her episodically, largely unbeknownst to himself, from the time the sight of her bathing in the woods causes him to faint and crack his head, though he spends a great part of the novel courting other women. Baron von Tuchheim has an unwanted visit from the king and the crown prince; the latter molests Silvia, whereupon Leo seizes his arm. The baron has a son, devious, conniving Henri, who is to become one of Leo's most persistent enemies, and a daughter, Amélie, with whom Walter falls in love across the class barrier. Fritz's sister, Sara, lives in the royal palace as the »housekeeper« of a bachelor minister and has become a scheming courtesan. Sara and the baron's brother, the esteemed General von Tuchheim, it turns out after many hundreds of pages, have a secret illegitimate son, an unprincipled and unstable young fop named Lippert, private secretary of the royal prince.

The baron is attempting to modernize agriculture on his estate, but he is not very expert or effective, and the workers oppose him because they fear unemployment. He therefore forms an uneasy partnership with his widowed brother-in-law Sonnenstein, ennobled son of a baptized Jew, who urges building factories because laborers can be obtained at minimal cost. Sonnenstein has a daughter, the affected Emma in the form of »eines jungen, sehr brünetten Mädchens« (*AR* 1, 6: 278), who loves Leo, and a feeble, unpromising son Alfred. Here one senses in the background Gustav Freytag's best-selling novel from the previous decade, *Soll und Haben*; although Alfred does not have the intellectual qualities of Freytag's Bernhard Ehrenthal, he is similarly tubercular, and when he dies, Sonnenstein no longer knows what he has worked for.[33] Eventually Henri von Tuchheim

---

[32] Katherine Roper, »Imaging the German Capital: Berlin Writers in the Two Unification Eras,« *1870/71–1989/90: German Unifications and the Change of Literary Discourse*, ed. Walter Pape (Berlin and New York, 1993), 175; Roper, »1848 in the Early Novels,« 442.

[33] Another echo from *Soll und Haben*, besides the conflict between the less competent, agrarian nobleman and the more ruthless Jewish industrialist, and the loss of the son for whom the Jew has labored, may be the scene in which the forester Fritz Gutmann is able to advance 10,000 talers to the baron (*AR*, 1, 7:

marries Emma for money even though he dislikes her. Leo comes under the influence of a schoolteacher, Conrad Tusky, son of a cowherd, a violent and vengeful revolutionary. Like Münzer, he calls up historical memories of the Peasant's War. He is the sort of character who reappears in Spielhagen's novels and comes to be identified as a nihilist: beset with a sense of the intolerable injustice of the world and the need for change but utterly contemptuous of the common herd and convinced of its need to be led by men of morally unfettered genius and iron will. Thus the radical's view of the people is the same as that reactionary general's: »Denn Sie wollen mir doch nicht sagen, daß die quer- und plattköpfige, schaufelhändige, breit-mäulige, durch und durch brutale Masse im Stande sein sollte, sich selbst zu regieren?« (*AR*, 1, 7: 284). Tusky instigates a failed revolt on the estate and must flee to America. His sister Eve is a demonic beauty who spends much of the second part of the novel trying to trade sex for information and influence, conspiring against Leo because he has rejected her.

When we encounter Leo seven years later in the *Nachmärz* gloom »einer Reaction, die aller Freiheit und allem Leben Tod und Verderben geschworen« (1, 6: 249), he is a physician totally persuaded of a vocation as an incomparable leader of the masses he despises. He has come to number Walter among the philistines because he argues for collective democratic action »in Reih' und Glied« (1, 6: 267). The crown prince, whom Leo attacked as a boy, has now been king for four years; Leo at first scorns the king but then imagines that he could lead the revolution, proclaim the republic, have himself elected president (270); perhaps one should think here of Louis Napoleon. Leo, jailed after having been involved in a failed strike in Tuchheim, advises striking workers, whom he privately thinks of as the »verdumpfte[ ] Masse« with which he is experimenting (512), to turn to the king instead of the capitalists. Sara, hoping to make Silvia the king's mistress, has induced her to reside in the palace; through her intervention she gets Leo released, and he gradually gains influence over the king, persuading him to form an alliance with the workers against the power of money; Leo frightens Silvia by telling her of a dream he had of the king

---

178), recalling Book 4, Chapter 4 of the earlier novel, where the hard-drinking laborer Sturm advances 1,900 talers to Baron Rothsattel's spendthrift son. Both scenes seem unrealistic and improbable. Young Nietzsche was much impressed by *In Reih' und Glied*; his teacher seems to have sensed a link with *Soll und Haben*, for Nietzsche reports him as declaring Spielhagen's novel ten times better than all of Freytag (Henning, *Friedrich Spielhagen*, 187).

serving him.[34] Baron Tuchheim, who, under Leo's influence, has opposed a confrontational policy toward the workers, is for that reason killed in a duel by the brother of the king's despotic minister Hey. Leo offers to buy the Tuchheim factories for the king; Sonnenstein is sure that, once the socialist experiment fails, he will be able to buy them back at half price. Leo imagines himself getting more and more powerful, seeks to become minister and gets himself ennobled, though he is told by the scorned Walter that he has moved »aus dem bürgerlichen Leben in eine abenteuerliche Scheinwelt« (1, 7: 272). He thinks of separating Emma from Henri, but becomes engaged, listlessly and aimlessly, to the general's soulless daughter Josephe von Tuchheim.

Everyone tries to use Leo; the king besieges Silvia, who gets a reputation as his mistress. The factories are failing and all ends in catastrophe; the king, who has become mystical and mentally unstable, dies; the workers rebel and form factions against one another; a badly tended furnace sets the factory on fire; Silvia, dismayed at the badness of the world, drowns in the same pond in which the young Leo had seen her bathing; he sees he has brought misery and guilt to the workers but Tusky turns up, urging him to stay the course or escape with him to America to free the slaves; the good Fritz is killed by a shot from the gun of the most radical worker and Leo is mortally wounded in a duel with Lippert. The novel ends in a funeral oration drawing the moral that workers can be saved only by themselves, must preserve the sacred order, whatever that may be, and remain good soldiers »in Reih' und Glied« (620). Thus the title phrase means »Zusammenrücken der Tugendhaften gegen Feudalismus und gegen Sozialismus.«[35] However, the evil Henri von Tuchheim, of whom Leo, who does not live long enough to duel with him, says, »würde er noch am Leben bleiben, meinem Vaterlande, ja vielleicht Europa noch viel Blut und Thränen kosten wird« (1, 7: 609), lives on as the favorite of the reactionary prince.

The more thoughtful critical attention the novel has received has been mainly focused on Leo as a further figuration of the Lassalle problem. Certainly he is heightened almost to caricature, more megalomanic, more

---

[34] See the stimulating observation on the function of dreams in the novel by Katherine Roper, »Friedrich Spielhagen,« *Dictionary of Literary Biography*, vol. 129, *Nineteenth-Century German Writers 1841–1900*, ed. James Hardin and Siegfried Mews (Detroit and London, 1993), 353.

[35] Dieter Kafitz, *Figurenkonstellation als Mittel der Wirklichkeitserfassung. Dargestellt am Roman der zweiten Hälfte des 19. Jahrhunderts (Freytag · Spielhagen · Fontane · Raabe)* (Kronberg, 1978), 115.

lusting for a virtually monarchical power of his own, and more contemptuous of the workers he is endeavoring to lead than Lassalle ever was; it has been remarked that he »never wins more than a conditioned interest and sympathy; in the end he becomes so odious that the reader rejoices at his downfall.«[36] But the problem of the alienation of the *Weltanschauung* of impatient and ambitious bourgeois revolutionaries from the real existence and experience of the working class is a genuine one and intensely if somewhat melodramatically elaborated in the novel. The wise Fritz, who has studied economics, has come to understand that a master like the baron cannot raise wages by himself if the competition does not, and the competition cannot if goods made more expensive cannot be sold on the world market (176); Lassalle, too, incidentally, came to an acknowledgment of the iron law of wages.[37] Spielhagen's democratic liberalism, though opposed to radical activism, could still be regarded as subversive; the novel was threatened with prosecution, though nothing came of it (*AW*, 191).

However, the novel has another significant complex that is usually only brushed upon: the character and role of the king. The reader is tempted to associate him with Friedrich Wilhelm IV.[38] Spielhagen himself even exaggerated the resemblance, »nach einem nicht mehr lebenden Modell mit großem Fleiß gezeichnet« (189). There are some rather clever scenes that visualize what it may have been like for the hopeful intelligentsia to attempt to engage with Friedrich Wilhelm IV: his bonhomie and humor, his apparent but unsteady interest in modern ideas, his flickers of attention to social issues, his drift into religious mysticism.[39] The mental stability of Spielhagen's king is precarious and there is an expectation that his rival, the more militaristic and reactionary, otherwise unidentified »prince« (whom

---

[36] Hewett-Thayer, »Ferdinand Lassalle,« 190–91.

[37] Wehler, *Deutsche Gesellschaftsgeschichte*, 3: 159.

[38] Julian Schmidt promptly noted resemblances to the king, »von dem beiläufig einzelne Züge genial und meisterhaft abconterfeit sind« but was puzzled by the deviations in the portrayal: »Friedrich Spielhagen,« *Westermann's Jahrbuch der Illustrirten Deutschen Monatshefte* 29 (1870–71), 440–41. Schumacher, *Ferdinand Lassalle*, 114–18, supplies a detailed list of resemblances. Klemperer, *Die Zeitromane Friedrich Spielhagens*, 100, following other authorities, takes the portrayal as a given, as does Anderson, »Spielhagen's Problematic Heroes,« 116, who remarks that the »reader ... should have no difficulty in ... recognizing the king«; his further observation that »the reader may substitute Bismarck for Wilhelm Friedrich [sic] IV« is less well taken.

[39] Friedrich Wilhelm IV's policy toward the poor resembled Eugène Sue's suggestions; he inquired about industrial reform in *Le Juif errant*. See Norbert Bachleitner, *Der englische und französische Sozialroman des 19. Jahrhunderts und seine Rezeption in Deutschland* (Amsterdam and Atlanta, 1993), 140, 142.

Leo exposes in public to the king's delight) will replace him as regent; one thinks necessarily of the Prince of Prussia, later regent, king, and Kaiser Wilhelm I. But Spielhagen, as was his custom, explicitly alters the model. His king must be about Leo's age, making him a good generation younger than Friedrich Wilhelm IV. He succeeds to the throne after the Revolution, in 1850, while the historical king succeeded in 1840. He has an infant heir, as Friedrich Wilhelm IV did not, and, as for his sometimes frantic and weepy wooing of Silvia, Friedrich Wilhelm IV was popularly reputed to be impotent. While he did dream of forming a direct bond with the »people,« circumventing the detested liberals and the constitution, he was obsessed with divine right, ruling by the grace of God, a style he restored after his more commonsensical father, Friedrich Wilhelm III, had dropped it.[40] This pervasive issue does not come up in Spielhagen's novel.

Rather it seems to me that what he has done is to turn the liberal monarchism endemic in nineteenth-century Germany, so to speak, inside out. Unable to contemplate the prospect of popular sovereignty, bourgeois liberals longed for an alliance of the royal power with themselves to the exclusion of the aristocracy. The notion goes back to the eighteenth century, expresses itself in Heine's Bonapartism, in the Young German movement, and in the patriotic novels of Willibald Alexis, was disastrously applied in the offer of the imperial crown to Friedrich Wilhelm IV by the National Assembly in 1849,[41] reemerged in the hopes invested in the crown prince, so sadly dashed in his ninety-nine day reign as Friedrich III, and was extinguished only by the no longer evadable reality of the character of Wilhelm II. Spielhagen's novel suggests what this alliance might have looked like in practice. The royal power is a chimera, grounded in a neurotic personality and constrained by a rigid social order. The king's momentary liberal affects are fleeting and shallow; in fact, he hopes his stupid subordinates will discredit constitutional government (*AR*, 1, 7: 30). His apparently lively aesthetic interest expresses itself in admiration for a picture of Pharaoh building the pyramids; he dubiously compliments the

---

[40] See the essays in *Friedrich Wilhelm IV. in seiner Zeit. Beiträge eines Colloquiums*, ed. Otto Büsch (Berlin, 1987). Roper, »1848 in the Early Novels,« 442, notes the only partial resemblance and suggests that it might be owing to fear of censorship, but the alteration of models was Spielhagen's constant custom.

[41] In *Ein neuer Pharao*, Dr. Brunn, a former forty-eighter who has made his pragmatic peace with the Wilhelminian order, is presented as a member of the delegation that offered the crown to the king (*AR*, 3, 3: 135). The father of the narrator of *Was will das werden?* recalls his youthful view that the king had no right to refuse a crown offered by the people (*AR*, 3, 4: 106).

painter by declaring that he is derivative of Horace Vernet and brooks no opposition to his critical opinions (88–89). The king and the radical form no real alliance but are trying to exploit one another; the king indulges Leo in order to win Silvia, pretending to offer the prime ministership, while Leo, like Schiller's Marquis Posa, imagines that he is just making use of the king for his own purposes. The king does not even have enough money to maintain the factories Leo has acquired to bind the workers to him; Leo must mortgage the villa the king has given him in a futile effort to stem the economic collapse. The sovereign king is no mightier than the Wizard of Oz and Leo's ambitions are no more realistic. In Leo's last, rueful thoughts when the king has repudiated him, the motif of the pyramid reappears: »Ich habe eine Pyramide aus Schlamm bauen wollen ..., wie kann ich mich wundern, daß der Regen sie weggewaschen hat!« (610). Here Spielhagen has crafted something that has not been clearly seen but is not without a degree of bitter intelligence. In a somewhat wry retrospect, he gave himself credit for prophecy: »ein gutes Stück Kathedersozialismus und die Lehre vom sozialen König, die heute als ein *novum* gilt, vor dreißig Jahren antizi-pierend« (*AW*, 190).

e: *Hammer und Amboß*

In Reih' und Glied does not appear to regard industrialization very positively. During the catastrophe Fritz Gutmann says to himself: »Soll denn die Un-glücksfabrik uns noch Alle verderben?« (*AR*, 1, 7: 568). Thus the author seems to put himself in the tradition of conservative, idealistic resistance to industrialization most eloquently inaugurated by Karl Immermann in his novel *Die Epigonen* over thirty years before, at the end of which the grimly described industrial enterprise is dismantled.[42] Spielhagen, however, did not stop with this resistance, but attempted a more encouraging view of industry in his next novel, *Hammer und Amboß*, which appeared in 1869, shortly after it had been serialized in the *Neue Freie Presse* in Vienna;[43] it

---

[42] This ending has been much debated. For my view of it, see *Six Essays on the Young German Novel* (Chapel Hill, 1972), 138–39. On the continuation of the Luddite attitude in *Vormärz* writing, see Ilsedore Rarisch, *Das Unternehmerbild in der deutschen Erzählliteratur der ersten Hälfte des 19. Jahrhunderts. Ein Beitrag zur Rezeption der frühen Industrialisierung in der belletristischen Literatur* (Berlin, 1977), 150–55.

[43] Lamers, *Held oder Welt?*, 38. Lamers also reports that it was published as a school text in 1912 (38–39).

had grown out of an undistinguished novella, *Breite Schultern,* five years before (*AR,* 2, 8: 257–81; also in *AmSk,* 337–61). Because of the longing of German critics to find something »modern« in literary history, the novel has attracted some attention in our time; it was published in paperback in a »Nostalgie Bibliothek« by Heyne in Munich in 1975. The question is, however, whether it can meet the hopes invested in it. Once again the title is taken from Goethe: »*Hammer* zu sein scheint jedem rühmlicher und wünschenswerter als *Ambos,* und doch was gehört nicht dazu, diese unendlichen, immer wiederkehrenden Schläge auszuhalten!«[44] Once again the phrase echoes as a leitmotif, here and elsewhere, and once again more significance is required of it by incantation than it can actually deliver. The allusion had already appeared in *Die von Hohenstein* and *In Reih' und Glied,* will be reified in the nailsmith scenes in *Was will das werden?* and will recur in *Ein neuer Pharao* (*AR,* 1, 2: 71, 87; 1, 6: 434; 3, 4: 98, 527; 3, 3: 138). Here, however, in keeping with the concept of a self being forged either by acting or being acted upon, the first-person novel has the linear pattern of the *Bildungsroman* and is thus more easily recounted, despite various subplots and digressions.

In the early 1830s a young man, Georg Hartwig, of uncommon size and strength, becomes alienated, in part through a quite one-sided friendship with a class-conscious noble boy, Arthur von Zehren, son of a *Steuerrath,* from school and family; when Georg's father throws him out, he is taken up by Malte von Zehren, the black sheep of the noble family, who lives from smuggling in partnership with his apparently respectable brother, Arthur's father, imagining himself, in his scruffy circumstances, as a daring, aristocratically sovereign robber baron of a fictional past. After some disorderly adventures, properly deplored by the retrospective narrator, tax officials ambush Malte, who flees and takes his life rather than be captured, while Georg, who, when he realizes he is wanted for a murder he has not committed, turns himself in and, partly on the testimony of his »friend« Arthur, is sentenced to seven years in prison. There he encounters another von Zehren, the warden, who with kindness and wisdom rehabilitates Georg by accustoming him to labor. Georg wins his support by saving his life during an escape attempt and makes friends with the warden's fourteen-year-old daughter Paula, a serious girl who aspires to be an artist, nurses him from the wounds obtained in the struggle, and contributes to his *Bildung* by placing volumes of Goethe, Schiller, and Lessing in his cell. Georg learns

---

[44] From a conversation in April 1806 reported by Friedrich Wilhelm Riemer, *Goethes Gespräche,* ed. Flodoard von Biedermann et al. (Leipzig, 1901–11), 1: 409.

office work, various trades, mathematics, and physics. He acquits himself well on the occasion of a dangerous storm during which the warden, against the orders of the authorities, allows the prisoners to strengthen the sea wall and rescue a ship, thus showing that a world without masters and slaves is possible. The already ill warden dies in the effort, but not before he has led the willing prisoners back to their cells.

Released, Georg, who has learned ship machinery in prison, is able to prevent a disaster at sea, an act witnessed by Hermine Streber, the daughter of the local capitalist; she mediates his employment in her father's factory, where Georg learns industrial work from the bottom up and pursues his *Bildung*. He notes that the workers consider themselves to be the anvil, while the owners see no reason why they should not be the hammer. Georg must persuade an unwilling Streber of the importance of locomotive manufacture for the future and, like a socialist-realist hero, solves a mechanical problem that the engineers were unable to master, leading to his promotion to foreman. Streber, he suspects, despite the luxury in which he lives, is failing in business. Georg himself has a phase of seduction by luxury that he must overcome; he marries the shallow and immature Hermine. Like his competitors, Georg must find his way through the industrial problems with which Germans have little experience; he cannot make the concessions to the workers that he would prefer. Streber poisons himself; Hermine dies in childbirth. Through hard work Georg rescues the enterprise, involving the workers in profit sharing, and marries his true love, Paula, a successful artist.

There can be no doubt that *Hammer und Amboß* represents a literary-historical advance; it is one of the first German novels to carry the narration onto the factory floor. It has been observed that Spielhagen has relieved the machine of its demonic aspect as soulless automaton and alien monster, beginning to treat it as a tool in the labor process.[45] He had well developed technical interests, initially born in his admiration for his engineering foster brother Mons, who gave him his first introduction to railroad building and took him on a visit to the Borsig locomotive works, an experience he explicitly connects to *Hammer und Amboß* (*FuE*, 1: 226–28). It was perhaps with Mons in mind that in the early novella *Auf der Düne* the dredging machine is explained to the visitor, but he is too unmathematical to understand it (*AR*, 2, 1: 170). There is an imaginative description of marble-cutting machinery in *Sturmflut* (*AR*, 1, 8: 148–49). Spielhagen several times

---

[45] Joachim Worthmann, *Probleme des Zeitromans. Studien zur Geschichte des deutschen Romans im 19. Jahrhundert* (Heidelberg, 1974), 101.

commented on the difference in consciousness technology had brought; in 1873, that the railroad and the telegraph have made us into Prometheus (*BT*, 39); in 1890, that Pegasus was losing the race with the locomotive (*FuE*, 1: viii); in 1898, that the telegraph and the telephone, railroads and steamers, and electricity in the most remote village must change literature (*NB*, 9–10). Telegrams come to be common in his fictions. The pneumatic post, introduced in Berlin in 1876, appears in *Stumme des Himmels* in 1895 (*NF*, 2: 155); in *Sonntagskind*, two years earlier, there is continuous use of the telephone, put into general use in Berlin in 1881 (*NF*, 1: 466–67). But it is in the penultimate novel, *Opfer* of 1900, where these devices proliferate: the telephone, the pneumatic post, a restaurant lit by electric flames, a party illuminated by hundreds of electric bulbs that almost create daylight, a hotel serviced by an elevator (not in general use until the preceding decade); an airship is employed as a simile while it is said of a fleeing thief that, in the age of the telegraph and telephone, he will not get far, which turns out to be true (*NF*, 6: 72, 181, 279, 249, 274, 296, 341, 422, 273–74). I have no idea how pioneering these occurrences are; I imagine there are many examples in the magazine fiction of the time, but they do not appear in the texts of the canonized realism and are early in my reading experience.

Spielhagen's view of labor relations seems forward-looking as well, especially the insight that industry will thrive best if employers and workers cooperate. The profit-sharing solution looks quite prophetic to us today, although a modern observer has complained that Spielhagen has not told us how this was to be done.[46] Rather, Georg is a visionary:

> ich sah die Flammen aus den großen Essen sprühen und die hohen Schlote rauchen; ich hörte den Schlag des Hammers auf den Amboß und sah die dunklen Schaaren der Arbeiter über die weiten Höfe wimmeln und sich in den Gassen eines neuen Quartiers verlieren, wo sie in einem der reinlichen Häuser ein freundlicher, warmer Heerd empfing, an dem sie sich ausruhen konnten von des Tages schwerer Mühe. (*AR*, 1, 4: 229)

Emancipatory labor and mutual brotherhood are the watchwords (374–75). Still, in 1869, all this must look very utopian, and the narrator admits the reader may think »daß jene goldene Zeit, von der ich spreche, heute noch wie damals in dem Schooße der Götter liege« (374), and in fact, as with most matters, Spielhagen's optimism had diminished by the end of his

---

[46] Rémy Charbon, »Der Homo œconomicus in der Literatur von 1830 bis zur Reichsgründung,« *Der literarische Homo œconomicus. Vom Märchenhelden zum Manager. Beiträge zum Ökonomieverständnis in der Literatur,* ed. Werner Wunderlich (Bern and Stuttgart, 1989), 150.

career. The narrator of *Frei geboren* declares that the factory portal should bear the motto: »laßt alle Hoffnung draußen« (*NF*, 7: 269). Similarly, Spielhagen's humanistic, nurturing prison warden must look quite fantastic, not only in 1869, but to the present day. Still, a tale was once told that a criminalized peasant boy was rehabilitated while in jail by a doctor who gave him *Hammer und Amboß* to read and thereby changed his life.[47] In any case, Spielhagen wanted to introduce an argument about criminal justice. The warden opposes the doctrine of the unnamed Hegel that punishment is the justice of injustice, the right of the criminal. Almost all the prisoners, he says, are physically ill and mentally retarded; almost all are children of social misery, pariahs of egotistical society. Some day (though not soon) this principle will be cast off along with that of death as the wages of sin. To-day we live with the ugly remains of the past: »überall das kaum versteckte, grundbarbarische Verhältniß zwischen Herrn und Sclaven, zwischen der dominirenden und der unterdrückten Kaste; überall die bange Wahl, ob wir Hammer sein wollen oder Amboß« (*AR*, 1, 3: 357–60). In the century-long debate in Germany about criminal justice these are very advanced positions.[48]

To be sure, reviewers from that time to this have complained about improbabilities and irrelevance.[49] While the American translator found a new strength in the novel, exceeding the then prestigious Auerbach in breadth, a reviewer of the translation concluded that the moral was to marry a rich

---

[47] *Friedrich Spielhagen. Dem Meister des deutschen Romans zu seinem 70. Geburtstage von Freunden und Jüngern gewidmet. Herausgegeben auf Veranlassung der Verlagshandlung vom Festausschuß der Spielhagen-Feier* (Leipzig, 1899), 85–87.

[48] Contextualized by Rainer Schröder, »Hegels Rechtsphilosophie im realistischen Roman. Zu *Hammer und Amboß* von Friedrich Spielhagen,« *Erzählte Kriminalität. Zur Typologie und Funktion von narrativen Darstellungen in Strafrechtspflege, Publizistik und Literatur zwischen 1770 und 1920*, ed. Jörg Schönert with Konstantin Imm and Joachim Linder (Tübingen, 1991), 413–28. Schröder complains (418) that Hegel has been simplified. The issue had been raised more briefly but in similar terms in *Clara Vere* (*AR* 2, 1: 26).

[49] For a good example of measuring the novel's inadequacies by today's ideological certainties, see Rolf Geissler, »Verspielte Realitätserkenntnis. Zum Problem der objektiven Darstellung in Friedrich Spielhagens *Hammer und Amboß*,« *Deutsche Vierteljahrsschrift* 52 (1978): 496–510; Geissler sniffs that, by turning himself in, Georg reenacts the gesture of Schiller's Karl Moor (503); in fact, he had evaded the opportunity of allowing a pair of gendarmes to earn the reward for him (*AR*, 1, 3: 254–55). Harro Segeberg, *Literatur im technischen Zeitalter. Von der Frühzeit der deutschen Aufklärung bis zum Beginn des Ersten Weltkriegs* (Darmstadt, 1997) sees little more than the adaptation of a skilled commercial writer to his public: »zum kongenialen Einfühlen und Harmonisieren zeitgenössischer Entwicklungstrends« (192). That the reader »wird in den endlosen Gesprächen ... von den beteiligten Personen ebenso tendenziös wie intensiv belehrt« he understands as violation of the principle of objective narration, thus signalling the insecurity of the validity of the ideal (194).

wife.[50] Although one might grant that Spielhagen's novel exhibits a healthy influence from Dickens, Heinrich Hart, of whom we shall hear more before long, complained that Spielhagen merely imitated the two marriages of David Copperfield.[51] It was a very common device of critics, especially Klemperer, to search for borrowings in Spielhagen from other novels, as though he were a poacher on other writers' property; a sense that intertextuality might enrich a literary work had not yet developed. A contemporary critic complains about the triviality of the adventures with Malte, a contradictory attitude toward bourgeois values, a hope for overcoming class conflicts but not the classes themselves, the representation of labor itself restricted to one scene of riveting a boiler, a rise to capitalist status more rapid than that of Freytag's Anton Wohlfart, the passivity of the workers who are used to being anvils, and the impossibility of poeticizing bourgeois work.[52] Another has observed that we do not hear the sounds of industry or of the railroad, only the talk about them, while most of the sounds are from nature, indicating a rootedness in Romantic topoi and a premodern landscape.[53] This litany of complaint seems to owe its origin to critics not having found what they wished for, as though the writer were responsible for all the manifold evils of the bourgeoisie. It seems fairer to point out that the riveting of the boiler and the thematizing of immediately contemporary issues enter »poetisches Neuland.«[54]

Spielhagen's progress as a novelist thus far had brought him up to the threshold of German unification. That epochal event, as we shall see in Part III, was to give his career quite a turn.

---

[50] Browne, »Spielhagen's Novels,« 213–14; Anonymous, [review of *Hammer and Anvil*], *Atlantic Monthly* 26 (1870): 636–37.

[51] Heinrich Hart, »Friedrich Spielhagen und der deutsche Roman der Gegenwart,« in Heinrich and Julius Hart, *Kritische Waffengänge*, ed. Mark Boulby (New York and London, 1969), 54. The alleged borrowing had already been complained of by Julian Schmidt, »Friedrich Spielhagen,« 440–41. Klemperer, *Die Zeitromane Friedrich Spielhagens*, 109–10, remarked that Spielhagen, like Dickens, took the easy way out by having the first wife die. For a more analytic view of the disappearance of Hermine after having made Georg heir to the means of production and of the handling of the marriage pattern, see Claudia Streit, *(Re-)- Konstitution von Familie im sozialen Roman des 19. Jahrhunderts* (Frankfurt am Main and Berlin, 1997), 161–79.

[52] Paul Jackson, »Friedrich Spielhagen: Hammer und Amboß,« *Bürgerliche Arbeit und Romanwirklichkeit. Studien zur Berufsproblematik in Romanen des deutschen Realismus* (Frankfurt am Main, 1981), 230–64.

[53] Gabriele Henkel, *Geräuschwelten im deutschen Zeitroman. Epische Darstellung und poetologische Bedeutung von der Romantik bis zum Naturalismus* (Wiesbaden, 1996), 141–91.

[54] Lamers, *Held oder Welt?*, 57.

3. The Decline of Reputation

In February of 1899 a segment of the German literary community organized a seventieth-birthday celebration for Spielhagen. Such occasions had become customary in German cultural life, although sometimes they seem to have been more gratifying for the celebrants than the celebrated. Twelve years earlier, Theodor Storm, struggling with the cancer that would end his life in less than a year, had endured a celebration that was practically an apotheosis; nevertheless he took the occasion to complain of the public's neglect of him as a lyric poet and wrote to Gottfried Keller that it would have been a nice birthday if it had not been the seventieth.[1] As for Keller, two years later, he avoided his simply by going out of town.[2] Two years after Spielhagen's, Wilhelm Raabe approached his with considerable trepidation. Although the event came off all right, some of the antecedent anxiety is evident in his posthumous, fragmentary novel *Altershausen.*[3] While Spielhagen had experienced such occasions since his fiftieth birthday,[4] he too, was uneasy, as he reports in a reminiscence entitled »*Post Festum*«; he felt he had been forced into the affair by his friends and wanted to escape; »mit seiner Dichterwürde,« he says of himself, »stand es mißlich.« There are, after all, lots of writers, »wie Sand am Meer. Unter ihnen welch fragwürdige Gestalten *masculini* und *feminini generis*!« (*AW*, 34–37). In verse he wrote that whoever reaches seventy experiences nothing new under the sun (*NG*, 177).

---

[1]   Karl Ernst Laage, *Theodor Storm Biographie* (Heide, 1999), 232–41.

[2]   See Emil Ermatinger, *Gottfried Kellers Leben* (Stuttgart and Berlin, 1924), 669–73. At the end of that year, Spielhagen reportedly gave the opening greeting at Theodor Fontane's seventieth-birthday banquet: *Fontane-Handbuch*, ed. Christian Grawe and Helmuth Nürnberger ([Stuttgart], 2000), 915.

[3]   See Sammons, *Wilhelm Raabe*, 46–47, 320–22.

[4]   Lamers, *Held oder Welt?*, 13–14. Berthold Auerbach gave a speech on the occasion: Anton Bettelheim, *Berthold Auerbach. Der Mann – Sein Werk – Sein Nachlaß* (Stuttgart and Berlin, 1907), 377. On Spielhagen's sixtieth, we are told, he was felicitated by the Prussian minister of education as »*au plus grand romancier de l'Allemagne,*« for which the minister received an official reprimand on account of Spielhagen's critical treatment of Bismarck in *Sturmflut*: Edouard de Morsier, *Romanciers allemands contemporains* (Paris, 1890), 6, 93 (emphasis in original).

But his distress must have been even greater than he indicates with this deflective humility. For, although a street was named for him in his birthplace of Magdeburg and his drama *Liebe für Liebe* was revived by the Royal Theater in Berlin,[5] by then the evidence had become unavoidable that his once gleaming career, the rise of which has just been chronicled, was by now in ruins. Some of the effect can be seen from the ninety-nine-page album that accompanied the celebration. First of all, no responsible editor is named; it was probably Gustav Karpeles, who had published an intensely idealizing little book on Spielhagen in the year of his sixtieth birthday[6] and who signed the introduction to the album. The contributions tend to light verse and bread-and-butter notes, many of them quite terse, doubtless telegrams. A toast by the eminent literary historian Erich Schmidt lectured Spielhagen on Goethe;[7] Klemperer, who knew Spielhagen personally, says that it made him feel like a schoolboy.[8] A modern commentator has deprecated the volume »mit seinen vielfach schnell und schäbig und immerfort auf der Hut vor zu viel Herzlichkeit zusammengeschriebenen Gratulationsversen und Prosawidmungen.«[9] Some colleagues are conspicuous by their absence, notably Raabe, whose own event was much more productive of honors.[10] On other such occasions Raabe tried to work up some politeness, but not for this one, although he was well aware of it (for details, see the Epilogue: »Spielhagen and Raabe«). Spielhagen knew a great many people in the literary world but may not have cultivated much intimacy with them. His biographer reports the rather striking fact that Karl Frenzel was the only one with whom he exchanged the pronoun »du,« and that only after many years, when Spielhagen was sixty-eight.[11]

His fall from canonical status was dramatic, especially when compared with his apparent public eminence. *Problematische Naturen*, which was republished nearly a half-century later in a two-volume, illustrated luxury edition (see the advertisement facing *NF*, 1: 598), achieved successes of a magnitude of which many authors can only dream. The early novels were

5 Müller-Donges, *Das Novellenwerk*, 11; Henning, *Friedrich Spielhagen*, 175. For his eightieth birthday in 1909 a plaque was put on his birth house (2–3).
6 Karpeles, *Friedrich Spielhagen*.
7 *Friedrich Spielhagen. Dem Meister des deutschen Romans*, 6–7.
8 Klemperer, *Curriculum vitae*, 1: 475.
9 Müller-Donges, *Das Novellenwerk*, 11.
10 See Werner Fuld, *Wilhelm Raabe. Eine Biographie* (Munich, 1993), 349; Walter Hettche, »Nach alter Melodie: Die Gedichte von Julius Rodenberg, Wilhelm Jensen und Paul Heyse zum 70. Geburtstag Wilhelm Raabes,« *Jahrbuch der Raabe-Gesellschaft* (1999): 144–45.
11 Henning, *Friedrich Spielhagen*, 142.

translated into all the major languages. In Russia, a committee celebrating Gogol's one-hundredth birthday in 1909 elected Spielhagen as an honorary member.[12] The French Swiss literary historian Edouard de Morsier in 1890 opened a 120-page chapter on Spielhagen with the somewhat anachronistic declaration that for twenty years he had been the most celebrated of contemporary German writers.[13] In 1914 it could be asserted that in addition to being popular in Russia he was one of the best-loved German writers in America and France.[14] The Norwegian-American scholar and novelist H. H. Boyesen stated: »His works, which extend over the last thirty-five years, though some of them deal with earlier periods, are to my mind the most valuable and faithful chronicles of German life and thought during the last quarter century that we possess.«[15] American periodicals kept track of him, down to notices of his death.[16] One of the widely used American histories of German literature concluded: »Certain it is that no novelist of Spielhagen's time, born, bred, and living in Germany, surpassed, or even equalled his attainments as a national novelist.« Those of others, like Freytag, »are without the grand significance which one must ever couple with the name of Spielhagen.«[17] The reception was not always positive. In Henry James's story »Pandora« (1884), »a very intelligent girl, who came from Boston,« rather insistently engages Count von Vogelstein, a pleasantly dim young diplomat, in a conversation on the novels of Spielhagen, »a voluminous writer,« without eliciting much response; the count is glad when the subject is changed.[18]

In England in 1880 it was observed that he »has been unanimously considered as the greatest of contemporary German novelists; and rightly so, for he embodies in his work all the merits and failings of his countrymen's ro-

[12] Henning, *Friedrich Spielhagen*, 117.
[13] Morsier, *Romanciers allemands contemporains*, 4.
[14] Hermann Schierding, *Untersuchungen über die Romantechnik Friedrich Spielhagens (Unter Benutzung unveröffentlichter Manuskripte)* (Borna-Leipzig, 1914), 138.
[15] Hjalmar Hjorth Boyesen, »Studies of the German Novel,« *Essays on German Literature* (New York, 1892), 258. The essay was originally published in 1884. Boyesen was a protégé of Spielhagen, as we shall see.
[16] For a particularly encomiastic example, see Harold Berman, »Friedrich Spielhagen: The Novelist of Democracy,« *Twentieth Century Magazine* 4 (1911): 347–49.
[17] John Firman Coar, *Studies in German Literature in the 19th Century* (New York, 1903), 293–94. I owe this reference to Thomas Tyrell, »Theodor Fontanes ›Effi Briest‹ und Friedrich Spielhagens ›Zum Zeitvertreib.‹ Zwei Dichtungen zu einer Wirklichkeit« (Diss. Rice U, 1986), 4.
[18] Henry James, *The Complete Tales*, ed. Leon Edel (Philadelphia and New York, 1963), 5: 387. On James's insuperable dislike of things German, see Evelyn A. Hovanec, *Henry James and Germany* (Amsterdam, 1979). She concludes that Spielhagen is an »imaginary writer« whose name James made up (100), a particularly striking instance of our hero's disappearance from the cultural memory.

mances, their careful observation and thoroughness, their inordinate length and tendency to sentimentalism. His novels are social photographs, that admirably reflect the manners and ideas of his time and country.«[19] Twelve of his novels were serialized in Austrian newspapers, ten in the *Neue Freie Presse*, beginning with *In Reih' und Glied* in 1865–66, and two in the *Wiener Presse*.[20] As for Germany, his former student friend Strodtmann declared flatly in 1879 that Spielhagen was the most brilliant novelist of the present.[21] Such statements are occasionally encountered even after they ceased to be strictly true. Peter Rosegger's son affirmed upon Spielhagen's death that he was incontestably the greatest German novelist of the time.[22] His books are found in the library of Empress Elisabeth and, for that matter, in Raabe's.[23]

Today there is barely a trace of all this glory. Only very recently has there been a sign here and there of the reemergence of the view of him as »dem zweifellos wichtigsten Zeitromanautor der zweiten Jahrhunderthälfte.«[24] There is, as I mentioned in the introduction, no modern edition and we have but a few scattered publications of his correspondence. Only a couple of his works are currently in print, and those in little-known publishing houses.[25] The decanonization has been thorough. Literary critics and historians regularly assure us that Spielhagen's fiction is of no value and that there is no need to become acquainted with it. Franz Mehring

---

[19] Zimmern, *Half-Hours with Foreign Novelists*, 1: 189. This praise might seem even more left-handed if joined to an introductory comment that »contemporary Germany boasts few novelists of first-class merit, and her current fictitious literature has never yet found much favour in this country« (1: vii).

[20] See the tables in *Quellen zur Rezeption des englischen und französischen Romans in Deutschland und Österreich im 19. Jahrhundert,* ed. Norbert Bachleitner (Tübingen, 1990), 106–107, 102.

[21] Strodtmann, *Dichterprofile,* 195.

[22] [Rosegger], »Briefe von Friedrich Spielhagen,« 608.

[23] Volker Neuhaus, »Der Unterhaltungsroman im 19. Jahrhundert,« *Handbuch des deutschen Romans,* ed. Helmut Koopmann (Düsseldorf, 1983), 408; Gabriele Henkel, *Studien zur Privatbibliothek Wilhelm Raabes. Vom »wirklichen Autor,« von Zeitgenossen und »ächten Dichtern«* (Braunschweig, 1997), 121.

[24] Göttsche, *Zeit im Roman,* 577.

[25] The only titles I can find in print at this writing are *Platt Land* (Recklinghausen, 1996), and *Sturmflut,* ed. Wolfgang Gabler (Rostock, 1996). The latter is abridged, but its extensive afterword (313–59) offers fresh and unprejudiced if somewhat psychologized perceptions. The paperback edition of *Hammer und Amboß* mentioned earlier appears to be out of print. According to Hans Heinrich Klatt, »Friedrich Spielhagen. Republikaner im Herzen,« *Gestalten der Bismarckzeit,* Vol. 2, ed. Gustav Seeber (Berlin, 1986), 189, n. 7, 190, n. 58, an East German edition of *Problematische Naturen,* published in Berlin in 1965 with an afterword by Therese Erler, immediately sold out 8,000 copies.

remarked that one seemed like a boor when one spoke of him at all.[26] An observation nearly forty years ago that it was »unlikely that Spielhagen will ever be widely read as a novelist again ... a renascence seems improbable«[27] has been borne out. As Mehring observed, the process, especially as applied to nineteenth-century German realism, leads inexorably into the catacombs of literary history.[28]

However, Spielhagen was not immediately abandoned by his public; notwithstanding the decline of his stature among the tastemakers, he did not disappear from public literary life. The ambitious late *Bildungsroman, Was will das werden?* (1887) was serialized in the venerable *Gartenlaube* in 1885, in, as has been pointed out, respectable company: the preceding year the periodical had brought Theodor Fontane's *Unterm Birnbaum*, Raabe's *Unruhige Gäste*, and Heinrich Heine's recently discovered memoirs.[29] There was a public celebration also of his eightieth birthday with recitations and poems.[30] A statistical survey of popular reading habits in 1900 put Spielhagen in sixth place, before his good friend Auerbach and after Heine.[31] The evidence indicates that he continued to be read into the 1930s, especially by the working class.[32] Consequently there has been a tendency for left-wing critics to defend him, although sometimes in a qualified way.[33] His last ill-

---

[26] Mehring, *Beiträge zur Literaturgeschichte*, 216.
[27] Anderson, »Spielhagen's Problematic Heroes,« 6. This short-sighted dismissal continues to the present day, as in Hugh Ridley, »›Der Halbbruder des Vormärz‹: Friedrich Spielhagen. Reflexionen zu den Kontinuitäten seines Werkes.« *Formen der Wirklichkeitserfassung nach 1848. Deutsche Literatur und Kultur vom Nachmärz bis zur Gründerzeit*, I, ed. Helmut Koopmann and Michael Perraudin (Bielefeld, 2003), 213–31. Ridley's information is second-hand and his knowledge of Spielhagen's fiction seems to end with and sometimes begin with *Sturmflut*.
[28] Mehring, *Beiträge zur Literaturgeschichte*, 216.
[29] Neuhaus, »Der Unterhaltungsroman im 19. Jahrhundert,« 410–11.
[30] Henning, *Friedrich Spielhagen*, 223–24. The remark of Schierding, *Untersuchungen über die Romantechnik Friedrich Spielhagens*, 138, that the eightieth and neunzigtieth birthdays were celebrated is an error in arithmetic.
[31] Ulrich Ott, ed., *Literatur im Industriezeitalter. Eine Ausstellung des Deutschen Literaturarchivs im Schiller-Nationalmuseum* (Marbach am Neckar, 1987), 1: 215–17; table, 1: 226.
[32] Ernst Alker, *Die deutsche Literatur im 19. Jahrhundert (1832–1914)*, 3rd edn. (Stuttgart, 1969), 124.
[33] Mehring, *Beiträge zur Literaturgeschichte*, 216–17; Leo Löwenthal, *Erzählkunst und Gesellschaft: Die Gesellschaftsproblematik in der deutschen Literatur des 19. Jahrhunderts* (Neuwied and Berlin, 1971), 137–75; Kuczynski, *Gestalten und Werke*, 1: 194–203. A flicker of interest, taking its cues from Mehring, seems to have emerged in the German Democratic Republic shortly before its demise. Klatt, »Friedrich Spielhagen,« 174–91, is, however, unpromising, copying for the most part from Henning's biography and Spielhagen's autobiographical memoirs, otherwise

ness was followed in the press, there were many notices and condolences upon his death, and his funeral was a public event. Along with numerous articles on his hundredth birthday in 1929, there was a publication of excerpts by an admirer, the feminist author and private scholar Dr. Ella Mensch, entitled *Er lebt noch immer!* The somewhat nationalistically colored citing of nuggets out of context from the author's »Weisheitsschatz,« along with a photograph, type *ehrwürdiger Greis*, may remind us of the Raabe reception of the time, although the assertions »daß die ursprünglichen Neigungen Spielhagens der demokratischen Seite sich zuwenden« or that his portrayal of women »bis an die Grenze der *erfüllten* Frauenemanzipationsbestrebungen [reicht]« will not.[34] But the declaration that he still lives looks more like a wistful farewell, for by that time it was acknowledged that he was no longer much read.[35] Some of the literary historians remained respectful of him or at least acknowledged his preeminence as a critic of his times and »Agitator.«[36] Rather the fatal blows to his reputation, the impulses to today's oblivion, came out of the literary community.

A curious case is that of Thomas Mann. In 1926, Bert Brecht, with a perfect instinct for what would cause Mann pain, implied that he was Spielhagen's retrograde successor.[37] In a testy and haughty retort, Mann asserted that though Spielhagen might not have been so bad, he, Mann, was unable to read him and, in fact, never had read a line because he knew in advance that all German prose from that period was unreadable.[38] In 1939

indifferently informed, especially in an inaccurate synopsis of *Problematische Naturen*, and generally exhibiting little intimacy with the texts. See also Gudrun Klatt and Hans Heinrich Klatt, »Zur Romantheorie Friedrich Spielhagens,« *Zeitschrift für Germanistik* 10 (1989): 34–44.

[34] Ella Mensch, ed., *Er lebt noch immer! Ein Spielhagen-Brevier* (Leipzig, 1929), 18, 12, 16–17.

[35] Lamers, *Held oder Welt?*, 12–14.

[36] E. g., Hellmuth Mielke, *Der Deutsche Roman des 19. Jahrhunderts*, 3rd edn. (Berlin, 1898), 289–302; Richard M. Meyer, *Die deutsche Literatur des Neunzehnten Jahrhunderts*, Volksausgabe (Berlin, 1912), 424. Meyer commented that Spielhagen was first overestimated, then underestimated: Goessl, »Die Darstellung des Adels,« 3.

[37] Verbatim, »was für ein Revolutionär Thomas' Vater Spielhagen war«: Bertolt Brecht, *Werke. Große kommentierte Berliner und Frankfurter Ausgabe*, ed. Werner Hecht, Jan Knopf, Werner Mittenzwei, and Klaus-Detlef Müller (Berlin, Weimar, and Frankfurt am Main, 1989–2000), 21: 159. In fact, Brecht asserted in an unpublished manuscript that Mann was a worse writer than Spielhagen (161–62) and in a published response to Mann's protest: »Ich fand Dinge bei Spielhagen, die mich angingen,« in contrast to what he found in Mann (165).

[38] Thomas Mann, *Gesammelte Werke in zwölf Bänden* ([Frankfurt am Main], 1960), 11: 753–54.

he declared to an audience of American students that Spielhagen's works were so insipid that one could not consider them a contribution to the European novel.[39] Had Mann, then, read him in the meantime? It seems unlikely. Here is a striking example of the way in which his worthlessness had become a received opinion, relieving readers of any direct experience with him. Such assurance is often reiterated. Only occasionally does one encounter a suggestion (such as Brecht's) that he has been too lightly dismissed.

The usual account is that the rebellion against Spielhagen came from the Naturalists. Sometimes mentioned in this connection is Carl Bleibtreu, who dashed off an attack on a defensive open letter Spielhagen had published in 1887.[40] One of his objections is to what he regards as erotic excess. We shall have more to say about this in Chapter 10. The suspicious ease with which the protagonists, such as Oswald Stein in *Problematische Naturen*, attract the devotion and passion of women of all stations drew censorious comment[41] and became one of the objects of Mauthner's literary parodies.[42] Julian Schmidt, whom one might have expected to find on this line, while remarking that Spielhagen's representations of female characters were not as pure as one might wish, nevertheless acknowledged his warm sensuality and defended Oswald.[43] But to claim, as Bleibtreu did, that the erotic is the kernel of the œuvre is absurd.[44] A somewhat more modernist tack was taken by the humor writer Hans Merian, who delivered a lecture vigorously propagating the European context of Zola, Dostoyevsky, and Ibsen while defending contemporary, vaguely Naturalist authors against the established writers, whom he lumps together as suppliers of fodder for women readers, portraying asexual men for »Backfischchen« in succession to »[d]ie gute Jungfer Marlitt.... An Nachfolgerinnen männlichen und weiblichen Geschlechts fehlt es ... nicht.« He includes Spielhagen in this succession along with Heyse, Ebers, and Dahn, and conventionally charges him with merely resuscitating the ideas of 1848 as though they were of contemporary relevance and of portraying displaced bourgeois youths who turn out to be

---

[39] Hans Mayer, *Von Lessing bis Thomas Mann. Wandlungen der bürgerlichen Literatur in Deutschland* (Pfullingen, 1959), 301.

[40] Carl Bleibtreu, *Revolution der Literatur*, ed. Johannes J. Braakenburg (Tübingen, 1973).

[41] See, for example, Klemperer, *Die Zeitromane Friedrich Spielhagens*, 72, 83, 134.

[42] Fritz Mauthner, *Nach berühmten Mustern. Parodistische Studien*, 6th edn. (Stuttgart, [1878]), 75–84.

[43] Schmidt, »Friedrich Spielhagen,« 424, 428, 430.

[44] Bleibtreu, *Revolution der Literatur*, 28.

»adelige Bankerte.«[45] As usual, there is little sign of sustained attention to the progress of his career.

The pivotal event was a seventy-four-page philippic delivered by Heinrich Hart in 1884.[46] The very length and intensity of this screed suggests something about Spielhagen's continued standing; one does not usually beat a dead horse so vigorously. The rambling, repetitious polemic turns on a few main points. The novel itself is an inferior genre that will never reach the ideal of poesy. The generic touchstone is the Homeric epic, embodying a totality to which a modern literature cannot aspire; the only »modern« works Hart acknowledges as approaching the ideal are the *Nibelungenlied*, Cervantes's *Don Quixote*, Grimmelshausen's *Simplicissimus*, and, somewhat oddly, Fielding's *Tom Jones*. The ideal is objective narration, free of any partisan purpose, creating the world in imitation of God; authorial intrusion undermines illusion and makes us aware of fictionality. Spielhagen's tendentiousness depresses the aesthetic and inhibits totality, defined as comprehending the whole people and universal human feeling; Hart links him in this connection with Zola. Spielhagen is a wordy phrasemaker like Auerbach. Such symbolism as he employs is forced upon the reader, as in *Sturmflut*. He was a poor prophet in his skepticism about Bismarck, for it is now evident that the chancellor realized the dreams of the masses, even if against their will; the democratic idea that actuates Spielhagen's writing is false. He is monotonous, writes the same novel over again; one could melt his œuvre down to one novel; his setting is always the same, his imagination limited to a space from Stralsund across the Baltic to the island of Rügen; his plotting is melodramatic, sensationalistic, and improbable. Like Bleibtreu, Hart complains that every novel exhibits sensual and passionate women. Spielhagen lacks the idealistic humor that looks upon the apparent contradictions of the world from a sublime height of equanimity. His style is complex,

---

45 Hans Merian, *Die sogenannten Jungdeutschen in unserer zeitgenössischen Litteratur. Ein Vortrag gehalten am 20. Februar 1888 in Leipzig* (Leipzig, [1889]), 11–12. »Jungdeutsche« refers here not to the Young Germans of the 1830s but to the younger generation of Merian's time, among whom, however, he appears to include Gottfried Keller and Conrad Ferdinand Meyer, both of whom were older than Spielhagen. It is amusing that he criticizes Bleibtreu for excessive portraiture of loose women (24–25).

46 Julius and Heinrich Hart are usually treated as coauthors of the *Kritische Waffengänge*, but Boulby assigns the Spielhagen essay to Heinrich on good grounds (Hart, *Kritische Waffengänge*, viii) and I shall follow his expert opinion. The segments are paged separately in Boulby's reprint; references are to the sixth one, entitled »Friedrich Spielhagen und der deutsche Roman der Gegenwart.« Interestingly, Julius Hart published a eulogy upon Spielhagen's death (Ott, ed., *Literatur im Industriezeitalter*, 1: 110–13).

too difficult, too elevated, lacking in vividness. His Goethean model is not *Wilhelm Meisters Lehrjahre*, which is a novel, but *Die Wahlverwandtschaften*, which is actually a novella. Thus he lacks a basic grasp of genre.[47]

This portrayal is a caricature for polemical purposes, but it is not wholly impertinent. There is a problem about style, though, as I shall suggest in the next chapter, I locate its origin in a different place; complaint about melodrama and sensationalism persists to the present day.[48] Whether the regional specificity characteristic of many though certainly not all of his texts is a weakness or a strength might be debated; I do not believe that it should be tarred with the brush of the suspect genre of *Heimatkunst*.[49] Any reader will discover similarities in situation, characterization, and plotting in many of the novels. Such complaints indicate an unwillingness to gauge the variation within the continuity,[50] though it is only too characteristic of Spielhagen's dilemmas that *he* complains of repetition of plots, conflicts, situations, and characters in *Thackeray's* novels (*VS*, 254). But the intertextuality among some of Spielhagen's might as easily be regarded as a fabric of integration in the œuvre as a whole. His novels are certainly not as complexly linked as Balzac's *Comédie humaine* and do not form a genealogical chain like Zola's Rougon-Macquart series, but they do echo and reflect one another in places. Spielhagen could have found less comprehensive examples in French novels that he knew; for example, the permanently unemployed actor Delobelle from Alphonse Daudet's *Fromont jeune et Risler aîné* (1874) reappears two years later as a character in *Jack*.

Spielhagen has a recurrent figure of a »Prince Prora,« sometimes with the same first name, but not always the same character; it is evidently taken from the Prorer Wiek, a bay on the shore of Rügen. Elsewhere »Prora« appears as a place name. Evil or disdained aristocrats are often named »Axel«; at the other end of the social scale, the plotting servant is regularly called »Jean.« A retired, depraved, parasitical, Frenchified Swedish diplomat named

---

47 Hart, »Friedrich Spielhagen,« 9, 73, 12, 20, 22, 57, 38, 52, 15–16, 16–17, 33, 46, 28, 50–51, 52, 58, 63, 51, 63, 64–65, 70.

48 See, for example, Lamers, *Held oder Welt?*, 120; Eda Sagarra, *Tradition and Revolution: German Literature and Society 1830–1890* (London, 1971), 216; Martin Swales, *Epochenbuch Realismus: Romane und Erzählungen* (Berlin, 1997), 102–03. Swales draws a comparison with soap operas.

49 On this point I disagree with Martha Geller, *Friedrich Spielhagens Theorie und Praxis des Romans* (Berlin, 1917), 96.

50 E. g., Schierding, *Untersuchungen über die Romantechnik Friedrich Spielhagens,* 120–22; Julian Schmidt, »Friedrich Spielhagen,« 424, remarks on »Monotonie.« Worthmann, *Probleme des Zeitromans*, 109, phrases it this way: »da die Wirklichkeit seiner Romanwelt immer auf denselben Grundmustern basierte, brauchte er nur wenige seiner ›Wirklichkeits-Clichés‹ auszuwechseln.«

Lindblad appears in *Platt Land* and again in *Uhlenhans*; he had already been mentioned in passing as an adulterer in *Das Skelet im Hause* and is doubtless a product of bitter memories of Swedish rule over Pomerania and Rügen before 1815. Essentially the same character can also appear under different names.[51] The two last novels, *Opfer* and *Frei geboren*, share characters, as noted irritably by Klemperer.[52] In fact, *Frei geboren* is a kind of Balzacian prequel to *Opfer*, as is indicated in the preface (*NF*, 7, iii).

Along with the names of local people, place names also recur, often altered: »Nedur« for Ruden, »Sundin« for Stralsund, »Grünwald« for Greifswald, although Spielhagen advises us not to seek anywhere on Rügen »Schloß Grenwitz,« a place and personal name that recurs in various contexts, starting with *Problematische Naturen* (*FuE*, 2: 427). Six years after Spielhagen had stayed at the Hotel Quisisana on Capri (*Vnbs*, 101–14), the heartsick fifty-year-old man in the novella *Quisisana* sets out for it, but never reaches it; instead, the young woman he loves and her husband honeymoon there (*AR*, 2: 8, 12–13, 250–52). Another thirteen years later, Isabel in *Sonntagskind* writes to her friend Justus from there (*NF*, 1: 334–36). Spielhagen also came to like certain phrases so much that he would repeat them. One of these characterized the gossipy community where everyone knew everything as a place of keen »acoustics«: it appears in *Sonntagskind* as »die ausgezeichnete Akustik von Karlsbad« and recurs in variations in *Selbstgerecht*, *Zum Zeitvertreib*, and *Faustulus* (1: 436; 5: 155; 3: 85; 4: 137). In *Zum Zeitvertreib*, the feckless would-be playwright summarizes his dramatization of a novella he has published, recognizable to the experienced reader of Spielhagen as his own *Das Skelet im Hause* (3: 63). In these and numerous other examples that could be catalogued, one might with some good will identify a degree of authorial recursiveness and narrative irony that one would not expect from his theories.

There are several peculiarities of Hart's critique that have not always been clearly registered. Conventionally it has been seen as a manifesto of the younger generation of Naturalists against a mode of literature still rooted in idealism and moralism, the sort of displacement of the fathers by the sons routine in literary history. But, apart from the reproach of stylistic artificiality, there is little of Naturalism in Hart's attack. The principles are, in fact, deeply conservative. The allegiance to objectivity and totality, the rejection of tendentiousness, the nostalgia for the epic, and the skepticism about the

---

[51] Examples noted by Zinken, *Der Roman als Zeitdokument*, 112 and n. 44. A good many more could be accumulated.

[52] Klemperer, *Die Zeitromane Friedrich Spielhagens*, 167–68.

genre of the novel are all grounded in the aesthetics of the age of Goethe. To this has been added a substantial dose of Wilhelminian nationalism, evident in the defense of Bismarck against Spielhagen's skepticism, in the dismissal of democratic ideas as antiquated,[53] and in the quite correct implication that Spielhagen had been unable to get with the program of the Reich.[54] Far from contrasting Spielhagen unfavorably to the Naturalists, Hart yokes him to the arch-Naturalist, Zola, the chief example for all those resistant to the modern of how not to write, with the additional taint of being *French*, that is, heartlessly and materialistically reproducing the vulgar, the ugly, and the salacious. One might dismiss this performance as an eccentricity if it had not been so influential – as late as 1928, the premier American Germanist, Kuno Francke, declared that, while Hart was not Spielhagen's equal in cosmopolitanism, the critique of his technique was fully justified[55] – and if it were not so illustrative of the bitter ironies that beset his reputation and must have dismayed him almost beyond bearing.

For the most diabolical aspect of the critique is that it turns his own values against him in a way that anticipates large areas of the case against him from his own time to the present. He placed an extremely high value on poesy and aspired to the sublime status of *Dichter*, yet he found himself accused of pursuing a debased and popular mode of subliterature. Eduard Engel charged him with descending with a work like *Angela* to the level of journalistic reading matter for boarding-school girls; *Susi* (1895) has also been declared a newspaper novel.[56] Spielhagen was strongly opposed to Naturalism, especially in the drama, imported as it was, via Ibsen, from abroad. He asserted hyperbolically that the whole world found *A Doll's House* distressing to any healthy spirit (*BT*, 299). On the matter of foreign literature he was often in substantial agreement with Hart, writing near the beginning of his career that the Germans were falling victim to the

---

[53] This view was taken also by Schmidt, »Friedrich Spielhagen,« 448. By the end of the century a critic was complaining of the persistence of »der verjährte liberale Parteistandpunkt« in *Opfer* and *Frei geboren*: Lamers, *Held oder Welt?*, 163.

[54] On the Harts' nationalism, see Boulby's introduction (Hart, *Kritische Waffengänge*, iv–v, x, xvii) and, with particular stress, Rolf Sältzer, *Entwicklungslinien der deutschen Zola-Rezeption von den Anfängen bis zum Tode des Autors* (Bern and Frankfurt am Main, 1989), 79–80.

[55] Kuno Francke, *Weltbürgertum in der deutschen Literatur von Herder bis Nietzsche* (Berlin, 1928), 116.

[56] Eduard Engel, »Stenographischer Bericht über die Gerichtsverhandlungen im Prozesse: ›Angela.‹ Roman von Friedrich Spielhagen,« *Magazin für die Literatur des In- und Auslandes* 50 (1881): 401, 414; Goessl, »Die Darstellung des Adels,« 199. We shall return to the *Angela* affair and Engel's commentary on it in Chapter 10.

sensationalism and coquetry in the French novel (*VS*, 302, 305), and near the end that, despite the achievements of foreign nations in the novel, the Germans were still superior (*NB*, 88); even Thackeray and Dickens are shallow compared to Auerbach and Freytag, not to speak of the French (*BT*, 262). He persistently combatted Zola, though with the further irony, as I shall suggest in Chapter 11, that Zola came nevertheless to infect his later writing; still, Hart's linking of him to Zola strikes one as a particularly perfidious maneuver.

Similarly perfidious is the crack about not understanding the difference between novel and novella; Spielhagen was fanatically concerned with genre definition and demarcation. His allegiance to the aesthetics of the age of Goethe, most particularly of Wilhelm von Humboldt, was copiously on the record;[57] the commitment grew stronger as his situation worsened,[58] until just before the end of his career he began at last to doubt that there were eternal laws of art (*NB*, 11). This initial commitment compelled the elevation of Homer as the unreachable model of the epic genre, along with the goal of totality, the dubious admissibility of the genre of the novel to poesy, and the demand for objective narration. Hart does not attack Spielhagen's theoretical convictions from a modernist and Naturalist position; from a conservative and at least implicitly antimodern position he associates himself with them and charges Spielhagen with gross failures to adhere to them. Particularly in the matter of objective narration Hart is able to mark up, with the greatest of ease, any number of violations in Spielhagen's practice.[59] Thus he is caught in a pincer: while for modern literary historians he was too much oriented on the past and old verities,[60] for Hart he was insufficiently oriented on the past or faithful to old verities.

The impeachment of Spielhagen as a novelist has led to claims that his real significance is to be found in his theoretical work. To this question we shall turn in the next chapter.

---

57 See Arthur H. Hughes, »Wilhelm von Humboldt's Influence on Spielhagen's Esthetics,« *Germanic Review* 5 (1930): 211–24.
58 Lamers, *Held oder Welt?*, 158.
59 See John R. Frey, »Author-Intrusion in the Narrative: German Theory and Some Modern Examples,« *Germanic Review* 23 (1948): 277.
60 See, for example, Geller, *Friedrich Spielhagens Theorie und Praxis des Romans*, 10; Hugo Bieber, *Der Kampf um die Tradition. Die deutsche Dichtung im europäischen Geistesleben 1830–1880* (Stuttgart, 1928), 472; Martini, *Deutsche Literatur im bürgerlichen Realismus*, 431; Günter Rebing, *Der Halbbruder des Dichters. Friedrich Spielhagens Theorie des Romans* (Frankfurt am Main, 1972), 30, 99; Worthmann, *Probleme des Zeitromans*, 100.

4. The Demon of Theory

It is hard to think of any post-Romantic German writer, except perhaps Otto Ludwig, who wrote as much and as insistently about literary theory as Spielhagen. These writings are wide-ranging, dealing with, among other things, genre definition, the relationship of authorial experience and imagination, character models and typology, along with a large body of practical criticism. They are best known, however, for a reiterated and, one might fairly say, fanatical insistence on the doctrine of objective narration. Since few in our time seriously believe in objective narration, it turns out that the theoretical work, though declared to be his most important achievement, is for most observers a historical curiosity of no intrinsic value. With this move, Spielhagen is catapulted into the black hole of decanonized oblivion from which no known force has been able to recuperate him.

His fixation on objective narration began at a fairly young age with what he initially thought of as a doctoral dissertation. In it he meant to apply an allegiance to Wilhelm von Humboldt's aesthetics, as developed in his book-length essay on Goethe's *Hermann und Dorothea*, to the refutation of Schiller's distinction of naive and sentimentive poetry.[1] This need to combat a sixty-five-year-old essay with the aid of a doctrine from the same era is in itself an indication of the burden of immobility that the achievements of the age of Goethe imposed on Spielhagen's generation. The corollary to the principle, argued against Schiller's dualities, that there is and can be only one poetic substance (*BT*, 112), came to be the precept of objective narration, which Spielhagen continued to affirm, though with sometimes confusing variations, practically to the end of his life. The principle is of suspect simplicity: the writer of prose fiction may not intrude into the text in his own authorial voice. The author must be silent and invisible; the poet has nothing to do with the reader and nothing to say to him (91). Authorial utterance speaks directly from the author's to the reader's understanding (*Verstand*), disillusions the imagination, and is therefore unpoetic

---

[1] Henning, *Friedrich Spielhagen*, 73–74; see *FuE* 2: 202–12, 222.

(*VS*, 209). No exceptions or variations are permissible; objectification is, in fact, the task of *all* the arts (*BT*, 41). To Spielhagen this was law; he could not understand why it was not universally acknowledged. He grieved that he lacked the ability to convince others of what was absolutely certain to him (*FuE*, 2: 222). Late in life he wrote that it was as clear to him as two plus two equals four; why would it not go into the heads of the teachers of literature and aesthetics?[2]

Today, after a century of narratology, it is difficult to regard these propositions with any seriousness at all.[3] One of the pioneers of narrative theory in Germany, Käte Friedemann, began her programmatic study with an attack on Spielhagen's position.[4] However, even earlier, the distinguished literary scholar Wilhelm Scherer had defended Goethe's flexible narrative practice and explicitly contradicted Spielhagen.[5] Almost all modern commentaries are exercises in displaying the theory's untenability.[6] Spielhagen seems to have had little or no idea of the author's voice as a created one,

---

[2]   Mensch, »Erinnerungen an Friedrich Spielhagen,« 359.

[3]   An exception is the eccentric effort of Andrea Fischbacher-Bosshardt, *Anfänge der modernen Erzählkunst: Untersuchungen zu Friedrich Spielhagens theoretischem und literarischem Werk* (Bern and Frankfurt am Main, 1988) to see him as anticipating modern theory in the abolition of the empirical author/narrator, sometimes exhibiting in her critique of Spielhagens's imperfect practice judgments no less dogmatically inflexible than his own. Il-Sop Han, *Spielhagens Ich-Roman-Theorie* (Diss. Heidelberg 1977) similarly takes the position that Spielhagen knew perfectly well that objectivity was only a device and that the narrator was fictive.

[4]   Käte Friedemann, *Die Rolle des Erzählers in der Epik* (Berlin, 1910; reprint Darmstadt, 1965), 3–6.

[5]   Wilhelm Scherer, *Geschichte der deutschen Litteratur* (Berlin: Weidmann, 1883), 682; *Poetik* (Berlin, 1888), 249–50. It has been argued that Scherer later modified his position under Spielhagen's influence: Frey, »Author-Intrusion in the Narrative,« 275. Spielhagen had an »ausgesprochen freundschaftliches Verhältnis« with Scherer and valued his criticism, supplying him with copies; see Wolfgang Höppner, *Das »Ererbte, Erlebte und Erlernte« im Werk Wilhelm Scherers. Ein Beitrag zur Geschichte der Germanistik* (Cologne, Weimar, and Vienna, 1993), 153, 185 and n. 123, 187 and n. 130. In Scherer's library, acquired after his death by what is today Case-Western Reserve University, there are a number of Spielhagen first editions, including one autographed to Lina Duncker. Spielhagen mediated the friendship between Scherer and the Dunckers (150 and n. 7). On the purchase of the library, see S. B. Platner, »Wilhelm Scherer's Library,« *New Englander and Yale Review* 46 (1887): 383–86.

[6]   E. g., Winfried Hellmann, »Objektivität, Subjektivität und Erzählkunst: Zur Romantheorie Friedrich Spielhagens,« *Deutsche Romantheorien*, ed. Reinhold Grimm (Frankfurt am Main, 1968), 165–217; Rebing, *Der Halbbruder des Dichters*, with greater tolerance Rhöse, *Konflikt und Versöhnung*, 176–204, and Worthmann, *Probleme des Zeitromans*, 104, 112. On the general impossibility of logically grounding »objectivity,« see Stephan Kohl, *Realismus. Theorie und Geschichte* (Munich, 1977), 108.

part of the fiction, and only intermittently recognized that the author's organization, setting of values, and moral system are forms of voice. For Bakhtin, Spielhagen's principles could result only in »unnovelistic novels.... As a theoretician Spielhagen was deaf to heteroglot language and to that which it specifically generates: double-voiced discourse.«[7] At times, to be sure, he admitted that the »Homeric« objectivity is no longer achievable in the more disparate, class-riven modern world (*NB*, 53) – a lesson he might have learned from Schiller – but he was unable to sever the genre of the novel from the model of the ancient epic. He exempts first-person narration from his strictures altogether, for in that mode he can recognize the fictionality of the narrator (*BT*, 131–32, 208); thus Georg in *Hammer und Amboß* can ask the reader to suspend judgment, assure him the book is not written to depress him, considers whether he has reached a stopping place, and again address the reader as his friend (*AR*, 1, 3: 300–01; 1, 4: 288, 393, 394). There is a trace of Raabe's instinctual awareness of the porous boundary between first and third-person narration in the fleeting comment that, compared to Homer, every modern novel is subjective and first-person (*BT*, 132; cf. 203) and in the recognition that *Problematische Naturen* had the external form of a third-person novel but was first-person in its essence (*FuE*, 2: 394, 443). But he cannot integrate these insights and can only conclude from them the inferiority of the novel genre (*BT*, 133–34).

As pointless as his theory may seem to us today, it was not eccentric in his own time, even if some contemporaries were inclined to evade his nonnegotiable stance in propagating it. Everyone after 1848 agreed on the exclusion of tendentiousness.[8] Otto Brahm, when comparing a novel of Julius Wolff unfavorably with Spielhagen's *Uhlenhans*, expressed his amazement that in 1883 it was possible for an author to address his characters.[9] Oskar Walzel claimed that by 1900 the ban on the author's voice had become »wie etwas Selbstverständliches,« and blamed Spielhagen for this »Mißbrauch.«[10] René Wellek went so far as to claim that »›objectivity‹ is certainly the other main watchword of realism [along with type],« only to add: »objectivity is hardly ever achieved in practice. Realism is didactic,

---

[7] M. M. Bahktin, *The Dialogic Imagination: Four Essays*, ed. Michael Holquist (Austin, 1981), 327.

[8] Rhöse, *Konflikt und Versöhnung*, 176.

[9] Otto Brahm, [review of *Uhlenhans*], *Deutsche Rundschau* 38 (1884): 310–11. Today we would speak of the narrator addressing his characters, not the author, but this distinction was unknown to the critical practice of the time.

[10] Oskar Walzel, »Objektive Erzählung,« *Das Wortkunstwerk. Mittel seiner Erforschung* (Leipzig, 1926), 184–85.

moralistic, reformist.«[11] Fontane acknowledged the objective principle while, characteristically, trying to be less rigid about it. He wrote to Spielhagen on February 15, 1896, that authorial intrusion is always a failing, but it is not always easy to tell when it is occurring, for the author has to *do* things; on the following November 24 he sent a copy of *Die Poggenpuhls* (1896) with a puckish apology for having violated Spielhagen's principles but adding that rules are there to be broken.[12] Still, one observer has concluded that Fontane reduced his level of authorial intrusion under Spielhagen's influence.[13] There were many who regarded the standard of narrative objectivity as axiomatic.[14] Its survival seems to be a conservative marker. In the revision of Tony Kellen's novel theory by the anti-Semitic Heinrich Keiter, Friedemann's critical position on objectivity is said to be an obvious error.[15] As late as 1959, Heimito von Doderer – oddly, a notably intrusive and digressive narrator – acknowledged Spielhagen's insistence on objectivity as one of the fundamental propositions of novel-writing.[16] A version of it may be thought to survive in the modern critical doctrine that the narrator must show, not tell.[17] But Lubbock's elaboration of this doctrine, exemplified in Flaubert's impersonality (occasionally mentioned in our connection) is incomparably subtle, flexible, and sensitive compared to Spielhagen's obstinacy.

As we have seen, Hart did not oppose the principle, but marked up Spielhagen's own violations of it. This is childishly easy to do. Anyone could see that Spielhagen, the enemy of the authorial voice and of tendentiousness in literature, was a crowdingly insistent evangelist, urging his world-view on the reader, and a liberal-democratic partisan evolving from a bourgeois class allegiance to an independent affinity for Social Democracy.

---

[11] René Wellek, *Concepts of Criticism*, ed. Stephen G. Nichols, Jr. (New Haven and London, 1963), 247, 253.

[12] Theodor Fontane, *Briefe*, ed. Walter Keitel and Helmuth Nürnberger (Munich, 1976–94), 4: 533, 615. Spielhagen, incidentally, in one of his literary-critical distichs, caught Fontane's achievement of making much out of little in *Die Poggenpuhls*: »Liliputanische Welt! nie würde das Aug' dich erblicken, / Träfe dich nicht ein Strahl herrlichsten Dichterhumors« (*NG*, 205).

[13] David Turner, »Marginalien und Handschriften zum Thema: Fontane und Spielhagens Theorie der ›Objektivität,‹« *Fontane-Blätter* 1 (1968–69): 265.

[14] E. g., Hart, »Friedrich Spielhagen,« 20; on the generally positive response, see Rhöse, *Konflikt und Versöhnung*, 193.

[15] Heinrich Keiter and Tony Kellen, *Der Roman. Theorie und Technik des Romans und der erzählenden Dichtung, nebst einer geschichtlichen Einleitung*, 4th edn. (Essen:, 1912), 288. It is not mentioned that Friedemann was Jewish, but this might have contributed to the curt dismissal.

[16] Heimito von Doderer, *Grundlagen und Funktion des Romans* (Nuremberg, 1959), 17–18.

[17] Percy Lubbock, *The Craft of Fiction* (New York, 1957), 62, 67.

»Unpleasant characters are sentenced to death by their creator, political opinions are discussed at large from different standpoints and the reactionary or pseudoliberal participants denounce themselves by stupidity and ridiculousness and the absurdity of their convictions.«[18] An American obituary commented that he was »so strong in his feelings that he could not be wholly objective in his portrayal of the world about him.«[19] The modern orthodox view that these attitudes cannot be charged to a nonexistent, empirical narrator, only to the created fictional consciousness,[20] I regard as pettifogging and unrealistic in regard to reception, for all that Spielhagen made a late claim that the method had nothing to do with *Weltanschauung* (*FuE*, 2: 220). In fact, he was often regarded as a successor to the generation of activist Young German writers and particularly to Karl Gutzkow, in whose periodical Spielhagen's first publication appeared.[21] Thus it was evident to the naked eye that the prohibition was purely formal,[22] directed against an explicit narrative »I« or visible, self-conscious management of the text, and had nothing to do with a severe objectivity of tone.

Spielhagen as a theoretician might have had fewer difficulties with his younger contemporaries and become less notorious today if he had not been so fiercely insistent on his position and so extreme in his critical application of it. (He also says in one place that aesthetics is not an exact science [*AW*, 111], an indication of the way his endless, garrulous thinking out loud generates inconsistencies.) Gottfried Keller thought he should study Spielhagen's theories but found he could not read »den verkehrten Gallimathias,« and the narrator of the first version of *Der grüne Heinrich*,

---

[18] Volker Neuhaus, »Friedrich Spielhagen – Critic of Bismarck's Empire,« *1870/71–1898/90*, ed. Pape, 139.

[19] Anonymous, »Friedrich Spielhagen,« *The Dial* 50 (1911): 200.

[20] Fischbacher-Bosshardt, *Anfänge der modernen Erzählkunst*, 43 and passim.

[21] Karpeles, *Friedrich Spielhagen*, 29–30; Henning, *Friedrich Spielhagen*, 65; see Rudolf von Gottschall in *Friedrich Spielhagen. Dem Meister des deutschen Romans*, 24; Heinrich Spiero, *Geschichte des deutschen Romans* (Berlin, 1950), 319; Alker, *Die deutsche Literatur*, 124; Bernd Neumann, »Friedrich Spielhagen: Sturmflut 1877. Die Gründerjahre als die ›Signatur des Jahrhunderts,‹« *Romane und Erzählungen des Bürgerlichen Realismus: Neue Interpretationen*, ed. Horst Denkler (Stuttgart, 1980), 261. Sometimes he was seen as overcoming Gutzkow's bad example: e. g., Fr. Kreyssig, *Vorlesungen über den Deutschen Roman der Gegenwart. Literar- und culturhistorische Studien* (Berlin:, 1871), 216–43. Cf. Spielhagen's denial of discipleship to Gutzkow, *FuE*, 2: 338–39, and the distinction drawn from Gutzkow's practice by Göttsche, *Zeit im Roman*, 586, »daß die dargestellten Konflikte (anders als später bei Spielhagen) nur zum Teil sozialer, politischer oder überhaupt spezifisch gesellschaftlicher Natur sind.«

[22] Friedemann, *Die Rolle des Erzählers*, 5; Geller, *Friedrich Spielhagens Theorie und Praxis des Romans*, 39.

with his customary self-satire, could describe his muted feelings at Anna's funeral »nicht anders, als mit dem fremden und kalten Worte ›objektiv‹ ..., welches die Gelehrsamkeit erfunden hat.«[23] Some of Spielhagen's censorious literary criticism can be extremely irritating and in places gives an impression of self-imposed obtuseness. Given his allegiance to the age of Goethe and his profound veneration of Goethe himself, one might suppose that he would relax a bit when he finds Goethe at odds with the principle, for example in the famous opening of *Die Wahlverwandtschaften*: »Eduard – so nennen wir einen reichen Baron im besten Mannesalter.«[24] No, no, no; one may not do such a thing (*BT*, 92). This opening seems to have soured him on what he regards as an overgrown, disordered novella, starting with the title; thus it is bitterly ironic that Hart declared it to be Spielhagen's model.[25] His recommendation would have been to get rid of the chemical symbolism, tighten the text, title it *Ottilie*, and excise Ottilie's diaries (*NB*, 96; *VS*, 215). Goethe should have avoided the editor's intrusion at the end of *Werther* as well (*NB*, 70).

Spielhagen's literary criticism often sounds like this. He read widely, in English, American, French, Scandinavian, and Russian as well as German literature. But he seems to have liked little of what he saw; no one knows how to do it. An example is a lengthy reckoning with George Eliot's *Middlemarch* as a botched novel, an almost unbelievable display of narrative barbarism, patched together from novella pieces (*BT*, 65–100).[26] One may be inclined to think that a reader who cannot appreciate *Middlemarch* is disqualified as a literary critic; Otto Ludwig praised Eliot precisely »for her

23 To Paul Heyse, January 30, 1882, *Gottfried Kellers Briefe 1861–1890*, ed. Emil Ermatinger (Stuttgart and Berlin, 1925), 447–48; Gottfried Keller, *Sämtliche Werke*, ed. Thomas Böning et al. (Frankfurt am Main, 1985–96), 2: 536.
24 Johann Wolfgang von Goethe, *Werke* (Hamburger Ausgabe), vol. 6, *Romane und Novellen*, ed. Benno von Wiese and Erich Trunz, 3rd ed. (Hamburg, 1958), 242.
25 Hart, »Friedrich Spielhagen,« 70.
26 Spielhagen was much concerned in a number of places with the distinction between novel and novella, which he regarded as a theoretical distinction of the Germans. It is not a matter of length; some of his novellas, such as *Auf der Düne*, are the length of short novels, and he himself commented, correctly, that novellas were getting longer. The key distinction is that the novella shows a conflict of finished characters in a chain of events; the novel represents the breadth of human life with developing characters (*BT*, 263, 279, 245–46). This indicates that Spielhagen's generic model for the novel was the *Bildungsroman*. In *Sonntagskind*, a kind of anti-*Bildungsroman*, we can observe Justus expanding a novella into a novel (*NF*, 1, 280). For a thoughtful new beginning on the *Middlemarch* review and the distinction of novel and novella, see Lothar Schneider, »Die Verabschiedung des idealistischen Realismus und die Kritiker,« *Formen der*

skill of interposing reflections in her story.«[27] Erich Schmidt took the occasion of the birthday celebration to preface his minilecture on *Die Wahlverwandtschaften* with the remark that Spielhagen had not upset *his* partiality for *Middlemarch*.[28]

Spielhagen was not a stupid man; such fervor on such a recondite topic demands explanation. Several considerations, which he regarded as imperatives, converged in the particular historical moment of his consciousness. The one usually highlighted is his allegiance to the German »classicism,« sometimes regarded as a symptom of the stunted maturation and resistance to modernization of the German bourgeoisie. To this it might be said, as a corrective to today's attitudes in this matter, that it was the great age of Goethe, with values reinforced by the Revolution of 1848, that certified, for the cultured bourgeoisie, the status of the inchoate German nation, a status that was widely acknowledged throughout the civilized world and of which, in Spielhagen's view, the Reich was a far from adequate successor and conserver, a status, finally, that he was obviously not wrong in conjecturing that the Reich might at length ruin in the world at large. If the Germans were to disappear, he wrote, they could be recreated from Goethe, who was more truly German than Luther, Frederick the Great, or Bismarck (*AW*, 90). It is perhaps optimistic to equate German idealism and humanism with a tradition of civil rights,[29] but Spielhagen did assert that the real strength of the German nation lay in humaneness; Germany will never start a war (91, 197–98).

Yet he was anything but rigidly classisistic, as appears from a witty sequence of poems, »Nach antiken Motiven,« in which he travesties the lofty texts with modern interpolations. The first of these, »Kalypso,« is a parodistic account of Odysseus freeing himself from submission to the goddess, concluding with a Heinesque observation that sex was freer then than in our Christian age (*G*, 93–105; the designation of the sequence as an »Intermezzo« may also obliquely refer to Heine). In the second, »Circe,« the archetypical *femme fatale* quotes Goethe (»Diesem allergrößten Heiden«) and

---

Wirklichkeitserfassung nach 1848. Deutsche Literatur und Kultur vom Nachmärz bis zur Gründerzeit in europäischer Perspektive, I, ed. Helmut Koopmann and Michael Perraudin (Bielefeld, 2003), 233–44.

[27] Frey, »Author-Intrusion in the Narrative,« 277. With another of the many ironies, an American reviewer ascribed the »clumsy form« of *Sturmflut* to the influence of *Middlemarch* and *Daniel Deronda*: Anonymous, [review of *Sturmflut*], *Atlantic Monthly* 40 (1877): 383.

[28] *Friedrich Spielhagen. Dem Meister des deutschen Romans,* 6.

[29] Neuhaus, »Friedrich Spielhagen – Critic of Bismarck's Empire,« 138–39.

declares she and Odysseus have »[e]ine holde Wahlverwandtschaft,« but he declares that, from his own experience, he is able to resist »[d]einem holden Hokuspokus« (105–18). In »Der Fall Brisäis,« Achilles, who died, according to Patroklos, unnecessarily »[i]n dem Leutnantsalter,« is still grouchy, compares himself to Hamlet, and quotes Goethe's *Tasso*, only to have Patroklos predict

> »Mädchen giebt es viel auf Erden,«
> Wird einst Heinrich Heine singen;
> Mehr als du und ich versteht er,
> Glaube mir, von solchen Dingen,

and conclude with instruction in Schiller's aesthetics, declaring Achilles's emotions inappropriately »sentimentalisch,« while »soviel ich weiß, wir leben / Noch in den naiven Zeiten« (119–25). The fourth poem is an adaptation of Horace's ode 2: 8, »Ulla si juris tibi pejerati,« in which faithlessness is unpunished and still thrives, an attitude that looks forward to Spielhagen's *Susi* (126–27; see Chapter 17). He experimented with a similar conceit in his second volume of poems with »Der Läufer von Marathon,« which modernizes the famous run with references to Heine and Moltke, along with the young lieutenant's embarrassment at the obligation to run naked (*NG,* 15–25). By the end of his career Spielhagen seems to have unwittingly approached Brecht with an insight that one cannot bring people to beauty when they are beset with poverty: »erst gilt's, sie satt zu machen« (173).

It is puzzling that a writer capable of such freedom would handcuff himself as a post-Romantic, realist novelist by submitting himself to models from the Classical-Romantic era, but it is impossible to exaggerate the extent to which he did so. Subsumed under the category of the »epic,« the modern novel could never hope to equal »Homeric« totality or unity of creation and reception. It *had* to be an inferior genre, a symptom of cultural decadence. Spielhagen made this matter as difficult as possible for himself by taking the most normative possible position in genre theory: literary genres are fixed once and for all; there never could be, he once wrote, a new genre (*BT,* 108). He has this attitude from the essay of Humboldt, the most harmful possible mentor Spielhagen could have chosen for himself, as, indeed, Goethe's *Hermann und Dorothea* is the least useful model for the modern novel. Humboldt's whole discourse is suffused with insistence on the stability of enduring human values, as though the Homeric model could be called upon to arrest the historical flow. Goethe's poem was meant to be an antidote to the disruptive threat of the French Revolution: »Es muss also von allen Seiten *Ruhe* hervorgehen.« The purpose of the epic is »den

Menschen mit dem Leben zu versöhnen und ihn für das Leben tauglich zu machen,« that is, one might be inclined to say, to accept injustice and adapt to the existing order. Humboldt makes his purpose explicit in his concluding admonition that »es nie nöthiger war, die innern Formen des Charakters zu bilden und zu befestigen, als jetzt, wo die äussern der Umstände und der Gewohnheit mit so furchtbarer Gewalt einen allgemeinen Umsturz drohen.« Objectivity restores the past, as in the heading to section XXXIX: »Die Verbindung reiner Objectivität mit einfacher Wahrheit macht dies Gedicht den Werken der Alten ähnlich.« Realism is the enemy: »Das Reich der Phantasie ist dem Reiche der Wirklichkeit durchaus entgegengesetzt.« The moderns are threatened by the truth of reality and by culture, »zu einer Wahrheit und Natur herabzusinken, die kaum noch künstlerisch heissen darf.... Daher ist nichts dem epischen Geist in so hohem Grade zuwider, als die blosse *Cultur.*«

The rhetoric is normative and prescriptive, particularly in regard to genre definitions; the essence of art and of its possible forms is to be defined; therefore, despite all the insistence upon totality, the effect is exclusive and constrictive. For totality does not mean comprehensiveness: »Der epische Dichter hat ... alles Bunte und Schreiende, alles Grelle und Contrastirende zu vermeiden.« It is through this »vollkommene und strenge Gesetzmässigkeit« that epic objectivity is achieved; in such moments we see the origin of the connection of Spielhagen's doctrine of objectivity with his intolerant critical practice. There is a single, dismissive remark about the novel:

> ... dass der Roman, der immer Begebenheiten darstellt, ob er gleich in Absicht seines Umfangs und der Verknüpfung seiner Theile zum Ganzen eine unverkennbare Aehnlichkeit mit dem epischen Gedicht an sich trägt, dennoch so wesentlich von demselben verschieden ist, dass, da diess auf der höchsten Stufe aller darstellenden Poesie steht, es von ihm unausgemacht ist, ob er nur überhaupt ein wahres Gedicht und ein reines Kunstwerk genannt werden kann.[30]

Spielhagen's anxiety about the status of the novel came to be focused on a perhaps more casual than systematic remark of Schiller in *Ueber naive und sentimentalische Dichtung* that the novelist was the »Halbbruder« of the poet.[31] Karpeles attempted a clumsy effort to free Spielhagen from the

---

[30] Wilhelm von Humboldt, »Über Göthes Herrmann und Dorothea,« *Werke in fünf Bänden,* ed. Andreas Flitner and Klaus Giel (Stuttgart, 1960–81) 2: 263, 265, 356, 214, 139, 299, 261, 177, 257.

[31] Friedrich Schiller, *Nationalausgabe,* ed. Julius Petersen et al. (Weimar, 1943-), 20: 462.

dilemma: »Ihm sind Epos und Roman nicht Halbbrüder, sondern Zwillingsbrüder und er kennt keinen Unterschied in den Bedingungen antiker und moderner epischen Poesie.«[32] Would that this had been the case. Spielhagen declared that he was ashamed of the novel-reading of his youth, of his attachment to the half brother (*FuE*, 1: 327). This half brother turns up constantly in his writings; he even jokes about him wryly in his fictional texts, for example, in *Sturmflut* and *Die schönen Amerikanerinnen* (*AR*, 1, 8: 324; 2, 4: 150). Since his only conceivable ambition was to be a poet, a *Dichter*, a permanent dissonance came to be installed in his conception of himself, which goes some way to explain the nonnegotiable character of his theoretical writings and what has been dismissed as his comic pedantry.[33] Early in his career he accepted that the novel was farthest genre from art's center, lying on the periphery of the history of art (*VS*, 210).

He never gave up trying to sort out this matter of status. After the seventieth-birthday celebration he tried to weigh himself fairly, as though he were another person: »Er war nämlich Dichter. Das heißt *cum grano salis*. Will sagen: er hatte in seinem langen Leben eine endlose Reihe von Romanen und Novellen geschrieben. Damit kann man, nach Schiller, die Halbbruderschaft des Dichters beanspruchen – *non meno*, aber auch *non più*« (*AW*, 36). Anyway, his modest status is not his fault but the novel genre's, which he tried to raise from its self-incurred degradation to the level of an art work (41). Even though at one point he hoped that Schiller might not have been entirely serious and was not referring to the master writers (*NB*, 54–55), Spielhagen never overcame the scruple that the novel was, in fact, poetologically inferior, degrading the prose specialist to the »Halbbruder des Dichters« (*AmSt*, 59). Preoccupied as always with the anxiety of influence, he quotes at length the letter to Goethe of October 20, 1797, where Schiller, with his customary irritating forthrightness, declares that the form of *Wilhelm Meister*, like that of any novel, is utterly unpoetic (*BT*, 198–200).[34] This view was widely shared in Spielhagen's time.[35] One index of this is the custom of depreciating what are perceived as sensational or melodramatic elements as »novelistic« (*romanhaft*), a locution that occurs in critiques of Spielhagen up to the present day.[36] In Germany, at any rate,

[32] Karpeles, *Friedrich Spielhagen*, 15.
[33] Klemperer, *Die Zeitromane Friedrich Spielhagens*, 151.
[34] Schiller, *Nationalausgabe*, 29: 148–50.
[35] E. g., Hart, *Kritische Waffengänge*, xlvi; »Friedrich Spielhagen,« 9.
[36] E. g., Goessl, »Die Darstellung des Adels,« 147; Martini, *Deutsche Literatur im bürgerlichen Realismus*, 405; Anderson, »Spielhagen's Problematic Heroes,« 142, n. 4; Jackson, *Bürgerliche Arbeit und Romanwirklichkeit*, 240.

the novel may not be novelistic; it must strive to be something other than it is, an effort in which it can, of course, never succeed except in eccentric cases, which then come to be canonized and create the impression that the German novel tradition is essentially different from that of other nations. For his part, Spielhagen intended to free the novel from the novelistic, only to be perpetually charged with this very fault.[37]

Other problematic elements of Spielhagen's theoretical efforts are related to the aporia of realism he shared with his literary generation: how to achieve mimetic fidelity without violating aesthetic canons of beauty and propriety. One expression of the problem is his extensive rumination on the relationship of experience and imagination, of finding and inventing, a dialectic that provided the title of an autobiography (*FuE*; see also *AW*, 93). Experience is the principle of realism, and it must be one's own (*BT*, 180); invention is the principle of poiesis; the real cannot be unmediatedly represented, but must be given shape, perhaps idealized, in the imagination. So much is clear, but beyond this I cannot provide any help. I still do not understand how the relationship actually works; it seems to oscillate opportunistically between contrary commitments without ever providing a formula of realistic poiesis. Something similar is the case with another element, his insistence that characters must be derived from real-life models, persons one knows or has seen. But, of course, the characters cannot be the same as the models – most people, he remarks are too mediocre to be useful (*AW*, 106–07) – but must be different. He understands, of course, that the author must submerge himself into an alien being (*BT*, 21). In wrestling with this topic he approaches without actually developing the concept of typology we know in the tradition from Friedrich Engels to Georg Lukács (180). In my opinion, this whole matter of character models is »objectively« a red herring in Spielhagen's theory, designed to maintain the alleged balance between *Finden* and *Erfinden*, to obscure the supremacy of imagination over mimesis so as to retain realist credentials. In the one place where we can control this best, *Zum Zeitvertreib*, where we know a great deal about the »model« figures, we can see that the fictional characters bear no resemblance to them (see chapter 19).

Finally, there is the contradiction between »objective« narration and the pronounced political and socially critical commitment of Spielhagen's fiction. The only explanation for this is an assumption that the liberal view is the true and real one; as reality narrates itself,[38] objective representation will

---

[37] Rebing, *Der Halbbruder des Dichters*, 92.
[38] Hellmann, »Objektivität, Subjektivität und Erzählkunst,« 184.

permit the liberal truth to emerge unencumbered by mere personal opinion or subjective intention, as though seen through still, transparent water (*BT*, 211). The »idea« is supposed to speak for itself, a view exactly contrary to the modernist literary aesthetic.[39] Tendentious writers, on the other hand (with a tag from *Faust*), do not allow »den Geist der Zeiten« to speak, only »ihren eigenen Geist,« the assumption being that the spirit of the times is objectively knowable (59). Strodtmann agreed that the illusion of reality conjured by the objective narrator, despite his *engagement*, is never tendentious.[40] Spielhagen's social novels, Karpeles noted on the occasion of the birthday celebration, pursued the goals of the progress of freedom, becoming increasingly objective and nonpartisan.[41] Early in his career, in a letter of 1862, Spielhagen allowed that the hermaphroditic nature of the novel must be borne, for it was the art of the present whose content was the emancipation of the poor and the simple from the curse of the common and the obsolete.[42] Thus objectivity is a device for dealing with contemporary problems. »If your purpose is to *outdo* a threatening or at least bewildering historical reality by remaking it imaginatively,« writes Robert Alter, »the last thing you want to remind yourself of is that everything you write is, necessarily and ambiguously, artifice.«[43] When the representation of the value-laden world is identified with reality itself, »objectivity« is duplicity, though quite unaware of itself, for Spielhagen in his conscious being was the most honest of men. Nothing else, I believe, calls the quality of his intellect and perspicuity more cruelly into question than this consideration.[44]

---

[39] Rhöse, *Konflikt und Versöhnung*, 185. Serendipitously I came across an excellent contrasting definition: »*der Text soll als das Produkt quasi-empirischer Produzenten in einer quasi-pragmatischen Situation transparent sein, er soll vor allem nicht als natürlich vorhanden, vom Himmel gefallen oder sonstwie eingegeben erscheinen. Die Reden sollen nicht als Ausfluß einer absoluten, das Publikum einbeziehenden Subjektivität, sondern als fremde Reden eines Anderen wirken*«: Jürgen Link, *Elementare Literatur und generative Diskursanalyse* (Munich, 1983), 133. The formulation is applied here to Brecht but is applicable to modernism generally. Note that what for Spielhagen was »objective« appears here as »subjective.«

[40] Strodtmann, *Dichterprofile*, 208.

[41] *Friedrich Spielhagen. Dem Meister des deutschen Romans*, 3; see also Karpeles, *Friedrich Spielhagen*, 17–18, 72, 84.

[42] Adolf Stahr, *Aus Adolf Stahrs Nachlaß. Briefe von Stahr nebst Briefe an ihn*, ed. Ludwig Geiger (Oldenburg, 1903), 258.

[43] Robert Alter, *Partial Magic: The Novel as a Self-Conscious Genre* (Berkeley, Los Angeles, and London, 1975), 98.

[44] It is piquant to read in Otto Pflanze, *Bismarck and the Development of Germany* (Princeton, 1990), 2: 197, that among statesmen »Bismarck was unique in that he viewed himself a complete realist, an observer of the actual world and the forces that moved it, unprejudiced by personal motives or ideological passions,« and to

Even if his self-imposed regimen of »objectivity« was illusory and, fortunately, infeasible, his theoretical preoccupations did exercise qualitative constraints. Peter Demetz has observed acutely that »objectivity« compels scenic narration that tends to the dramatic, the melodramatic, and the theatrical, thus subverting probability and, one might add, Spielhagen's rigid genre distinctions.[45] The demand for transparency is also inhospitable to creativity at the level of style, for the writing is not supposed to get in the way of the representation of reality; the word is not an end in itself, he wrote, but a means to an end (*AW*, 136). The virtuosity of French literary style he regarded as a defect (*VS*, 302). Justus in *Sonntagskind* has trouble retaining what another character says because she is so well-spoken that her style distracts from the content (*NF*, 1: 260). Opinions on Spielhagen's own style range widely from piquant and effervescent or, while unremarkable, pleasant and cultivated, to gleaming but empty, garrulous and trivial, bloated and theatrical, or banal.[46] There has been a good deal of complaint about its bookishness regardless of the speaker's cultural level or dialect,[47] a charge that he brought against Goethe's *Die Wahlverwandtschaften*, recommending instead a stylized everyday language (*NB*, 118–19). In a late verse he defends himself obliquely by satirizing those who would complain that all the polyglot characters in *Wallensteins Lager* speak only »das Schillersche Deutsch« (*NG*, 199). He tells us that he had never mastered Low German (*FuE*, 1: 26) and he does not try to reproduce the dialect speech of many of his settings, but the narrator will sometimes call attention to its use, a narrative intru-

---

reflect that the two objective realisms came to quite divergent perceptions of that world.

[45] Peter Demetz, *Formen des Realismus: Theodor Fontane. Kritische Untersuchungen* (Munich:, 1964), 24. A similar observation was made earlier by Wilhelm Scherer, »Zur Technik der modernen Erzählung,« *Kleine Schriften zur neueren Litteratur, Kunst und Zeitgeschichte* (Berlin, 1893), 2: 168: objectivity »rückt den Roman möglichst in die Nähe des Dramas,« leading to monologues and dialogues. Spielhagen seems to have inherited his legislative rigidity from Humboldt, for example, in such absurd pronouncements as that a novel cannot have two heroes (*AmSt*, 332) but must have one; if Thackeray pretended he had written *Vanity Fair* without a hero, he must have been kidding (Becky is the hero, *BT*, 71–72). Spielhagen claimed that no novel employing illegitimate means could survive (*BT*, 294).

[46] Gottschall in *Friedrich Spielhagen. Dem Meister des deutschen Romans*, 24; Schmidt, »Friedrich Spielhagen,« 423; Bleibtreu, *Revolution der Literatur*, 26–27; Engel, »Stenographischer Bericht,« 401–02; Goessl, »Die Darstellung des Adels,« 65; Kuczynski, *Gestalten und Werke*, 1: 194–95.

[47] Hart, »Friedrich Spielhagen,« 66; Meyer, *Die deutsche Literatur des Neunzehnten Jahrhunderts*, 397.

sion, to be sure.[48] A coachman in *Platt Land* tries to speak standard German for the benefit of the visitor, who muses that in the homeland of *Plattdeutsch* speakers one is truly on the flat land, thus metaphorizing the title of the book in which he is a character (*AR*, 2, 5: 1–2). In a review of *Platt Land* Scherer observed perspicaciously that »der gleichmäßige Charakter der Sprache« detracts from objectivity, because the reader constantly hears the author's voice; Spielhagen »hat immer Handschuhe an. Seine Sprache überrascht nicht. Er fährt uns angenehm dahin, wie auf Gummirädern.«[49] My own opinion is that, since Spielhagen was a high-strung, to some degree neurotic personality, his style has a certain edge and vivacity, but in general it is undistinguished, even programmatically so. I think, incidentally, that this is a problem with German realism generally and may partly account for its modest standing in general literary history.

Similarly, the insistence on transparency is unfriendly to symbol and metaphor, for to do anything artistic with the surface of narration is a form of intrusion, of the author calling attention to himself and his fiction-making.[50] Spielhagen was generally impatient with symbolic devices, as appears in his ambivalence toward Goethe;[51] symbol and allegory, he remarked in connection with *Die Wahlverwandtschaften*, cannot reflect the real world (*NB*, 81). A doctor in *Quisisana* comments on the metaphoric evasions of his patient: »es geht [Ihrem Bild] wie allen Bildern: es deckt die Sache nur teilweise« (*AR*, 2, 8: 246), which, of course, is irrefutably true. This reticence may owe something to Humboldt, who praises *Hermann und Dorothea* for avoiding »Colorit,«[52] by which he seems to mean description and adjectival

---

48 Schierding, *Untersuchungen über die Romantechnik*, 131–32, relates that he learned from an interview with Henning that when Spielhagen read aloud, he pronounced in Low German the dialogues meant to be Low German but written in standard German on the page.

49 Scherer, »Zur Technik,« 169. He contrasts the »Element der Ursprünglichkeit, ein naives, wild leidenschaftliches Greifen nach der Sache« of the often rough stylist Gutzkow, adding that the reader does not always want to be rocked in a cradle (170).

50 Rebing, *Der Halbbruder des Dichters*, 61, points out that for Humboldt language was supposed to vanish in the picture of what is represented before the reader's imagination. Lilian R. Furst, *All is True: The Claims and Strategies of Realist Fiction* (Durham, NC and London, 1995), 148–49, observes fairly that transparency need not mean an absence of style.

51 On the relationship of »objectivity« to the loss of Goethean symbolism, see Jürgen Kolbe, *Goethes »Wahlverwandtschaften« und der Roman des 19. Jahrhunderts* (Stuttgart, Berlin, Cologne, and Mainz, 1968), 146. Kolbe remarks, 148, that it is easy to make fun of a critic who cannot grasp symbol and leitmotif.

52 Humboldt, »Über Göthes Herrmann und Dorothea,« 238.

ornamentation. Spielhagen's most overt effort at employing a symbol as an objective correlative, the flood in *Sturmflut*, made him uncomfortable; he confesses apologetically that, in reality, the events linked by the symbol, the inflationary flood of French gold reparations after the Franco-Prussian War and the inundation of Germany's north shore, had nothing to do with one another chronologically (*NB*, 220). Much later, he was to hate the »Mummenschanz der Allegorie« in Gerhart Hauptmann's *Die versunkene Glocke* (312), a view with which I must say I have some sympathy.[53] Others shared the suspicion of symbol; Julian Schmidt wrote that Spielhagen should have left the hammer and anvil out of *Hammer und Amboß*; Hart, too, felt that a true *Dichter* would have spared us these tools.[54] But Swales, who sees the relative absence of symbol as a marker of Spielhagen's inferiority to Balzac and Dickens, singles out the scene of the flooding storm as a uniquely successful passage.[55]

Of course symbols do occur; it is hard to imagine fiction without them. As is practically universal in nineteenth-century prose, weather often serves as an objective correlative to mood. A scene in *Platt Land*, where a falcon attacks a flight of doves and kills a faltering white one, certainly has the character of symbolic foreshadowing (*AR*, 2, 5: 20–21). Swallows are naturally ubiquitous in *Was die Schwalbe sang*. Of the leitmotivic use of a fairy tale figure of an ogre in *Sonntagskind*, more will be said in Chapter 16. In that same novel, the appearance of a ship with black sails when Justus and Isabel begin their ill-fated marriage fills her with fear; they try to ignore it as a perfectly normal coastal sight, but unsuccessfully (*NF*, 1: 450–51, 501, 508). Justus, trying for weeks to find an ending for a character in his story, decides to reify the metaphor of life as a pulverizing machine by flinging him into a »real« machine (323–24). The very use of title phrases as leitmotifs calls attention to authorial management.

---

[53] In a series of literary-critical distichs, Spielhagen passed judgment on several Hauptmann works: *Die Weber, Kollege Crampton* positively; *Hanneles Himmelfahrt, Die versunkene Glocke, Der Biberpelz* with mixed judgment; *Florian Geyer, Fuhrmann Henschel* negatively (*NG*, 202–03, 206–09).

[54] Schmidt, »Friedrich Spielhagen,« 441; Hart, »Friedrich Spielhagen,« 29–30.

[55] Swales, *Epochenbuch Realismus*, 103–07. Recently the novel has received an unusually literary treatment as an example of the integrative function of symbol for »kollektive Bildlichkeit«: Axel Drews and Ita Gerhard, »Wissen, Kollektivsymbolik und Literatur am Beispiel von Friedrich Spielhagens ›Sturmflut,‹« *Bürgerlicher Realismus und Gründerzeit 1848–1890. Hansers Sozialgeschichte der deutschen Literatur vom 16. Jahrhundert bis zur Gegenwart*, vol. 6, ed. Edward McInnes and Gerhard Plumpe (Munich, 1996), 711.

In fact, it may be Spielhagen's very violations of strict objectivity that rescue a degree of literary quality that the theory seems determined to strangle.[56] Sometimes there are recursive references to fiction-writing. The narrator of *Hammer und Amboß* asserts that he is not writing a novel but the history of his life (*AR*, 1, 3: 281), but Walter, Spielhagen's alter ego in *In Reih' und Glied*, is writing a self-indulgent novel of his own life (like *Problematische Naturen*?) and finds reality less shapely than fiction (1, 6: 299–304; the novel is criticized in various discussions). The criticism of Justus's novel by a professor of literature in *Sonntagskind* might possibly be Spielhagen's own self-criticism (*NF*, 1: 289–92). Reinhold Schmidt in *Sturmflut* muses about the coincidences he has experienced: »Das ist wie in einem Roman, und geht doch alles mit so natürlichen Dingen zu!« (*AR*, 1, 8: 106), while a character in *Ein neuer Pharao* remarks that the family might be good novel material (3, 3: 43). A visiting princess in *Quisisana* analyzes the configuration of characters, telling the protagonist it is as obvious as »die Geheimnisse eines Dutzendromans« and calling his passion for a young woman »eine kompliziertere Fabel«; he in exasperation accuses her of describing people as though they were novel characters and creating »das Arrangement, das den Herren Poeten so viel Kopfzerbrechen verursacht«; she really should make a book out of it. He adds that »der geistreiche Autor gewinnt auch einem alten Stoffe neue Seiten ab,« which seems like a recursive irony, since the novella is self-consciously a rewriting of Goethe's *Der Mann von fünfzig Jahren* (2, 8: 115–16). Münzer in *Die von Hohenstein* peers into an aristocratic house and »dort schöne Gestalten geschaut, wie sie der Dichter in anmuthigen Novellen braucht« (1, 2: 152), and Sven's busybody of a landlady in *In der zwölften Stunde* gives Mrs. Durham's diary to her admirer, »denn ich wußte aus den Romanen, daß in so einem Tagebuch immer alles steht, was man nur zu wissen wünschen kann« (2, 1: 472). Lothar broods in *Was will das werden?* that a novel hero could overcome all of his troubles, »nach seines Dichters hohem Ratschluß,« but he is not a novel hero, just slogging along, and in another place he remarks that what he has to relate would be regarded as exaggerations if found in a novel (3, 5: 63–64, 222). Ironic expectations of a reader are addressed by Escheburg of *An der Heilquelle* to his secret beloved when he sees her lose interest in a book:

---

[56] I find curious the formulation of Worthmann, *Probleme des Zeitromans*, 112: »Spielhagens Praxis straft gleichsam seine Theorie Lügen, sie verschüttet Ansätze, die zu einem großen realistischen Zeitroman hätte führen können,« as though the theory were superior to the creative practice. My view is the opposite.

Du willst es den armen Autor nicht entgelten lassen. Er hat gewiß sein Bestes gethan, in langer mühevoller Arbeit sein kunstreiches Gespinst webend, Faden klug durch Faden schlingend und alle wieder zum sorgsam berechneten Mittelpunkte leitend. Er kann verlangen, daß du mit offenen Sinnen ihm entgegenkommst, mit gutem Willen, dich seiner Schöpfung zu freuen, und nicht ihn stumpf und poesielos nennst, weil du es in dir selber bist. Es ist ja nur so schon zu viel Undank in der Welt. (3, 1: 120).

Here, in 1885, one suspects a *pro domo* utterance on the part of the author. Such gestures occur in a number of other places. A highly symmetrical plot disposition, such as we shall point out in connection with *Alles fließt*, clearly signals an authorial presence (see chapter 17).

Other devices foreground fictionality. Leaving aside early works, in which Spielhagen is said not to have found his way to narrative discipline, we are viewing narrative craft exposed when one narrator in *Platt Land* stays outside Gerhard's mind, not knowing why he behaves as he does, but at the end gets inside his deliriously distorted vision (2, 5: 54, 534–36); when one says a character is faking, as in *Allzeit voran* (2, 2: 219) or suspends judgment on a character's sincerity, as in *Faustulus* (*NF* 4, 7); when one tells us what will happen in the future, as in *Noblesse oblige* (*AR*, 3, 2: 78). Since it was just the symbolic conjunction in *Sturmflut* that made the author uneasy, it is interesting that when the storm and the financial collapse coincide, the narrator jubilates, then, with an ironic twist, takes us inside the luxurious but doomed house: »Es soll der Dichter mit dem König, und es muß der Künstler mit dem Gründer gehen. Das sind Gesetze, die wir zu respectiren haben« (1, 9: 227–29). Fictionality is ironically exposed as dwelling in the imagination at the end of *Die schönen Amerikanerinnen* when the narrator invites the »lieber Leser« to join him a visit to his friend's estate, giving directions to take the train to the sea and steer the boat »Nord-Nord-Ost, oder Süd-Süd-West, oder wie der Wind gerade weht« (2, 4: 211–12). By the last phase of his career Spielhagen had come to care much less about narrative abstinence than his still spinning theoretical prayer wheel would indicate; the narrator of *Zum Zeitvertreib* repeatedly comments on Albrecht in a superior way, while the narrator of *Susi* takes a hard line on the heroine, like Thackeray on Becky Sharp, with a similar result, that the reader develops an affection for the bad girl and begins to share some of her disdain for her honest, loving oaf of a husband (see Chapters 19 and 17).

For all of the weight of the case that can be maintained against Spielhagen and the agreement to keep him in the decanonized outer darkness, from time to time there have been voices suggesting a reconsideration. Usually such arguments are made on political and ideological grounds, giving him credit for maintaining a discourse on social problems in inhospitable times.[57] He was, after all, one of the most democratic writers in German literature of the nineteenth century, especially recognized as such in foreign countries. Löwenthal from his left-wing position asserted that Spielhagen had been silenced by the dominant order and that this was to his credit.[58] That judgment may be excessive, but more recently he has been described as »one of the most important literary representatives of a liberal Germany which would be ruled through political participation and democracy.«[59] Perhaps a consideration of some of his themes, to which we shall turn in Part II, can contribute to a fairer assessment.

[57] Rhöse, *Konflikt und Versöhnung*, 191.
[58] Löwenthal, *Erzählkunst und Gesellschaft*, 175.
[59] Neuhaus, »Friedrich Spielhagen – Critic of Bismarck's Empire,« 135.

II.
THEMES

5. The Aristocracy

> Ein Adelshasser, ich? Wenn, adlig sein,
> Gleich: vornehm sein – ich schwärme für den Adel
> Der Geistesritter ohne Furcht und Tadel.
> Mein Haß gilt nur den frechen Junkerlein. (NG, 167)

Most people who know a few things about Spielhagen are likely to know that his fiction is much preoccupied with the aristocracy, often in a critical, sometimes satirical or lampooning way, but also sometimes with a degree of envy, perhaps an undercurrent of accommodation. »Die Auseinandersetzung mit dem Adel ... bildet in fast allen Prosawerken Spielhagens das Grundthema.«[1] Like everything else prominently connected with him, this thematic preoccupation has drawn much negative comment.[2] A good deal of it has been motivated by an opposition to »tendentiousness,« a conviction that social and class conflicts should not be roiled up in literature.[3] But other

---

[1] Alfred F. Goessl, »Die Darstellung des Adels in Prosaschriften Friedrich Spielhagens« (Diss. Tulane U, 1966), 13.

[2] Ernest K. Bramsted, whose *Aristocracy and the Middle-Classes in Germany: Social Types in German Literature 1830–1900*, rev. edn. (Chicago and London, 1964), famously associated the evolution of the theme in the social novel with the political accommodation of the bourgeoisie to the aristocracy, found Spielhagen's representations inferior in realism to those of Gutzkow and Freytag (80, 121). However, it has been argued more recently that, although the aristocracy provided social models to be imitated by the bourgeoisie (a pan-European phenomenon), the latter's feudalization is doubtful; marriage into the upper class was not common: Hans-Ulrich Wehler, *Deutsche Gesellschaftsgeschichte*, vol. 3, *Von der »Deutschen Doppelrevolution« bis zum Beginn des Ersten Weltkrieges 1848–1814* (Munich, 1995), 474, 1270, 718–20.

[3] See Rosa-Maria Zinken, *Der Roman als Zeitdokument. Bürgerlicher Liberalismus in Friedrich Spielhagens »Die von Hohenstein« (1863/64)*, (Frankfurt am Main and Bern, 1991), 45–47. It is curious to see one of Spielhagen's American reviewers take a conservative line on this on other matters, deriving the treatment of the aristocracy from »personal hatred,« noting that it »has been by some of his critics ascribed – unjustly, as we think – to mere *bourgeois* envy of aristocratic privileges and social honors«: Wm. Hand Browne, »Spielhagen's Novels,« *New Eclectic Magazine* 7 (1870): 211. The journal was a publication of the deep South.

observers have complained of a static fixation on a problem of the past, when the true conflict of modern times was that of the capitalist bourgeoisie with the proletariat.[4] Spielhagen was not above a certain self-satire of his proclivity, as with the foolish antiaristocratic affect of the petty-bourgeois *Literat* Gönnich in *An der Heilquelle* (e.g, *AR*, 3, 1: 198). In the late phase, the social status of the aristocracy has become, like so much else, an object of satire, as in the assertion of the rich Jewish parvenu Philipp Bielefelder in *Frei geboren*: »ein Graf ist immer ein netter Schmuck für eine bürgerliche Gesellschaft« (*NF*, 7: 339). In the long run Spielhagen was certain he had been right. In a late sonnet, »Vergebliche Warnung,« he declares that years before he had warned: »Ihr wackern Bürger, traut den Junkern nicht!... / Man lachte höhnisch mir ins Angesicht.... / Wie hat seitdem das Blättlein sich gewandt: /›Will uns denn niemand vor den Junkern retten ....‹ / Nun erntet auch, die ihr gesä't, die Saat!« (*NG*, 116).

No conscientious sociopolitical fiction in late nineteenth-century Germany could have avoided the problem of the power and prestige of the aristocracy.[5] Dr. Paulus in *In Reih' und Glied* supports the writer Walter Gutmann (the author's alter ego, one is inclined to think) in his »Verhöhnung der ›Regierung,‹ wie sich die brutale Polizeiwirtschaft, unter der wir leiden, naiv genug nennt« (*AR*, 1, 6: 304). It has been said that Spielhagen's early novels were written at a time when there was a near civil war in Prussia between the bourgeoisie and the monarchist aristocracy.[6] If anything, these entitlements were reinforced in the course of the nineteenth century and, in the Reich, were shored up, legally and by dominant practice, perhaps just because the nobility's real *raison d'être* was eroding, so that a variety of social fictions and sanctions was required to maintain its privileges and immuni-

---

[4] Alexander Robinson Anderson, »Spielhagen's Problematic Heroes« (Diss. Brown U, 1962), 177; Victor Klemperer, *Die Zeitromane Friedrich Spielhagens und ihre Wurzeln* (Weimar, 1913), 116. Dieter Kafitz, *Figurenkonstellation als Mittel der Wirklichkeitserfassung. Dargestellt an Romanen der zweiten Hälfte des 19. Jahrhunderts (Freytag · Spielhagen · Fontane · Raabe)* (Kronberg, 1978), 116, argues that by *Opfer* at the end of his career Spielhagen had lost interest in the conflict with the aristocracy and become concerned with the problems of an ethical socialism.

[5] See the sensible contextualization of Spielhagen's theme by Patricia B. Herminghouse, »Schloß oder Fabrik? Zur Problematik der Adelsdarstellung im Roman des Nachmärz,« *Legitimationskrisen des deutschen Adels 1200–1900*, ed. Peter Uwe Hohendahl and Paul Michael Lützeler (Stuttgart, 1979), 245–61. Herminghouse sees *Problematische Naturen* distinguished by its sense of ambiguity in Oswald's character and an awareness of the political dimension less foregrounded by other novelists (254, 256).

[6] Franz Rhöse, *Konflikt und Versöhnung. Untersuchungen zur Theorie des Romans von Hegel bis zum Naturalismus* (Stuttgart, 1978), 194.

ties. The historian Hans-Ulrich Wehler has shown that increasing prosperity made the landed nobility optimistic and arrogant, but as its indebtedness grew it became pessimistic behind the scenes. Although its true significance had been falling since the Napoleonic Wars and 1848, it maintained its privileges for seventy years; the *Junker* enforced a veto power in the Prussian parliament down to 1918. The wars of the 1860s and 1870s upgraded the aristocratic class, which developed a pathological arrogance. Wehler speaks of a »Klassenkampf von oben.«[7] At the same time, it is not surprising that the aristocratic caste should have inspired envy, what in Spielhagen's case has been treated as the love-hate of the parvenu,[8] especially in regard to its power position in politics and the military, but also because of its perhaps more imagined than real conditions of freedom to fashion the self. Here the truly »classical« text is the famous passage in *Wilhelm Meisters Lehrjahre*:

> Ich weiß nicht, wie es in fremden Ländern ist, aber in Deutschland ist nur dem Edelmann eine gewisse allgemeine, wenn ich sagen darf, personelle Ausbildung möglich. Ein Bürger kann sich Verdienst erwerben und zur höchsten Not seinen Geist ausbilden; seine Persönlichkeit geht aber verloren, er mag sich stellen wie er will. Indem es dem Edelmann, der mit den Vornehmsten umgeht, zur Pflicht wird, sich selbst einen vornehmen Anstand zu geben, indem dieser Anstand, da ihm weder Tür noch Tor verschlossen ist, zu einem freien Anstand wird, da er mit seiner Figur, mit seiner Person, es sei bei Hofe oder bei der Armee, bezahlen muß, so hat er Ursache, etwas auf sie zu halten und zeigen, daß er etwas auf sie hält.[9]

Goethe, of course, is not to be identified with Wilhelm's naïveté here; his hero learns better during his theater troupe's sojourn on the estate of a count, among the most comic scenes in the novel. But, looking at the matter contemporaneously, Julian Schmidt observed: »Ich finde es vielmehr sehr natürlich, daß die Neigung jedes Dichters ihn aus dem alltäglichen, engen bürgerlichen Leben und seinen Pflichten hinaustreibt in eine Sphäre glänzender Farben, kühner Striche, gewaltiger Leidenschaften.«[10] There is a

---

7 Wehler, *Deutsche Gesellschaftsgeschichte*, 3: 39, 167, 171, 204, 815, 822, 834.

8 Goessl, »Die Darstellung des Adels,« 15. Gustav Karpeles, *Friedrich Spielhagen. Ein literarischer Essay* (Leipzig, 1889), observed with uncharacteristic perspicacity (35) that Spielhagen found himself in the middle between these affects.

9 Johann Wolfgang von Goethe, *Werke* (Hamburger Ausgabe), vol. 7, *Romane und Novellen*, ed. Erich Trunz, 3rd edn. (Hamburg, 1957), 290.

10 Julian Schmidt, »Friedrich Spielhagen,« *Westermann's Jahrbuch der Illustrirten Deutschen Monatshefte* 29 (1870–71): 438. On the same page he complained that the treatment of the nobility in *Die von Hohenstein* »macht doch einen sehr widerwärtigen Eindruck, da nicht *ein* versöhnender Moment eintritt.«

passage in *Sonntagskind*, addressed to the narrator by the intellectually and literarily alert Frau Körner, that might almost be a gloss on the passage from *Wilhelm Meister*:

> Immerhin wird sich Ihr Talent mehr zur Schilderung der höheren gesellschaftlichen Klassen eignen, als der der niederen; und die psychologische Analyse gebildeter Geister und feingestimmter Herzen Ihnen besser gelingen als die unwissender Seelen und roher Gemüter. Aber gerade daraus erwächst sich nach meinem Dafürhalten für Sie die Nötigung, dem Unfreien, Unschönen, Häßlichen mutig zu Leibe zu gehen, es doppelt sorgfältig zu prüfen und zu studieren, damit Sie es, wo es nötig ist, in Ihren Darstellungen verwerten können.... Ihre Menschheit darf nicht, wie die Feuillets, mit dem Baron anfangen, aber auch nicht, wie die Zolas und seiner Nachbeter und Nachtreter, bei dem Baron, oder schon weit vorher, aufhören, – sie muß Ihnen bestehen aus allem, was Menschenantlitz trägt. (*NF*, 1: 292)[11]

The awareness that the life of the aristocracy is itself a kind of social theater that needs to be analyzed and exposed is a driving motivation in Spielhagen's œuvre from beginning to end.

He seems to have had relatively little direct experience of the aristocracy in his youth and young manhood. While an upper-middle-class Jewish student like Heine in the preceding generation could have a surprising number of noble friends and acquaintances, few such persons turn up in Spielhagen's biography. He does, however, give a picture of class inequality in the north of Germany; because he does not want to augment »den Verdacht des Adelshasses, in welchem ich stehe,« he quotes a couple of pages on the oppression of the peasants from Ernst Moritz Arndt, »den jetzt wohl niemand mehr des Radikalismus zeihen wird« (*FuE*, 1: 176–79). Spielhagen tells us that his parents had social relations with a family in a manor house on Rügen, but we are assured that these were perfectly kindly people who do not resemble his fictional figures (197–98). He made some observations as a tutor in the house of a landowner, who also seems to have been an innocuous person (2: 105–13). His models for Melitta von Berkow and Helene von Grenwitz were women he observed from a distance (431). Evidently he made critical and, it has been claimed, accurate observations of the Pomeranian *Junker* in his neighborhood,[12] and he certainly developed perceptions of

---

[11] This passage is cited in what seems to me an exceptionally fair and perceptive treatment of the question by Leo Löwenthal, *Erzählkunst und Gesellschaft. Die Gesellschaftsproblematik in der deutschen Literatur des 19. Jahrhunderts* (Neuwied and Berlin, 1971), 143, 157, 173–74.

[12] Hermann Schierding, *Untersuchungen über die Romantechnik Friedrich Spielhagens. (Unter Benutzung unveröffentlichter Manuskripte)* (Borna-Leipzig, 1914), 9.

aristocratic officers during his military service, though that, as we shall see, came to be a special topic. On the whole, his environment, as he himself indicates, was intensely bourgeois. His critique of the nobility is not fueled by any personal conflicts or bitterness but is ideologically motivated, thus located on a broad social base. From the outset Spielhagen records very hostile attitudes. Oswald in *Problematische Naturen*, when trained in shooting by his alleged father, was taught to imagine every bull's eye as the heart of a nobleman (*AR*, 1, 1: 195–96).

The initial tendency is to portray aristocrats as either fools or knaves. The most notorious example of the former may be Baron Cloten in *Problematische Naturen*, the stupidest man of all of Spielhagen's characters, who is persuaded of an alternative version of the Book of Genesis in which the aristocracy and the common people have distinct first parents. The knaves appear in full force in *Die von Hohenstein*: oppressors, a thief, even a murderer – a hostile representation in some quarters perceived as a libel. A baron turns out to be a thief in *Quisisana* and another in *Uhlenhans*. Many versions of these types appear in the œuvre; when such persons are in power they are genuinely dangerous, enemies of the moral progress of mankind, but when left to their own devices often helpless in the modern world. The landed aristocrat who is incompetent in modern agriculture is introduced in *In Reih' und Glied* and reappears in *Platt Land*. The kind, shy Count Guido Wendelin in *Stumme des Himmels* confesses that he knows nothing of agriculture and lets the tenants run his estate, adding that in Farther Pomerania »viel Geist wird bei uns nicht konsumiert, es liegt nicht in der Rasse, glaube ich« (*NF*, 2: 109). The problem of making a landed estate support a noble family in the fashion to which it would like to be accustomed reappears in the late *Selbstgerecht* (5, 69–70). In that novel a baroness is aware that her depraved husband's violent death »brachte das Publikum um das Vergnügen, die *chronique scandaleuse* der *upper ten thousand* um einen kostbaren Fall bereichert zu haben« (131–32). Another type is the amiable good-for-nothing, an unemployable wastrel who piles up debts and sponges off others or tries to marry well, perhaps a rich Jewess. An example in pure culture is Falko von Falkenburg in the late novel *Opfer*.

The female of the species is often beautiful and haughty, sometimes prideful and in need of comeuppance, sometimes empty-headed, luxury-loving, and frivolous. The older women can be scheming wives and mothers. Camilla von Hohenstein's mother hopes her daughter will become a prince's mistress after her marriage (*AR*, 1, 2: 741–42). In *Opfer*, Ebba von Falkenburg, who is supposed to marry her cousin Wilfried (though the reader suspects from the beginning that she will not), cannot believe that he actually means to live and work on his estates, and dislikes his being an *Assessor,* that is, an unpaid junior legal official; it makes him seem like a bumpkin (*NF,* 6: 55–56). The stupid countess in *Sonntagskind* loves her stupid son Armand but not her bright daughter Sibylle, a woman of refinement and strength of character such as can also emerge from the privileged class.

This is true of men also. An early example is Baron von Oldenburg, one of the problematic natures; it is he, after all, who hoaxes Baron Cloten with the alternative Bible yarn. But such men come to be Byronic renegades, alienated from their class, and so they drop out of the power grid. In a worst case, a nobleman can become preoccupied with imaginary feudal atavisms, turn Bohemian and eventually sociopathic, as does Malte von Zehren in *Hammer und Amboß,* who tries to sell his own daughter for a gambling debt. Yet it is his brother, the prison warden, who is one of the most ideal figures in all of Spielhagen's fiction. In *Röschen vom Hofe,* written at the same time as the caustic *Die von Hohenstein,* a deeply reactionary nobleman can be converted by love and decency to acceptance of a politically progressive, oppositional count as a son-in-law.[13] Wilfried von Falkenburg in *Opfer* is another nobleman who comes to be alienated from his class. As he observes its pettiness and money-grubbing, he muses: »das war nun das moralische Rückgrat dieser Leute, die sich einreden, die unzerbrechliche Stütze von Thron und Altar zu sein« (211). Sometimes, however, class determination is indomitable; Angela, in the novel of that name, believes Edward, son of an Irish noblewoman crazed with class obsessions, to be above considerations of class and wealth, but she is mistaken.

Aristocrats can also find themselves in a kind of schizophrenic identity, not so much between the classes as between the times. Major Degenfeld in *Die von Hohenstein* mulls the internalization of class difference, which he detects in himself, and when he finds himself on the side of the rebels, attacked by his own battalion in the tactics he has taught them, he feels that he has been doubled, that he is on both sides simultaneously (*AR,* 1, 2: 661–62, 691). An elaborately developed case is Ulrich von Vogtriz in *Was will das werden?,* a strong, bluff, impetuous, well-intentioned chap called »Schlagododro« after the giant Schlagadodro in Immermann's mock-

---

13 As pointed out in a somewhat caustic comment of his own by Jürgen Kuczynski, *Gestalten und Werke. Soziologische Studien zur deutschen Literatur,* vol. 1 (Berlin and Weimar, 1969), 201. The story had been earlier adduced by Adolf Strodtmann, *Dichterprofile. Literaturbilder aus dem neunzehnten Jahrhundert* (Stuttgart, 1879), 209, as proof that Spielhagen was not always unfair to the nobility.

epic, *Tulifäntchen*.[14] Spielhagen's Schlagododro befriends Lothar Lorenz, but through complicated plot developments becomes alienated from him, ostensibly through rivalry in love affairs, but in fact as a result of Schlagododro's reversion to aristocratic traits, even as he is ostracized by his family for associating with a carpenter's son. He tries to study and learn economics, but a professor, a liberal voice in the novel, declares that one cannot be a monarchist and an economics scholar at the same time (3, 5: 441). In that same novel there appears a new, distinctly *fin-de-siècle* type, the pale, elegant, aloof, intellectual Adalbert von Werin, with whom Lothar also makes friends although Schlagododro is instinctively hostile to him. He comes to be one of Spielhagen's nihilists, implacably radical and contemptuous of mankind, who, when arrested, takes his life.

Much comment has been addressed to the cases of secret noble origin in Spielhagen's fiction. Mauthner in his parody had a fine time with it; Edgar, who, it is suddenly discovered, »war mütterlicherseits adelig!,« leads the workers on the barricades with his hairy right hand and the nobles with his elegant left.[15] Because the device is thematic in his earliest works, *Clara Vere* and *Problematische Naturen*, is hinted at in *In Reih' und Glied*, then recurs in the major novels *Was will das werden?* and *Sonntagskind*, it is thought to be more pervasive than it actually is. It is difficult to get the right perspective on this trope. Secret family relationships are a familiar plotting device in this era of the novel, partly because families themselves are so important to the web of events, but largely, I suspect, because they make the novelist's task of maintaining suspense across large narrative expanses easier. That they should cross class boundaries brings an attractive *frisson* of the illicit but also makes the secrecy more plausible. They are not peculiar to Spielhagen; for example, the carpenter in Karl Gutzkow's *Die Ritter vom Geiste* is actually a prince.[16]

That they reflect in Spielhagen's case subliminal attraction and accommodation to the privileged class I rather doubt. Klemperer made the important point that the convention of secret family relationships illuminates the senselessness of hereditary legitimacy.[17] The revealed aristocratic heritage

---

[14] Karl Immermann, *Werke in fünf Bänden*, ed. Benno von Wiese et al. (Frankfurt am Main, 1971–77), 1: 448.

[15] Fritz Mauthner, *Nach berühmten Mustern. Parodistische Studien*, 6th ed. (Stuttgart, [1878]), 81, 83.

[16] Norbert Bachleitner, *Der englische und französische Sozialroman des 19. Jahrhunderts und seine Rezeption in Deutschland* (Amsterdam and Atlanta, 1993), 446.

[17] Klemperer, *Die Zeitromane Friedrich Spielhagens*, 70–71.

is a burden and distraction for the hero, who regularly rejects it, as in the paradigmatic case of Oswald Stein. The returned »Smith« in *Ein neuer Pharao* is smelled out by the doctor as a born aristocrat – »Wir geborenen Plebejer haben eine scharfe Witterung für euch Aristokraten« – but he had long since renounced his title before going into American exile (3, 3: 363, 512–15). The count in *Röschen vom Hofe*, having evolved to enlightenment, understands that *Geist* has come to replace *Blut* as the mark of personal value (2, 1: 598–99). Subsequently he serves as a mediator between the court and a non-noble ministry, doubtless a liberal wish dream of the young author (624). The hapless, unstable landowner Zempin in *Platt Land* hates the local count because he himself would like to be count, prince, or king (2, 5: 440) and is thus a cautionary example of such envy. The movement is, if anything, the other way, toward embourgeoisement, as in the case of Walter von Hohenstein, product of a mixed marriage, who abandons his class and makes a bourgeois marriage of his own; this kind of marriage across class boundaries on bourgeois terms is characteristic of the social novel generally.[18] Other positive aristocratic figures evolve in this direction, such as Major, later Colonel von Vogtriz in *Was will das werden?*

However, the secret class origin seems to have deterministic psychological effects; some form of superiority or delicacy is detectable before the circumstances of birth are revealed. Oswald Stein in *Problematische Naturen* developed, despite the influence of his fiercely class-conscious alleged father, initially incomprehensible aristocratic instincts, a love of fine clothes and comfort, an attraction to refinement and poesy (1, 5: 10). Something similar happens in *Sonntagskind*, though in a more complicated way. Justus, who is rather estranged from his difficult, alleged father, becomes reconciled in admiration for him when he stands up to the count, whom he regards as a thief, refusing his money and job; yet when Justus finds himself in the garden of the manor, he feels a longing for beauty and elegance (*NF*, 1: 39–43, 51). This pattern recurs: the carpenter who is Lothar's stepfather in *Was will das werden?* always regarded princes as »gräßliche Wütheriche,« but Lothar is instinctively attracted to the elegance of the officer von Vogtriz, who grieves at the gap between classes and whose private secretary Lothar becomes; ultimately Vogtriz is forced to resign, an outcome for which Schlagododro blames Lothar (*AR*, 3, 4: 105, 27; 3, 5: 194, 197, 323–24). The inner ambiguity can work the other way, to the bourgeois advantage; I commented in

---

[18]   Claudia Streit, *(Re-)Konstruktion von Familie im sozialen Roman des 19. Jahrhunderts* (Frankfurt am Main and Berlin, 1997), 98.

Chapter 2 that Bella's claim in *Die von Hohenstein* that Walter, apropos of his marriage to her daughter Ottilie, has »ein Schmitz'sches Herz« (1, 2: 494–95) suggests a virtually biological inheritance. It is always difficult to tell in the late nineteenth century whether implications of blood inheritance are merely a metaphorical usage or are precursors of genetic ideas. I cannot see that Spielhagen ever shows any interest in the emergence of race theory in his time; we shall ask this question again in Chapter 8. The obsequious spa director in *Die schönen Amerikanerinnen* identifies »Rasse« in a Hungarian count who turns out to be a Viennese billiards hustler and swindler (2, 4: 104). But notions of genetic inheritance are grounded in ancient folk perceptions and I do not think Spielhagen entirely free of them in his understanding of class determinants. One observer has remarked that his »critique is seriously weakened by countervailing hints that the notion of inborn superiority might have merit.«[19] Perhaps in many cases, however, they should be put on the account of fictional characters, such as the protagonist of *Selbstgerecht*, who feels that, as a democrat, he has no fear of falling for a beautiful baroness who believes that aristocrats are a category of natural history, »eine Rasse ..., so streng geschieden von den bürgerlichen Menschen, wie nur immer eine Rasse von der andern sein kann« (*NF*, 5: 36–37); the experienced reader knows, of course, that things will not be quite that simple. Nor is aristocratic blood an essential substance; in that same novel, the protagonist, with an application of *Bildung*, removes the traces of aristocratic prejudice from the blood of the baroness's son (200). Origin does not always replicate itself deterministically; one of the characters in *Ein neuer Pharao* makes an observation that corresponds to my own, particularly among academics, namely that he is a monarchist because he was born poor, while the exiled forty-eighter »Smith« is a radical because he was born an aristocrat (*AR*, 3, 3: 364–66).

Finally, I should like to call attention to what seems to me an estimable insight into the reality of aristocracy in Germany: that it was not fully subordinated to the royal or princely power. German monarchies never annexed the nobility as the French monarchy had done long before. Norbert Elias has pointed out that the aristocratic dueling ethos conducted according to a code external to the laws of the state broke »the royal monopoly of violence« and has concluded that aristocrats »never really defined themselves

---

[19] Katherine Roper, »1848 in the Early Novels of Friedrich Spielhagen. The Making of a German Democrat,« *German Studies Review* 23 (2000): 431.

as subjects of the ruling prince.«[20] Consequently, while some of Spielhagen's aristocrats can be dangerous and powerful personalities, even if seriously flawed, his kings, princes, and reigning dukes tend to be ineffectual. The clearest example, already mentioned in Chapter 2, is the king of *In Reih' in Glied*. It is not he who is the dangerous man in the kingdom, except through incompetence and inadvertence, but his minister Hey, sometimes, equally imprecisely, linked to Bismarck, but more probably modelled on the ferocious Prussian police director Karl Ludwig Friedrich von Hinckeldey (1805–56).[21] In *Allzeit voran*, as we shall see in Chapter 12, a conflict between a count, powerful in his personality, and a weak ruling prince is thematic to the novel. A count in *Platt Land*, who is presented as a harmless ass, claims to have the ear of the king and is determined to make his province what it should be, »eine Hochburg der Königstreue, eine feste Wehr conservativer Gesinnung gegen die trübe Flut des königs- und gottlosen Liberalismus, welchen vom Rhein, von Schlesien herandrängt, und überall in den großen Städten ihre Hydrahäupter erhebt« (2: 5, 244). However, it appears from the further narration that aristocratic class identity across national boundaries is more important than loyalty to the nation.

In *Opfer*, the Falkenburg family estate on Rügen is failing owing to economic laws; Wilfried von Falkenburg's brother is a prince, but he is powerless to help. The petty prince in *Die schönen Amerikanerinnen*, »Serenissimus,« who tries to restore ancient hunting privileges, is satirized as »Sr. Hoheit, Herman de[r] Hundertsiebenundneunzigste[ ]« (2, 4: 68). The ruling duke in *Was will das werden?* turns out to be poor in spirit for all that he tries to help and support Lothar, his son, as it emerges; the type recurs as the count in *Sonntagskind*.[22] Lothar pities the duke, who deserved

---

[20] Norbert Elias, *The Germans: Power Struggles and the Development of Habitus in the Nineteenth and Twentieth Centuries*, ed. Michael Schröter (New York, 1996), 64–65.

[21] See Adolf Schumacher, *Ferdinand Lassalle As a Novelistic Subject of Friedrich Spielhagen* (Diss. U of Pennsylvania, 1910), 115–16.

[22] The duke in *Was will das werden?*, who is anxious for Lothar's approbation of his poetry and tries to involve him in theatricals, has sometimes been identified with Ernst II, duke of Saxe-Coburg (1818–93), an unusually liberal and artistic ruler who wrote operas: Schierding, *Untersuchungen über die Romantechnik*, 109; Kuno Francke, *Weltbürgertum in der deutschen Literatur von Herder bis Nietzsche* (Berlin, 1928), 113–14. Spielhagen refused a decoration from Duke Ernst: Hans Henning, *Friedrich Spielhagen* (Leipzig:, 1910), 151–52. One might also think of Duke Georg of Saxe-Meiningen (1826–1914), whose theater troupe, founded in 1874, set national standards of performance, especially for Naturalistic drama. But, as always, such identifications can only be approximate.

better than to have been born a prince; for his part the duke tends to feel sorry for himself and, at the end, when he wants to take credit for a drama Lothar has written (on Thomas Münzer!), becomes genuinely pitiable (3, 4: 499; 3, 5: 425, 427). In *Susi*, the ruling duke would like to get rid of Susi's husband Baron Astolf, previously his best friend, but those days are over; duke or not, now he is no better than the last of his vassals; he resents the now institutionalized political opposition (*NF*, 3: 314). Here, to be sure, it is not the aristocracy but the prince who frustrates him by interfering with his amour with Susi; he rages against the fish-blooded prince, asking himself if one is not allowed to make love any more (339); such troubles are unbearable for a ruling lord (373). The cuckolded husband thinks that, despite the princely blood in the duke's veins, he is worse than a plebeian (375). In the end, after the husband has been killed in an ironic accident, the prince, who sees the duke has been at fault, smooths things over, persuaded of the sacred duty of »die Solidarität der fürstlichen Interessen« (408). In *Uhlenhans*, the idle, superannuated Swedish diplomat Lindblad, who has dealt with Napoleon and Talleyrand, is enraged at being patronized by the local prince, »von diesem Duodezfürsten, diesem obersten von ein paar Dutzend anderen Krautjunkern ... und ein Französisch sprach wie eine *vache espagnole!*« (*AR*, 2, 7: 179–80).

Spielhagen's critical representation of the aristocracy can be fairly judged as perceptive, timely, and differentiated. Furthermore, it does not exhaust his interest in the politically increasingly relevant class differences in his time, as I shall try to show in the next chapter.

6. Class Identity, Liberalism, and Social Democracy

Zöglinge alle wir fürs Himmelreich;
Doch sehr verschieden sind die Institute:
In diesem: Essen gut, Behandlung sammetweich;
In jenem: schmale Kost, ausgieb'ge Rute. (*NG,* 174)

Friedrich Spielhagen is regularly identified as a liberal, frequently as a demo-crat, and sometimes as a socialist. But the meaning of these terms, to him and to others, can be a little fuzzy. Querying him and his texts will not make them precise, but will indicate a kind of ongoing controversy in his mind that in turn reflects the sometimes rather diffuse political discourse in the German educated classes. Given his preoccupation with narrative »objec-tivity,« the discourse is distributed among a large number of interlocutors, debaters, and speechmakers. In general, the views expressed are class-specific, but there are also class mutants now and again.

That Spielhagen began as a »liberal« as this term was commonly un-derstood in mid-nineteenth-century Germany no one is likely to dispute.[1] In general this implied a desire for constitutional government, that is, for curbs on the exercise of power of absolutism and for the responsibility of ministers to an elected assembly, and »freedom,« a term the content of which could be a little unclear, but for the educated middle class eminently included freedom of the press and expression; freedom of assembly was also important to those more politically inclined. Many nineteenth-century German liberals were monarchists, hoping for an alliance of the educated

---

[1]   Victor Klemperer, »Die Juden in Spielhagens Werken. (Eine Studie zu seinem achtzigsten Geburtstag),« *Allgemeine Zeitung des Judentums* 73 (1908/09): 104, stated that Spielhagen »gehört ... mit Leib und Seele der freisinnigen Partei.« It is not clear whether this means the *Deutsche freisinnige Partei,* founded in 1884, or the *Freisinnige Volkspartei* that, under Eugen Richter, split off from it over the military budget in 1893. The latter is likely. At the time Klemperer was writing both parties had come close to the vanishing point, though in the election of 1907 they had shown some signs of life.

middle class with the crown against aristocracy.[2] This does not seem to be Spielhagen's case, given his unflattering portrayals of rulers; personally, he seems, on the whole, to have stayed away from princes and courts, unlike some of his literary colleagues such as Freytag or Auerbach. The only ones with whom he seems to have had much association were the Prussian crown prince, whose ninety-nine day reign as Friedrich III in 1888 bitterly disappointed the elaborate hopes liberals had invested in him, and the culturally lively Duke Ernst of Saxe-Coburg, by whom Spielhagen was offered a decoration that he refused.[3] One might conclude from this that he tended more to the republican end of the spectrum. »Republican« was an explosive and potentially dangerous word at that time, so that prudence tended to avoid it.[4] He, however, believed he was admired as a republican in America and Russia (AW, 42). In his last novel, Frei geboren, the narrator, the free-thinking Baroness Antoinette, publicly declares that she would rather live in a republic than a monarchy, and when she is chided by her husband, the Jewish entrepreneur Philipp Bielefelder, she simply ignores him (NF, 7: 248, 250).

Liberals understood themselves as descended from the Enlightenment, supporting intellectual and scientific progress, which in many cases came to mean a discipleship to Darwinism. In consequence they were, for the most part, irreligious and, in some cases, antireligious. The period from the decline of Romanticism until the modernist searchings for alternatives to reason and science probably represented the low point of the prestige of religion among the educated in the whole history of the German people. Spielhagen took a firm position on this ground. He is the most

---

[2] Andrew Lees, *Revolution and Reflection: Intellectual Change in Germany during the 1850's* (The Hague, 1974), 22: »Many men who called themselves republicans assumed that the republic would simply be a democratic monarchy.«

[3] Both the crown prince and Duke Ernst were interested in *Problematische Naturen*. See *FuE* 1: 366–72 and Henning, *Friedrich Spielhagen*, 113, 151–52, 187.

[4] One of the earliest studies on him declared that he was a republican at heart, but added that a republic was not suited to Germany: Schierding, *Untersuchungen zur Romantechnik*, 18, an assertion of the still unsettled Major Vogtriz in *Was will das werden?* (*AR*, 3, 4: 289) and of a very liberal elderly lieutenant-general in *Opfer* (*NF*, 6: 418). In his time Spielhagen was much criticized for holding to political views regarded as obsolete. As early as the time of the unification, Julian Schmidt ranted about ugly partisanship, unbearable praise of revolution at a time when what was needed was bourgeois work to combat anarchy (»Friedrich Spielhagen,« 423, 436). Spielhagen projected such attitudes back to his youthful environment in the *Vormärz*: »Preßfreiheit, Geschworenengerichte, Konstitution – diese alten Marotten ... sollte der König da nicht endlich die Geduld verlieren?« (*FuE*, 1: 115).

proactively irreligious German-language writer in this period with whom I am acquainted. Even Gottfried Keller, an out-and-out atheist, did not campaign against religion but appropriated religious legends and contexts in a secularized, humorous spirit. Spielhagen tells us that his parents were not religious and that he would have refused confirmation (as Lothar will do in his place in *Was will das werden?*, *AR*, 3, 4: 113) but did not want to hurt anyone's feelings (*FuE*, 1: 77–79). Art has replaced religion (*AmSt*, 27; see also *AR*, 3, 5: 18); he thought religion the death of lyric poetry in America, for only a literary work emancipated from religion can be true art (*VS*, 347).[5] Bemperlein in *Problematische Naturen* gives up a clerical career because of loss of faith (*AR*, 1: 149–51). The artist in *Was die Schwalbe sang* asserts that it is easier to pass a theological examination than to make a good picture (2, 3: 8). Religion perpetuates class distinctions; Spielhagen praised his friend Auerbach for resisting Christianity, renouncing a heaven that would not have a place for everyone (*BT*, 332). Indeed, religion can be dangerous to life itself. The eccentric Frau von Werin in *Was will das werden?* trains children on principles that seem to resemble Christian Science; when she denies them a doctor and they die, she drowns herself (*AR*, 3, 5: 161, 380). In *Problematische Naturen*, Dr. Braun, an ideal liberal on the barricade in 1848, sees the basic revolutionary issue not as the proclamation of the republic but as combat against »dem dumpfen Pfaffenglauben« (1, 5: 452). Earlier in the novel, Oswald encounters a poor old lady all of whose children and acquaintances are dead but who does not believe in the Resurrection, while the peasants ignore a pastor who is an ally of the rich; Oswald thinks optimistically: »Nun, nun, wenn selbst die Einfältigen und Friedfertigen anfangen, sich zu besinnen, daß sie Augen zum Sehen und Ohren zum Hören haben, so ist ja wohl der letzte Tag der Dunkelmänner gekommen« (55). The most positive figure in *Hammer und Amboß*, the prison warden, objects to the pastor preaching on the meaning of a storm; he wants it explained to the people as a natural event (1, 3: 472–73). Events destroy the faith of both lovers in *Noblesse oblige*. The meaning of *Frei*

---

5 Perhaps owing to his *Goethezeit* allegiance, with this view Spielhagen deviates from that described by J. W. Burrow, *The Crisis of Reason: European Thought, 1848–1914* (New Haven and London, 2000), 48–49: »residual piety towards Christianity was decisively replaced by the gospel of science, including Darwinism.... The universe itself was the ›highest idea,‹ and in it we recognize order and goodness and rationality, and we surrender ourselves to it ›in loving trust.‹« ... »[I]t became common, most particularly it seems in Germany, having expelled God and even, ostensibly, teleology from nature, to invest nature itself with at least some of the attributes of divinity.« The quotations are from David Friedrich Strauss, *The Old Belief and the New* (1872).

geboren is to be free of religion (*NF*, 7: 81, 398–99); earlier, in *Selbstgerecht*, religion is said to be a system »das die edelsten Kräfte lähmt, freigeborene Menschen in Sklavenketten schlägt« (5: 158).

Clergymen are regularly toadies of the rich and powerful, sinister, disingenuous intriguers, and in many cases morally depraved. When the young Leo Gutmann of *In Reih' und Glied*, who has religious yearnings as part of his effort to find himself, turns to his pastor, Dr. Urban, for advice, he is told that faith is necessary for the mob, not for enlightened people like ourselves (*AR*, 1, 6: 115). Urban has quite a career in the rest of the novel, becoming the chief preacher in the capital as a reward for his role in suppressing rebellion; there he demands a policy that will help capitalists while appearing to help the workers. When Leo, desperate for political leverage, tries to form an alliance with him, it is a clear sign of the deterioration of his character and situation. A figuration with which Spielhagen may have overreached himself, the malevolent Catholic layman Giraldi in *Sturmflut*, caused much offense in a variety of quarters.[6] Even so, much later, in *Was will das werden?*, another scheming priest has alienated Justus's mother from him and made her unloving. In the same novel, religion is one of the matters that come between Lorenz and Schlagododro, who denounces Lorenz for his lack of faith, for he who does not love God does not love the king and should be shot (3, 4: 370).[7]

One of the few exceptions is the well-meaning priest alienated from the authorities and his congregation in *Die von Hohenstein*; this pattern had already appeared in *Clara Vere*. In *Sonntagskind* there is a kindly but deteriorated, alcoholic, unpriestly priest whose housekeeper Anna is possibly his concubine; after he is suspended, the new priest sermonizes against alcohol and kicks Anna out; not an improvement, as the reader is meant to understand.[8] Even good intentions come to be doubted, as in the case of

6   Objections, for example, from Theodor Fontane, »Friedrich Spielhagen. *Sturm-flut*,« *Sämtliche Werke*, ed. Edgar Gross et al., vol. 21.2 (Munich, 1974), 201; Strodtmann, *Dichterprofile*, 207; Hellmuth Mielke, *Der Deutsche Roman des 19. Jahrhunderts*, 3rd ed. (Berlin, 1898), 376; Heinrich Hart, »Friedrich Spielhagen und der deutsche Roman der Gegenwart,« in Heinrich and Julius Hart, *Kritische Waffengänge*, ed. Mark Boulby (New York and London, 1969), 60–61; Kafitz, *Figurenkonstellation als Mittel der Wirklichkeitserfassung*, 108.
7   Officers regarded an insult to the monarch as one to themselves and an occasion for a challenge to a duel. See Ute Frevert, *Ehrenmänner. Das Duell in der bürgerlichen Gesellschaft* (Munich, 1991), 95.
8   Of course, this sort of thing all depends. The pastor in *Was die Schwalbe sang* believes in keeping the rich warm, cheats on a book sale for the poor, passes out drunk, exhibiting »das stupide Wüstlingsgesicht des Hallenser Corpsburschen,« and lives with an »üppige Dirne« (*AR*, 2, 3: 10, 31, 200–01).

Pastor Römer and his virtuous wife in *Opfer*, who are Christian socialists, not in the anti-Semitic sense, but in a sense more akin to the worker-priest movement in France, committed to active, sympathetic ministry to the working class; nevertheless, the protagonist cannot fully ally himself with this initiative because for him it is vitiated by religious belief, which cannot bring a better future (*NF*, 6: 338). The narrator of *Frei geboren* regrets that the Jewish patriarch Bielefelder, »ein Mann von Scharf- und Tiefsinn, von der peinlichsten Gewissenhaftigkeit und skrupulösesten Wahrheitsliebe,« in the sorrows of his old age has returned »zum alten Kinderglauben« (7: 312). Every positive hero and heroine tends to be irreligious if not antireligious when the matter comes up at all.

Most liberals were persuaded that progress in the issues of liberty, enlightenment, progress, and humane government could be achieved only in a unified nation; they developed »the feeling that half a loaf was better than none and ... once unity had been achieved political freedom would inevitably follow.«[9] Thus they became national liberals, and the task of creating the nation turned out to be so difficult and, in fact, so indifferent to the ideals and efforts of the liberals themselves, that in many cases the nationalism came to absorb the liberalism and to invest German identity with superior self-worth.[10] That Spielhagen shared the nationalist sentiment characteristic of his class there can be no doubt; Karpeles surely thought he was being helpful when he declared that Spielhagen was »ein Patriot vom Wirbel bis zur Zehe, trotz seines Weltbürgerthums, ungeachtet seiner kosmopolitischen Tendenzen.«[11] Spielhagen recalled a time when German disunity hindered railroad building, and tells an anecdote of a poor boy, Julius Schmidt (1825–84), who became a famous astronomer collaborating with Alexander von Humboldt from Athens because Germany had no use for him (*FuE*, 1: 229–30, 358). Spielhagen hoped for a national, populist art, »das Ziel ... das wir alle herbeisehnen, erhoffen, erharren ... wie auf den Messias,« to gather the people to the promised land where they might live in joy and peace (*AmSt*, 45). In his last memoir, published in 1903, he

---

[9] Lees, *Revolution and Reflection*, 132.
[10] For a conventional view, see Alexander Schwan, »German Liberalism and the National Question in the Nineteenth Century,« *Nation Building in Central Europe*, ed. Hagen Schulze (Leamington Spa, Hamburg, and New York, 1987), 66: »German liberalism – upon which the development of an original democratic culture might have been expected to depend – was actually ruined between 1867 and 1871 by its own ill-conceived nationalism. The causes of this lie not only in the superior skill of Bismarck but also in its own tradition.«
[11] Karpeles, *Friedrich Spielhagen*, 21.

noted with gratification that Germany was a world power that could no longer be ignored, while continuing to believe that its real strength was »Menschlichkeit« (*AW*, 91). The affect appears most pointedly in his literary criticism with its tendency to devalue the foreign. He also occasionally expresses the notion that the Frenchified aristocracy is cosmopolitan and internationalist, putting its shared class interests above those of the nation.

But he exhibits a flexibility in such matters not found everywhere at this time. Particularly unexpected is his historical novel of the Wars of Liberation, *Noblesse oblige*, written in the decade after unification. Politically, this novel is a revisitation of the lost opportunity for freedom in the uprising against Napoleon. The Hamburg book dealer Friedrich Christoph Perthes (1772–1843), a historical figure who is a consistent national-liberal voice in the novel, declares that the sacrifices of the people are useless without the liberation of Germany (*AR*, 3, 2: 185). The plot line is the tragedy of an unachievable union between a French officer of high noble descent and a woman of the Hamburg patrician class; she is destroyed by her own father and a vile suitor she is forced to marry, while her brother, a rabid, uncompromising nationalist and anti-Bonapartist, appears as rigid, heartless, and extreme. To be sure, the heroine, who bravely faces down French insolence, is obliged to learn that one cannot change one's nationally determined self, and on reading her lover's last letter concludes that men will never overcome national enmity, but these are sorrowful insights (447, 506). As for the Franco-Prussian War, the protagonist's former teacher in *Was will das werden?* sadly sees its necessity, but loves Paris, France, and the French, to whom the Germans owe much; now they will be cut off (3, 4: 336). The would-be liberal duke in that same novel objects to Major von Vogtriz's »Deutschtümelei« and polemicizes against the hobbyhorse of nationalism, which Europe must get over and for which he blames Napoleon III (456–57). By the time of *Opfer*, internationalism is projected as possible, but it will take time; nationalism has come to seem like an ever heavier armor (*NF*, 6: 353). The true superiority of the Germans, of which they are losing track in the Reich, we read in *Frei geboren*, is cosmopolitan idealism (7: 315).

This view was not always easy to maintain. When in 1895 writers were asked to protest a proposed *Umsturzgesetz* that would repress political crimes along with criticism in science and art and attacks on Christianity, Spielhagen wrote an extremely sarcastic essay in which he declared that the government was right to get rid of the people of »Dichter und Denker« along with superfluous literature on society and politics, to impress the world with tyranny and violence, and to let the government do the thinking (*AW*,

181–93); from the unusually fierce tone in this piece one may sense the pain in his heart.[12] He understood the accommodation of former forty-eighters to the Bismarckian regime but could not approve of it, as appears in the figure of Dr. Brunn in *Ein neuer Pharao*.[13] The heroine of that novel, who studies the 1848 revolution and the evolution of politics, decides that today (1878) patriotism has become a mask for power lust and selfishness (*AR*, 3, 3: 298). In *Opfer*, the protagonist is offended at nationalist tones in a funeral for an old general who was a reader of Darwin and Haeckel with a tendency toward atheism and republicanism (*NF*, 6: 473).

Although Spielhagen was, in retrospect, somewhat sheepish about his nonparticipation in the Revolution of 1848, I would venture the suggestion that his lack of a personal history of engagement may have been an advantage, insofar as it left him with an understanding of the *Nachmärz* depression without being victimized by it. Münzer in *Die von Hohenstein* remarks: »mir ist, als kämen wir nicht aus der Stelle, als ob die Revolution im März gestorben wäre und wir schmückten einen Leichnam, ohne es zu wissen« (*AR*, 1, 2: 278). The former forty-eighters, who are icons of rectitude, devotion to liberty, and bourgeois virtue, can also become rigid in their grieving and unable to form new alliances. The model figure is the printer Peter Schmitz in *Die von Hohenstein*, an admirable character in many respects, whose family forms »das politisch-moralische Zentrum des Romans,«[14] but ineffectual in his righteousness and somewhat pathetic in the failure of his newspaper because of the evanescence of democratic attitudes in the *Nachmärz* public, at the same time opposed to socialism because it is international, thus leading away from German unity (500–01). Another such character, Uncle Ernst in *Sturmflut*, comes, through dialogue with his ideological antipode, an aristocratic general who was on the other side in 1848, to a relaxation of his commitments, recognizing that »der Grundsatz schrankenloser Freiheit und absoluter Selbstbestimmung in seiner äußersten Consequenz schwächere Geister zu Abwegen führen kann, vielleicht führen muß« while the general comes to understand that his concept of honor has narrowed his horizon (1, 9: 340, 343). This passage has been critically cited

---

12 On this episode, see Wehler, *Deutsche Gesellschaftsgeschichte*, 3: 1007. It is interesting to learn that the storm of protest caused the defeat of the proposal.

13 Dirk Göttsche, *Zeit im Roman. Literarische Zeitreflexion und die Geschichte des Zeitromans im späten 18. und im 19. Jahrhundert* (Munich, 2001), 730, points out that Dr. Brunn discourses on his »versöhnliche Geschichtsperspektive« at the railroad station, the scene of modernity, and finds that his views and those of the uncompromising »Smith« »glücklicherweise unaufgelöst nebeneinanderstehen.«

14 Göttsche, *Zeit im Roman*, 692.

as an example of bourgeois accommodation to the ruling order;[15] I think it is an attempt on Spielhagen's part to project fairness, a dialogic way out of the impasse left behind by 1848; furthermore, it is an unusual moment without much echo in the later novels.

The rigidified, mourning forty-eighter comes to be displaced by the younger activist who is most likely to be an aspiring writer. Thus the type converges with Spielhagen's own persona. Eventually, however, we encounter liberals in electoral and parliamentary politics. One of these is the protagonist's mentor Professor von Hunnius in *Was will das werden?* He, too, is a former forty-eighter, who sat on the Left in the Frankfurt Parliament but now sees that republicanism is not the right way to national unity (3, 4: 85); he becomes a representative in the North German *Reichstag*, defeating one of Spielhagen's odious pastors, though it is said that the liberals can be distinguished from the conservatives only by »das Auge des Eingeweihten« (260). Hunnius, incidentally, recognizes the decline of the liberal parties, pinned between Bismarck's state socialism and Social Democracy, a bind that Spielhagen thought was squeezing out the individual, rescuable only by poesy (3, 5: 348; *FuE*, 2: viii).[16] With one of those speeches with which he likes to end his novels, Hunnius is made to say that liberalism can save itself only if it gives up its fear of freedom and democracy (*AR*, 3, 5: 348, 451). In another of these perorations, the temporarily returned forty-eighter »Smith« in *Ein neuer Pharao* declares that the new generation was wrong to reject the republican idea, for it would be the only bulwark against the radicalism gaining ground under the surface (3, 3: 526).[17] Spielhagen does not directly portray parliamentary scenes, about which he may not have known very much from experience; he knew some parliamentarians, however, and he shows a speech against corruption of Eduard Lasker causing consternation in the upper classes in *Sturmflut* (*NB*, 220; *AR*, 1, 9: 244–45).[18]

---

[15] E. g., Bernd Neumann, »Friedrich Spielhagen: *Sturmflut* (1877). Die ›Gründerjahre‹ als die ›Signatur des Jahrhunderts,‹« *Romane und Erzählungen des Bürgerlichen Realismus. Neue Interpretationen*, ed. Horst Denkler (Stuttgart, 1980), 270. Neumann's unfriendly view of Spielhagen as an enemy of the working class and propagator of class accommodation is restricted to this one novel. The constellation here is not permanent, though it is tendentious, for one would have to ask who the promulgators of unbridled freedom were.

[16] Löwenthal, *Erzählkunst und Gesellschaft*, 174, identifies Spielhagen himself as a representative of the disappearing middle.

[17] Wehler, *Deutsche Gesellschaftsgeschichte*, 3: 870, observes that opposition to democratic suffrage was harmful to liberalism in the long run.

[18] For Lasker's role, see Schierding, *Untersuchungen zur Romantechnik*, 39–40; Kafitz, *Figurenkonstellation als Mittel der Wirklichkeitserfassung*, 102.

As I have indicated, he was thought of, and thought of himself, as a democrat. He was always, he says, »ein Schwärmer für die Freiheit gewesen, wie ich sie eben verstand« (*AW*, 7). American obituaries particularly stressed this point.[19] During his lifetime, the Norwegian-American writer H. H. Boyesen stated bluntly: »Spielhagen is fiercely democratic, a thorough radical, loves barricades, and preaches revolution.«[20] Recently he has been declared »one of the most important literary representatives of a liberal Germany which would be ruled through political participation and democracy«[21] and credited with a »lifelong commitment to use fiction to summon his readers to the cause of a democratic Germany.«[22] The question is what this meant at this time. Democracy means the rule of the people. But who are the people? Certainly they are not the aristocracy and their allies, the clergy, in the seamless ruling alliance of throne and altar. Indeed, Spielhagen was to say that even the officials, like his father, were not part of the people but the governors of it (*FuE*, 1: 114). But nor are the people the members of the underclass, of which the proletariat was coming to be a substantial though not the only component. For these have not been gentled by bourgeois *Bildung*, by the ethos of renunciation, the commitment to spiritual imperatives above self-interest, the motivation to do things for their own sake, a virtue Germans came to ascribe exclusively to themselves. Even a Yankee official acknowledges this last virtue in the German settlers of *Deutsche Pioniere* (*AR*, 2, 4: 585). Perhaps in some century the underclass could be educated to *Bildung*, but as they were then, primitive in morality, lacking in deferred gratification, easily duped by demagogues, and consumed with greed and resentment, they were not ready to participate in active governance (see, e.g., 1, 2: 499–500). In Italy Spielhagen found occasion to comment: »Der natürliche Mensch, bevor die Bildung seine brutalen Instincte gebrochen, ist eine grausame Bestie, und der gemeine Italiener, der ein sehr natürlicher Mensch ist, eine sehr grausame« (*VNbS*, 193). When unfettered the underclass seeks plunder and rapine, scenes that recur in *Die von Hohenstein*, *In Reih' und Glied*, and elsewhere. »Waren die trunkenen, lärmenden Gesellen,

---

19   Anonymous, »Friedrich Spielhagen, A Mirror of German Life,« *American Review of Reviews* 43 (1911): 623; Harold Berman, »Friedrich Spielhagen: The Novelist of Democracy,« *Twentieth Century Magazine* 4 (1911): 347–49.

20   [Hjalmar Hjorth Boyesen], [review of *Ultimo*], *North American Review* 120 (January-April, 1875): 197.

21   Volker Neuhaus, »Friedrich Spielhagen – Critic of Bismarck's Empire,« *1870/71–1989/90: German Unifications and the Change of Literary Discourse*, ed. Walter Pape (Berlin and New York, 1993), 135.

22   Roper, »1848 in the Early Novels of Friedrich Spielhagen,« 427.

die er heute um Tusky sich drängen sah,« worries the would-be revolutionary Leo Gutmann, »waren sie die Menschheit, der er das Evangelium des Friedens und der Liebe hat predigen wollen?« (*AR*, 1, 6: 221).

The trouble was that the *Bildungsbürgertum* was never more than a tiny minority of the population, recently estimated at under one percent.[23] It could not ally with the historical backbone of the bourgeoisie, artisans and guild workers, because liberal policies of free trade and free labor were anathema to them, with the result that they were more likely to become invested in the stasis of monarchist conservatism.[24] The financial and capitalist bourgeoisie was of no use, either, for it was constituted of men ungentled by idealistic *Bildung*, exclusively concerned with wealth and power, perverting the very idea of liberalism into the doctrine of *laissez-faire* with which it has come to be identified in European politics to the present day. When Münzer hears music coming from an elegant house, he assumes that monied hands cannot play the piano and, sure enough, discovers the musician is the aristocratic Antonie (1, 2: 152). Thus liberal government in Germany could not be democratic and, with the numerical expansion and accelerating organization of the working class, democratic government could not be liberal. Dr. Holm, a voice of moderation in *Die von Hohenstein*, observes that the cause of the people is not very rooted in the people (126). Lurking in the background is the fear of broad-based popular revolution, which is always imagined as an orgy of destructive, lawless terrorism, still associated with historical memories of the first French Revolution. Spielhagen never escaped from this pincer, for he could not conceive how a humane civilization could be preserved without commitment to the values of *Bildung*. At the same time he understood the social dynamics of the problem. As early as *Die von Hohenstein* he has Münzer explain the failure of the Revolution

---

23 Wehler, *Deutsche Gesellschaftsgeschichte*, 3: 127–28. Wehler's remark (868) that they were all leaders and no troops could be illustrated in numerous places in Spielhagen's fiction.

24 See on this what I have found to be one of the most enlightening studies of German history I have ever encountered, Mack Walker, *German Home Towns: Community, State, and General Estate 1648–1871* (Ithaca and London, 1971). It has been pointed out that Robert Prutz's novel *Das Engelchen* (1851), before *Hammer und Amboß*, restores the guild artisanship against industry, while Max Kretzer's *Meister Timpe* (1888), after Spielhagen's novel, looks back on the guilds in nostalgic despair: Walter Hinderer, »›Die Schornsteine müssen gestürzt werden, denn sie verpesten die Luft.‹ Diskurse über Industrialisierung und Natur im deutschen Roman des 19. Jahrhunderts,« *Literatur und Demokratie. Festschrift für Hartmut Steinecke zum 60. Geburtstag*, ed. Alo Allkemper and Norbert Otto Eke (Berlin, 2000), 109–14.

as class betrayal: »Die Kleinbürger haben das Proletariat an die Geldsäcke verrathen, die sich bereitwillig der frechen Faust des Adels öffnen, der sie zugleich vor dem Proletarier und dem Kleinbürgerthum beschützen muß« (666). Still, the consequences of government without the participation of the working class and without consideration of the condition of the poor, who still constituted the majority of the population, were unacceptable to him, so he became what one might call a fellow traveler of Social Democracy. The Social Democrats were the only force in society that cared about the conditions he cared about (in fact, the leadership was much more committed to *Bildung* than those in his position may have realized).

Since, as has been said, no one at this time took freedom, democracy, and equality as seriously as the Social Democrats,[25] Spielhagen necessarily acquired something of a reputation, even occasionally in his own mind, of being a socialist. He associated himself, he said, with the »politisches-religiöses Programm ... des linken Flügels der Radikalen der Paulskirche in 1848« and moved leftward over the years until he approached the Social Democrats (*AW*, 42–43). At the same time he saw himself as occupying a temporary place in the flux of political obsolescence: »So sieht der Realpolitiker von heute den republikanischen Schwärmer von Achtundvierzig in demselben vollen Lichte der Naivetät, in welcher er möglicherweise dem Sozialdemokraten der Zukunft erscheinen wird« (*FuE*, 2: 206); thus the future belongs to Social Democracy. One cannot imagine him joining the party, and there is a constant anxiety in the texts of what Social Democratic political power might actually mean. He is supposed to have said in an interview that he had no objection to be called a socialist but the party was impossible with »allerhand leere und utopische Schrullen.«[26] In an essay on

---

[25] Wehler, *Deutsche Gesellschaftsgeschichte*, 3: 804.

[26] Hermann Bahr, *Der Antisemitismus. Ein internationales Interview*, ed. Hermann Greive (Königstein, 1979), 18.

[27] In *Opfer*, Wilfried's brother, Prince Dagobert, when lecturing him on the impracticality of Social Democracy and the likelihood that it will evolve into a reform party, and urging him to apply his wealth and standing to progressive purpose, quotes from Goethe's *Faust*, ll. 1824–25: »Wenn ich sechs Hengste zahlen kann, / Sind ihre Kräfte nicht die meine?« (*NF*, 6: 353–54; Spielhagen has »meinen«). He cannot have known that Marx applied the same passage to the power of money in the *Ökonomisch-philosophische Manuskripte* of 1844, as they had not been published. See Karl Marx, Friedrich Engels, *Über Kunst und Literatur*, ed. Manfred Kliem (Berlin, 1967), 1: 385–90. Similarly, in *Was will das werden?*, the sympathetic Maria von Werin encourages Lothar with the prediction that »In dem Staat der Zukunft wird jeder Poet zugleich Handwerker sein« (*AR*, 3, 5: 168), which reminds one of a passage from the also unpublished *Deutsche Ideologie*: that it shall be possible »in der kommunistischen Gesellschaft, wo Jeder

Social Democracy he developed a Heinesque worry about the survival of art (shared even by the charitable Frau Brandt in the novel that examines Social Democracy in the greatest detail, *Opfer*, *NF*, 6: 219): literature survives its time »für die *happy few* einer exquisiten Bildung, deren geringe Zahl mit der Zeit immer geringer werden dürfte« (*NB*, 5, 9). Here it is remarked that the only Social Democratic leader worth listening to is Bebel. In a review of Gerhart Hauptmann's *Die Weber* Spielhagen mentions Bebel along with Marx and Lassalle (283); if I am not mistaken, an awareness of Marx is unusual among the writers of this period.[27] A worker opposing Christian socialism in *Opfer* surprises Count Wilfried with a precision and command of the material unusual in an unschooled man; Wilfried recognizes in his discourse »ein Auszug der Marxschen Lehre« (*NF*, 6: 238–39).

Within this complex we must try particularly to understand what the term »socialism« means. It has little or nothing to do with a systematic political doctrine or a would-be scientific analysis of class relations. It means an active sympathy for the condition of the working class and the poor, and a demand that this sympathy shape the attitudes and policies of governance.[28] Academics who took this position were tagged »Kathedersozialisten,« and in an early dissertation the term was applied to Spielhagen also.[29] Count Wilfried in *Opfer*, after a painful evolution driven mainly by his sympathy for others, acquires the reputation of a socialist when he makes a speech denouncing the indifference to and oppression of the poorer classes, causing him to be ostracized as a class traitor, lampooned in a sonnet as a salon socialist, patronized by a policeman who says one cannot have a count in this situation, repudiated by his proletarian protégés, and sorrowfully disinherited by his wealthy aunt. Like several of Spielhagen's protagonists, among them Lothar in *Was will das werden?*, Wilfried tries to become a worker himself, though his employer thinks Social Democracy unbearable nonsense and that equality encompassing the range from the lumpenproletarian Schulzes to Bismarck is ridiculous; Wilfried is too learned and complicated, as well as too radical, to write for the socialist *Vorwärts*, and

---

nicht einen ausschließlichen Kreis der Tätigkeit hat ... morgens zu jagen, nachmittags zu fischen, abends Viehzucht zu treiben, nach dem Essen zu kritisieren, wie ich gerade Lust habe, ohne je Jäger, Fischer, Hirt oder Kritiker zu werden«: Karl Marx and Friedrich Engels, *Werke*, ed. Institut für Marxismus-Leninismus beim ZK der SED (Berlin, 1956–68), 3: 33.

[28] Bachleitner, *Der englische und französische Sozialroman*, 383: »Noch immer galt jede arbeiterfreundliche Geste als ›sozialistisch.‹«

[29] Martha Geller, *Friedrich Spielhagens Theorie und Praxis des Romans* (Berlin, 1917), 116.

he comes to see his sacrifice as useless (387, 423, 483–84). These efforts to alter one's class-determined identity never succeed. Even Georg Hartwig in *Hammer und Amboß*, who, owing to the chaotic circumstances of his youth, does not have much of a determined identity, rises *through* the working class to entrepreneurship. Everyone tells Lothar that he cannot be a worker; Schlagododro accuses him of only playacting, though he does become a kind of learned artisan at the end (*AR*, 3, 5: 84, 436). At times the »socialist« sympathy might sound like a form of charity, but this issue is brought up critically in *Frei geboren*, where the narrator realizes that, given the dimensions of poverty, charity is a drop in the bucket; she throws herself into charity to cope with her personal despair, which she understands does not compare with real suffering; she muses that if the rich cannot learn, revolution will have to teach them, while acknowledging that she does not dismiss her own maids or get rid of her two riding horses (*NF*, 7: 158, 372–75). However, much is made of selfless and energetic charitable work in *Opfer*. The husband of the rational and stable Frau Brandt says that she helps »Les misérables,« there being no adequate word in German (6: 45). Wilfried goes through a psychological process of self-redemption through charity, though his assistance to the Schulz family, with whose daughter Lotte he becomes infatuated, may be doing more harm than good; at least she thinks so.

A person of strong intellect and heroic instincts may respond to this frustration by becoming what came to be called a »nihilist.« The term is misleading because it suggests a rejection of all values, when in fact it denotes the absorption of most values by one or a few intense commitments. As we know, it gained currency from Turgenev's novel *Fathers and Sons*, practically contemporaneous with *Problematische Naturen*; Turgenev was a significant presence in German literary life in the nineteenth century. Actual Russian nihilists appear in *Stumme des Himmels* and *Opfer*. The nihilist is a revolutionary convinced of his own elite superiority and the need for the violent destruction of existing power relations along with conventional morality while remaining contemptuous of the masses he intends to liberate. Professor Berger in *Problematische Naturen* approaches nihilism in his episode of madness, a symptom of which is his effort to convert Oswald to a philosophy that appears to be derived from Schopenhauer (*AR*, 1, 5: 53–54). There is a slumbering potential of the pattern in Spielhagen's early figurations of Lassalle, later in *Opfer* said to be »ein Nietzschescher Löwe im Marxschen Schaffell« (*NF*, 6: 248), and in Tusky of *In Reih' und Glied*, who sees ordinary people as zombies (*AR*, 1, 6: 187–88), but it becomes definitive in either renegade aristocrats, like Adalbert von Werin in *Was will das werden?*, or a type of grim striver of native intellect, Hermann Schulz in *Opfer*, who passes through proletarian existence and Social Democracy via Nietzsche to complete radicalism and then crime. An American girl, Anne Curtis in *Ein neuer Pharao*, who cannot find an object for her boiling desire for heroic purpose, becomes a terrorist, bound in her passion to the illegitimately born, marginalized clerk Selk, a dubious, vengeful Social Democrat who Anne believes has attempted to assassinate the Kaiser in order to ignite popular revolution, but then finds he is merely robbing her father; when he insults her, she knocks him down with her whip, then takes her life (3, 3: 498–507). Spielhagen's characters of this kind cause harm and end catastrophically, and there is a suggestion that the disastrous personal outcome is a logical result of radical ideas; but there is an undertone of admiration for their refusal of compromise with endemic injustice and moral slovenliness.

Thus personal options seem limited, while the prospect of collective action is frightening. The modern observer will say that Spielhagen is in a characteristic ideological bind that hinders insight and prevents active solutions. But from the perspective of his own time his location looks quite different; his sympathies become increasingly oppositional as the alliance between the bourgeoisie and the aristocracy against Social Democracy undermines his basis in the public.[30] His way of dealing with the epochal social crisis was to give increasing attention in his late novels to the character and condition of the working class, the debates for and against Social Democracy, and the ambiguity of industry as both the quintessence of progress and the destroyer of lives and environments; this is particularly the case in *Sonntagskind*, as we shall see when we come to speak of that novel in more detail.

---

[30] Rhöse, *Konflikt und Versöhnung*, 202.

7. The Military and the Ethos of Dueling

Normally one would think that the topic of the military would be subsumed under those of aristocracy and class. In nineteenth-century Germany, the military was the domain of the aristocracy, which monopolized the officer corps, especially in Prussia.[1] The military, the monarchy, and the state seemed to constitute a unit of dominance. Wilhelm I, by his attitude and bearing, put himself into a tradition of Prussian soldier-kings interrupted by the vacillating Friedrich Wilhelm III and the quite unsoldierly Friedrich Wilhelm IV. At the same time, Emperor Franz Joseph liked nothing better than the role of a soldier, slept in an iron field bed, and regularly wore a lieutenant's uniform; it was thought of him in some quarters that as a lieutenant he might have reached his level of competence. But the military also sought an immunity exterior to the state; the frustrated efforts of parliamentary government to control the military through the budget constitute a substantial segment of the history of the politics of the Reich. The swagger, irresponsibility, arrogance, and impunity of some officers generated a bitterness in class relations thematized innumerable times in fiction. At the same time, the military was a theater of the regularly alleged assimilation of the bourgeoisie to the aristocracy. The brusquely curt style of aristocratic-military command extended into industry and business.[2] It became extremely important for the sons of the bourgeoisie to have at least a year of military training and a reserve-officer status unreachable, of course, by the lower classes. It has been observed that the cooperation of officer and bourgeois noncom in *Die von Hohenstein* represents the hope for a new order, »deren Hierarchie nicht mehr durch Tradition, sondern durch Tüchtigkeit legitimiert ist.«[3] Bourgeois men demanded to be regarded as *satisfaktionsfähig* on a footing with the officer caste in affairs of honor, and, although this aspiration was resented, it was generally achieved, not least through the dueling

---

[1]   There were bourgeois officers in Bavaria, Württemberg, and Saxony, but not in Prussia. See Wehler, *Deutsche Gesellschaftsgeschichte*, 3: 178.

[2]   Wehler, *Deutsche Gesellschaftsgeschichte*, 3: 726.

[3]   Zinken, *Der Roman als Zeitdokument*, 202.

ethos of the student fraternities. The ordinary merchant captain Reinhold Schmidt in *Sturmflut* owes a good deal of his standing, especially with his eventual father-in-law General von Werben, to his military service and his battlefield promotion to reserve lieutenant in the field during the Franco-Prussian war; he himself sees himself as a man of military discipline in civilian life and is very impressed with the respectful way the general treats him (*AR*, 1, 8: 116–17, 334).

From what has been said so far, we might imagine what to expect from Spielhagen in such matters: a critical view of the officer caste and its values, perhaps the inclusion in his packet of liberal demands and expectations the taming of the military by civilian control. That this is not entirely the case is one of the peculiarities of the Spielhagen complex that invites a certain dissection. His views appear to have been compounded by personal experience. He came to enjoy his year of military service, beginning in October 1851, with »ungeschminkte herzhafte Freude« (*AW*, 256; see the autobiographical account, *FuE*, 2: 3–8).[4] Encouraged by his commanding officer, he even thought of making a military career until he considered the loss of his freedom (*FuE*, 2: 377–79). He regretted that he had no war experience and believed that he would have made a good soldier (98, 101). He was called up again during the brief French-Italian-Austrian war of 1859 and admitted sheepishly that he was disappointed not to see action (372–74). Psychologically, this may not be such a great mystery. The picture we have obtained of him as a student is of a pale, bookish, introverted, perhaps sedentary, and somewhat gauche young man. Military service challenged him with physical education and discipline, and he found that he could meet the challenge, thrive, and take his place in a comradely community. I believe his military experience was a gratifying maturation process. The adult Spielhagen, as far as we can see, was a reasonably healthy and sturdy man; he may well have been toughened by his military training. Sometimes the military atmosphere can be exhilarating against one's better judgment. Military display, after all, is designed to arouse enthusiasm. Even Social Democrats, Spielhagen remarked, like parades (*AW*, 258). From the experience he developed several fictional figures of positively drawn officers; since they do not seem modelled on his own rather disagreeable commanding officer, one may suspect them of being imagined selves or perhaps father figures of the author. However, in order for them to play this role, they must themselves develop a critical attitude toward the military and embody

---

[4] See also Henning, *Friedrich Spielhagen*, 63–64.

progressive hopes for a liberalized ethos. It is significant that none succeeds in exerting such an influence.

At first the prospect seems hopeless from the outset, in the case of Wolfgang von Hohenstein. As we have had occasion to remark, he reluctantly attempts to find his way as an officer and realizes he is on the wrong side, combatting democracy, concluding: »Zwischen dem Geist der Zeit und dem Geist, der in dem Stande gepflegt wurde, zu dem er jetzt gehörte, gab es keine Versöhnung; – sie mußten sich bekämpfen wie Ormuz und Ariman, die Götter des Lichts und der Finsternis«; when he admits to democratic convictions he is arrested (*AR*, 1, 2: 453, 560–62). *Die von Hohenstein* also brings the first of Spielhagen's rebellious regular officers, Wolfgang's commander Major von Degenfeld. He hopes for a national citizen military force, a *Volksheer*, a concept that goes back to the Wars of Liberation and was influenced by, for those who had eyes to see it, the unprecedented loyal strength of Napoleon's armies. The common man will be given pride as a soldier, enabling him to stand up to those who molest and demean him (443). Degenfeld and Wolfgang are both hated by the other officers as renegades, becoming the object of particular zeal in the skirmishes with regular troops; Degenfeld ends as a suicide (659–60, 691), Wolfgang in exile.

The most important example of this type is a mentor in Spielhagen's most elaborate *Bildungsroman, Was will das werden?*: Major, later Colonel von Vogtriz. He becomes almost a surrogate father for the narrator Lothar Lorenz, who, as a boy, is filled with admiration for him when he first sees him, describing him in a way that he admits sounds like a hero of a novel (3, 4: 27). The major is kindly disposed toward Lothar, despite a realization that his stepfather was on the other side in 1848, because the major has lost a son of his own whom the bright, serious Lothar resembles. Lothar, in turn, declares he wants to be a soldier like the deceased boy (29). As a child he plays soldier, forcing his quite unmilitary Jewish friend Emil Israel to play with him; he obliges Emil to call him »Herr Major« because Vogtriz has become a heroic ideal for him (42). At one point Lothar is determined to struggle for Vogtriz's blessing like Jacob for the angel's (3, 5: 57). Vogtriz is another of the officers who becomes alienated from his caste; he grieves at the gap from the rest of mankind, observes that »das Junkerhafte ... nicht schöner wird, weil es uniformiert ist,« and tries to make a distinction from the real soldiers who perfect themselves in their profession in order eventually to make it superfluous (194–95). Lothar becomes Vogtriz's private secretary, in which capacity he makes the acquaintance of intelligent, humanistically educated young officers, whose tone he likes, but not their opinions (197); here I think we can observe the clash between Spielhagen's wish dream of a modern officer and the persistent realities of the military caste.

In Book VIII, Chapter 2, Vogtriz narrates the experiences that have led to his inner revolution. He tells of twice being obliged to fire upon the people. The first occasion was in 1848, when he led an attack on the barricade where Lothar's stepfather was fighting. The second was an action against rebellious workers. Although convinced that this was an uprising that »künstlich-frevelhaft genährt war von einer fanatischen Partei,« nevertheless he feels that his duty made him »zum Totschläger meiner Brüder« (204). Thus military service puts him on the wrong side in the two great social conflicts of the age: against the liberals and against the working class. At one time he believed that the end of national unity justified the means, but where, echoing Degenfeld in *Die von Hohenstein*, is the transformation into a *Volksarmee*? Must we wait another fifty years for it? (206–07). The worthiness of the German Reich to endure longer than other empires of history, he declares, »ist einzig und allein und es kann auch nur bestehen, was aus der humanen Idee herausgewachsen ist und deshalb nicht bloß den Griechen, Römern oder Germanen, sondern der ganzen Menschheit zu gute kommt« (207). With this formulation, Spielhagen has converted the colonel to classical *Humanitätsphilosophie*. He goes on to say that it must be a nation for everyone, not just a minority of the people while the majority is condemned to poverty and ignorance; with a critical allusion to the unnamed Bismarck, he adds that the theory of »Blut und Eisen« cannot be Christian (207–08). Thus, though Vogtriz immediately declares that he is not a republican and is convinced of the need for monarchy, Spielhagen has moved him toward what he understood as socialism.

As for war, Vogtriz declares that anyone who wants another after having experienced one campaign has no heart or is a braggart (202). Lothar's teacher has already taught him that war in his time is a »Steigerung der materialistischen Tendenzen,« damaging »die internationale Solidarität des geistigen und moralischen Interesses«; every war is a »Bruderkrieg« (3, 4: 336). It might be mentioned in passing that Spielhagen has few scenes of actual warfare, except for a climactic battle scene in *Allzeit voran* and skirmishes in *Noblesse oblige* and *Deutsche Pioniere*, all of which are set in wartime; doubtless this is because he had not had such experiences. The chapters toward the end of *Die von Hohenstein* recounting Wolfgang's flight and command of a batch of unreliable irregulars strike me as less adventurous than tedious, holding up the progress of the long novel. For a time, Vogtriz is protected from the consequences of his dissension by his membership in an old noble family, »lauter Grafen, Barone, Herren von!« (3, 5:

206). This, too, he recognizes as unjust. But the privilege of birth cannot protect him indefinitely. His eventual entanglement with a subversive publication by Lothar's rather sinister nihilist friend Adalbert von Werin forces his resignation (319). What we are witnessing here is the opposite of the assimilation of the bourgeoisie to the aristocracy; rather the evolution of an aristocrat to progressive bourgeois values, to be sure, in an optative fiction that may not for all readers have the quality of mimetic realism. That this hope can be invested in a professional military man comes out of Spielhagen's peculiar perspective. Of course, he was not uncritical of the military spirit. Even before his service, in 1848, the unpoliticized young man, on a journey in the spirit of Eichendorff, was arrested as a »Freischärler,« in a situation, he remarks sarcastically, that only a noncom could misunderstand (*FuE*, 1: 346–49). As part of the prehistory of the events in *Platt Land*, we hear of a forester who in 1815 stabbed an officer who had insulted him; only because of his valor as a soldier was his sentence commuted to ten years of fortress imprisonment, but he believes that a noble officer would have got just a couple of months (*AR*, 2, 5: 235, 504). The protagonist of that novel, Gerhard von Wacha, who himself belongs to the lower landed nobility, is opposed to military service (48). The rather censorious correspondent in the novella *Mesmerismus,* comparing Roderich's past bravery in battle with his current laxness in an adulterous relationship, observes:

> Ich sehe jetzt freilich klärlich, was ich immer behauptet: der soldatische Mut ist noch lange, lange nicht der höchste. Vor den Augen von hunderten Braver nicht feig zu sein, was ist denn das? Aber brav sein im stillen Kämmerlein, die Zähne aufeinander beißen und mit der Leidenschaft, die uns angepackt hat, ringen die Nacht hindurch und nicht von ihr lassen, bis wir ihr die Knie auf die verkeuchende Brust setzten können – das, *mon cher,* ist wahres Heldenthum, und es thut mir weh, zu sehen, wie weit du von ihm entfernt bist. (*NF,* 5: 293–94)

Perhaps the most deleterious influence of the military on general social life was the practice of dueling, derived from a rigid and primitive aristocratic honor code. Dueling episodes are commonly encountered in nineteenth-century German social realism. Sometimes I suspect that they are devices for getting rid of characters no longer needed by the author, as when in *Frei geboren* an evil-spirited former forty-eighter emerges to shoot down a Count R., who is causing plot difficulties (*NF,* 7: 261). But in fact dueling was a fact of social life. Norbert Elias has commented:

> Underlying both the training provided within the student fighting fraternities and the life as a member of the imperial upper classes at which it was aimed is an implicit picture of human social life as a struggle of all against all which was

almost Hobbesian in character. But, as it developed in Germany, it was not a logically thought-out philosophy, but rather an unplanned tradition of behavior and feeling produced by the blind fate of history.[5]

Spielhagen's first major work, *Problematische Naturen*, has a number of dueling events of various kinds, including Oswald's failed efforts to provoke a duel with anyone, Baron Oldenburg challenging everyone in Oswald's name, Oswald invaliding Felix von Grenwitz for life, and a fake Polish count evading challenges.

The dueling ethos grew stronger with the increasing militarization of the society of the Reich,[6] and it has been connected to the subjugation of women, for many dueling affairs were nominally fought in defense of a woman's honor, but in fact were motivated by a need to compensate before the public for the unmanly condition of cuckold.[7] We will see a pure example of this when we come to Spielhagen's novella about the Ardenne scandal, *Zum Zeitvertreib* (1897). The correspondent of *Mesmerismus*, published in the same year, declares that dueling is just a device to maintain a woman in a dependent condition, »eine Salonpuppe ..., die man zu adorieren vorgiebt, um sie zu zerbrechen, sobald sie sich einfallen läßt, ein Mensch sein zu wollen, wie der Mann auch« (5: 302). The dueling principle was thought to be eminently German: Treitschke regarded the practice as »a bulwark against ›the penetration of French views of married life and relations between the sexes.‹«[8] Still, women were sometimes drawn into an excitement about or enthusiasm for the duel.[9] The beloved Erna in *Quisisana* seems to support the dueling ethos (*AR*, 2, 8: 242). In *Opfer*, the profligate Count Lessberg, who is mad for Ebba von Falkenburg, declares he will kill her intended Wilfried and marry her; she thinks this might be a good idea (*NF*, 6: 59, 62). As for Wilfried, when he gets into a duel with an officer who has called him a »Salonsozialist,« his landlady is relieved to hear that he has found his

5 Elias, *The Germans*, 112.
6 Wehler, *Deutsche Gesellschaftsgeschichte*, 3: 474; Frevert, *Ehrenmänner*, 89.
7 See Kevin McAleer, »Les Belles Dames Sans Merci,« *Dueling: The Cult of Honor in Fin-de-siècle Germany* (Princeton, 1994), 159–81. This is an informative book despite its bumptious, insistently adolescent style, which impairs judgment. A calmer and more comprehensive version of the chapter will be found as »Les Belles Dames Sans Merci: Woman and the Duel in Fin-de-Siècle Germany,« *Tel Aviver Jahrbuch für deutsche Geschichte*, 21 (1992): 69–97. Frevert, *Ehrenmänner*, 61, lists among seven arguments offered in favor of dueling: »Das Duell schützt die Männlichkeit vor der Weiblichkeit.« For a more composed discussion than McAleer's of women's adaptation of the ethos, see 228–32.
8 McAleer, *Dueling*, 169.
9 McAleer, *Dueling*, 172–73; Frevert, *Ehrenmänner*, 228–30.

way back to his class role (479). As he lies mortally wounded, his friends are angry that the officer should have taken Wilfried's »socialdemokratische[ ] Eskapade« seriously and find it tasteless that the victor immediately afterwards gets himself engaged to Wilfried's implacable enemy Frau von Haida as a reward for his deed (486–87). When Schlagododro in *Was will das werden?* gets into a duel, the lower-class Christine, whom he has abandoned, hopes he will be killed (*AR*, 3, 5: 377).

Satisfaktionsfähigkeit appears to have been a tricky matter. The Prince of Prora in *Hammer und Amboß* dies in a duel with an actor who willfully insulted him and to whom satisfaction must be a granted because he is of ancient lineage. The peaceable Bemperlein in *Problematische Naturen*, vulnerable to dueling challenges despite his modest origins because he was student, fears them, not out of cowardice, but because he has maintained his class values:

> Den ganzen sogenannten Comment hielt ich nämlich von jeher für den abominabelsten Unsinn, verderblich für die Gesundheit, viel verderblicher aber noch für die Moral, denn er zwingt die jungen Gemüther, ihr eigenes Denken und Fühlen heroisch dem Moloch eines barbarischen Ehrbegriffs, der lächerlichsten Carricatur eines Codex der Moral, der je erfunden ist, zu opfern, und gewöhnt sie auf diese Weise systematisch an jenes blinde, katholische Gehorchen, welches mir die eigentliche Sünde gegen den heiligen Geist zu sein scheint. Ich weiß nicht, ob wir hierin einer Ansicht sind, Herr Collega?

To which Oswald replies: »Vollkommen« (1, 1: 139). For those who were on the periphery of the dominant system, like intellectuals or dissidents of various kinds, an insistence upon admission to the dueling ethos clearly had a sociopsychological compensatory motivation. Heinrich Heine, who had no skill with weapons and was not credited with much physical courage by those who knew him best, was involved in the course of his life in at least ten dueling affairs; most were settled by reconciliation, but his last one, just after his marriage, was genuinely dangerous.[10] One thinks also of the death of Lassalle in a duel, often regarded, perhaps not unfairly, as pathetically absurd. I have seen no evidence that Spielhagen himself, who, as I have mentioned, cared little for the student culture, was ever involved in such an affair.

By and large, duels are a positive evil in his fiction, as in the lieutenant's killing of the decent Gustav in *Auf der Düne*. In the eerily effective,

---

[10] See Jeffrey L. Sammons, *Heinrich Heine: A Modern Biography* (Princeton, 1979), 74, 241–42.

climactic Chapter 10 of the tragic early novella *In der zwölften Stunde*, Mr. Durham creates a kind of alternative to a duel by taking the protagonist Sven, who has declared his love for Mrs. Durham, out on the stormy Rhine in a newly purchased boat, which, after the Englishman declares that Sven, as a German, has no concept of gentlemanly honor, he crashes into a steamer, losing his life, while Sven is rescued. Later, this question of national honor undergoes a couple of curious twists in the historical novel *Noblesse oblige*, where Minna's fanatically nationalist brother Georg attempts to goad her French lover Hypolit into a duel; Minna forbids it, causing Hypolit to remark that the Germans are a barbaric people, which Minna takes as an insult, motivating her to renounce him; earlier, Hypolit has killed a fellow French officer who has harassed Minna (3, 2: 457, 465, 356–58). The well-meaning, would-be industrialist Baron von Tuchheim of *In Reih' und Glied* is killed by the royal minister Hey. An involved plot element of the ironically titled *An der Heilquelle* concerns the devices of Professor Dr. Escheburg to prevent and subvert a duel. In the more comic *Die schönen Amerikanerinnen*, a duel is effectively stalled by a search for pistols, difficult to find in a vacation resort. One of the saddest of these affairs is the threatened encounter between the quondam friends Schlagododro and Lothar Lorenz in *Was will das werden?* Schlagododro has already attacked Adalbert von Werin for refusing to drink to Bismarck; Lothar, trying to intervene, is seriously wounded and lamed in one arm (3, 4: 391–92). Later Schlagododro threatens a duel with Lothar, who demurs, observing gently that between a giant and a cripple only an »American« duel is possible, that is, with pistols (3, 5: 355). This does not occur, but Schlagododro is finally mortally wounded in a duel with the Jewish theater director Lamarque, a particularly demeaning end for a nobleman.

One dissonance in the dueling ethos is the asymmetry between those who would treat it as a symbolic act for which readiness is sufficient and those who actually wish to kill or maim their opponents. (Americans may think of the duel between Alexander Hamilton and Aaron Burr.) Dueling manuals strictly opposed shooting in the air or missing intentionally as a denial of *Satisfaktion* to the opponent, but such gestures occurred anyway, if rarely.[11] An example is found in the concluding duel between Gerhard von Vacha and the confused landowner Zempin in Book VI, Chapter 5 of *Platt Land*, where Gerhard fires into the air while Zempin aims directly at him but instead is shot by his wronged forester. Similarly, in the duel

---

[11] Frevert, *Ehrenmänner*, 207.

between Schlagododro and Lamarque in *Was will das werden?*, Schlagodo-dro fires into the air but Lamarque does not (408); here we may imagine the accumulated resentment of the despised Jew and socially peripheralized theater impresario. In *Was die Schwalbe sang*, two schoolboys who are to be enemies have an anticipatory duel at age fifteen; the protagonist of the novel inadvertently wounds his opponent and lowers his rapier, whereupon the other boy hits him twice (2, 3: 55–56), an act that is not promising for his future character. Justus in *Sonntagskind* manages to neutralize an obnoxious malcontent by winging him in the shoulder, disappointing the novel's fairy princess Isabel, who comments: »Ihr Männer sind eben zu weichherzig« (*NF*, 1: 420), another example of female acceptance of the dueling ethos.

Dueling was illegal, regarded in the law as murder or manslaughter, but there was an explicit ambiguity about this, at least as far as the aristocracy and the military caste were concerned, for whom punishment was a formality. For those in the dominant class, victors in duels were rarely inconvenienced very long in the conduct of their lives. This was, for example, notoriously the result in the case of Baron von Ardenne, as well as of his counterparts Innstetten in Fontane's *Effi Briest* and Viktor von Sorbitz in Spielhagen's *Zum Zeitvertreib*. In a curious coincidence, a debate on tightening the laws against dueling began in the Reichstag on the very day of the Ardenne duel, in connection with which Kaiser Wilhelm I demanded that officers defend their honor; officers are above society.[12] A similar pattern is touched upon in passing in *Frei geboren*: the nobly born protagonist Antoinette Bielefelder sympathizes with a widow of an official who had an affair with an officer's wife and was killed by him; while her uncle regards this outcome as quite in order, indeed unavoidable, Antoinette grieves for the bereft widow and for the officer's wife, despite her guilt, for her children have been taken away from her (7: 48–49).[13] Henri von Tuchheim of *In Reih' und Glied*, trying to think of a way to get rid of Leo Gutmann, recalls an anecdote of a fellow nobleman who shot a liberal relative for refusing a toast to a prince; the court of honor exonerates the noble so that the king is obliged to pardon him despite hating him personally (*AR*, 1, 7: 433). Subsequently Leo is, indeed, mortally wounded in a duel with Henri (616). In *Ein neuer*

---

[12] Manfred Franke, *Leben und Roman der Elisabeth von Ardenne, Fontanes »Effi Briest«* (Düsseldorf, 1994), 154–57.

[13] The dueling ethos was explicitly believed to supersede responsibilities to wife and children; see Frevert, *Ehrenmänner*, 194–95. Although there is no direct indication of it, the details suggest that Spielhagen is here once again thinking of the Ardenne affair.

Pharao, Reginald von Ilicius kills his former friend Count Axel Karlsburg, who has had an affair with Reginald's married sister Stephanie; it is assumed that Reginald will not be in prison long, nor will his engagement to marry be harmed, while Stephanie and her husband will be obliged to stay together (3, 3: 460–64).

The picture that develops from this topic redounds to the credit of Spielhagen's integrity as a writer. Impelled in part by personal, »subjective« experience, he developed a hypothesis that a certain type of military officer could evolve into an effective defender of the humane virtues and enlightened politics that alone could embody value in the German Reich. As he tests this hypothesis in the logic of his fiction, it is shown to be illusory. This, it would seem to me, is an example of the useful work that realism can do.

8. Jews and »the Jews«

The most elementary principle when considering the discourse about Jews in nineteenth-century Germany – I do not know how far this may apply to other countries – is that there are two contiguous but distinct categories. First there are Jews, people one knows, associates with, acknowledges in professional or public life, people one may like or perhaps not like but with whom one has more or less normal human relations. Then there are »the Jews,« a more abstract collective with characteristics that mark them as aliens: a restless, sometimes nervous ambitiousness; a preoccupation with material gain; lovelessness and heartlessness in personal relations; cosmopolitanism rather than national patriotism and a sometimes frivolous attitude toward the symbolic values esteemed by the nation; a knack for appropriating learning and culture without depth; and especially a lack of those attributes that make of the German an elevated being: idealism, honesty, earnestness, introspection, and the readiness to do a thing for its own sake rather than for advantage. They are likely to be swarthy, sometimes ugly in appearance (this last does not always apply to females, the ubiquitous *belles juives*, preferred, for example, by Falko von Falkenburg in *Opfer*, to Jewish men, whom his cousin Wilfried agrees are »mein Genre auch nicht« [*NF*, 6, 84; cf. 412 at Karlsbad]). The pattern has been identified in Goethe's attitudes: »seine Verehrung für einzelne, herausragende Juden und für die Kulturleistungen des Judentums hielten ihn nicht davon ab, die Masse der Juden zu übersehen und ihre Emanzipation abzulehnen.«[1] Since the educated bourgeoisie in this era did not take religion seriously, it did not take Jewish religion seriously; in fact, it often seems that the very existence of Judaism has not been registered, and there certainly is no curiosity or general knowledge about it. These views are not anti-Semitic in the strict terms of racial doctrine; in the communities of writers, intellectuals, scholars, and the educated generally, racist anti-Semites are rare, fringe figures often regarded as crackpots. The attitude is a version of a generalized group

---

[1]   Klaus L. Berghahn, »Ein klassischer Chiasmus: Goethe und die Juden, die Juden und Goethe,« *Goethe Yearbook* 10 (2001): 212

prejudice such as we find in almost all human societies anywhere and any-time, but one that softened the ground for its occupation by a systematic, would-be scientific, purposeful, and, in time, violent anti-Semitism, which is why, in historical retrospect, these symptoms have acquired a much larger significance than they appeared to have to people in their own time.

In fiction, and no doubt also in real life, individuals can be transferred from the second category to the first, usually on the ground of assimilation to *Bildung* and majority values. This fluidity sometimes makes writers seem more ambiguous and confused to us than they probably did to themselves and their own public. The consequence is that one can comb authors and texts in order to make a case, depending on one's argumentative purpose, for friendly or hostile attitudes to the Jews. Taking account of, without, of course, accepting, the distinction between Jews and »the Jews« would make inquiries in these matters more exact and less tendentious than they often are. Spielhagen's case, as usual, exhibits typical features as well as some com-plications of its own. As far as I can see, he had no problem with Jews in the first sense. He speaks of the publisher of the newspaper he worked for in Hanover as an amiable old Jew (*AW*, 10). He was proud of his friendship with the Jewish liberal politician Eduard Lasker, his exact contemporary (*NB*, 220).[2] Like Wilhelm Raabe, whose ambiguities in this matter are, if anything, more pronounced, Spielhagen had Jewish admirers.[3] The most fer-vent of these was Gustav Karpeles, a Hapsburg crown-lander by origin who was certainly assimilated but who devoted a large proportion of his efforts as a literary historian, essayist, and journalist to Jewish concerns. For a time he was associated with Spielhagen in the editorship of *Westermanns*. Karpe-

---

2   »In 1871 he [Lasker] helped to form a literary-political club that, during its short life, attracted writers like Berthold Auerbach, Karl Frenzel, Friedrich Spielhagen, Julian Schmidt, and Ernst Dohm, along with politicians like Rudolf von Bennig-sen, Max von Forckenbeck, Ludwig Bamberger, and Friedrich Kapp«: James F. Harris, *A Study in the Theory and Practice of German Liberalism: Eduard Lasker, 1829–1884* (Lanham, MD, New York, and London, 1984), 10. Harris has this from Julius Rodenberg, »Briefe von Eduard Lasker. Nebst persönlichen Erinnerun-gen,« *Deutsche Rundschau* 38 (1884): 444. Bamberger was also Jewish, as was, of course, Auerbach; Dohm was a baptized Jew. We know little of associations like this in Spielhagen's life.
3   See my essay, »Wilhelm Raabe and his Reputation Among Jews and Anti-Semi-tes,« *Identity and Ethos: A Festschrift for Sol Liptzin on the Occasion of his 85th Birthday*, ed. Mark H. Gelber (New York and Bern, 1986), 169–91. The claim of Schierding, *Untersuchungen über die Romantechnik*, 137, that Spielhagen lost »die Sympathien gewisser literarischer Kreise« because of his exposure of the disadvan-tages to liberalism from its association with Jewry lacks credibility and says more about Schierding's attitudes in the atmosphere of 1914.

les refuted those who might find a breath of anti-Semitism in *Was will das werden?* on the grounds that, as a poet, Spielhagen was far above that.[4] The defense suggests that there might be a question there, after all.

Among Spielhagen's best and, as it seems to me, relatively few friends in the literary community was Berthold Auerbach, the very model of what came to be called a »deutscher Staatsbürger jüdischen Glaubens,« a vigorous proponent of assimilation who was nevertheless determined to maintain an intact Jewish identity. For years Spielhagen and Auerbach lived on the same street in Berlin with only one house between them (*AmSt*, 206). No other contemporary writer is praised as fulsomely and frequently by Spielhagen, who, in a poem celebrating Auerbach's sixty-fifth birthday, called him »viellieber Meister mein« and wondered how he maintained his remarkable cheerfulness (*G*, 248–49). His typically cheerful last letter, written four hours before his death, was addressed to Spielhagen, his literary executor.[5] He acknowledges Auerbach's companionship in the preface to his major theoretical work (*BT*, viii). In a memorial oration, Spielhagen declared: »wenn ein moderner Dichter den vollen epischen Atem hatte in der mächtigen, von überquellender Empfindung geschwellten Brust, und auch wahrlich die Stimme gehabt hätte, diesen Atem auszuströmen in klangvoll hallendem, glänzend geprägten Wort: dann war es Berthold Auerbach« (322). Auerbach seems to have been the one author after Spielhagen's heart. In a memorial written ten years after Auerbach's death, Spielhagen quotes the observation in Auerbach's last letter that it was a difficult task to be a German writer and a Jew at the same time (*AW*, 123). Elsewhere he stressed that Auerbach had found his way out of traditional religion to the »Religion des reinen Menschenthums« and that it was unfair to make the same reproaches to »der gebildete Jude« as to »dem polnischen Schacherjuden und dem aus dem Schacherjuden in die Berliner oder Wiener *haute-finance* transponirten Börsenbaron!« (*AmSt*, 226–27).

---

4   Karpeles, *Friedrich Spielhagen*, 72. Heinrich Spiero, of Jewish origin but a convinced and active Protestant who survived the Nazi era, wrote in his posthumously published *Geschichte des deutschen Romans* (Berlin: de Gruyter, 1950), 323, that the novel gave an accurate picture of the anti-Semitic mood that had been on the rise since the 1870s.

5   See Anton Bettelheim, *Berthold Auerbach. Der Mann – Sein Werk – Sein Nachlaß* (Stuttgart and Berlin, 1907), 382. Spielhagen wrote a foreword to a selection of Auerbach's letters to his closest friend, *Berthold Auerbach. Briefe an seinen Freund Jakob Auerbach. Ein biographisches Denkmal*, ed. Jakob Auerbach (Frankfurt am Main, 1884). It is reprinted in *AW*, 129–77; a much expanded version had already appeared in *AmSt*, 199–272. Bettelheim (374) tells us that he and Spielhagen found galleys of a novel directed against »Sozialdemagogie,« which they decided not to publish.

If I understand him correctly, these are culturally determined and not racial categories. He saw clearly that, since religion was no longer an issue, the anti-Jewish discourse falls back on an irrational concept of race easily satirized: »Blut ist eben ein besonderer und Rasseblut ein ganz besonderer Saft.... [Es] läßt sich das nicht mehr in Worte fassen, man muß es fühlen. Fühlen, daß ein jüdischer Justizminister ... eine Absurdität, ein jüdischer General eine Lächerlichkeit sein soll, und so mit Grazie *in infinitum*« (229). Although in many places he indicates an admiration for Heine, he nevertheless associates himself with Auerbach's attack on Heine as a cancer on literature, understanding correctly that it was a gesture of dissociation from what was perceived as Jewish in Heine's destructive satire (234–36). The extremely fulsome praise of Auerbach, a writer today held in very limited regard, may well affect our evaluation of Spielhagen himself (a point not surprisingly picked up by the hostile Heinrich Hart[6]), but I think there is a slight incongruity here. It has sometimes seemed to me that Spielhagen's literary theory and critical practice, if followed to all its implications, would give one Auerbach rather than Spielhagen as a writer. In his elegy upon Auerbach's death, he pairs their writings chronologically, the last *Dorfgeschichten* with *Problematische Naturen*, *Auf der Höhe* with *In Reih' und Glied* (to which, we are told, Auerbach supplied the title), *Das Landhaus am Rhein* with *Hammer und Amboß* – »Schulter and Schulter, Schritt für Schritt« (*BT*, 318). These parallels seem very inexact to me.[7] When Spielhagen argues that

---

6 Hart, »Friedrich Spielhagen,« 17.
7 As one might expect, Spielhagen was not actually an admirer of the genre of the *Dorfgeschichte.* Near the beginning of *Die Dorfcoquette*, which might be a kind of parody, a lady expresses the hope that the narrator is »kein Dorfgeschichtenschreiber« and continues by criticizing the genre as disagreeable to the peasants, uncomprehending of their real lives, and redolent of class dominance (*AR*, 2, 4: 334–35). The narrator, a writer, tries to defend the genre. The lady narrates her story as an alternative *Dorfgeschichte*, »keinen Roman..., sondern nur ein Stück Menschengeschichte« (352), very likely owing to its inordinate cruelty: the jilted lover cut off the coquette's ears in the hope of making her unattractive to others, eventually marrying her. In the interpolated diary of *Sonntagskind*, Justus tells himself that he only needed to write down the tragic story of Albinka »um Berthold Auerbach und Gottfried Keller paroli zu bieten,« only to find that real events do not have the neat shape of fiction (*NF*, 1: 308). When, in *Opfer*, a clerk in the Bielefelder bank absconds, the expected cover-up is called »Eine Bielefelder Dorfgeschichte« (6: 273). Spielhagen, like Justus, tried his hand at the genre itself in *Hans und Grete*, where a poor girl's narration is praised »als lese sie eine Dorfgeschichte, von Meisterhand geschrieben« (*AR*, 2, 4: 320); the master hand is probably Auerbach's but the story itself, in which almost everyone is petty and quarrelsome, has a sour tone. Jürgen Hein, *Dorfgeschichte* (Stuttgart, 1976), 94, cites an opinion that *Die Dorfcoquette* and *Hans und Grete* are failed

the best way to read Auerbach is get past his faults to his underlying harmony and find his great heart, it may be the way Spielhagen himself hoped to be read (*AmSt*, 269). If so, the partiality for Auerbach lies near the core paradoxes in his literary imagination.

As we can already see, with »the Jews« things are rather different. In a discussion of Lessing's *Nathan der Weise*, we are told that »the Jews,« because of their suffering, to be sure, are loveless; only love can save them (*AW*, 71). A review of a biography of Rahel Varnhagen acknowledges her as an individual, but she is also said to exhibit the most pronounced features of »the Jews« (172). Still, there are moments of sympathy with »the Jews« also; for example, in 1894 Spielhagen declared himself opposed to the exclusion of *Ostjuden* because there are so many outstanding doctors, lawyers, writers, and financiers among them (271). In the previous decade, in *Noblesse oblige*, which takes place during the Wars of Liberation but was written in the context of the rise of political anti-Semitism, the patriot Georg Warburg praises the *Ostjuden* (*AR*, 3, 2: 129).[8] The American Ralph Curtis in *Ein neuer Pharao* thinks an officer is joking when he wants to exclude Jews from the army (3, 3: 141).

If there is a paradox in Spielhagen's relationship to the Jews, it is bracketed by two singular moments at the beginning and the end of his career. The first is a matter of origins, for Spielhagen stated in an early letter that his mother had »von väterlicher Seite jüdisches Blut in ihren Adern.«[9] Nothing is said about this in any other memoir. The second, near of the end of his life, is Victor Klemperer's certification of Spielhagen as a »Philosemit« in an article of 1909 in the *Allgemeine Zeitung des Judentums*. Klemperer discusses a number of the Jewish figures, indicating that some are better, some worse, but ascribing the differentiation to a »Prinzip des Ba-

---

   Dorfgeschichten because of Spielhagen's urban perspective, but this judgment may fail to understand his intention.

8   I am puzzled by the choice of the name Warburg for the protagonists' family. It is, of course, the name of a Jewish banking family that was established in Hamburg by the time of the Wars of Liberation and by Spielhagen's time had become very prominent. His Warburgs, however, are certainly not Jewish. The standard of Jewish wealth and luxurious entertainment in the novel is Heine's Uncle Salomon (*AR*, 3, 2: 242–43).

9   To Adolf Stahr, February 18, 1862, *Aus Adolf Stahrs Nachlaß. Briefe von Stahr nebst Briefe an ihn*, ed. Ludwig Geiger (Oldenburg, 1903), 258. The fanatic anti-Semite Adolf Bartels charged Spielhagen with having »Judenblut,« but he might have said that of anyone of whom he disapproved. See Rolf Sältzer, *Entwicklungslinien der deutschen Zola-Rezeption von den Anfängen bis zum Tod des Autors* (Bern and Frankfurt am Main, 1989), 267, n. 789.

lancierens, der ausgleichenden Gerechtigkeit,« and then, inevitably, to »ein heißes Bemühen der Objektivität.«[10] There are some reasons to be a little skeptical of this effort. In the first place, Klemperer, as we know from his now famous memoirs, had hardly any sense of Jewish identity until one was imposed on him by the Nazis; what is he doing writing for the *AZJ*, one of the central organs of German-Jewish identity? At this time he was trying to ingratiate himself with Spielhagen (and his daughter Toni), perhaps to become his literary executor; in any case, Klemperer wanted to write Spielhagen's biography but was forestalled by Henning.[11] In his dissertation, a surrogate for the dissertation in the Romance field that he would have preferred to write, he is, in general, much less positive, gives less credit to Spielhagen for his alleged echoes of Shylock than to Freytag, and complains that both his good and bad Jews are exaggerated.[12] The *AZJ* article seems to be a bit of a whitewash. In 1893, in an interview by Hermann Bahr, Spielhagen appears at best ambiguous, claiming that usurers are, as a rule, Jewish; that their religious and national aspects are masks and illusions; that Jewish students are superior in competition, thus a danger for »our« lazy youth; that they are superior in industry and intelligence but »[d]as Höchste in den Wissenschaften, in den Künsten bleibt ihnen freilich versagt«; Heine is a high point in literature but, compared with Goethe and Schiller, »gering«; Spielhagen is, to be sure, a Spinozist, but Spinoza is an exception that only confirms the rule.[13]

To trace all the occurrences of Jews and Jewishness in Spielhagen's works would yield a bulky monograph; however, as usual, there is a good deal of repetition. His most concentrated portrayals represent Jews in families: the Sonnensteins of *In Reih' und Glied,* the Israels of *Was will das werden?,* and the Bielefelders of *Opfer* and *Frei geboren.* The elder, ennobled Sonnenstein,

---

10 Klemperer, »Die Juden in Spielhagens Werken,« 104, 117, 118.

11 Victor Klemperer, *Curriculum vitae. Jugend um 1900* (Berlin, 1989), 1: 473–76.

12 Klemperer, *Die Zeitromane Friedrich Spielhagens,* 66, 94, 131, 169. In *Curriculum vitae,* 2: 35, Klemperer says that the dissertation was written in eight weeks, which one can easily believe.

13 Bahr, *Der Antisemitismus,* 18–19. Bahr was developing anti-Semitic tendencies at this time, so that the interview might be somewhat colored by them. See Mark H. Gelber, *Melancholy Pride: Nation, Race, and Gender in the German Literature of Cultural Zionism* (Tübingen, 2000), 254–56. Gelber, 259–61, also discusses the odor of anti-Semitism around Spielhagen's admired colleague and correspondent Peter Rosegger. Spielhagen wrote a sonnet in praise of Spinoza, beginning: »Wenn ich dich liebe, Gott, was geht's dich an?« and alluding to Novalis's famous phrase: »Du, gottheitstrunk'ner, großer, heil'ger Mann« (*G,* 90).

grandson of a baptized Jew, who talks his reluctant brother-in-law Baron von Tuchheim into constructing factories on his estate, has a rather weak-willed son Alfred, who tries to copy the baron's mean and arrogant son Henri, and an affected, Frenchified daughter Emma, whom Henri marries for her money even though he dislikes her and wants to teach a lesson to »[d]iese feigen Judenseelen«; at one point her father tries to pair her to the rising Leo Gutmann as »eine Geschäftsfrage,« since liberalism is good for business (1, 6: 457, 425).[14] The relationship with the baron is burdened by his distrust of Sonnenstein's Jewish ancestry, as Sonnenstein well knows, but also by the latter's greater dexterity in business matters, which he applies to the baron's disadvantage. Emma becomes miserable at Henri's treatment of her, and Alfred feels he would be a worthless Jew if his father were not a millionaire; the elder Sonnenstein, for his part, resents being regarded as a Jew (1, 7: 366; 6: 366). Sonnenstein fears losing his son and, when the son dies, no longer knows what he is working for (1, 7: 116–17, 466). There has been occasion to comment on the similarity of this pattern to that in Gustav Freytag's *Soll und Haben*. We may be reminded of this connection by the ancillary characterizations of Markus, an employee of Sonnenstein who, while presenting accounts to Leo, comports himself with fake elegance and a nasal voice, or of the dirty, noisy quarters of a conniving »Wucherer« to whom Leo must mortgage his house at the bottom of his fortunes (1, 6: 536, 7: 512). But Spielhagen at this point is less concerned with Freytag's national and ethnic preoccupations than with the association of Sonnenstein with rapacious industrial enterprise. At one point the father tries to explain his ambition to his daughter from family and personal history: his descent from an impoverished peddler who became prosperous out of a decision for vengefulness that came to him while sitting on a warm stone in the sunlight – thus his name – and his inherited determination to make his children and grandchildren as rich and powerful as will be necessary to quell the persistent anti-Semitic hostility (1, 7: 242–43).

The Israels of *Was will das werden?* are, as has been pointed out, more differentiated but still associated with the commercial spirit of the *Gründerzeit*, of which they are the only representatives in the novel.[15] The

---

[14] The marriage of the nobleman to the rich Jewess in order to strengthen his fortunes is a recurring motif. When the conniving Count Golm in *Sturmflut* is advised to marry, he replies: »Nennen Sie mir die betreffende jüdische junge Dame!« (*AR*, 1, 8: 203).

[15] Henrike Lamers, *Held oder Welt? Zum Romanwerk Friedrich Spielhagens* (Bonn, 1991), 113.

protagonist Lothar Lorenz and Emil Israel are boyhood friends; we have already seen how Lothar obliges the unwilling Emil to play soldier, for Jews are unmartial; none of the Israels, including Emil, can understand why Lothar wants to enlist in the Franco-Prussian War (3, 4: 352). Lothar protects Emil against bullying (119), a motif that may again come from *Soll und Haben* and perhaps from Wilhelm Raabe's *Der Hungerpastor*. Emil's sister Jettchen is a kind, gentle, plain girl who hopelessly pines for Lothar for much of the novel. Their father, Isidor Israel, not very affectionately known in the community as »I. I.,« is a tougher version of Sonnenstein; he gets rich on army supplies for the Franco-Prussian War, which he hopes will not end soon (324, 349). His redevelopment of the harbor generates distress, which causes at first attacks on the construction workers as surrogates for the Jews but eventually a rebellious riot in front of Israel's house, in the course of which he dies (3, 5: 46, 50). In the past he has forced Vogtriz *père* to pledge a distillery to him, leading the father to conclude that it is the Jews, not the French, who are the enemy and motivating his son Schlagododro's hostility to Emil, which Lothar tries to mitigate by sharing an essay on Lessing's *Nathan der Weise* with him (3, 4: 276, 294, 145, 148). Lothar is shocked by I. I.'s manners and especially his praise of money – Lothar, with his idealistic contempt for money, has never imagined anyone could express such a sentiment, though this is an ironic retrospect, for, with more experience, he wishes he had some (135, 346). Lothar is ashamed to pretend friendship for I. I. while I. I. pretends kindness to him (346). He continues to hold I. I. in contempt even when the latter insists on paying the convalescent costs after Lothar has been accidentally wounded by Schlagododro; Lothar is determined to pay him back from what he believes to be his earnings as a writer, but is obliged to discover that they are being secretly supplied by Jettchen (404, 411).

Emil is kinder and more humane than his father but, for just that reason, not as capable as a businessman. He would like to help the Vogtriz family that had been squeezed by his father, but his partner, a Polish Jew named Löbinsky, will not allow it (3, 5: 245). With Löbinsky, Emil becomes for a time a successful speculator, taking risks, as he says, that Bismarck's banker Bleichröder would not have taken (258), and acquiring a luxurious way of life, abetted by his wife, Löbinsky's sister, a vulgar parvenue renamed Lili, who has an affair with a visiting English Jew, Fred Simon, and eventually runs off to London with him. Owing to Löbinsky's dishonesty, Emil's firm suffers a spectacular crash. His selfless, compassionate sister Jettchen develops into an angelic, virtually unearthly character on her deathbed, where she praises Lothar for seeing Jews as human beings, not just ugly creatures, and claims that he should be the messiah to redeem the Jews »aus unserm Elend, als Juden geboren zu sein,« adding that association with Jews has been important to his *Bildung*: »sie haben Dich zu dem machen helfen, wozu Du die Bestimmung in Dir trugst: ein Mensch zu werden, dem nichts Menschliches fremd ist.« Lothar understandably declines this mission, but the terms of Jettchen's further appeal to him can be disturbing to today's reader. She goes on to say that »the Jews« must reform, become free, emancipate themselves from the tribe, which is »ein Schmarotzergewächs am Baum der Menschheit.« The drift is that the oppression of »the Jews« is their own fault; »the Jews« do not love the Christians, as the Christians do not love them: »Wir thun auch manches, weshalb sie es wohl nicht können.« »The Jews« use oppression as an excuse to remain stuck »in den angeborenen Vorurteilen« and eschew any activity other than »Geldmachen und Reichwerden« in order to allow »dem eingeborenen, egoistischen Triebe zügellose Freiheit.« She concludes by saying that her belief in Lothar is her religion. This curious speech allows Lothar to mull the difference between Jews and »the Jews«: »welch sonderbarer Menschenboden dieser jüdische doch sei, der so unschmackhafte Früchte bringe und dann wieder andere von so berauschender Süßigkeit, gerade wie in ihrem heimischen Orient hart am Rande der steinigen Wüste die Zweige der Dattelpalme wehen« (270–73).

This discourse, ascribed to a Jewish woman, might today be identified as »eliminationist.« It has been often pointed out how dangerous the Enlightenment emancipation from religion came to be for the Jewish cause. If Christianity no longer commanded belief, except as a general term for Western culture, what reason could there be for the retention of Judaism? Recently it has been observed: »To many during the Enlightenment, Judaism was the archetype of a clerical religion, and as such, it seemed inimical to the values of freedom and autonomy. This view made it possible for them to extend a hand to individual Jews while at the same time carrying on a cultural war against Judaism.«[16] As Heine put it in his own behalf: »man wendet sich nicht an die überwelken Reize der Mutter, wenn einem die alternde Tochter nicht mehr behagt.«[17] If Judaism had been rendered nugatory, what point could there be to retaining Jewish identity? In *Ultimo*

---

[16] Steven B. Smith, *Spinoza, Liberalism, and the Question of Jewish Identity* (New Haven and London, 1997), p. 25.
[17] Heinrich Heine, »Über den Denunzianten,« *Sämtliche Schriften*, ed. Klaus Briegleb et al. (Munich, 1968–76), 5: 38.

(1873), the Jewish father wants his daughter to marry a Jew and tries to prevent her marriage to a Gentile, saying that he does not want to her marry a Christian. To this the Gentile replies: »So kann sie getrost mein Weib werden, der ich mich längst von jeder positiven Religion losgesagt habe« (2, 3: 455). The implication is, I think, that Jewishness is the equivalent of no religion.

The Jewish self-criticism expressed by Jettchen in *Was will das werden?* had already appeared in *Was die Schwalbe sang*, here in the form of self-persiflage that is meant to make the character, Gotthold Weber's business agent and, to some extent, surrogate father, Emil Wollnow, amiable to the reader. He has married the Jewish girl Ottilie Blaustein, with whom the young Gotthold had danced when nobody else would, but Gotthold is surprised to learn that Wollnow, too, is of Jewish origin; »Reinster Race,« he says ironically; »haben Sie das nicht gesehen, als ich vorher Ihr Geld so eilig wieder in den Schrank schloß? – reinster polnischer Race«; he had wanted to marry Gotthold's mother but could not because he was a Jew. For the sake of his wife, he says, »die hinreichend unter dem Judenthum gelitten zu haben erklärte,« and for business reasons he has converted to Christianity, »den für mich sehr leichten Schritt aus einer positiven Religion, die mir gleichgültig war, in eine andere, die mir nicht minder gleichgültig war, gemacht habe« (36). This passage curiously seems to paraphrase the still unpublished defense Heine made to his conventionally irreligious friend Heinrich Laube of the late change in his religious posture.[18] Ottilie, like Jettchen, mulls the Jewish condition, though in a more sympathetic way: »die Stellung der Juden, mußt Du wissen, war damals, vor dreißig Jahren, noch ein wenig precärer und ungemüthlicher als jetzt, trotzdem auch jetzt vielleicht noch nicht Alles ist, wie es sein sollte« (216).

Was will das werden?, published in 1887, shows signs of its location within the increasing intensity of anti-Semitism in the German public discourse

---

[18] Heine to Laube, January 25, 1850, *Heinrich Heine Säkularausgabe*, ed. Nationale Forschungs- und Gedenkstätten der klassischen deutschen Literatur in Weimar and Centre National de la Recherche Scientifique in Paris (Berlin and Paris, 1970), 23: 23–24. The full passage reads: »Es hat sich in meiner religiösen Gefühlsweise gar keine so große Veränderung zugetragen und das einzige innere Ereigniß, wovon ich Dir mit Bestimmtheit und mit Selbstbewußtseyn etwas melden kann, besteht darin, daß auch in meinen religiösen Ansichten und Gedanken eine FebruarRevoluzion eingetreten ist, wo ich an der Stelle eines frühern Prinzips, das mich doch früherhin ziemlich indifferent ließ, ein neues Prinzip aufstellte, dem ich ebenfalls nicht allzu fanatisch anhänge und wodurch mein Gemüthszustand nicht plötzlich umgewandelt werden konnte.« The letter was published in 1906.

of that decade. Here the Jews are caught in a pincer between radicals and liberals. Lothar's intellectually elegant, eventually nihilistic friend Adalbert von Werin is vociferously anti-Jewish and tries to separate Lothar from Emil. Adalbert gets himself a bad grade with a school essay on Lessing's *Nathan* by claiming that it caused much harm by persuading so many Jews that they were Nathans when they were really »Stockjuden«; that Nathan was opposed to »die dogmatische und nationale Beschränktheit des Judentums« and generally human, so that Lessing could have made him »einen Christen, Mohammedaner, Hindu, Feueranbeter, Wilden à la Seume«; that Lessing made him a Jew is just a joke. Adalbert then rants against the emancipation campaigns, which have left behind »bis auf den heutigen Tag der uralte, vertrocknete, wurmstichige Kern des bornierten, vaterlandslosen, nur auf Gewinn spekulierenden, durch und durch materialistischen, ganz gemeinen Juden« (3, 4: 164–65). Lothar's mentor Professor Hunnius goes on at some length on the harm done to liberalism by association with »the Jews.« Emancipation has brought nothing but an obsession with wealth, luxury, unscrupulous ambition, and a pretense of supporting freedom while exploiting one's fellow man (3, 5: 349). This passage has been disturbing to those who would like to see Spielhagen in the best light in these matters. It is sometimes ascribed to his »objectivity,« his own voice allegedly suppressed. But this will not quite do. Hunnius is a positive figure; he has been attacked from the right as »Gottesleugner, Judenfreund« (48), sure signs of his political virtue. The oration is placed very close to the end of the novel. Furthermore, Hunnius predicts that »the Jews« will make common cause with reactionaries in disparaging Lothar's drama *Thomas Münzer*. Hunnius has observed in the theater foyer a pack of journalists »das die schwarzen Köpfe zusammensteckte und den kritischen Kurs Ihres Münzer für morgen feststellte« (351).[19] This prophecy turns out to be correct; the drama is slated by those same, presumably Jewish, »ehrlichen Maklern des Foyer«; only the director Lamarque is spared, who, we have learned, is the son of Polish Jew named Markus and began life as a barber (369–70, 8).

Sonntagskind, which comes between *Was will das werden?* and the last pair of novels, does not have a typological Jewish family but features Spiel-

---

[19] Spielhagen several times employs a reference to dark-haired or black-haired men as a sign of Jewish infestation. For example, Israel's assistant is »ein[ ] sehr brünette[r] junge[r] Mann,« and in Emil's firm, Lothar observes barred enclosures »in welchen dunkelhaarige junge Herren schweigsam über ihre Pulte gebeugt kritzelten« (*AR*, 3, 4: 346 and passim; 5: 257). Similarly, in *Opfer*, the Bielefelder sons are spotted in a café as »zwei jüngere, sehr brünette Männer« (*NF*, 6: 16).

hagen's most evil Jew, the Polish smuggler Löb, to whom Justus's father, a forester muddled by misfortune and oppression, wants to apprentice his son, and from whom his mother earns a hard living with embroidery. Löb eventually contrives the father's murder, for which he is slowly brought to justice. In a subplot we have once again the marriage of a depraved young aristocrat to a Jewish girl for money, in this case Count Armand, whose father refuses to pay his huge gambling debts and who therefore has them paid by Isidor Seligmann in exchange for taking his daughter Christine. When Christine is so badly treated that she wants a divorce, Seligmann is furious: a deal is a deal; the aristocrat had cost him millions (*NF* ,1: 474); he forces his daughter to return but she eventually drowns herself. An English governess has no sympathy for her plight, regarding her as just one of those Jews for whom everything is a business deal and who wanted to be a countess (475). This is not very fair, as the forlorn Christine seems actually to love her worthless husband (480). The short novel *Herrin*, which turns crucially on the plan of a beautiful Jewish girl to marry a count, is one of those peculiar late works that will have to be dealt with separately in Chapter 17. It might be mentioned in passing that in *Ultimo* the shoe is somewhat on the other foot. Here the vain coquette Melanie Goldheimer wants to marry a Gentile doctor, but her father wants her to marry Eugen Silbermann, whose father will not extend a credit of 100,000 marks unless she does so by tomorrow noon (*AR*, 2, 3: 386–87). Melanie's mother takes a different tack, commiserating with her daughter that Jewish women can't do what they wish; the love of Christian men doesn't last any more than that of Jewish husbands, but the former have no money; the latter do, even if we don't love them; that is »die Hauptsache« (431). This complicated and implausible tale has a comic tone and everything turns out all right, but the comedy is at the expense of the scorned »Geldjuden« (455).

The plots of *Opfer* and *Frei geboren* are in reverse chronological order; the second is a kind of prequel to the first. The elder of the Bielefelders, Samuel, a former fur dealer who has traveled in America, Canada, and Siberia, is a decent and lovable man who eschews luxury and is perceived as Nathan the Wise (*NF*, 7: 132). The admirable Jewish patriarch had already appeared in the form of the honest Samuel Hirsch in *Noblesse oblige*. Though Hirsch speaks in the Yiddish syntax sometimes employed by German authors to diminish Jewish figures,[20] particular stress is put upon his

---

[20] See Jeffrey A. Grossman, *The Discourse on Yiddish in Germany from the Enlightenment to the Second Empire* (Columbia, SC: 2000).

patriotic opposition to Napoleon, an attitude not shared by all Jews at the time, who placed some hopes of emancipation in him. Thus of Hirsch, who is one of the few in the novel who remain loyal to the family of Minna Warburg and attends the funeral of her failed father, it is said: »Gab es jemals einen Israeliten, in dem kein Falsch ist, so ist er es« (*AR*, 3, 2: 346), with a possible hint that falseness is to be expected of Jews. However that may be, in *Opfer* and *Frei geboren*, Samuel Bielefelder and his unchic, kind, religious wife are the very models of good Jews; they are the only loving couple in either novel. But with the Bielefelders, Spielhagen introduces another pattern, moral decay through the generations. We have already seen the beginnings of this with Alfred and Emma von Sonnenstein of *In Reih' und Glied*, a degeneration that parallels a similar development in the family of Baron Tuchheim. That the Jewish son is meaner and more ruthless than the father is suggested also in Fritz Reuter's *Ut mine Stromtid*, Wilhelm Raabe's *Der Hungerpastor*, and Theodor Fontane's *Der Stechlin*. Like the degeneration of aristocratic families, the parallel development in Jewish families is a sign, it seems to me, of the decline of humane values in the dominant classes of the Reich, with which »the Jews,« because of the control of wealth and credit ascribed to them, are rather perversely associated. Samuel Bielefelder's younger son Philipp, a businessman and an initially but inconstantly liberal politician who stresses his Germanness and *kleindeutsch* patriotism, is a self-centered, inconsiderate man. Out of convenience he marries, then disregards the Baroness Antoinette Kesselbrook, who in *Opfer* is a neglected invalid, visited by Wilfried von Falkenburg but hardly by the members of her own family; she is, however, the narrator of *Frei geboren*, which tells how these things came about. Philipp's older brother Arthur is a more unpleasant man, »der unerfreuliche Typ seiner Rasse« (7: 312), who marries a rather stupid but seductive and luxury-loving Englishwoman, Jane Lilifield (originally Rebekka Lilienfeld), with whom Philipp has an affair.

There is further deterioration in the next generation. Philipp's sons, Arthur and Leonor, are unloved by their mother because they take after their father: »Kaufmannsgesichter ... kleine *matter-of-fact-men*« (327). Even as children they are inaccessible to literature, read only war stories, care only for money, and despise the poor (362). Arthur Jr. is a man who, despite living in luxury, can vulgarly name the price when offering a cognac (6: 298). The sons weaken the firm by speculation, which fails when a clerk, the proletarian striver Hermann Schulz, who has passed through Social Democracy to nihilism, absconds with a million and a half; Wilfried von Falkenburg, who had tried to befriend Hermann, comes to believe that the Bielefelders are the greater thieves (313). Antoinette's friend Adele had warned her against marrying even a baptized Jew, for her children would still have »Judenblut in den Adern« and »Auf das Blut kommt es an; Blut ist alles« (7: 246); for all that this may be aristocratic superstition from Spielhagen's normal point of view, it seems to have been prophetic in this case. On the other hand, Antoinette, on reading Lassalle, decides »the Jews« really are the chosen people (289). The coquettish daughter Else and her cousin, Arthur's daughter Chlotilde (who may actually be Philipp's child with Jane) are Jewish versions of the haughty beauty Ebba von Falkenburg (6: 26). The girls discuss which noblemen they will take; Else is glad that at a party (which will end disastrously as so often in Spielhagen's fiction), there will be so many »Herren von« (277, 280). Else will get Falko von Falkenburg, who needs the money. He thinks it is too bad that she is a Bielefelder; he likes her well enough and could love her if she didn't have a penny, but in that case would not marry her (320, 323). As a consequence of this marriage he is transferred to a provincial regiment despite his Gentile, noble mother-in-law (414).

One sees how these issues gain density in Spielhagen's later novels. Clearly they have been affected by the intensifying environmental discourse of anti-Semitism. When a police lieutenant recognizes Wilfried von Falkenburg at a Social Democratic meeting, he offers to take him to an anti-Semitic meeting instead, as presumably more appropriate for a man of his class (232). Spielhagen tried to maintain the distinction of Jews from »the Jews,« whom he came to associate almost exclusively with ruthless and rapacious finance capitalism. Doubtless this view derived from unanalytic experiential observation. It has been estimated that half of the entrepreneurs in Berlin were Jewish at the time Spielhagen was living there.[21] But the transformation of such observations into narrative is affected by race-based typologies, partly inherited from traditional attitudes concerning alien, non-German attributes, partly enhanced by the environmental discourse. The case that Karpeles and Klemperer tried to make on Spielhagen's behalf in such matters requires revision and nuance. With his tolerant and humane instincts, he tried to maintain an even keel. But, in a sense, his keel is too even; viewed in retrospect, at any rate, he allowed too much credit to affects and attitudes that are irrationally biased and ultimately harmful.

---

[21] Wehler, *Deutsche Gesellschaftsgeschichte*, 3: 116.

9. America

As we have seen, young Spielhagen acquired, through personal connections, a knowledge of English, then taught the language for a time in a school. English was becoming more important for Germans and especially for German writers than it had been earlier in the century because of the increasing interest in and orientation upon the English novel. Wilhelm Raabe, for example, had also taught himself English, in the first instance to read Thackeray. Spielhagen claims he chose English because it was the easiest modern foreign language – a young girl in *Stumme des Himmels* learns to read *The Vicar of Wakefield* in four weeks (*NF*, 2: 190) – but his choice of Goldsmith, Dickens, and, of course, Shakespeare as texts on which to practice clearly show the literary direction of his interest (*FuE*, 1: 333, 335). English novelists, notably Scott and Dickens, were rapidly translated into German, but there was a desire and a need to read the originals. An entire publishing house, Tauchnitz, was founded in Leipzig to specialize in English-language publication, nor was it the only one of its kind, merely the best known and most enduring.[1] Spielhagen tells us of young ladies for whom the *Tauchnitz Edition* came immediately after the Gospels (2: 366). Scraps of English words and phrases are found in many places in his fiction, sometimes imitating the imperfections of German speakers of English. In *Alles fließt*, a man in a train compartment responds to a request to »Shut the window, please!« with a conversational gambit: »The world is all a fleeting show, says Thomas Moore. Think, he is right. Do you not?« (*MAF*, 283). Spielhagen should have liked to visit England, but never did (*FuE*, 2: 307).

As with other writers, Dickens is a presence in the background. The bad childhood years of the printer Peter Schmitz making ink in *Die von Hohenstein* remind one of Dickens's youthful sufferings in the blacking factory (*AR*, 1, 2: 85). From a phrase of Thackeray Spielhagen took the title

---

[1] See Thomas Keiderling, »Leipzig als Vermittlungs- und Produktionszentrum englischsprachiger Literatur zwischen 1815 und 1914,« *Beiträge zur Rezeption der britischen und irischen Literatur des 19. Jahrhunderts im deutschsprachigen Raum*, ed. Norbert Bachleitner (Amsterdam and Atlanta, 2000), 3–76.

of *Das Skelet im Hause* and there is an allusion to *Pendennis* in *Sonntags-kind*; the gentle-spirited Count Wendelin in *Stumme des Himmels* prefers Thackeray to Dickens, while his royal-blooded Norwegian mother prefers Byron and Shakespeare (*AR*, 2, 8: 412; *NF*, 1: 456, 461; 2: 170). When visiting Pompeii, Spielhagen was not surprisingly reminded of Bulwer-Lytton (*VNbS*, 39). Spielhagen was interested in poetry as well. We have seen how he extrapolated his first novella from a poem of Tennyson, though in this case mediated by Freiligrath's translation. *Mesmerismus* begins with the protagonist Roderich trying to translate Browning's poem, »Mesmerism,« not without difficulty, in view of the English poet's notoriously cryptic manner; the translation of the first seven stanzas and the twenty-fourth appears near the end of the story (*NF*, 5: 354–55). There is also a complete translation of »In a Gondola,« which takes up a good deal of printed space, but Roderich's friend is reminded of the painting spectacles of Makart and objects to »die Hyperbeln einer verstiegenen Phantasie« (281, 314–20, 312–13).[2] The translation is eventually burned. The young girl learning English in *Stumme des Himmels* finds Browning to be her favorite poet, although »[e]r ist nicht leicht zu lesen« (2: 190); one might well say so.

At an early point Spielhagen also developed a noteworthy interest in American literature. Within a year of the end of his life, he sent a greeting on the occasion of the seventy-fifth anniversary of the *New Yorker Staats-Zeitung*, expressing his regret that he had never been able to visit America, stressing his life-long habit of reading American literature and particularly his early translations.[3] Germans had been very much concerned with the United States since the latter part of the eighteenth century and readers were well acquainted with James Fenimore Cooper and Washington Irving. But Spielhagen turned to more recent writers, eventually contemporary ones, for criticism and especially for translation. The most venerable of these was Ralph Waldo Emerson, whose *English Traits*, a series of lectures delivered in 1848 and published in 1856, was translated by Spielhagen as

---

[2] Both poems belong to the »Dramatic Romances,« published in the collection *Bells and Pomegranates* in 1846; the first begins: »All I believed is true!«; the second: »I send my heart up to thee, all my heart.« *The Poems and Plays of Robert Browning*, ed. Saxe Commins (New York, 1934), 103–07, 123–29. In the second poem the translation suppresses Browning's, I presume, metaphorical line, »I am a Jew.« The translation also appears in *NG*, 245–53, with the same line missing. It is possible that Spielhagen was attempting in *Mesmerismus* to replicate something of Browning's obliqueness, as most of the story is told in the friend's replies to Roderich's letters, so that the reader must work some to piece it together.

[3] »Friedrich Spielhagen's Gruß an die ›New Yorker Staats-Zeitung,‹« *New Yorker Staats-Zeitung*, Sunday supplement of April 24, 1910, 3.

Englische Charakteristiken in the following year. He thought of himself as a bit of a pioneer, commenting in retrospect that all Germans know Emerson now, even if they have not read anything, but he was then unknown (*FuE*, 2: 300–01). In that same year Spielhagen published a translation of George William Curtis's (1824–92) *Nile Notes of a Howadji* (New York: Harper, 1851; »howadji,« Curtis tells us on the flyleaf, is Arabic for merchant and therefore traveler). A transcendentalist influenced by Emerson, Curtis was on his way to becoming a prominent writer, essayist, and orator, concerned with patriotism, labor relations, and women's suffrage; he became chancellor of the University of the State of New York and editor of *Harper's*. Spielhagen, however, encountered Curtis at the beginning of his career and commented on the struggle he had with the humorous style of the American's first book – »erste Bücher sind manchmal in einem krausen Stil geschrieben« – and recalled that while the translation had been ignored by the critics, he received an appreciative letter from the author (294). To make up for the book's obscurity, nearly forty years later a character in *Stumme des Himmels* refers to it (*NF*, 2: 41). When Spielhagen wrote his own travel work, the circumstances of this early publication came to mind again (*VNbS*, 199). In 1861 he translated the Englishman William Roscoe's widely read and often reprinted biography of Lorenzo de' Medici, dating from 1795.

These translations were the first publications of his career, potboilers commissioned from a fledgling writer, so that it is difficult to say how important they were to his mental furniture. Strodtmann indicated that he undertook them when his novellas did not succeed.[4] Of more evident weight was his project of translating a selection of American poems, which appeared with an introduction as *Amerikanische Gedichte* in 1859 and again in the *Vermischte Schriften* (see *FuE*, 2: 288–91). Spielhagen, as he puts it, was not burdened by a honorarium; a friend had secretly financed the publication (320–21). There are fifty-eight poems by fifteen poets, including Bryant, Longfellow, Poe, Bayard Taylor, and Emerson, along with some others whom we nonspecialists in American literature have to look up. Among those new to me was Park Benjamin (1809–64), one of whose poems is quoted without identification by the protagonist of *In der zwölften Stunde* (*AR*, 2, 1: 367). Notable, perhaps, is the absence of Whitman, whose fame, however, was fairly recent. He seems to have been obscure in

---

4   Strodtmann, *Dichterprofile*, 200.
5   See Walter Grünzweig, *Constructing the German Walt Whitman* (Iowa City, 1995), 11–19. For Freiligrath's Whitman translations, see the entries in Fleischhack, *Bibliographie Ferdinand Freiligrath*.

Germany until Freiligrath began to make him known in translation in the following decade.[5]

Spielhagen consulted R. W. Griswold's book on American poetry;[6] however, the choice of poems is not exclusively taken from that volume, so there must have been other sources. Griswold is mainly remembered for his attempt to destroy Poe's reputation. This is not without interest, as Spielhagen, with his theoretical bent, wrote an eighty-page essay on the differences between Poe and Longfellow, which typically rambles into a number of his preoccupations (*AmSt*, 99–179). Its initial impetus seems to have been a charge of plagiarism Poe had brought against Longfellow some forty-five years earlier; Spielhagen recapitulates this dispute in some detail, translating as he goes. On the whole, he comes down on Longfellow's side, an example of the tendency of his criticism to prefer the solid and reliable to the experimental and adventurous; he cites Longfellow in a number of places throughout his œuvre. Spielhagen, given his submission to Homer, is especially worried about Poe's claim that there was no such thing as a long poem. While he grants Poe a point here and there, ultimately he ascribes Poe's critique of Longfellow's moralism to a hatred of the latter's purer, clearer genius (176–77). However, in *In der zwölften Stunde*, when an American praises the independence and virtue of his countrywomen, Sven replies that women cannot produce works of genius but crush those who do, like Poe (*AR* 2, 1: 387–90). Sven then recites from »ein Bändchen Uebersetzungen amerikanischer Gedichte,« doubtless Spielhagen's own, the latter's translation of »To Helen« (390–93). In his late greeting to the *New Yorker Staats-Zeitung*, he speaks, of all the poets he has translated, including Longfellow, »vor allem von meinem Liebling, Edgar Poe.«[7]

Spielhagen indicates in his introduction to the American poems, as usual, that he knows everything and has an opinion about it. He is convinced that Americans cannot have an epic for they have no youthful phase of their history or »Gemeinsamkeit«; this was not the view of his guide Griswold, incidentally, who asserted that »we have no lack of themes for romance, poetry, or any sort of writing.«[8] Cooper is the prosaic epigone of Homer, but real Indians, as Spielhagen knows (from Gerstäcker?) are dirty and cruel, not ideal; there are very few social and philosophical novels owing to the lack of culture; *Uncle Tom's Cabin* was a success for other reasons. Poesy

---

6 Rufus Wilmot Griswold, *The Poets and Poetry of America with an Historical Intro-duction* (Philadelphia, 1842).
7 »Friedrich Spielhagen's Gruß,« 3.
8 Griswold, *Poets and Poetry of America*, »Preface,« unpaged.

and idealism have a difficult time (this from a man who had just translated Emerson): »Der Aufschwung des geistigen Lebens in Amerika wird vorläufig von den Fesseln eines geistlosen, unbarmherzigen Materialismus darnieder-gehalten«; poetry is a necessary reaction against the »brutale Herrschaft der physischen Kraft ... des Verstandes,« »ein sehr fragliches Lob,« to be sure. Religion, he adds characteristically, is the death of lyric poetry; only works that are emancipated from religion can be called art (*VS*, 340–48). Much of this falls into the imagological category of preconceived notions of the foreign other; it rather confirms Spielhagen's theoretical view that one does best to write about what one knows.

Later in life he became more appreciative of American writing. He quite liked Mark Twain, one is relieved to discover; unfortunately, Spielhagen was inspired by him to a leaden discourse on humor (*AmSt*, 181–98). The rise of reputation of Bret Harte is noted (318). Two other writers caught his particular attention. One was the Norwegian-American Hjalmar Hjorth Boyesen (1848–95), like Spielhagen a writer who enjoyed a considerable reputation in his own time that has all but disappeared today. He was pro-fessor of northern European literature, later of German, at Cornell, writing popular studies on Goethe, Schiller, and other German topics.[9] Spielhagen was among the writers he praised, noting especially his objective theory of the novel. Boyesen declared, as other American observers did, that his novels »are to my mind the most valuable and faithful chronicles of German life and thought during the last quarter century that we possess.«[10] Spielhagen took Boyesen up, despite the fact that, while acknowledging Spielhagen as a democratic writer, Boyesen had written an unfriendly review of *Ultimo* in the *North American Review*.[11] Spielhagen translated Boyesen's »The Story of an Outcast«[12] and opened the pages of *Westermanns* to him for an essay on literary life in the United States.[13] He praised Boyesen's objectivity and

---

[9]   See Clarence A. Glasrud, *Hjalmar Hjorth Boyesen* (Northfield, MN, 1963); Robert S. Fredrickson, *Hjalmar Hjorth Boyesen* (Boston, 1980).
[10] Hjalmar Hjorth Boyesen, *Essays on German Literature* (New York, 1892), 258.
[11] [Boyesen], [review of *Ultimo*]. I am not sure that Spielhagen knew that Boyesen had written this, as the review is unsigned.
[12] As »Glitzer-Brita,« with introduction, *Westermanns Monatshefte* 46 (April-Septem-ber 1879): 673–90. Spielhagen published this translation, along with one of »The Man Who Lost His Name,« in *Engelhorn's allgemeine Roman-Bibliothek* (Stuttgart: Engelhorn, 1885). An advertisement in the front matter asserts: »Daß *Friedrich Spielhagen* es für der Mühe wert gehalten hat, diese Novellen selbst zu übersetzen, ist wohl die beste Gewähr für deren ungewöhnliche Bedeutung.«
[13] Hjalmar Hjorth Boyesen, »Literarisches Leben in den Vereinigten Staaten,« *Wes-termanns Monatshefte* 48 (April-September, 1880): 447–57; 50 (April-September, 1881): 383–93.

admired particularly his exposure of the corruption of American life by the spirit of business, achieved through the perspective of »seine normännische Geradheit und Ehrlichkeit« (*NB*, 173, 180). Boyesen was a clever and sensible man who developed a felicitous style in his assiduously learned American English, but there is no hope of reviving admiration for his idealistic, sentimental, indifferently structured fiction.

Matters are rather different with the other American who caught Spielhagen's attention, »Julien Gordon,« the pen name of Julie Grinnell Storrow, a grandniece of Washington Irving, who was known in private life by her first married name, Julia van Rensselaer Cruger (died 1920). Like Boyesen, she enjoyed a vogue in her time that has since vanished, but, unlike Boyesen, she has so thoroughly vanished that it is difficult to find out anything about her; for example, although I have learned that she was born in Paris, I have been unable to find out the year.[14] This obscurity seems a pity, as she strikes me as a much better writer than Boyesen, a cosmopolitan, witty, pointedly feminist, high-society novelist; she was evidently quite wealthy, experienced from Manhattan to Oyster Bay and in foreign capitals from Paris to St. Petersburg; she knew French, Italian, German, and later Russian. A set of fan letters following her novel, *A Diplomat's Diary* (1890), indicates how enthusiastic readers could become about her.[15] The novel consists of the diary entries of an aging, ironically pompous Austrian ambassador at the Russian court who falls absurdly in love with a beautiful American girl who could be one of Henry James's innocents abroad.

Spielhagen praised this work, along with *A Puritan Pagan* (1891), a story of how a very fine but morally severe young woman is urbanely and painstakingly mentored to a reconciliation with her decent, devoted husband, who has revolted her with a fleeting infidelity (186–87). Julien Gordon's *fin-de-siècle* finesse, her sexual and social knowingness, make Spielhagen's interest in her in his late phase particularly intriguing. His translation of *A Diplomat's Diary* appeared under the girl's name, Daphne, perhaps for commercial reasons, even though the novel is focused on the inner life of the

---

[14] My main sources have been an entry in the *National Cyclopaedia of American Biography* (Clifton, NJ, 1893-), 14: 160–61, under her second married name, Julia Chance, which cites Spielhagen's praise of her, and a brief but pithy obituary, »Julien Gordon, dies. Widow of Col. S. Van R. Cruger and ex-Wife of Wade Chance, Wrote Vampires,« *New York Times* (July 13, 1920): 11.

[15] »Some Letters to Julien Gordon,« *Lippincott's Monthly Magazine* 47 (January-June, 1891): 652–57. Since Lippincott was her publisher, these are obviously advertising materials.

curmudgeonly, painfully self-aware ambassador.[16] Spielhagen also translated the novella *Mademoiselle Réséda*,[17] published together with *Vampires* in 1891; it tells of how worldly-wise and somewhat *ennuyées* ladies observe a young woman capture an artist, or vice versa.

Americans appear, of course, in Spielhagen's novels. As is often the case with German writers, they frequently turn out to be Germans or some kind of Central Europeans, such as »Smith,« the returned forty-eighter in *Ein neuer Pharao* who cannot adapt to the moral environment of the Reich and goes back to America. The actual Americans here are the rapacious Curtis,[18] a former slave dealer and, as it emerges, murderer and cannibal; his stupid wife, the only person Curtis loves; his son Ralph, professor of German at Columbia, who is in feeble health; and his rebellious daughter Anne, who ends up as a nihilist and would-be terrorist. Perhaps one will note here parallels to the fictional pattern of the Jewish family, particularly the strong ruthless father contrasted to the well-meaning, idealistic but physically impaired son, who dies in the course of the novel, along with the various plans of German aristocrats to marry the allegedly rich Americans. Observers have occasionally noted a structural similarity of European anti-Americanism to anti-Semitism.[19] The common denominator is the lawless ruthlessness of finance capitalism. Curtis is engaged in an elaborate, ultimately criminal plot to defraud the German Ilicius with a phony investment scheme. He crows, too soon, as it turns out, that he has outsmarted the stupid Germans (*AR*, 3, 3: 472). In this scheme, Curtis expects the support of the American minister in Berlin, »sonst in geschäftlichen Dingen ein großer Esel« (150). Curtis has no success with this, and a high official warns Ilicius that the minister understands *Faust* better than the affairs of his own country (428).

---

[16] *Daphne. Nach A Diplomat's Diary deutsch bearbeitet von Friedrich Spielhagen*, in *Engelhorn's allgemeine Roman-Bibliothek* (Stuttgart, 1891–92), with the only photograph of the author I have seen. The translation is somewhat abridged, as Spielhagen indicates in his preface (8).

[17] Julien Gordon, *Mademoiselle Reseda*, in the series *Michow-Bücher*, vol. 16 (Charlottenburg, 1898). The Engelhorn series had already published it in 1891 as *Fräulein Reseda*, along with her first novel, *Ein Mann der Erfolge* (*A Successful Man*), but these do not seem to be Spielhagen's translations.

[18] Spielhagen was already familiar with the name from his early translation. Always parsimonious with names, he employed it also for the young American of *In der zwölften Stunde* (*AR*, 2, 1: 387).

[19] See my comments and citations on this in »Zu den Grundlagen des Antiamerikanismus in der deutschen Literatur,« *Alte Welten – neue Welten. Akten des IX. Kongresses der Internationalen Vereinigung für germanische Sprach- und Literaturwissenschaft*, vol. 1, *Plenarvorträge*, ed. Michael S. Batts (Tübingen, 1996), 41–42.

Though nowhere named, this man is undoubtedly Bayard Taylor (1825–78), the prominent American poet who was revered in Germany as the author of the most prestigious translation of *Faust* into English of his time and, in general, as an enthusiast for German literature, and who was United States minister to Berlin from May 1878 to his death in December (see Chapter 15).

In the novel there is a certain ambiguity about the meaning or possibly the threat of America to Germany. The spirited Anne admires American men who retire from military service to civilian pursuits in a country where a backwoodsman can become president (thinking perhaps of William Henry Harrison), and complains of the authoritarian obsequiousness and lack of initiative of German men (183). »Smith« treats Curtis as an aberration and directly confronts him: »Du Auswurf Deiner edlen Nation!« (474). But Anne is an unstable woman, and a voice of liberalism in the novel, Dr. Brunn, tells the idealistic »Smith« that he does not belong in materialistic America; he belongs in Germany, where the ideals of 1848 will be harvested (528). Earlier Brunn has said that Ralph's nervous ailment is typical of the noble American's flight from the worship of money, and »Smith« himself declares that the orgies of greed and selfishness that have engrossed America are now infecting Germany (278, 406). America is the source of the mysterious millions of Lothar Lorenz's aloof mother in *Was will das werden?*, money that Lothar long endeavors to avoid. However, the notion that all Americans are rich can be misleading. When the subproletarian Schulz in *Opfer* learns that a long-lost brother who emigrated to America forty years before is seeking his family through the embassy to share his prosperity, he becomes very excited; his level-headed daughter thinks he is hoping for millions. When the brother sends $1,000 and invites the family to join him on a farm, Schulz is very disappointed; he feels that it is »unerhört ... eine Perfidie, die dicht an Betrug grenze« that his brother is not rich (*NF*, 6: 426–27, 437).

In the earlier comical tale *Die schönen Amerikanerinnen* of 1868 there are, it turns out, no Americans, although at first there appear to be. The first-person narrator, identifiable as a persona of the author, is visiting a wealthy friend, Egbert, at a spa in the Thuringian forest, a setting that permits satire of literary types. Also at the spa is the family of Augustus Lionel Cunnigsby, called the »Jaguar,« allegedly driven from the Confederacy by war, his plantations sequestered; consequently he is short of cash and has to borrow on the strength of a draft on »T. Grauröder« in Berlin (*AR*, 2, 4: 93; obviously we are to think of Bismarck's banker Bleichröder). Hateful at first sight, he is imagined by a guest that he might have been one of Lincoln's assassins (23). He has two daughters, Virginia and Ellen, the latter a great beauty.

The narrator so often reiterates that he cannot possibly be attracted to her because of his wife and children at home that his protestations become totally transparent; however, he loyally mediates a love relationship between Ellen and Egbert and tries to teach Egbert some English so he can speak to her. An opulent Hungarian count appears as a rival suitor, preferred by Cunnigsby. In the course of a number of amusingly trite recognition scenes, these identities begin to disintegrate. The count is revealed to be a confidence man, originally a Viennese »Billardcaspar« (170). Ellen, it turns out, not only spells English poorly but speaks German. At first it is believed that she cannot be the daughter of the horrible American. But then it turns out that Cunnigsby, first exposed as the perpetrator of a swindle in Berlin under the name of Jones and then as a fugitive threatened by legal action in New York, was originally a German tailor named Gottlieb Lebrecht König who had emigrated in 1857 and, in one of Spielhagen's patented narrative coincidences, is the long-lost brother of a local artisan. So as not to compromise the union of Egbert and Ellen (properly called, it now appears, Lenchen), Spielhagen has »Cunnigsby« escape, leaving behind a message that his current name will be »Philip Phillips aus Boston« (200–07).

Although the rapacious, indeed, criminal Cunnigsby turns out to be a German, he is still perceived as an American, particularly a Southern one; he clearly prefigures the native American Curtis in *Ein neuer Pharao*. A common way of articulating reservations about America was to refer to slavery. One might think here of the odious Sonnenkamp of Auerbach's *Das Landhaus am Rhein*, which appeared prepublication in the *Neue freie Presse* in the same year as Spielhagen's story;[20] he is a *ci-devant* American Mormon slave trader, originally from Warsaw, who carries in a ring a tooth he has taken from a slave he has strangled.[21] The narrator of *Die schönen Amerikanerinnen*, amazed that Cunnigsby would force his daughter to a liaison with the dubious count, muses: »was weiß ein Sclavenzüchter von Ehre und Rechtlichkeit« (177). He recalls Longfellow's treatment of a similar case »in einer kleinen, schauerlichen schönen Ballade ... wie ein Pflanzer seine Tochter an einen Sklavenschiffscapitän verkauft,« then cites, without further identifying it, the penultimate stanza of »The Quadroon Girl« from *Poems of Slavery* (1842):

> But the voice of nature was too weak;
> He took the glittering gold!

---

[20] Thomas Scheuffelen, *Berthold Auerbach 1812–1882*, *Marbacher Magazin*, Sonderheft, 36 (1985): 81.

> Then pale as death grew the maiden's cheek,
> Her hands as icy cold (178).[22]

Thus the association of Americans with the inhumane pursuit of profit and wealth remains intact despite the exposure of Cunnigsby's German identity.

The other text in which Americans appear as Germans is the historical novel *Deutsche Pioniere* of 1870, a work that has puzzled me and that I am not fully able to explain. The story takes place during an episode of the French and Indian War in 1758 in the area around Oswego, New York. Except for a friendly Colonial official named Brown, all the important characters are German settlers. The plot concerns a farmer named Lambert Sternberg, equipped with »die großen, blauen, guten deutschen Augen« (411), who, on a visit to the city, observes the debarkation of starving German immigrants, among them a very thin but finer-featured, beautiful girl, Katharine Weise, whose father, a pastor, has died on the voyage, and whose indenture contract Lambert purchases from the avaricious shipmaster. Needless to say, Lambert and the courageous, trustworthy Katharine are eventually joined, though not before disruptions caused by the attack of the French and the Indians on the settlement and by the rivalry of Lambert's brother Konrad, a hot-tempered giant who lives with Indians (in fact, he is a better Indian than the Indians themselves [453–54], calling inescapably to mind Karl May's Old Shatterhand).

Deutsche Pioniere is not a very distinguished novel, certainly not one to recommend to a reader with little knowledge of Spielhagen. But it is unexpected and enigmatic for three reasons. First, he was opposed to historical fiction on theoretical grounds. The requirements of historical exactness, he complained, resulted in puppetizing statues (*BT*, 15–16). Historical novels, he scoffed, give information as though they were doctoral dissertations (*VS*, 214). He cited with approval Auerbach's dismissal of the historical novel as »eine Willkürlichkeit, in der Bibliothek erzeugt« (*AmSt*, 263 n.). Doubtless Spielhagen was reacting against the mode of the scrupulously researched, professorially footnoted historical romance that was becoming a fashion in his time. Second, he was insistent that fictional characters should be modeled on people one has known. There is no obvious way to do this when

---

[21] Berthold Auerbach, *Das Landhaus am Rhein*, in *Schriften*, 2nd ser. (Stuttgart, 1871). Göttsche, *Zeit im Roman*, 729, has also made this connection. Curtis in *Ein neuer Pharao* twenty-one years later may also be in this descent, though he is a native American.

the setting is in the past (*AW*, 105). Thus, any modern novel must take place in the present (*BT*, 58). He wrote only two historical novels himself, *Deutsche Pioniere* and *Noblesse oblige*, though it must be said that both his efforts dispense with learned apparatus and erudite disquisitions, allowing setting and circumstance to emerge from his »objective« devices. The American novel reaches farther back into the past than any other fiction he attempted. Third, the German novel about America was a mode that was growing passé. It was in large part impelled by a decades-long, often disputatious public concern about the emigration. Although the emigration was not to reach its peak until 1882, the increased confidence of Germans in themselves after unification caused the worry and the debate about it to recede. The last important nineteenth-century German novel about America of my acquaintance, Gerstäcker's posthumous *In Amerika*, appeared in 1872. With so many disincentives, one wonders why Spielhagen, who was not in need of projects to fill up his time, published such a novel in 1870.

A further puzzle is where he got his information. Some of the environmental description suggests an influence from Cooper,[23] and he refers in passing to Charles Sealsfield's *Lebensbilder aus beiden Hemisphären* (from whom the heroic defense of a blockhouse in Chapter 15 might have been taken), and to Gerstäcker's *Die Regulatoren in Arkansas* (*NB*, 41). But, although Spielhagen is reported to have told a German-American inquirer that the novel was »völlig erfunden,«[24] it is quite exactly detailed, down to the stages of the French attack on the settlements and the fort, as well as to the correct names of the French commander, Belletre, and a local officer called here variously Herkheimer and Herckheimer, »ein rechter Israelit, in dem kein Falsch ist« (*AR*, 2, 4: 471, 537), but known to American history as Nicholas Herkimer (1728–77), who, as a brigadier general, died a hero's death on the battlefield in the Revolutionary War.[25] But at the time of the events of the novel he was a captain in the militia, nowhere nearly as prominent as he was to become later; nor does the whole episode loom large in

---

[22] Cited verbatim. See Henry Wadsworth Longfellow, *The Complete Poetical Works* (New York, 1902), 28.

[23] Julian Schmidt, in the revised and expanded version of his essay in *Westermanns Jahrbuch*, previously cited, in *Neue Bilder aus dem Geistigen Leben unserer Zeit* (Leipzig, 1873), 241, remarks that Cooper »dieselbe Zeit und dieselben Orte schildert« (ibid.), but he could not have supplied the details of the novel.

[24] Henning, *Friedrich Spielhagen*, 167.

[25] Herkimer County in New York was named for him. A couple of my ancestors when serving under him had an adventure that got into the history books and thence into a youth novel.

general histories of the war.[26] After a good deal of searching and inquiry, I managed, more by luck than skill, to find the source: Friedrich Kapp's history of the Germans in New York State, the first and only volume of a projected history of the German immigration, published in plenty of time for Spielhagen in 1868.[27]

The only explanation for the novel on record was given by Spielhagen's daughter: »In den ›Deutschen Pionieren‹ ist mein Vater im Jahre 1871 schon, also kurz nach dem Kriege, für die erste soviel später begonnene Kolonial- politik eingetreten, da er schon damals klar erkannte, daß das wachsende, starke Deutschland Raum nach außen brauchte.«[28] Although she should know better than we do, I remain skeptical of this explanation. In the first place, she has the date significantly wrong by one year. Since the book was published in 1870, most if not all of it must have been written before the outbreak of the war in July. The date seems too early for colonialist concerns. In an essay taken into the *Neue Beiträge* in 1898, Spielhagen remarks that the Germans are an inland, not a seafaring people, otherwise »unsere Kolo- nialbestrebungen müßten denn mit ganz anderen Erfolgen als bisher gekrönt werden« (*NB*, 42). In a muddled lecture delivered in Vienna in December 1900, »Was unseren Kolonien not tut,« he climbs, as he often does, onto his hobbyhorses, complaining about the foreign occupation of the drama and the novel. Like many Europeans of the time, he does not acknowledge that there are any native peoples in the potentially colonizable territories; he speaks of the virtues and characteristics needed to open up »die Öden des dunklen Erdteils« (*AW*, 203). As for the Germans themselves, they will never start a war. They lack personal initiative and want a »Führer,« preferably of royal blood. The English colonies were strong because of self-reliance:

Nur die Initiative, der Wagemut, das feste Aufsichselbstruhen, welche die Pilgrim- väter aus der Heimat mit in die Urwälder des amerikanischen Ostens nahmen, sich dort eine neue, größere, schönere Heimat zu erkämpfen, ohne jemals einen hilfesuchenden Blick rückwärts zu wenden – wie steht es damit? Wie mit der

---

26 George A. Hardin with Frank H. Willard, *History of Herkimer County New York* (Syracuse, 1893), gives in the first chapter an account that agrees encouragingly with the events in Spielhagen's novel.
27 Friedrich Kapp, *Geschichte der deutschen Einwanderung in Amerika*, vol. 1: *Die Deutschen im Staate New York bis zum Anfang des neunzehnten Jahrhunderts* (Leip- zig, 1868), 159-64. Kapp describes the Battle of Oriskany, where Herckheimer (Herkimer) received his fatal wound, 241–49, and provides a biography of him, 250–53.
28 Antonie Spielhagen, »Zum 80. Geburtstag Friedrich Spielhagens,« *Gartenlaube* [57] (1909): 167. The similar observation of Henning, *Friedrich Spielhagen*, 166, very likely came from her.

Kraft und dem Talent der Selbstregierung, die aus dem kalifornischen Chaos, in welchem Büchse und Revolver die *ultima ratio* waren, in bewunderungswürdig kurzer Zeit ein geordnetes Gemeinwesen machten? (203).

Militarism and authoritarianism will not do it (204). From these fleeting remarks one can surmise that Spielhagen accommodated to the colonialist fervor that beset Germany after unification, but without a great deal of zeal or concern with detail.

One passage in *Deutsche Pioniere* might support the colonialist interpretation: a prayer in which the settlement is said to be »an der äußersten Grenze der von Menschen unseres Stammes bewohnten Erde« (*AR*, 2, 4: 496). But the novel is better understood as a product of the nationalist pressure cooker on the threshold of unification. The war in this rendition is not a conflict between British and French colonial interests but between the decent, peace-loving Germans and the perfidious, aggressive French that just happens to be taking place in North America. Near the beginning, Mr. Brown asserts that the settlers help the English »im beständigen Kampf mit unsern Erbfeinden, den Franzosen«; the »hereditary enemy« is labeled again by Herckheimer (411, 536). He adds the old complaint that the Germans lack unity and don't stick up for themselves. When the settlers become quarrelsome among themselves, Herckheimer observes that freedom does not preclude unity (497), a sentiment of particular relevance to the Germany of Spielhagen's time with its memories of 1848. A patriarchal old farmer, with seventy-year-old memories going back to 1689, denounces the settlers for quarreling while »die fränkischen Wölfe« are marauding in the same way that they murdered his family and burned their house in Heidelberg, and he renews his curse on the »Henker und Mordbrenner« (499–500, 513).[29] But today the German settlers are giant, powerful men, no longer pale, emaciated immigrants (489) and should be able to defend themselves.[30] Katharine reflects that the struggle is »ein ehrlicher Kampf für Haus und Hof, für Leib

---

[29] Cf. Kapp, *Geschichte der deutschen Einwanderung,* 162: »Die Kinder der armen Ansiedler, die vor den Banden der Turennes, Melacs, Villars und wie alle jene Mordbrenner heißen mochten, Sicherheit überm Meer gesucht hatten, mußten vor den Söhnen und Enkeln jener Barbaren dieselben Niederträchten, ja noch Aergeres in der amerikanischen Wildniß erdulden.«

[30] Cf. ibid., 231: »... diese Männer waren im Kampfe mit dem Leben gestählt, ihr starker Arm, ihre treue Büchse hatten ihnen Selbstvertrauen, den Stolz des freien Bürgers eingeflößt, sie hatten durch den kleinen und großen Krieg mit den Elementen gelernt, daß nur der Mensch verloren ist, welcher sich selbst aufgiebt, daß aber der Alles gewinnt, der im rechten Moment sein Alles, sein Leben für seine Sache einsetzt.... In der That, prächtige Leute waren es, hoch vom Wuchs und kräftig von Gestalt.«

und Leben! derselbe Kampf in anderer Form, der ihren alten guten Vater mit seiner ganzen Gemeinde aus Deutschland vertrieben!« (455). A French officer, irritated at having to speak German because none of the settlers speaks French, is a pompous blowhard who runs away after making empty threats (564–65). Five years later, after »der Held des Jahrhunderts, der alte Fritz,« is victorious in the Seven Years War, Herckheimer welcomes »Alles, was deutsch war.« The government official Brown admires the Germans while admitting that Yankees do nothing except for profit. The Germans here are a wall against the French and the avant-garde of Germany; what strength, exclaims Mr. Brown, there is in »dieser Rasse« that has risen from poor immigrant slaves to strong free men: »deutsche Pioniere, wie Mr. Brown sagt, die dem Heere vorausziehen, das nach uns kommen wird.« They wonder whether they will be able to remain German; Lambert and Katharine hope to go back (578, 580, 585, 586, 589); consequently they are less colonists or immigrants than exiles.

Thus Spielhagen's »American« novel is his most immoderately nationalistic, with messages directed to his own time and place, just before the false dawn. It is perhaps not too much of a speculation to suggest that his other historical novel, *Noblesse oblige*, eleven years after the false dawn, indicates a revision of tone. Here, during the reoccupation of Hamburg by the French in 1813–14, patriotism is an important value, but it struggles within the rigidities of the class system; that Minna Warburg's liaison with a French officer turns out to be impossible and she is obliged to marry a cruel, disloyal German patrician hardly constitute a victory. Nine more years later, Spielhagen made a drama out of the material. Here the patriotic feeling and the atrocities of the French are heightened melodramatically, but the cosmopolitan, internationalist hope is also more explicit, expressed by the Huguenot physician Barbeyrac, with his combined identity: »ich bin ein Franzose, den das Schicksal zu einem Deutschen gemacht hat; ich bin ein Deutscher, der ein Franzose geblieben ist«; he declares in one of Spielhagen's programmatic set speeches that the conflict is »ein blutiger Schein, der uns die ewige, sonnenhafte Wahrheit verhüllen will, daß die Brüderlichkeit der Individuen, wie der Völker Endzweck der Menschheit, Ziel ihrer Geschichte, und Liebe der heilige Urgrund ist, in dem sie unerschütterlich wurzelt.«[31] The sequence is emblematic for Spielhagen's forced revision of his allegiances.

---

[31] Friedrich Spielhagen, *In eiserner Zeit* (Leipzig, 1891), 74-75. Barbeyrac also has the last word in the tragedy: »... ich höre einen Jubelsang durch die Ferne der kommenden Jahrhunderte. Er schallt zum Himmel empor von der Erde, die keine sich hassenden Völker mehr kennt, – nur Menschen – Menschen nach dem Ebenbilde Gottes, der die Liebe ist« (139).

10. Women, *Femmes fatales*, Love, and the Erotic

> In ihm haben wir den ersten ausgesprochen modernen
> Romanschriftsteller ..., der sehr eingehend sich mit
> dem Wesen der Frau und seinen verschiedenen Typen
> befaßt hat.
>
> Ella Mensch, *Er lebt noch immer!*

The most absurd event we know of in Spielhagen's literary career occurred
in 1881, when the newspaper serializing his novel *Angela* was confiscated for
what were taken to be lesbian insinuations in one episode; this in turn led
to a brisk, fictionalized satire of the courtroom proceeding by Eduard Engel,
directed against the censorship but even more against Spielhagen himself as
a long-winded bore who could not possibly titillate anyone.[1] *Angela* is a not
very successful novel about the frustrated love of a beautiful young woman
for Arnold, a married artist, while she is listlessly courted by Edward, an
emotionally subdued Irish aristocrat, son of Lady Ballycastle, a preposter-
ously raging and despotic madwoman, who, it turns out, shot her husband
to protect her lover, Edward's actual father, and so forth. The incriminated
passage would be unlikely to capture anyone's attention today. In it Angela
is embraced by the artist's wife, the flighty, emotionally unmoored Nanni,
who needs comfort and support:

> Sie war vor Angela, die sich auf das Sofa gesetzt hatte, niedergesunken und
> drückte den vollen Busen gegen deren Kniee. Das üppige blonde Haar, das sie
> eben, um es anders zu arrangieren, aufgebunden, umfloß sie wie ein goldener
> durchsichtiger Mantel.... Sie hatte, sich aufrichtend, Angela beide Arme um den

---

[1]   Eduard Engel, »Stenographischer Bericht über die Gerichtsverhandlungen im Prozesse: ›Angela.‹ Roman von Friedrich Spielhagen,« *Magazin für die Literatur des
In- und Auslandes* 50 (1881): 399–404, 413–17. On this episode, see Hellmuth
Mojem, »Literaturbetrieb und literarisches Selbstverständnis: Der Briefwechsel
Wilhelm Raabes mit Eduard Engel,« *Jahrbuch der Raabe-Gesellschaft* (1995):
63–64; Gabriele Henkel, *Studien zur Privatbibliothek Wilhelm Raabes. Vom
»wirklichen Autor,« von Zeitgenossen und »ächten Dichtern«* (Braunschweig, 1997),
117; cf. Spielhagen's own wry commentaries, *AW*, 192.

Nacken geworfen und küßte sie auf Haar und Stirn und Lippen mit bacchantischer Wut.

Ein sonderbar unheimliches Gefühl, wie sie es noch nie empfunden, überkam Angela. Ihr war, während sie, atemlos unter den wütenden Küssen, die Augen in seltsamer Beklommenheit schloß, als sei es Arnold, der sie in seinen Armen halte. Ein Schauer des Entzückens und Entsetzens zugleich durchrieselte sie – nur einen Moment; dann hatte sie mit einer gewaltsamen Anstrengung Nanni von sich gedrängt.... (*AR*, 2, 6: 361–62)

The sudden, unaccustomed carnal stimulation startles Angela and she repels it as ugly, scorning the saucy Nanni as impure. But later, feverish with sexual imaginings, Angela nearly yields to Arnold, sighing »Männerküsse, das ist noch ganz etwas andres« (378), before repelling him in a delirious rage, recoiling in disgust from the carnal surge, his and her own. By Victorian standards, these scenes may be somewhat venturesome; as will be suggested in the next chapter, there may be a French connection, if not to the text itself, then to the distress it caused in the public sphere.

Of course, there are no explicit sex scenes in Spielhagen's fiction; he once remarked that he did not, like some others, wish the intimacies in Fontane's *Effi Briest* more detailed, though not out of prudery, and he fulminated against what he regarded as French pornography, though also allegedly not out of prudery (*NB*, 104, 156–57; *VS*, 325). But a certain erotic excitement and fascination is detectable in many places; in this respect he may be close to a boundary of the conventional in the Victorian age. He once commented that all poets must be sensual like Goethe, Heine, even Schiller, not chaste like Lessing, who was, therefore, not a poet (*FuE*, 2: 407), and in another place he remarked quaintly that the writer must be scientifically informed about the physiology of love (*NB*, 231). Female forms are perceptible under clothing in many places. In fact, there is a touch of same-sex desire in *Ein neuer Pharao*, where Marie embraces Anne Curtis, »dessen herrliche Formen das feine Nachthemd kaum verhüllt,« though Anne responds with the countenance of Medusa, thinking only of her passion for the mad radical Selk (*AR*, 3, 3: 485), and in the girlhood of the narrator of the last novel *Frei geboren*, leading again to heterosexual desire (*NF*, 7: 26–27, 31). Early in his career Spielhagen picked up a little income with translations of Michelet, beginning with *L'Amour* (1858) and *La Femme* (1859), his »bizarre essays on woman,«[2] which might serve as unwitting parodies of the fabled patriarchal combination of the worship of and con-

---

[2]   Linda Orr, *Jules Michelet: Nature, History, and Language* (Ithaca and London, 1976), xiii.

descending guidance of the incompetent, formless female self. Fortunately, Spielhagen was not much influenced by »dem hyperidealistischen Michelet,« even while admiring his *esprit*. Of course, the success of *Die Liebe*, which was taken into Reclam's *Universalbibliothek*, was not displeasing (*FuE*, 2: 322–23). Spielhagen did point out in a review that »fast überall erscheint die Frau als sklavisch abhängig von den Einflüssen der eigenen Organisation; fast überall unter der Botmäßigkeit der Naturgewalten,« therefore necessarily under the strict guidance of a husband, who makes her into an idiot (*VS*, 264–65); these and other peculiarities he ascribes to the foreignness of the French character. Antoinette in *Frei geboren*, dismayed at being pregnant by her husband, thinks of Michelet's extensive and morbid lucubrations on »le travail de la maternité« (*NF*, 7: 376).[3]

Minna in *Noblesse oblige* patterns herself on Rousseau's Julie, who yields to her lover; she renounces the horrible book but keeps on reading (*AR*, 3, 2: 147–49, with several substantial quotations in translation). Spielhagen apparently did not hold the common view that cultivated women were incapable of sexual arousal, as he would have seen propagated by Michelet.[4] Becky Lombard in *Herrin* is determined to control her sexuality and use it only as a snare, yet finds herself lusting for the man she would like to capture (*NF* 4: 425). Valerie in *Sturmflut* explains her submission to the demonic Giraldi by a heart »das nach einer höchsten Lust begehrlich verlangte« so that she was »in Herz und Phantasie ohne Zucht und Scham« (*AR*, 1, 9: 204). For all that this account is submerged in a rhetoric of sullied purity and retrospective shame, it still acknowledges female sexual arousal. Later in that novel, in the midst of the storm, Carla von Wallbach responds erotically when the lecherous Count Golm kisses her passionately – »Du Wilder« – and when, even after having made her suspicious by his evident evasion of her demand that he promise marriage, he hauls her onto his horse, »sie warf sich wie eine Bacchantin rückwärts, ihn mit beiden Armen umschlingend: Mit Dir! mit Dir! nimm mich! nimm mich! Ich bin Dein, Dein, Dein!« (373, 376). Only when she recognizes his selfishness and cowardice in failing to protect her from the storm is her passion quelled, to his enraged frustration. As has been noted in Chapter 3, not only the philistines were made uneasy by Spielhagen's erotic tone.

The question of the value he accorded to the erotic is more difficult. He seems suspicious of passion; the erotic can be intense, but it does not

---

[3] See Jules Michelet, *L'Amour, Œuvres complètes*, ed. Paul Viallaneix et al. (Paris, 1971–82), 18: 126–31.

[4] Michelet, *L'Amour*, 120.

endure. Antoinette in *Frei geboren* is not the only one to suspect that love is stupid or perhaps an illness (*NF*, 7: 232–33, 268). Roderich's correspondent in *Mesmerismus* agrees with him that it is unimaginable that any man could see his inamorata without loving her, but then adds the sabotaging thought that hundreds of men have seen her without loving her; later Roderich curses »[d]as Gaukelspiel der Liebe, mit dem uns ein Teufel narrt, bis er uns in seiner Hölle hat« (5: 294, 346). The passion of Count Wilfried for the proletarian Lotte is subjected to a great deal of skepticism throughout *Opfer*, not least by Lotte herself, who extricates herself from the impossible mésalliance by escaping to America. Oswald in *Problematische Naturen* is remarkable not only for his magnetism to women but also for the brevity of these intense liaisons, of which Spielhagen said ruefully that they would have been all right for an opera (*FuE*, 2: 444–45). Ottomar von Werben in *Sturmflut* is quite intimidated by the passion of his beloved Ferdinande, beset by »ein Grauen vor der Glut, die ihn umloderte, eine Empfindung, wie der Ohnmacht, gegenüber einer Leidenschaft, die mit der Allgewalt eines Sturmes ihn umrauschte und erdrückte« (*AR*, 1, 8: 287). In *Ein neuer Pharao*, the American Amazon Anne Curtis, after having sex with the would-be revolutionary Selk, almost scares him to death; the short-lived erotic frenzy vanishes and he looks at her like a lion tamer who knows he will be ripped to pieces. When she offers to support him as a terrorist, he is torn between hate and lust for her (3, 3: 380–81, 395–98). Another sexual predator of this kind is the Greek woman Isäa in *Uhlenhans*, who offers sex to her husband's friend Axel, a »blonder deutscher Dummkopf,« if he will help her escape, but is so cold-blooded about it that Axel begins to feel she is too dangerous (2, 7: 307, 363).[5] Angela, who has nearly yielded to Arnold, recognizes, shortly before she intentionally sacrifices her life while saving one of his children from drowning, that he had always been »[e]in Trugbild ihrer Phantasie von dem Manne, den sie lieben könnte« and she perceives a morally empty universe: »sie sah den Himmel, wie er ewig war und ewig sein wird: ein hohles Nichts; und darunter die platte öde Erde, über welche Schatten huschen, die sich Menschen nennen und es tragen, daß sie geboren sind, um zu sterben und zwischen Wiege und Grab den nichtigen Kampf um ein nichtswürdiges Dasein zu kämpfen« (2, 6: 433–34),

---

[5] That Isäa, who has escaped to England after her husband has been murdered by her Greek stalker, marries a duke nicknamed »Lovelace« on account of his »tausend Skandalgeschichten« (*AR*, 2, 7: 432–43) I take to be a little literary joke on Spielhagen's part alluding to the great influence of Richardson's *Clarissa Harlowe* on the *Goethezeit*.

rather strikingly antiidealistic sentiments for an author of Spielhagen's provenance and theoretical claims.

An experienced man in the ironically titled *An der Heilquelle* observes that marriage cannot realize the dreams invested in it and must lead to disappointment (3, 1: 134), an insight that undergoes numerous variations in the novels. In *Selbstgerecht* marriage is defined as two heads on one pillow with their thoughts far away and as two hearts neither of which is aware how their beat differs (*NF*, 5: 174); in *Was die Schwalbe sang* there is a lengthy debate as to whether love and marriage are compatible, in which one of the opponents asserts that the unrealized dream of love makes marriage a hell (*AR*, 2, 3: 39). Spielhagen's views on sexual deviance seem to have evolved. Sara Gutmann of *In Reih' und Glied*, who becomes a royal courtesan, appears as a cruel intriguer who repudiates her illegitimate son and wishes she had killed him at birth (1, 7: 407). Georg Hartwig in *Hammer und Amboß*, who gets inveigled into a sexual interlude with the gypsy-like, disingenuously promiscuous Konstanze, illegitimate daughter of Malte von Zehren, only to be abandoned by her for a better placed man, feels sullied, condemned never to have a pure love relationship, though of course he does (1, 4: 132). Adultery is the sourly tragicomic theme of the novella *Mesmerismus*, a version of the old story of a man's affair with the young wife of an elderly husband. After their intimacy, the lover declares that they are man and wife without a priest, but she, thinking perhaps of Schiller's Luise Miller, postpones their union to the afterlife (*NF*, 5: 353); she does indeed die, with her unborn child, of what seems to be a willed heart attack, after which her lover shoots himself, melodramatically enough, although the atmosphere of morphine visions at the end indicate a convergence with a kind of decadence. In his play *Gerettet* of 1884 the adultery of the Baroness Leonore in the past turns out in a fairly conventional way to be a nemesis that exposes her to extortion and endangers those she loves, whom she can only extricate by taking poison. Nevertheless, a liberalization of the sexual code becomes detectable in the late work, particularly in *Frei geboren*, where the unhappily married Antoinette reminisces about near-adulterous affairs, first one with a traveling young man, and then an experience she recalls as »der Höhepunkt und die Quintessenz meines Daseins« (7: 325) with a Count Werneck, introduced by a fellow officer who dismissively comments to him on marriage with reference to *Die Wahlverwandtschaften*: »Das bißchen Ehe, Herr Baron in den besten Jahren, mit Ihrer fischblütigen Frau Gemahlin kann euch doch wahrlich nicht genieren« (331). At first Antoinette thinks Werneck a would-be poet, the man she has been searching for, and her husband encourages the liaison because a count is an ornament to a bourgeois household (339). But when she declares her desire for an open relationship without secrets, like so many of Spielhagen's men he grows timid, thinks of his career and the disapproval of his parents; Antoinette is also shocked at his Bismarckian militarism, so contrary to her beliefs (347, 349), and, in fact, he dies on the battlefield.

Interestingly, she tries for a time to be friendlier to her husband – it seems that the prospect of adultery has improved her character – but he is frightened, fearing a trap, and when she gets pregnant, she is ashamed at having had sex with him, feeling that she has betrayed her lover, then later perceives her unwanted pregnancy as the wages of sin (361, 375, 377). The motif is prefigured in *Noblesse oblige*, where Minna is ashamed of having had sex with her husband as disloyalty to her beloved, wonders if she can love a child if he resembles the despised father, and blames herself for infidelity in spirit when the baby dies (*AR*, 3, 2: 349–50, 377, 396–97). She, too, breaks with her husband and joins herself to her beloved French officer, who dies attempting to save her husband from a shipwreck. When Antoinette surprises her husband in an embrace with her sister-in-law Jane, she finds the situation comic, but, more upset than she thought, she falls on a step, the last event of her life, as it seems to her, for she never leaves her room afterward (*NF*, 7: 382, 385).

One motif very familiar from the literary tradition is marriage arranged for financial reasons. There are many examples of this and they go in various directions: aristocratic men trading status for Jewish wealth, women escaping from indigence, children coerced by parents. The paradigmatic case is Melitta von Berkow in *Problematische Naturen*, sold to her husband to cover her father's debts. Sometimes these patterns are familiarly sentimental but in other places, as in the late *Faustulus*, they imply a touch of cynicism about the way of the world. Such arrangements may be extramarital. In *Ein neuer Pharao*, Count Axel tries to buy Stephanie by paying her husband's debts; »elle l'a voulu,« shrugs Stephanie's pragmatic brother (*AR*, 3, 3: 255). The fairy princess Isabel in *Sonntagskind* cannot marry her faithful lover Justus, as she claims she would prefer to do, because he is too poor, so marries a Baron Axel instead, whose name she dislikes, so calls him »Daxel« (»*What is there to be done?*«) (*NF*, 1: 238–44); ultimately, as the baron's prosperous widow, she marries Justus, but to no lasting happiness, as we shall see. Another motif that recurs in several places is the sexless marriage, either a »white,« celibate marriage by design or the result of an estrangement between husband and wife; in either case, the situation is not a healthy one. In Chapter 12 we shall see an important example of a white marriage in *Allzeit voran*. Sexually disturbed, sometimes sexless marriages, often providing occasion for adultery, occur in *Angela, An der Heilquelle, Was will das werden?, Susi, Zum Zeitvertreib, Faustulus,* and indirectly in *Was die Schwalbe sang.* Minna in *Noblesse oblige* tries unsuccessfully to maintain a sexless marriage in order to keep her mean-spirited husband focused on patriotism (*AR*, 3: 2, 261–64). Ulrich von Randow in *Stumme des Himmels,* who has fallen in love with the beautiful Eleonore Ritter he has met at the shore, ceases to sleep with his cool, businesslike wife, who has let him down because she did not keep pace with him in expanding her *Bildung,* she herself feels she has been »bildungsunfähig« and pathetically thinks of learning English and French to surprise him (*NF*, 2: 224, 254, 345, 350). In a partial reconciliation, the sexual relationship is restored, but without love (382). Eleonore eventually gives herself to Ulrich, but it all ends in inevitable tragedy. Ulrich is a sad case, but his stubborn selfishness and his hardness to his innocent wife distance him from the reader. The motif of the wife who cannot reach to her husband's *Bildung* recurs in several places, such as *Selbstgerecht* (*NF*, 5, 150–51), and becomes critical, as we shall see in Chapter 19, in *Zum Zeitvertreib.*

Spielhagen has sometimes been criticized for submerging his political and social concerns in conventional plotting concerned with private life, love stories, the founding of families, and so forth. But this is the substance of most realist novels of the international Victorian age and part of a literary-historical development. It has been pointed out recently that the novel of contemporary time evolves »durchgängig in der Spannung von privater Sozialität und gesellschaftlicher Sozialstruktur« and that *Problematische Naturen* and *Die von Hohenstein* in particular herald a return to the form of the family novel.[6] Generally speaking, Spielhagen's families are no happier than Tolstoy's; in fact, the skeptical Isabel in *Sonntagskind,* remarking that the realists have brought some light into the darkness of the family, refers to Tolstoy's *Kreutzer Sonata* (*NF*, 1: 396). Doubts about the once firmly believed sacredness of the family cause Lothar in *Was will das werden?* to doubt the sacredness of all other institutions, »ob in denselben nicht ebenfalls der Schein sich breit mache, all das Unheilige zu verbergen, das sich dahinter versteckt« (*AR*, 3, 5: 22). Family members grate on one another; they intrigue against and betray one another; parents and children are unloving to one another; sibling hatred is not uncommon; the marriages formed for loveless reasons are often bitter; divorce becomes increasingly a desire or an option, though as an actual solution it encounters considerable

---

[6]   Göttsche, *Zeit im Roman,* 34, 607.

inhibitions. As one example among many: once Henri von Tuchheim of *In Reih' und Glied* has married his rich Jewish wife, he wants nothing to do with her and fantasizes her death (1, 7: 432, 446). The behavior of the aristocratic Vogtrizes at dinner in *Was will das werden?* reminds the narrator of the feast of Belshazzar; the handwriting on the wall seems imminent (3, 4: 294). Thus Spielhagen's claim that Ibsen was causing the family to degenerate (*BT*, 302) seems as typically dissociated from his narrative practice as his complaint that even qualified critics were falling under the »Bann des koquetten Zaubers« of the French (*VS*, 305).

The convergence of the political and social novel with the family novel results in hundreds of female characters; only typological examples can be adumbrated here. Even if we wanted to violate critical precepts by inquiring about Spielhagen's experience with women and his sexual psychology, we would have hardly any means for doing so. He informs us coyly that he may only hint at his »Herzenserlebnisse« and refers us, in the third person, »auf die Partien seiner Werke, in welchen er die Wahrheit dichterisch zu verwerten und zu verklären versucht hat« (*FuE*, 1: 232); in places one may feel that »verklären« is not quite the right term. Although his poems often recollect passion and loss in something other than tranquillity, there is no way to judge their connection to actual experience, especially since much of the tone is quite derivative of Heine. My guess is that his love experiences as a young man were in no way remarkable, except insofar as they always seem remarkable to oneself, and that he was as loving and faithful a husband as one might wish. He concludes his sketch of the brief amour that lay behind *Auf der Düne* with the observation: »Der Großmut auf Seiten des Weibes, des Kleinmuts auf der des Mannes – eine alte Erfahrung, dadurch um nichts erfreulicher, daß sie schon so alt ist und jeder Tag sie aufs neue bestätigt« (2: 144), not least, one might add, in his own fiction.

What went on in his fantasy life is another matter; it may have been fairly energetic. Since he rarely gives a detailed physical description of his female characters, one cannot say much about his ideal of beauty, except for one point that invites mention by reason of its repetitiousness and possibly its deviation from a conventional norm, especially of German writers: his most beautiful women are regularly provided with gleaming dark, black, or blue-black hair. Examples are Helene von Grenwitz in *Problematische Naturen* (where the bewitching Melitta von Berkow is also dark-haired), Antonie in *Die von Hohenstein*, Konstanze in *Hammer und Amboß*, the second, Jewish Toni in *Der Vergnügungskommissar* (»ein prachtvolles, dunkeläugiges, schwarzhaariges Geschöpf« [*AR*, 2, 8: 313]), Katharine in *Deutsche Pioniere*, Minna in *Noblesse oblige*, Anne Curtis in *Ein neuer Pharao*, Baroness Kardow in *Selbstgerecht*, Lili in *Mesmerismus*, Becky in *Herrin*, and the clear-minded proletarian Lotte in *Opfer*. There the ruthlessly emancipated, aristocratically sporty Ebba, by contrast, has »rotblonde[s] Männerfischerinhaar« (*NF*, 6: 195), obviously a significant feature, as is the Titian hair of the innkeeper's wild daughter Marie in *Selbstgerecht*, »das Modell zu einer Bacchantin oder Mänade,« who is irresistible to sensual men and banished after having sex with a subsequently murdered baron (5: 52, 97, 127); however, in *Sturmflut* the cheery, winsome Miete von Strummin is also red-blonde, while Else von Werben, less breathtakingly beautiful than simply perfect, has chestnut hair (*AR*, 1, 8: 77–78). The blondes, though, are often less valued as coquettes or geese, like Nanni in *Angela* or the disagreeable French tutor Margot, fiancée of the unhappy Dr. Müller in *Sonntagskind* (*NF*, 1: 152). The blonde, blue-eyed, fair-skinned girls in *Platt Land* all look alike to Gerhard, who despairs of telling them apart (*AR*, 2, 5: 37–38); in *An der Heilquelle*, three fair English girls look so much alike that they are known as the »drei Gleichen«; consequently it makes no difference which of them one courts (3, 1: 56–57 and passim). These are not rules, however. Leo's unloved fiancée, Josephe von Tuchheim of *In Reih' und Glied* is black-haired, and the mature, timelessly beautiful but cold and selfish Hildegard in *Quisisana* causes Bertram to exclaim to himself: »so leuchtend das bläuliche Schwarz des vollen Haares« (2, 8: 40). The saintly blind girl Cilli in *Sturmflut* is ash-blonde; the good Stine in *Faustulus* is also blonde. But it would be no surprise to discover that Spielhagen's beloved wife, who was of French descent, had beautiful dark hair.[7] I would not have spent so much time on this matter of hair color if Spielhagen himself had not foregrounded it so insistently. In general one might wonder whether he was resisting a conventional, affirmative iconography of the blonde German woman in her superior purity and elevation.

Before committing ourselves to so congenial an interpretation, we should consider the self-effacing women, such as Christine in *Ultimo*, who through self-sacrifice rescues her wayward, apparently inconstant beloved. A pure type appears in the acrid atmosphere of *Faustulus*. Stine, pregnant by the programmatically amoral Arno, who abandons her for a plainer but wealthier girl, decides to drown herself when she realizes that the love for which she lived was just a game to him and goes to great lengths to make her death appear an accident so that there will be no disturbance of scandal.

---

[7] All I have found is his remark in *AW*, 18, that when she came to Hanover from Thuringia she developed a taste for the people »mit dem schlichten, blonden Haar, den treuherzigen blauen Augen und den staatlichen Gestalten.«

This works pretty well despite some suspicions; the relieved Arno quotes Mephisto to himself –«Sie ist die erste nicht« – and muses that Goethe's Faust was a philistine to be shocked (*NF*, 4, 198). One might be reminded here of Stifter's ideal of a self-sacrificing wife, who allows herself to fall from a hanging bridge so as not to endanger her husband: »Still sich opfernd.«[8] But Stine's choice might be regarded as an act of autonomy, a rational acceptance of responsibility; one might also consider the evident decriminalization of Goethe's Gretchen. It is a more solemn conclusion to her life than Angela's drowning in a mood of frustrated passion and hallucination, and more soberly motivated than Lili's drowning in *Mesmerismus*. The more heroic Minna in *Noblesse oblige*, incidentally, decides that drowning herself before her wedding would be too easy (*AR*, 3, 2: 235).

The coquette is an unambiguously negative figure. This is because she is disingenuous, lacks the frankness and openness that is such a prominent value in Schiller's moral universe and the absence of which has tragic consequences in Kleist's. A woman can get an unfair reputation as a coquette just through independent conduct or by riding with men who are better horsemen than her husband, as happens to Antoinette in *Frei geboren* (*NF*, 7: 253). She can also come to a bad end, like Bertha in *Die Dorfcoquette*, who gets her ears cut off, or Zempin's wife in *Platt Land*, who learned the skills of a coquette and sold herself to him in the hope that he would raise her *Bildung*, but he turned out to be a brute who wanted only sex; she has become an unstable and somewhat lascivious woman. Isabel in *Sonntagskind*, the ultimate coquette *malgré elle*, expects to be the heroine of Justus's novel, but will never forgive him if she is portrayed as »eine raffinierte Kokette ..., *une mondaine furieuse*, eine Männerfischerin« (*NF*, 1: 287), an expression, no doubt, of the uneasiness in her own constitution, blithe on the surface, troubled beneath. The coquette is all the more threatening because men are so simple-mindedly and unobservantly susceptible. In the course of time Isabel grows quite tired of admirers, or so she claims, though she apparently cannot get rid of them: »Die Männer sind durchweg *a nasty set* – weißt Du, was das heißt? – *and really I have no longer patience with them*. Könnte ich sie nur loswerden! Aber das hängt an einem wie Kletten an einem Florkleide« (335). Later, after her marriage, when Justus's friends are still helplessly in love with her, she concludes that men are and remain schoolboys (503). As Spielhagen's social satire develops, some of these creatures can

---

8   Adalbert Stifter, *Die Mappe meines Urgroßvaters, Gesammelte Werke in vierzehn Bänden*, ed. Konrad Steffen (Basel and Stuttgart, 1961–72), 2: 56.

be quite comically portrayed. Kittie of *Stumme des Himmels* mulls the choice »das Heidenröslein zu sein, das sich mit stechenden Dornen umgibt, oder die Lotosblume, die mit gesenktem Haupte schweigend die Nacht erwartet,« depending on the character of the presumably witless male. In consultation with her mother, Kittie chooses »Lotosblume« (2: 290), though the allusions to Goethe and Heine seem a bit beyond her cultural horizon.

The *femme fatale* might be regarded as the superlative degree of the coquette. But Spielhagen is less sure about this type, of which he created too many examples to count. Some of them are quite innocent; like Hedwig in *Allzeit voran* or Isabel in *Sonntagskind*,[9] their enchanted beauty wreaks havoc through no fault of their own. Thus the problem again seems to be with the men, all of whom are declared by Zempin's wife to the visiting Gerhard in *Platt Land* to be motivated by lust and tyranny, which does not prevent her from exposing her breasts to him on another occasion (*AR*, 2, 5: 164, 213, see also 383). Angela is the Loreley type, »nur geboren, Unglück und Verderben zu bringen über alle, die sie liebten! Und war doch selbst so gut und liebevoll und barmherzig« (2, 6: 429–30). Susi, in the novella named for her, who is beyond good and evil, is said by the duke who lusts for her, as in the song popular in my youth, to be too beautiful for one man alone (*NF*, 3: 223). Justus, who has been learning in a sad school, ultimately tells Isabel that men misunderstand her attractiveness, as though it had something to do with them:

> Du hast nur von Natur ein so süßes Lächeln und so glänzende Augen. Da denken die Männer: das gilt ihnen: und ist doch nichts als Deine gottbegnadete Natur, für die Du nicht mehr verantwortlich bist als der Schmetterling für den Glanz seiner Flügel, die Nachtigall für ihren holden Sang, die Rose für ihren süßen Duft. (1: 587)

This effect is particularly pronounced in Isabel's case but not peculiar to it. When the doctor in *Das Skelet im Hause*, angry that his friend has been taken from him by a new wife, fulminates to her: »die Huldinnen mit den sammetweichen unschuldigen Rehaugen und den weißen beringten Nixenhänden – nur zu oft – fast immer – die Gelegenheitsursache zum Ausbruche des Leidens sind« (*AR*, 2, 8: 420), it seems quite clearly to be a problem he has with himself, as is the case with the misanthropic Karl in *Der Vergnügungskommissar*, who would be cheered by the sight of pretty girls at a resort

---

[9] Both Hedwig and Isabel are special cases who will have to be dealt with in more detail in the chapters on those novels. Isabel may also have a French connection, as I shall mention in the next chapter.

»wenn der Gedanke, daß es eben nur schöne Masken sind, die Seele nicht mit Bitterkeit erfüllte« (294). The duke in *Susi*, bewildered by his lust for her, decides she is a »verführerische kleine Hexe« (*NF*, 3: 339). Some *femmes fatales*, however, are actively wicked, intentionally employing their beauty to bewitch, like Clara Vere in Spielhagen's first work, who is said to have the evil eye (*AR*, 2, 1: 9). Even in her case, however, her falseness seems to be a kind of determined curse and she would like to improve her character (94, 146); we shall encounter a similar introspection of the *femme fatale* of *Zum Zeitvertreib* towards the end of Spielhagen's career. Gerhard in *Platt Land* is fairly warned against Maggie as a Loreley (2, 5: 35, 157). Others like her plot for wealth or status, such as Camilla in *Die von Hohenstein*. Of this Becky in *Herrin* is a special case requiring separate treatment. Some are driven to rage by frustrated jealousy, such as Eve Tusky of *In Reih' und Glied*, who offers sex to the besotted Ferdinand if he will kill Leo (1, 7: 304). The most successful of the wicked ones have the advantage of being unsusceptible to love. Isabel, who is not wicked, comes to conclude that she can love no one but herself (*NF*, 1: 394). In the underclass the *femme fatale* becomes a sex-crazed virago, Polish in the case of Albinka in *Sonntagskind*, who is frustrated to rage by her marriage to an older, bookish man; she hates her stepdaughter and nearly rapes the protagonist Justus, who escapes with a knife wound, wondering if he would have remained innocent (229–36). Eventually, seduced by a local man, she dies by drowning, Spielhagen's favorite disposal method (305). Isabel, however, who is said to be poetry incarnate, rather admires Albinka's erotic spunk (432). An American might have a similar character; the hard-riding Anne Curtis, who sleeps with a revolver and gets sexually out of control, is perceived as a »trunkene Bac-chantin« (*AR*, 3, 3: 352).[10]

There is a steady sequence of strong, confident, proud women in the œuvre. They long for men of equal stature, as imagined by Antoinette in *Frei geboren*: »Einer, der einen starken Geist, einen unbeugsamen Willen hatte, den Ehrgeiz und die Fähigkeit, Großes zu leisten«; when she sees Bismarck, whom she dislikes on political grounds, she murmurs, »Voilà un homme,« not failing to note the legend of Napoleon's meeting with Goethe (*NF*, 7: 66, 283). Such men are rarely found. There is an equally long se-

---

[10]   The narrator of *Die schönen Amerikanerinnen* thinks the American girls must be »die reinen Circen.... *As fair in form, as warm, yet pure in heart, love's image upon earth, without....*« (*AR*, 2, 4: 19–20); however, since the girls turn out not to be Americans, the point is blunted. The lines are cited, without attribution, from the prologue to Byron's *Childe Harold's Pilgrimage*.

quence of fops, narcissists, brutal egotists, and philanderers; Antoinette has no better luck. She writes in her diary of her future husband that it is not enough for a man to be beautiful and complains: »Daß so wenig Männer Männer sind!« (150–51). Even before her marriage, after his own mother has warned her against him, she tests him and finds him wanting; he looks like a Viking but lacks courage (218–19, 229). Men seem to need quite a lot of sustaining; Minna in *Noblesse oblige* muses that women must be brave so as not to undermine men in crisis. Her superiority irritates her family and in general she is found superhumanly frightening, but the narrator ascribes to her a powerful brain. After the war she evolves into a wise woman whom the common people would like to have as ruler of Schleswig-Holstein; then they wouldn't need the Danish duke (*AR*, 3, 2: 180–81, 211, 376, 287, 494). Rose of *Röschen vom Hofe* is a quite early example of this type, one of several reasons the story should not be dismissed as a failed *Dorfgeschichte*. Frustrated that she has not been more hostile to an amorous pastor, she gets sarcastic to the repressed count she will inevitably marry about men's alleged higher duties and angry at »die egoistische Starrheit des Männerstolzes«; her own father must bitterly acknowledge her emancipation from him (2, 1: 594, 597, 625, 608).

But this need not only be the attitude of women; as early as *In der zwölften Stunde*, Sven von Tissow, after observing his adored mother's marriage and that of other cultivated women, concludes that they had to suffer »überall ... von der Rohheit, zum mindesten Unkultur der Männer, deren einzige Lectüre oft nur das Amtsblatt und der Rennkalender war« (361). In one of Spielhagen's mock-classical verses, Odysseus acknowledges to Circe the female view of male imbecility often articulated in the narrative works:

> Für euch Frauen sind die Männer,
> Jung und alt, nur dumme Fische;
> Wollt ihr sie, ihr könnt sie haben:

> Für ein Lächeln eures Mundes,
> Für ein Zwinkern eurer Augen,
> Für ein Drücken eurer Finger
> Und dergleichen bill'ge Scherze.

> Denn der Männer *ruling passion*
> Ist die Eitelkeit, und steckt ihr
> Diesen Köder an den Hamen,
> Schnappen zu sie unbesehen. (*G*, 110–11)

Spielhagen nowhere directly addresses, as far as I can see, the women's movement of the later part of the century, but there are numerous deposits

of feminist ideas in his texts, always with a positive valence, though sometimes scorned by unregenerate males, like the duke in *Was will das werden?*,
who speaks dismissively of his illegitimate daughter Adele's »Emanzipations-
ideen«; later a newspaper scorns Ellinor von Vogtriz as a renegade in the
company of »überspannter emanzipierter Frauen« (*AR*, 3, 4: 552; 5: 434). On
the other hand, the inner narrator of *Selbstgerecht* reports himself as saying
to his beloved:

> das gang und gäbe Urteil der Männer über die Frauen ist einfach ein Vorurteil,
> ein unüberwundener Rest von Barbarei, für welche die Inferiorität der Frau ein
> Dogma war. Durch das zähe Kleben an diesem Dogma, durch das hartnäckige,
> hochmütige bornierte Widerstreben der Männer, die Frau an den Vorteilen der
> Bildung vollen Anteil nehmen zu lassen, wird dann allerdings die Frau in dieser
> Inferiorität vorläufig festgehalten. (*NF*, 5: 150–51).

The earliest specific mention of »Frauenemancipationen,« I believe, occurs
in *Alles fließt*, originally published one year later, in 1897, where the movement is paralleled to Stella's artistic emancipation as a poet (*MAF*, 172).
Spielhagen speculated that if Rahel Varnhagen had lived in his time, she
would have given up her salon and become a feminist leader (*AW*, 176).
The theme of the frustration of women with the limitations imposed on
them begins early in the novels and echoes throughout. The clever, observ-
ant Silvia of *In Reih' und Glied* wants to be something in the real world but
feels hindered as a woman, though at one point she tries to go secretly to
a political meeting; the tailor Rehbein, a true revolutionary figure in that
novel, expresses the view that women are »die wahren Sclaven der modernen
Zeit, besonders in den unteren Ständen; aber auch überall sonst« (*AR*, 1, 6:
276, 1, 7: 4–8; 1, 6: 414). Angela rebels against woman's lot, »geboren zum
Dulden und Dienen und Tragen und – Entsagen« (2, 6: 196). Antoinette of
Frei geboren at one point, paraphrasing Goethe's Iphigenie, finds her situation »eine Bestätigung der uralten Wahrheit, daß der Frauen Schicksal
beklagenswert ist«; already in her girlhood she resents the privileges of boys,
especially in learning things that girls could learn as well, like Latin, Greek,
or mathematics, whereas her friend Adele has taken from her teacher, Sister
Ambrosia, detestable like almost all of Spielhagen's religious figures, an enthusiasm for »das ›Ewig Weibliche‹« (*NF*, 7: 376, 28); in *Opfer*, Adele is
shown to have evolved into a good-hearted but silly woman. The high-
strung Hilde in *An der Heilquelle* wishes she had been a man so she could
have gone to the university (*AR* 3, 1: 87). Spielhagen could joke about these
matters, too; when it is suggested that the fluffy Poly in the same novel go
into parliament, a humorless radical begins to discourse on the suffrage
movement in America before he is cut off (55). A couple of Spielhagen's

rhymed aphorisms may not quite meet today's standards of correctness but still suggest that, for his time, he had his heart in the right place:

> 22. Ob der Natur Gesetz es sei:
> Die Frau gehorche blind dem Mann?
> Macht sie von jeder Fessel frei,
> Dann wird sie zeigen was sie kann.

> 23. Ein Fräulein-Doktor? Warum nicht?
> Gelehrsamkeit, sie schändet keinen.
> Und kommt dazu ein hübsch Gesicht,
> Wüßt nicht, weshalb ich d'rum soll weinen. (*NG*, 139)

As usual, Spielhagen's qualities of mind seem to break down somewhat when he turns to literary criticism. His dismissive attitude toward women writers may have some connection to the problem about women readers that I touched upon in Chapter 2. His endorsement of Marie von Ebner-Eschenbach as »zweifellos die größte unter den lebenden deutschen Dichterinnen« seems commendable until we get to his reasons: »sobald der Name *Marie von Ebner* genannt wird, umweht es dich wie Blumenduft aus einem Sommergarten; atmest du in einer Atmosphäre, in der es unerlaubt ist, ein häßliches Wort über die Lippen zu bringen, einer unlauteren Empfindung nachzuhängen« (*NB*, 63, 166, 169). Apart from being condescending, the prissy judgment is absurdly askew for such a thoughtful and penetrating writer, and must be added to the long tally of Spielhagen's critical solecisms, which contrast so oddly with his creative competence.

In his late work, some of his women begin to break out of the conventions limiting them toward more independent possibilities. Many of his female characters express a longing to do so. Eleonore in *Stumme des Himmels* explains that her education in a Lilliputian principality has prepared her for three female possibilities: »Lehrerin, Erzieherin, Gesellschafterin« (*NF* 2, 49). German women began to be teachers in the 1850s and 1860s;[11] the refined Maria von Werin in *Was will das werden?* becomes a private school teacher. In a poem in the mode of what is sometimes dismissed as *Armeleutepoesie*, »Die Lehrerin,« a poor schoolteacher is made to say, with great bitterness: »Und fühle mich eine Königin,« whereas in fact she cares for her sick mother and her sister's orphans, and having been engaged to a man for ten years, forlornly imagines the arrival of the swan boat (*NG*, 107–08). Spielhagen pushes some of his characters beyond this. Christiane

---

[11] Wehler, *Deutsche Gesellschaftsgeschichte*, 3: 405, 1198.

Kempe in *Ultimo* does office work (*AR*, 2, 3: 363). But his main device is to bring his more independent women into a paramedical profession. Midwifery is, of course, a traditional female role, but in *An der Heilquelle* the physician discovers the midwife reading his textbook on pathology, and so they come to be in a certain sense colleagues (3, 1: 250–51). In that same novel, an exposed fake English lady decides, with the practicality of her nation, to become a nurse, and the heroine wonders why she should not do the same (363, 366); in *Selbstgerecht*, a widowed baroness becomes a nurse (*NF*, 5: 194). At the other end of the social scale, Marthe in *Sonntagskind*, in order to escape marriage to a brutal workingman, becomes a nurse, eventually in Berlin's prestigious public-health hospital, the *Charité*, and the upper-class Sibylle would like to imitate her if she were not an invalid, even though the elegant world would think her crazy (1: 204, 273, 578–79).

We must understand this movement toward nursing in Spielhagen's time as an emancipatory step. The desire of the well-born Marie von Alden in *Ein neuer Pharao* to be a nurse is vigorously opposed by her family, which insists that she should be a governess or companion. The doctor tells her that nursing is »*contra naturam*,« no sort of work for a young, blooming girl (she is twenty-nine). Nevertheless, she nurses the dying Ralph like a professional (*AR*, 3, 3: 29, 328, 370). The potential for such skill appears early on, in *Röschen vom Hofe*, where Rose helps the local doctor so well, »[o]hne eine Spur weiblicher Schwäche und Prüderie,« that he calls her his »Herrn Assistenten« and cordially praises her with a kiss of the hand (2, 1: 621–23). But such generosity is not universal. Stine in *Faustulus* has picked up some nursing knowledge from her uncle, an unrespected paramedic, and is therefore sarcastically addressed as colleague by the »Faustian« physician Arno. He scorns her as a goose even though she is useful and efficient in his hospital and radiates healing during a typhus epidemic (*NF*, 4: 47–48, 127, 158–59). The unfashionable, practical wife of Dr. Brandt in *Opfer*, one of Spielhagen's most competent women, has been a nurse and shocks Count Wilfried when he discovers her reading a highly technical medical book (6: 43).

Thus Spielhagen's representations of women exhibit a number of conventional notions and recurrent preoccupations, but also an inquiring spirit, a sense of the variety of human experience, and a lively if sometimes subsurface sensual excitement. In this regard he seems to have remained unperceived, eclipsed particularly by Fontane's reputation as the most sensitive and appreciative portrayer of women. No doubt Fontane deserves the credit, but when one reads on his behalf:

Kaum ein Autor oder eine Autorin hat in der zweiten Hälfte des 19. Jahrhunderts vergleichbar über das Thema Frau und Weiblichkeit geschrieben, kaum jemand sonst hat in diesen Jahrzehnten derart dezidierte literarische Entwürfe fremd- und selbstbestimmten Frauenlebens vorgelegt .... [E]iner der wenigen Autoren, die sich in den 1880er und 90er Jahren überhaupt mit der Frage der Berufstätigkeit von Frauen und der ökonomischen Fundierung weiblicher Emanzipation befassen.... Fontanes ausschließlich positive Akzentuierung des weiblichen Andersseins dürfte innerhalb des männlich geführten literarischen Diskurses über Weiblichkeit wohl eine Ausnahme sein,[12]

then I would like to put up my hand to say that Spielhagen in his own way came as close to what at that time was the frontier in these matters as any German male writer of the age of my acquaintance.

---

[12] Sabina Becker, »Literatur als ›Psychographie.‹ Entwürfe weiblicher Identität in Theodor Fontanes Romanen,« »*Realismus*«? *Zur deutschen Prosa-Literatur des 19. Jahrhunderts,* ed. Norbert Oellers and Hartmut Steinecke, *Zeitschrift für deutsche Philologie* 120 (2001), Sonderheft: 90, 93, 94.

11. Sleeping with the Enemy: Zola and Other Frenchmen

Spielhagen was a wide-ranging reader of contemporary literature and wrote a large body of criticism; probably we do not know all of it, beyond what he himself collected in book form, because it has not been excavated from the periodicals. The objects of his criticism were by no means exclusively or even primarily German. As we have begun to learn, German literary life in the second half of the nineteenth century was broadly cosmopolitan, with widespread circulation of and attention to French, English, and American, but also Scandinavian and Russian publications.[1] But, as there has several times been occasion to observe, his criticism is not noteworthy for its elegance, judgment, or perceptivity. In general, German journalistic criticism in his time was not very distinguished; most of it one would not wish to read except for reception research. One can see in the case of Wilhelm Raabe how maddeningly obtuse and repetitious the critics were decade upon decade, wholly missing the evolution of his narrative inventiveness.[2] The reason for this was the insistently normative character of criticism, endlessly dissertating on how *Dichtung* must be constituted, what it may and may not represent, what formal devices were and were not permissible. In some cases the creative writers, like Friedrich Hebbel, exhibited greater insight and sensitivity than the academics and *Publizisten*, but Spielhagen was not among them, and for the same reason: when he put on his critical hat, it filled his head with all the constrictive normative precepts allegedly derived from the *Goethezeit* that seem only marginally relevant to his creative imagination. It has been said that this stubborn allegiance increasingly isolated him from the other writers of his time.[3] One should not exaggerate the point; he had

---

[1] See Bachleitner, *Der englische und französische Sozialroman*; Bachleitner, ed., *Beiträge zur Rezeption der britischen und irischen Literatur des 19. Jahrhunderts im deutschsprachigen Raum.*

[2] See Jeffrey L. Sammons, *Wilhelm Raabe: The Fiction of the Alternative Community* (Princeton, 1987), 39–40.

[3] Christa Müller-Donges, *Das Novellenwerk Friedrich Spielhagens in seiner Entwicklung zwischen 1851 und 1899* (Marburg, 1970), 1.

extensive connections in the literary world; furthermore, there were some who agreed with him in principle. But it is hard to imagine that he gained many friends through his critical practice.

A substantial part of this body of criticism is directed to French writing. If one were to take one's cues from the gatekeepers of morals and taste in nineteenth-century Germany, one might conclude that French literature and culture were regarded with unremitting horror and detestation. But just as the large body of shrill, sometimes fanatical denunciation of Heine implies his widespread popularity and success in establishing himself in the culture – otherwise, why would one bother? – so the fulminations about French frivolity, immorality, materialism, etc. suggest that French imports may have been widely read and appreciated, and so it was, as we have begun to learn. Spielhagen's attitude toward such matters, as in other matters, seems rather stressed and possibly incoherent. On the one hand, most patriotic Germans felt an instinctive hostility toward the French, the *Erbfeind,* as they were regularly called, including by Spielhagen in *Deutsche Pioniere.* The degenerate Malte von Zehren in *Hammer und Amboß* found his real element in the »Seinestadt,« luxuriating in the arms of a Frenchwoman while the *Erbfeind* ravaged the family estate (*AR,* 1, 3: 371). Nothing loomed larger in negative reception of Heine than his refusal to yield ground to German nationalism and the impression that in politics and morals he was an ally of the French. Twentieth-century experiences have caused the memory of why this was so to fade. For centuries France was the aggressor nation, the unified kingdom stronger than the congeries of German states. Raabe, hardly the most assertive of nationalists, constantly came back to this in his historical fiction: in *Höxter und Corvey,* the French are in the land, invited by German disunity; in *Die Innerste,* »die Franzosen waren im Lande«; in *Hastenbeck,* »die Franzosen waren, wie üblich, im Lande.«[4] Spielhagen, no less than anyone else, longed for a unified Germany that could maintain an even footing with France.

On the other hand, his allegiance to the *Goethezeit* brought with it a sense of shared humanity and international citizenship, and an underlying desire, often far from realized, for a posture of judicious tolerance. At the same time, German writers, rather than rejoicing in the international enrichment of the literary environment, saw the imports as damaging to their interests »in dem nachahmungssüchtigen Deutschland« (*AW,* 44).

---

[4] Wilhelm Raabe, *Sämtliche Werke,* ed. Karl Hoppe et al. (Göttingen, 1960–94), 11: 262–63; 12: 106; 20: 11.

Raabe complained bitterly about the neglect of native writers in favor of foreigners.[5] One can understand that his frustration was motivated by his constant difficulties in maintaining himself with his public and making a living from literature; the affect is perhaps less excusable on the part of the more commercially successful Spielhagen. He complained that Germany was »centrifugal,« drawn to foreign culture and morals (*BT*, 327). In his youth he was persuaded that German novelists could not compete with the English or with French writers such as Sue and Dumas *père* (*FuE*, 1: 71). These competing instincts, it seems to me, do not come to be synthesized, dialectically or otherwise, but ricochet and rattle about in a verbose, jittery, digressive discourse that combats rather than encompasses its object.

He began reading French literature during his days as a tutor; he was repelled by the Romantics, especially Victor Hugo, and disliked all the moderns with the exception of George Sand. Not atypically for German writers of this period, he preferred the English, *Gulliver's Travels* to *Gargantua*; *Tom Jones* to *Gil Blas*; Carlyle's history of the French Revolution to Lamartine's, *Vanity Fair* to *Madame Bovary*. He would even trade George Sand's beloved *Consuelo* for *David Copperfield* (I would, too).[6] The French relate to the English, he feels, as the Romans to the Greeks; in both cases he prefers the latter (*FuE*, 2: 158). The corrupt Sara Gutmann of *In Reih' und Glied* likes only eighteenth-century French novels; Silvia tortures her with Goethe (*AR*, 1, 7: 406). In *Opfer*, Ebba von Falkenburg's habit of reading French novels is similarly a bad sign (*NF*, 6: 54). In a somewhat listless forward to a translation of Madame de Staël's *Corinne*, Spielhagen shows himself at his most conventional in these matters. Declaring that literature is a reflection of the society in which and for which it is written, he asserts that French literature is no longer written to please women with »ein harmonisches, im besten Sinne keusches Gemüth« and has earned the »Vorwurf, die Sympathie der reinlichen Geister verscherzt zu haben und zu verscherzen«; Germans object to »die Frivolität und den Cynismus«; the French by contrast have not generated any of the great ideas of mankind. He exempts Madame de Staël from this appraisal, but mainly in regard to her book on Germany.

5   See Sammons, *Wilhelm Raabe*, 38.
6   The youthful attachment to *Consuelo*, a novel I find almost unreadable, might serve as a base for a more acute literary-historical, psychophilosophical inquiry than is pursued here. In any case it is a reminder that the object of a study such as this will always remain a stranger. Decades later, at a melancholy moment in *Sonntagskind*, Spielhagen has his protagonist cite *Consuelo*, in French (*NF*, 1: 262). He seems to have had a retentive memory for texts.

Corinne he finds overfilled with Italian travel material, doubtless a trite criticism but one with which I cannot help agreeing.[7]

He strove to be fairest to those French writers who seemed most assimilated to the Victorian norms of idealistic-realistic fiction. Among these was the less remembered Georges Ohnet (1848–1918), whose resemblance to Spielhagen has been noted; in his own time he was outsold in Germany by Hugo, Dickens, Sue, and Bulwer-Lytton, and it is not encouraging to learn that Kaiser Wilhelm II praised him at Zola's expense.[8] Spielhagen liked Ohnet well enough, but unfortunately he was one of those French writers who did not know the difference between novel and novella, a hobby-horse Spielhagen rides in what purports to be a review of Ohnet's *Serge Panine* (1881) but in fact is a rambling discourse on the incompetence of French narrative. A drama of Ohnet in which a mother kills her daughter's evil husband, lies about it, and pretends it was a suicide, outraged not only Spielhagen – »Welch brutaler Schlag in das Angesicht – nicht der Philistermoral, sondern – der wahren Sittlichkeit« (*BT*, 292), but also the Berlin police, and now he is in a difficulty, for he certainly cannot approve of censorship; it is too bad, he comments, when the police interfere in aesthetics, and even worse when they are right (292–93, n.).[9]

Another writer for whom he felt an affinity and on whom he published an obituary was Alphonse Daudet (1840–97), every one of whose books Spielhagen read when it appeared, though he knew that Daudet never read one of his (*AW*, 147–48). Each one encouraged Spielhagen to believe that he was on the right path (147); one of these was *Jack* (1876), whose hero becomes a stoker as Georg Hartwig had done in *Hammer und Amboß* before him. With *Fromont jeune et Risler aîné* (1874) one might think of one of Spielhagen's recurrent patterns, radicalized in *Susi*, of the kindly, elderly husband duped by his scornful, *femme fatale* wife. Spielhagen believed that he could oppose Daudet's imagination to Zola's *tempérament* (144).[10] Con-

---

[7] Friedrich Spielhagen, »Vorwort,« *Frau von Staël's Corinna oder Italien*, tr. M. Bock (Leipzig, n.d.), 5–9. I have not been able to learn the publication date. It can be no earlier than 1865, as he refers in a note to a book that appeared that year (7). I expect it is not much later, as the tone and attitude belong to his initial phase; probably it is one of the tasks he took on to earn a little cash.

[8] Bachleitner, *Der englische und französische Sozialroman*, 347, 374.

[9] Spielhagen was necessarily consistent on this matter. For all his doubts about Gerhart Hauptmann, he defended *Die Weber* against government repression (*AW*, 193).

[10] One wonders what Spielhagen would have thought had he known that Daudet subscribed to a nihilist journal, *La Révolte*. Burrow, *The Crisis of Reason*, 196.

cerning Octave Feuillet (1821–90), about whom Spielhagen wrote two essays, he was a little less certain, though again he seems to have read everything. The literary professor Richter in *Sonntagskind*, praising Justus's novel draft for sparing the reader the »tausendste Schilderung des Elendes der Fabrikarbeiter,« comments: »Es könnten aber nicht alle Emile Zolas sein; es müssen auch Octave Feuillets geben,« adding, however, that neither is a great writer. Richter's daughter, Justus's encourager Frau Körner, tells him that he may match Feuillet in elegance, »aber ich weiß, Sie werden sich tiefere Probleme stellen, und sein markloser moralischer Latitudinarismus kann nie der Ihre sein,« observing that a writer can't begin with the baron, like Feuillet, or stop with the baron like Zola (*NF*, 1: 290–92). Feuillet's novel of the social life of the »*upper ten thousand*,« of the »exklusive Welt der geschminkten Korruption und der fragwürdigen Tugend« made Spielhagen uneasy and, employing the mantra he applied to himself, he declared that, despite his art, Feuillet was a *Finder*, not an *Erfinder*, that is, he was merely mimetic, lacking imagination, a great writer in a genre that was not great (*AmSt*, 285, 290, 305). It was Spielhagen's view from his earliest acquaintance: »Seine Erfindungsgabe ist ... nicht eben bedeutend« (*VS*, 287). Within these limitations, however: »Welches Leben, welche Sauberkeit der Analyse, welche Feinheit der Zeichnung« (278). But he accused Feuillet in 1863 of adapting to the imperialism of his nation by giving ground to religion in the interest of Napoleon III's court; he should remember that an empress can grant many things, but not immortality (289–94). I wonder if Spielhagen, in his lengthy, ironic account of Feuillet's *Honneur d'artiste* (*AmSt*, 296–305), saw the comedy of empty people who cannot live without a fortune. He may have noticed, however, that in that novel Feuillet got in a little oblique dig at Zola: of a debauched viscount the narrator observes: »Les psychologues le regardaient probablement comme une victime du déterminisme. Mais, pour le vulgaire, c'était simplement un drôle.«[11]

Spielhagen's most ferocious attack on a French book was directed against *Affaire Clémenceau* of Alexandre Dumas *fils* (1866). It is an epistolary novel written from prison by a man condemned for murder. Much loved in his youth by his widowed mother, he becomes a skilled and successful sculptor who falls deeply in love with a beautiful, Polish-Russian model he first encounters when she is fourteen, Iza (Izabelle) Dobronowska, whose mother turns out to be a ruthless adventuress. He imagines himself to be Pygmalion, but his passion for the shameless, amoral girl turns out to be his

---

[11] Octave Feuillet, *Honneur d'artiste* (Paris, 1890), 65.

undoing; like some of Spielhagen's *femmes fatales*, she is unconscious of her own destructiveness. Toward the end she tells him she was unfaithful out of ennui and just wanted new sensations; Pierre was the only one she loved. She would have been content to be his mistress, and he comes to think, like some of Spielhagen's characters, that marriage was »un acte absurde, mais loyal et sincère,« and that, if it is foolish to marry at all, one need not be so foolish as to marry an exceptionally beautiful woman. He feels that his passion diminishes his art and that women kill artists. When a son, possibly not his, is born to them, Iza refuses to nurse him, and Pierre himself thinks he is not suited to be a father. Anonymous letters denounce his wife; she disappears with one of her lovers and her mother. When she returns, she buys a »hôtel« for two and a half million francs, where she receives fashionable people. Pierre, after demanding that she yield to him sexually one last time, stabs her and gives himself up.[12]

It is a little difficult to make out what enraged Spielhagen so much about this novel. Dumas *fils* is, of course, known as an author of dramas, not of novels, even though he wrote twelve, of which the allegedly autobiographical *Affaire Clémenceau* was the last. Even a specialist on his novels has conceded that »Dumas n'est pas romancier de vocation.« In retrospect he may look to us as a moralist, defending the family and condemning adultery, his »bête noire.« Especially in *Affaire Clémenceau* he strove for objectivity and eliminating the narrative self no less than Spielhagen.[13] In his essay he rants almost uncontrollably against the French. He dismisses Hugo's *Les Misérables*, Balzac's *Illusions perdues*, and Flaubert's *Madame Bovary* (*VS*, 298). As though associating himself with Gustav Freytag, whom he otherwise disdained, he complains that the French novel does not seek society in work, only in pleasure, apparently forgetting about David Séchard in *Illusions perdues*. Dumas's book in particular is an »Abgrund des Moders und der Verwesung« (326). Spielhagen complains that there is no denunciation of Pierre by his lawyer (330); that Pierre is profoundly critical of himself seems to have escaped him. Spielhagen almost makes of the novel a *casus belli*:

> In dem Augenblicke, wo Frankreich und Deutschland sich, bis an die Zähne gerüstet, gegenüberstehen, das französische Volk finster grollenden, eifersüchtig scheelen Blickes dem Wachsthum unserer Macht zuschaut, wo ein Funke vielleicht hinreicht, den verderblichsten Krieg zu entfachen, in welchem die beiden

---

[12] Alexandre Dumas fils, *Affaire Clémenceau. Mémoire de l'accusé* (Paris, [1909]), 65, 95, 103, 118.
[13] Octavian Gheorgiu, *Les Romans de Dumas Fils* (Paris, [1935]), 51, 79, 138–39.

größten Kulturvölker des Kontingents [sic] um die Suprametie ringen werden – in einem solchen Augenblick könnte ein schwaches Gemüth eine Art von Trost empfinden, und eine Art von Schadenfreude nähren über den Verfall des französischen Geistes, der in Büchern, wie das besprochene und in so manchen anderen ähnlichen an den Tag tritt. Denn der Geist ist es, der die Schlachten schlägt und in den Schlachten siegt und unterliegt; wie kann der gesunde und immer mehr erstarkende deutsche Geist von diesem kranken und immer kränker werdenden französischen Geist besiegt werden!

Aber fern sei uns jeder Gedanke dieser Art!

French barbarousness, imperialistic tyranny, the »freche Cultur der Frivolität und Selbstsucht, diese kindisch gewordene geist- und sittenlose Civilisation« are driving us to war; »sie schmettert in die Kriegstrompete, sie schreibt die Bücher à l'Affaire Clémenceau!« May no such seed fall on German ground, and yet – the admirers of the novel in Germany number in the thousands (332).

If one tries to extract the fundamental objection from this sinister jabberwocky, it appears to be the absence of sufficient poetic justice. But I think there may be an underlying irritant. Dumas, like Zola after him, tried to introduce a scientific method into literature.[14] What this means is the postulation of a genetic determinism that relativizes if it does not actually annul responsibility.[15] Pierre is the illegitimate son of a loving, saintly mother but a brutal father, a fateful heredity: »Tel père, tel fils.« The self is totally determined, with the father's character dominant. Individuals count for nothing; determinism has supplanted Providence.[16] This looks like a materialist doctrine that even the explicator of Dumas's novels declared »une théorie immorale et dangereuse.«[17] Germans had long been frightened of French materialism, perhaps even more than of French arms. Decades earlier, Schiller's Franz Moor in *Die Räuber* claims to see only accident in his birth as a second son, sired by his father in animal lust without any intention of creating Franz the person. Schiller meant to scare the audience, but he seems to have scared himself, for it turns out that he has no answer to Franz's, one supposes, French materialism; instead he brings the pastor from his boyhood onto the stage to threaten Franz with divine judgment, in which Schiller, of course, did not believe.[18] The fear is that German

---

[14] Gheorghiu, *Les Romans du Dumas Fils*, 138.
[15] »It was determinism as well as materialism which eventually came increasingly under attack«: Burrow, *The Crisis of Reason*, 58.
[16] Dumas, *Affaire Clémenceau*, 54, 97, 116.
[17] Gheorghiu, *Les Romans de Dumas Fils*, 151.
[18] Schiller, *Nationalausgabe*, 3: 19–20, 123.

idealism is too delicate and vulnerable to stand up before the uncouth but robust French materialism. This is part of the pattern of the Germans' self-understanding as perpetual victims. Spielhagen's assertion that the French are decaying into weakness from frivolity and salaciousness is, in my opinion, just whistling in the dark, and just the sort of collective self-hypnosis that leads to the brutality he instinctively abhorred. I offer this tentatively as an explanation for the Dumas review, in my experience the worst moment in all of Spielhagen's literary criticism, which is saying a lot.[19]

In any case, *Affaire Clémenceau* is the French connection to *Sonntags-kind* at which I hinted in the last chapter. Although a quarter of a century had gone by, I think there is no doubt that *Sonntagskind* was an attempt to rewrite or even undo Dumas's novel in a German spirit; in fact, even later, when the cuckolded Astolf in *Susi* thinks of killing his wife, he is prevented by the thought that he would be copying Dumas's novel, »dem widerlichen, von dem raffiniertesten Pinsel gemalten Schandbild der Wollust, die mit der Grausamkeit die gräßliche Ehe eingeht; dem Produkt der Fäulnis einer bis in das innerste Mark angefressenen Hyperkultur« (*NF*, 3: 380), unforgotten by Spielhagen nearly thirty years later. *Sonntagskind*, too, is the story of an enduring love for an evanescent beloved, the most faithful love of a man for a woman in Spielhagen's œuvre. She is also named Isabel and is also of Polish descent, and Justus also first encounters her when she is fourteen. Both begin to articulate their relationship in terms of a fairy tale, a feature about which there will be more to say when we come to the novel itself; Pierre perceives Iza's transformation from his beautiful beloved into a loathsome animal »comme dans un conte de fées.«[20] Unlike Pierre, Justus remains enamored of Isabel through all the vicissitudes of their lives, including her marriage for money to a baron. But when, after hundreds of pages, Justus manages to marry the widowed Isabel, their marriage, like Pierre's and Iza's, falls short of the imagined bliss. Isabel is not promiscuous like Iza, but needs many admirers for assurance as well as an elegant social life and luxuries that the struggling writer Justus cannot provide, so they must live from her inherited wealth, making him insecure. While Iza ignores her child of doubtful parentage, Isabel, who does not want children, dies in a childbirth that she knew would be dangerous to her, giving her

---

[19] It is characteristic both for the tone of the time and the way in which Spielhagen's criticism got him into a distorted relationship with it that this dreadful performance was particularly singled out for praise by Julian Schmidt, »Friedrich Spielhagen,« *Neue Bilder*, 246–47.

[20] Dumas, *Affaire Clémenceau*, 92.

life for Justus's unlikely happiness. One sees how Spielhagen gentles and softens, someone might say, sentimentalizes the French model. The reader can empathize with Isabel's existential erotic and aesthetic magnetism in a way that is not likely with Iza, whom Dumas seems to hate and, in any case, condemns. Isabel remains lovable despite all her faults, in part because of her candid awareness and acknowledgment of them. All the same, Spielhagen appears to remain much involved with the despised French book. In fact, Isabel is no less determined by congenital character than Dumas's figures, and the themes of the illusory nature of obsessive love and worship of beauty and the doubtful capacity of marriage to unite disparate individuals are comparable in the two novels.[21] It seems that one can combat an enemy so intensely that one succumbs to his influence.[22]

This comes to be to a certain extent the case with the most monstrous of literary enemies, Emile Zola, who served the German literary and critical community as the unsurpassed example of the impermissible and repulsive. Frustratingly, Zola was widely read in Germany, thus generating in a larger compass the same problem that Spielhagen had with *Affaire Clémenceau*, which must be loathsome to German sensibilities and yet found thousands of admirers.[23] One must suppose that Germans could not stop reading Zola

---

[21] One theme in the novel is the impatience of women with men. An Englishwoman married to a doctor complains that »Die Männer sind dumme Fische« while Isabel tells her that men's love comes not from the heart but from sensuality and fantasy (*NF*, 1: 506–07); when Isabel is exasperated by the antics of one of her many wooers, she sighs, »Die Männer sind einfach entsetzlich« (534). It is probably no more than a piquant, redoubled coincidence that Pierre's sigh in Dumas's novel, 103, »Ah, que les femmes sont bêtes,« seems to receive a comic gloss two years later in the couplet in act 2 of Jacques Offenbach's *La Périchole* (Paris, n.d.), 139–43, »Ah! Que les hommes sont bêtes.« Spielhagen's women often express this sentiment, e.g., Elma in *Liebe für Liebe* (Leipzig, 1875), 136: »Ach! Ihr Männer seid ja so schrecklich – ... schrecklich dumm!«

[22] Under this heading one might count as a detail that in *In Reih' und Glied* a French ballet dancer, a casual companion at a gambling evening hosted by the scheming Eva Tusky, wears a white camellia in her hair (*AR*, 1, 7: 296). Many readers will have been reminded of Dumas's *La Dame aux Camélias*, the novel version of which had appeared in 1848. Some of Spielhagen's social fiction, such as *An der Heilquelle* with its crisscrossing love and sexual relations and treatment of human foibles approaching the grotesque, also suggests a convergence with French fiction.

[23] One of these Zola admirers, curiously, was Raabe, who otherwise expressed antipathies to contemporary foreign literature and Naturalism similar to those of Spielhagen and others of the time. See Sammons, *Wilhelm Raabe*, 160, and Leo A. Lensing, »Naturalismus, Religion und Sexualität. Zur Frage der Auseinandersetzung mit Zola in Wilhelm Raabes *Unruhige Gäste*,« *Jahrbuch der Raabe-Gesellschaft* (1988): 145–67.

in order to assure themselves of how horrible he was: »The tremendous popularity of his novels not only amazed and irritated the critics, but, in some cases, drew their discussion and attack.«[24] Today it is easy to dismiss the hostility to Zola as an expression of bourgeois prudishness, constrictive normative principles, and philistinism generally. But it is only fair to remember that Zola was an extremely confrontational and lacerating writer, especially for readers accustomed to a certain amount of Victorian gentility.[25] There can be no doubt that he was a moralist – his great campaign in the matter of Captain Dreyfus sufficiently documents his devotion to principle – and he was no stranger to poetic justice. But reading him can be a grueling experience, as situations, especially of the working class, decline from bad to worse, even when it looks as though they could get no worse, human relations revert to the law of the jungle, and characters systematically and inexorably subvert their own hopes and possibilities.

The hostility to Zola was a part, though a prominent one, of the general worry about the advent of Naturalism. For a politically engaged social realist like Spielhagen, this was no easy problem. On the one hand, if poesy by its nature was an expression of the ideal, then the literary status of the realist novel was threatened by the incursions of the seamy side of life, the ills of society, the alienated meanness in human relations, especially in what used to be love relations, as well as subversive ideas of determinism, genetic

---

[24] Winthrop H. Root, *German Criticism of Zola 1875–1893 with Special Reference to the Rougon-Macquart Cycle and the Roman Expérimental* (New York, 1931), 10–11. For the dissemination of Zola's novels in Germany, especially in French among the educated, and the objections to him, see Bachleitner, *Der englische und französische Sozialroman*, 270–93. For an overview of the German reception, see Sältzer, *Entwicklungslinien der deutschen Zola-Rezeption.* Sältzer concentrates on the negative reception more than on the wide readership. His work is criticized in *Quellen zur Rezeption des englischen und französischen Romans in Deutschland und Österreich im 19. Jahrhundert,* ed. Norbert Bachleitner (Tübingen, 1990), 496–97.

[25] The resistance to Zola was, of course, not a peculiarity of Germans. In England his translator was attacked and imprisoned in 1889 and there was much outrage about determinism, sex, and the challenge to idealism, accompanied by great popularity among readers. See William C. Frierson, »The English Controversy on Realism in Fiction 1885–1895,« *Publications of the Modern Language Society of America* 43 (1928): 533–50. Zola himself ironically reflects the resistance by ascribing to the debauched Nana a revulsion at a novel about a prostitute: »elle disait que tout cela était faux, témoignant d'ailleurs une répugnance indignée contre cette littérature immonde, dont la prétention était de rendre la nature; comme si l'on pouvait tout montrer! comme si un roman ne devait pas être écrit pour passer une heure agréable! En matière de livres et de drames, Nana avait des opinions très arrêtées....«: Émile Zola, *Nana, Œuvres complètes,* ed. Henri Mitterand et al. (Paris, 1966–68), 4: 253.

inheritance, or supposedly Darwinian pitilessness; man is not a plant or an animal, Spielhagen objected (*AW,* 151). Who cares, he wrote in a critique of Ibsen's *Doll's House,* how Lear's daughters or Iago got to be how they are? (*BT,* 298). Citing Schiller but sounding a little like Plato, he declares the mere reproduction of the details of life inartistic, for what good is a pure reproduction of our ugly world? Anyone ought to be able to see »das ästhetische Fiasko« in the »Orgien des Naturalismus, in welchen Zola und seine Schule schwelgen« (*AmSt,* 243).

On the other hand, Naturalism seemed a logical extension of realism, especially if one believed one were in the service of revealing truth, and a writer like Spielhagen was sometimes thought of as a proto-Naturalist himself. He is said to have approached Naturalism while combatting it because it represented »ein Extrem der Spielhagenschen Forderungen.«[26] He tried to express his opposition in a more gingerly way than was his custom on other matters, explaining that, though he was fixed in his ways, he harmonized with the purposes of truth, democracy, and the expansion into areas that were closed to him (*AW,* 45). He declared »daß ich die Strebungen unserer jungen und jüngsten Litteratur mit größter Teilnahme verfolge« and that no literature should be forbidden to meet the needs of the time, only to continue with his reservations (*FuE,* 1: vii-viii). Naturalism, he declared magnanimously, had a right to exist. But then, what about the »ewigen Kunstgesetze«? Well, art and aesthetics are relative to their times (*NB,* 11–13). He concedes that »Verfasser des L'Assommoir oder des Raskolnikow« agree with Goethe that there is no limit on what is admissible to literature, and if they see »Sinn und Wesen der Armen und Elenden« differently than we do, it is a matter of a difference of experience (*AmSt,* 70).[27] Little by little he seems to give ground to the determination of consciousness, but two pages later he criticizes the scientific methods of the new writers (71–72; see also *NB,* 231). Justus in *Sonntagskind* writes an essay attacking scientific non-poesy, including six lines of Freiligrath beginning: »Lasse nur den Alltag nicht / Deine Dichtung dir verschütten« that he wants to set as a motto to his novel while wondering whether Isabel will find them tasteless or absurd (*NF,* 1: 363).[28]

---

[26] Müller-Donges, *Das Novellenwerk Friedrich Spielhagens,* 141.

[27] Sometimes it was argued that Zola was irrelevant to Germany because there were no such degenerate conditions there: Bachleitner, *Der englische und französische Sozialroman,* 320.

[28] The lines are from Freiligrath's exile poem, »Nach England« of 1846, included in the second part of his *Neuere politische und soziale Gedichte* of 1851: for the full text see Ferdinand Freiligrath, *Sämtliche Werke in zehn Bänden,* ed. Ludwig Schröder (Leipzig, [1907]), 6: 52–54.

In the last chapter I hinted that there might be a French connection to the miniscandal that developed in 1881 about the sensual moments between women in *Angela*. It has not been noticed that one of the most notorious of Zola's novels, *Nana*, appeared in the preceding year. Nana, for all her voluptuousness and sexual abandon, does not get very stimulated by men; it is this relative coolness that enables her to utilize her sexual allurement in a businesslike way. Rather, having worked up a tolerance for lesbian relationships after an initial disgust, she comments »que des goûts et des couleurs il ne faillait pas disputer, car on ne savait jamais ce qu'on pourrait aimer un jour«;[29] soon afterward she experiences her most intense sexual gratification with the depraved young streetwalker Satin in explicit scenes that extend over several chapters. Despite a possible temptation to link Spielhagen's »Nanni« with »Nana,« it is unlikely that he would have taken his cue from Zola's novel, but it might have charged the atmosphere that led to the prosecution. In any case, the circumstance suggests an unconscious and unwilling convergence with Zola. Gottfried Keller, after having read, not *Angela*, but a review of it, thought he sensed a French connection, that »es sich um Einführung der Pariser Errungenschaften handelt, und zwar bis auf das Argot.«[30]

Zola exhibits some similarities to Spielhagen of which the latter was probably unaware and that might have surprised him if called to his attention. Like Spielhagen, Zola was attracted by but not wholly enthusiastic about Social Democracy. More importantly, he was opposed to employing the novel to explicit ideological or political purpose and insistently viewed »art and politics as inherently separate realms.« Like Spielhagen, he modelled from observation and personal acquaintance, but he also ascribed a priority to the shaping and organizing imagination not too different from Spielhagen's distinction of finding and inventing.[31] It has been argued that his literary theory approached Zola's principles, but this claim presents chronological difficulties; nevertheless, there are parallels in the theory and practice of objective narration.[32] The convergence, it seems to me, is more

---

[29] Zola, *Nana*, 198.
[30] Gottfried Keller to Julius Rodenberg, March 28, 1882, *Gottfried Kellers Briefe 1861–1890*, ed. Emil Ermatinger (Stuttgart and Berlin, 1925), 453. See Rätus Luck, *Gottfried Keller als Literaturkritiker* (Bern and Munich, 1970), 546. The use of *argot* was one of the abrasive issues in the German reception of Zola; see Root, *German Criticism of Zola*, 15.
[31] Frederick Brown, *Zola: A Life* (New York, 1995), 110, 130, 151. Inevitably, Spielhagen declared that Zola was only a finder (*NB*, 81).
[32] Sältzer, *Entwicklungslinien der deutschen Zola-Rezeption*, 68–70. German critics with a positive view of Zola praised his objectivity; see Root, *German Criticism of Zola*, 61–62.

to be found in the evolution of Spielhagen's fictional practice, in which he may have been participating in a development in German reception: »Before 1880, there was as good as nothing but hostility toward Zola; from 1880 on, hostility and enthusiasm ran parallel, the enthusiasm gaining ground, until around 1885 it was in the ascendancy.«[33] Others have noted Spielhagen's movement.[34] The alleged Naturalist Heinrich Hart had already made the connection pejoratively.[35] Hart's attack was less a reasoned argument than a polemic designed to cause pain, and one can imagine how pained Spielhagen must have been to be linked with Zola in this way. Yet his persistent engagement with Zola indicates that he regarded the French author seriously as a competitor. For example, he takes the trouble to rewrite Zola's »schiefe Definition« of the novel: »Ein Stück Natur, gesehen durch ein Temperament« should rightly read: »ein Ausschnitt der Gesellschaft, gesehen durch die Phantasie« (*AW*, 108). Zola's concept of *tempérament* occupied and troubled German critics to an extraordinary degree.[36]

Other signs of convergence suggest themselves in Spielhagen's final phase. He once wrote, struggling as always to retain an idealistic faith, that one can be a radical skeptic in many vocations but not as an artist, »ein Zola wohl, aber kein Hans Sachs oder gar ein Goethe« (*AmSt*, 32), but the rising level of skepticism is inescapable in the late work. Spielhagen developed a rhetoric of acknowledging Zola in a left-handed way while repudiating him at the same time: »ich will sogar die Bedeutung Zolas in seinen grau in grau gemalten Unsitten-Gemälden anerkennen« (*BT*, 262), or: no one will say that his heaps of ugliness are not drawn from reality,

> und wenn Zola die Häßlichkeiten über die Wahrscheinlichkeit hinaus cumuliert und das in Wirklichkeit Zerstreute und Auseinanderliegende in übersichtliche Verbindung bringt, so übt er damit nur sein gutes Dichterrecht.... Aber in der übereifrigen Verfolgung dieses Rechtes vergißt er der Pflicht, die dem Recht zur Seite geht und seine Schroffheiten abmildert; der Pflicht, nicht nur die Wahrheit, sondern die ganze Wahrheit zu sagen. (*FuE*, 1: 186)

The form of argument often encountered in these matters, that the ugliness and misery are real, but are not the whole truth, is a weakened version of

---

[33] Root, *German Criticism of Zola*, xii.

[34] One of the earliest interpreters, Geller, *Friedrich Spielhagens Theorie und Praxis*, commented that »er nähert sich der Zolaschen Definition vom coin de la nature vu à travers un tempérament« (49; for the origin of this phrase, see Brown, *Zola*, 111); elsewhere she compares the last sequence of novels to the »Rougon-Macquart-Serie« (Geller, 110).

[35] Hart, »Friedrich Spielhagen,« 16, 55–56.

[36] See Root, *German Criticism of Zola*, 72–96.

the idealistic position that the mundane real is subaltern to higher truth. Yet one cannot ignore the magnitude of the phenomenon, the »Romane des gewaltigen Zola, der uns stets mit einem neuen gigantischen Vorwurf überrascht« (*NB*, 45); thus Spielhagen found himself obliged to acknowledge the force of the runaway train in *La Bête humaine* (49).[37] He counts Zola among the »recht glänzende Schriftsteller« of foreign nations, but adds: »*documents humains* sind keine Kunstgebilde« (89). He gets into a habit, when reviewing contemporary German books, of adducing comparisons to Zola, not always to his disadvantage (see 146, 150, 151, 163, 165).

But there are more specific indications of a movement toward convergence, among them signs of an acceptance of determinism and genetic inheritance.[38] In *Sonntagskind*, one of Isabel's admirers, as he prepares for a duel, explains his lightheartedness as a »Zolascher Atavismus« that has skipped a generation in his family (*NF*, 1: 407). One of Spielhagen's late verse aphorisms reads:

> Wer seine Ur-Ur-Väter sämtlich kennte
> Und seine Ur-Ur-Mütter in den Kauf,
> Er hätte dann vielleicht die Elemente
> Von seines Lebens irrem, wirren Lauf. (*NG*, 175)

The wise Antoinette who narrates *Frei geboren* similarly declares concerning her own noble descent:

> Es ist nicht gleichgiltig, von wem wir abstammen. Im Gegenteil! Wer die Reihen seiner Ahnen väterlicher- und mütterlicherseits nur weit genug zurückverfolgen könnte, würde sicher finden, daß er in allen seinen physischen, Temperaments-, Charakter- und seelischen Eigenschaften gar nichts Eigenes hat, sondern schlechthin der glücklich-unglückliche Erbe seiner Vorfahren ist. (*NF*, 7: 8)

This is not meant to be a value statement, I think, but one of fact, to explain how Antoinette's life turned out as unhappily as it did. In the preceding novel, *Opfer*, the quality of proletarian life in the Schulz family,

---

[37] Root, *German Criticism of Zola*, 74, observes: »*La Bête Humaine*, 1890, was the novel ... which gave the final impetus to the new conception of Zola as a vivid, romantic, and imaginative personality.«

[38] Wilhelm Scherer, in his review of *Platt Land*, seems to have regarded Spielhagen as still behind the times in this matter; he observes that the novel exhibits »eine ganz entschiedene sittliche Tendenz. [Spielhagen] will nichts wissen von der Erblichkeit der Schuld,« adding emphatically: »Aber Charaktereigenschaften *sind* erblich«: *Kleine Schriften zur neueren Litteratur, Kunst und Zeitgeschichte* (Berlin, 1893), 2: 164.

with the drinking, nonworking father, the abuse of children, one son driven out, a daughter as a *Fabrikmädchen* (which seems to be a euphemism for prostitute), and another daughter supporting the whole crew as a milliner, may remind one of family life in *L'Assommoir* (6: 78–80). The customarily lascivious life among the factory workers in *Sonntagskind* (1: 306) may also strike one as Zolaesque. The narrator Justus, imagining a novella or novel about his experiences as a worker, determines to take all possible care with the milieu, »[d]amit es mir ergeht, wie Zola mit seinem ›Germinal‹ in den Augen unseres Oberdirektors,« who declares that if one of his mining foremen were to commit the stupidities Zola ascribes to his people, he would be a foreman no longer (307–08; I think »nicht« is missing in the first clause). But Zola has not been quite disposed of in this novel. When Justus is worried about dealing with a strike, he broods: »Hätte ich eine Faser der herkulischen Kraft, die Zolas Muskeln schwellt, wenn es gilt, einen Augiasstall zu räumen, so müßte sie sich jetzt regen« (321). The misery of the coal-mining workers distinctly reminds one of *Germinal* (322–23). Later there is a joking exchange about the folly of adducing *Germinal* in an industrial accident case, concerning which Justus's literary mentor, Professor Richter, comments »daß der experimentale Roman und überhaupt die ganze realistische Poesie viel besser thäten, wenn sie ihr Geschäft aufgäben und es der Wissenschaft überließen, die es allein gründlich besorgen kann« (488). This appears to be a repudiation of the veridical value of a socially critical literature, but the passage and its whole narrative environment are not unambiguous and signify a vacillation toward and away from Zola on Spielhagen's part.

That he instinctively sought some sort of accommodation with the model of Zola is suggested to me by the scenes in the Hamburg harbor underworld in Book 5, Chapters 12 and 13 of *Was will das werden?*, where the fleeing Lothar intends to escape to South America, though he does not actually do so. Lothar is anxiously intimidated by the squalid, criminalized milieu, the bar girls and prostitutes who have no idea of virtue, the orgiastic sailors' dances, the garbage in the streets, the indescribable vice, »das scheusälige Elend« (*AR*, 3, 4: 584). The critics have been unimpressed by this excursion into an environment doubtless foreign to the author's experience. Klemperer, with his customary comparative captiousness, declared Spielhagen's portrayal of the criminal milieu inferior to Gutzkow's, with no feeling for the masses or for destitution.[39] Even a more recent critic has

---

[39] Klemperer, *Die Zeitromane Friedrich Spielhagens*, 135–36.

found the scenes superfluous.[40] Indeed, a reader might get an uncomfortable feeling of a sensationalism derived from Sue, or at least of an author striving for an effect that did not come naturally to him.[41] But I think the scenes are effective in their evocation of the claustrophobic impact on a young man unprepared for this level of reality and that they evince an effort to meet the Naturalists in general and Zola in particular on their own ground. Spielhagen was as fearful of Zola as Lothar is of the Hamburg underworld; had he been less burdened with the idealistic baggage of the *Goethezeit*, which he was almost but not quite ready to unload, he might have been able to follow his realistic instincts to a more productive and relaxed response to Zola.

---

[40] Lamers, *Held oder Welt?*, 110.
[41] Like any reader of his time, Spielhagen was aware of Sue from an early date. In his very first novel he has Oswald complain about Sue's ubiquity and object to Melitta's willing reading of *Les mystères de Paris* (*AR*, 1, 1: 94–95).

III.
After the Dawn – Spielhagen in the Reich

12. Beware of Your Wishes: *Allzeit voran*

Allzeit voran! – ein stolzes Wort
Zu jeder Zeit, an jedem Ort.
Nur hüte dich, voran zu sein
Beim Wettekriechen, Hurraschrein! (*NG*, 219)

During the 1860s one can detect a rising excitement in Spielhagen vibrat-
ing with the expectation of a showdown with France and the unification
of the nation, from the outbursts in his review of Dumas's *Affaire Clémenceau* in 1867 to *Deutsche Pioniere* in 1870. In this frame of mind he
was no doubt much in tune with his political and class environment; in
fact, it seems possible to me that the influence of the preunification atmosphere pushed him beyond his normal limits of liberality and circumspec-
tion. Of the constitution of his mind and manner during the Franco-Prussian War we know almost nothing. In retrospect he said of himself in the
third person:

> Die Aufrichtung des deutschen Reiches, die auch er mit Freuden begrüßt, war
> Vielen eine Abschlagszahlung gewesen, für die sie willig einen beträchtlichen
> Posten von der liberalen Rechnung, die sie einstmals der Regierung präsentiert
> hatte, streichen zu dürfen glaubten. Da er von diesem Abstrich nichts wissen
> wollte, vielmehr der Meinung war, es habe das Volk, das mit Strömen seines
> Blutes den Einheitsbau gekittet, jetzt doppelt und dreifach das Recht, die Einrich-
> tung im Innern nach seinen Wünschen und Bedürfnissen zu treffen, und er diese
> Überzeugung, wie er es gewohnt, mit Freimut nachdrücklich aussprach, gelangte
> er in den Ruf eines Mannes, der, wie er nichts vergessen, so auch nichts gelernt
> habe. Das entfremdete ihm viele alte Freunde und erwarb ihm keine neuen, die er
> nur in Kreisen hätte finden können, von welchen ihn jener Riß trennte, der zum
> ungeheuren Schaden beider Teile durch die Bildung unseres Volkes geht, und den
> zu beseitigen die Aufgabe und schwere Arbeit des kommenden Jahrhunderts sein
> wird. (*AW*, 43)

However, this formulation may compress a development that did not occur
at once, as it did with the more militant historian Georg Gottfried Gervinus, who died in March 1871 before unification had been proclaimed but
not before he had deplored the antidemocratic military might that would

make the Reich a danger for Europe.[1] In a series of sonnets, »Wir und die Brüder,« beginning »Was ist des Deutschen Vaterland?,« Spielhagen praises the founding of the Reich while threatening the resistant Czechs and Magyars (*G*, 201–06). But these are immediately followed in the volume of poems by three sonnets entitled »Dioskuren,« which optatively pair Goethe and Bismarck but warn the latter not to have only one soul in his breast, »gierig nur nach Plutos Schätzen rennen, / Nur für Apollos Lorbeerkranz entbrennen« (207–09; the poems are those that constitute Lothar Lorenz's first if somewhat dubious publication in *Was will das werden?*, AR 3, 4: 361–63). The following pair, »Junker« (*G*, 210–11), finds Spielhagen settling into his more familiar posture. I infer that his initial response was compounded of anticipation, anxiety, and disorientation, and I draw this inference from the first novel he published after unification, *Allzeit voran* of 1872.[2]

The reception or, rather, nonreception of this somewhat strange work may well be an illustration of the isolation he claimed to have experienced in his alienation from the Reich, even though the publisher must have initially thought it timely, because 2,200 copies instead of the usual thousand were printed.[3] The only appreciative German critic of the past I have found was, significantly, the Socialist Franz Mehring, who specially praised the novel as so strong in language and style as to be atypical for Spielhagen.[4] Otherwise, only in an American obituary was it recalled with »peculiar affection.«[5] Sometimes I wonder if those who dismiss it have actually read it, such as those who listed it among the »Jammerprodukte« of

---

[1] Hans-Ulrich Wehler, *Deutsche Gesellschaftsgeschichte*, vol. 3: *Von der »Deutschen Doppelrevolution« bis zum Beginn des Ersten Weltkrieges 1849–1914* (Munich, 1995), 330–31.

[2] Cf. J. W. Burrow, *The Crisis of Reason: European Thought, 1848–1918* (New Haven and London, 2000), 136: »In Germany the achievement, in the new Reich, of something like the nation state, though with Austria excluded, was necessarily disillusioning to many of the hope of national cultural and moral regeneration invested in it. The period of struggle for unification came, on the contrary, to seem like an heroic age, confronted with a mundane and materialistic contemporary reality.«

[3] Rosa-Maria Zinken, *Der Roman als Zeitdokument. Bürgerlicher Liberalismus in Friedrich Spielhagens »Die von Hohenstein« (1863–64)* (Frankfurt am Main and Bern, 1991), 16. Zinken speaks, quite expectedly, of »der offensichtlich mißlungene Roman« (ibid.). Hans Henning, *Friedrich Spielhagen* (Leipzig, 1910), 193, had already declared it »[e]in offenbarer Rückschritt.«

[4] Franz Mehring, »Friedrich Spielhagen,« *Beiträge zur Literaturgeschichte*, ed. Walter Heist (Berlin, 1948), 216–17. Mehring goes into no further detail supporting his view.

[5] Anonymous, »Friedrich Spielhagen,« *Dial* 50 (1911): 201.

»die kleinen und kleinsten Talente« celebrating 1870/71.[6] Only quite recently has one scholar shown some adequate understanding that the novel marks »den Umschlagpunkt von dem liberalen Optimismus der sechziger Jahre zu jener zunehmenden Enttäuschung über die Entwicklung der Gesellschaft und ihrer Mentalität im Deutschen Reich, die Spielhagen mit Raabe teilt und die sich in den Zeitromanen der siebziger und achtziger Jahre immer deutlicher zeigt.«[7] In the circumstances it will be necessary, first of all, to give an account of the novel.

It takes place in the summer of 1870 in a tiny, impoverished, disease-ridden, mediatized, apparently Saxon principality ruled, after a fashion, by Prince Erich von Roda,[8] who has been for three years morganatically married to the beautiful Hedwig, daughter of a serf, whom he espoused at sixty-two when she was seventeen. Hedwig, lonely and frustrated, but energetic in trying to do what good she can, is one of Spielhagen's unconscious *femmes fatales*, passionately loved by the prince, by a physician exiled from Hanover, Hermann Horst, and, as it emerges, by the prince's hated relative, Count Heinrich Roda-Steinburg, a military hero in Prussian service, like the prince descended from a Count Erich XXXIV, heir apparent to the principality and, inconveniently, married. His wife, Countess Stephanie, is pregnant, though the count can hardly imagine he ever felt anything for her (*AR*, 2: 2, 67). The prince and Hedwig have a »white« marriage as a result of a promise he made in order to win her. He now regrets this and is consumed with sexual longing, which Hedwig firmly repels. All these relationships have some depth in the past; particularly the count had loved Hedwig but abandoned her for a wife more appropriate to his class; he regards Stephanie with a condescension bordering on contempt, though she loves him, ruefully citing the French adage that in a love relationship there are two persons: »Einer, der liebt, und Einer, der sich lieben läßt« (91). The prince is depressed for other reasons, including the sorry state of his principality, about which he genuinely cares, and the looming threat to his auton-

6   Richard Hamann and Jost Hermand, *Deutsche Kunst und Kultur von der Gründerzeit bis zum Expressionismus*, vol. 1: *Gründerzeit* (Berlin, 1965), 219.
7   Dirk Göttsche, *Zeit im Roman. Literarische Zeitreflexion und die Geschichte des Zeitromans im späten 18. und im 19. Jahrhundert* (Munich, 2001), 721.
8   There is a real town with a ducal palace and a stream named Roda in Saxony. French visitors, of whom more in a moment, complain of the fictional principality's puniness of ten square miles (*AR*, 2, 2: 179). If these are German miles, as I assume, that would convert to about fifty-five square kilometers, small enough, to be sure.

omy from Prussia, to which he feels deeply hostile. The prince's father was a follower of Rousseau and an ultimately disappointed partisan of Napoleon I; the prince has to deal with emissaries of the nephew, the repetition of history as farce, as we recall from Marx. These French conspirators are Ludovic de Rosel, an Alsatian of dual nationality, whom Dr. Horst recognizes from Hanover as a fraudulent *Freiheitsschwärmer*, and a ridiculously vain Marquis de Florville, who supposes himself, quite unrealistically, a successful suitor of Hedwig. The plan is to draw the frustrated prince into a league of the middle states friendly to France and against Prussia; Rosel prates of liberty and equality while the marquis appeals to aristocratic solidarity and traditional sovereignty. The prince foolishly allows himself to be drawn into a negotiation with these popinjays, which, when revealed, causes the raging count to threaten him with arrest. When the prince, who has physical as well as metaphorical heart trouble, dies, the count succeeds him; soon he is gravely wounded in the crucial battle of Gravelotte (August 18, 1870). Hedwig nurses him with the rest of the wounded but firmly rejects his advances; she parts from the sorrowful Dr. Horst as well, and, after having refused the property the prince intended to settle on her, disappears.

This sketch typically leaves out much of Spielhagen's densely detailed narration, including a dimension of social criticism and satire. One ubiquitous figure is the rueful idler Oskar von Zeisel from Saxony, a kind of major domo of the miniature court, who spends much of his time pursuing marriage with one or another of the local daughters. There is a vast amount of malicious gossip and intrigue, much of it instigated by the chancellor's stupid wife, who wants to marry her daughter to the prince. For Hedwig's morganatic status is not taken seriously; one of the several intriguers against her states that it is hardly different from being a mistress (168). Class stress, as usual, pervades the community. Interestingly, it does not much involve Hedwig, who is too low-born to be taken seriously in this regard; rather, she is disparaged as »Prinzessin Hochmuth« and accused of hypocrisy and scheming (87). Particularly vulnerable is Dr. Horst, whom the count despises as a Hanoverian, a bourgeois democrat, and a rival for Hedwig. Horst has been caring for Countess Stephanie's pregnancy, but the count has him displaced with a haughty *Geheimrath* from Berlin, who scorns Horst as a frivolous and ignorant incompetent, opposes his report on public health, and blames him for the mortality in a typhus epidemic that Horst had actually stemmed, while the pastor hints at his lack of religion (325–26, 356). Needless to say, Stephanie has a childbirth crisis and Horst has to be called in to rescue the situation. The *Geheimrath* declares the prince to be in good health, only needing rest, not long before he drops dead.

It is not surprising that this novel, with its odd construction (»grotesk ersonnene Fabel«[9]) and insecurity of political tone, should have been disliked by the critics; one scholar remarked that everyone hates it.[10] But some of the objections seem peculiar. Klemperer complained that »in dem Augenblick, der ein Volk um seine Macht und Einheit ringen sieht, kann nichts gleichgültiger sein als das ohnmächtige Machtbegehren eines winzigen Regenten.«[11] But, apart from the fact that Spielhagen is using the tiny state as a kind of laboratory for the larger issues, the minor principalities were a unification issue; even after 1871 there remained twenty-two »Zwergstaaten [die] ihre bizarren Züge konservierten.«[12] Martini asserted that Spielhagen's »Abneigung gegen den Sieg der preußischen Monarchie machte ihn zum Anwalt eines ohnmächtigen Kleinfürstentums und trieb ihn so paradox in das Reaktionäre zurück.«[13] But this is clearly not the case; the principality is a problem, not a solution. Hedwig herself speaks eloquently of its limitations: »unsere Gewerbeschule mit den drei Schülern, unsere Fortbildungsanstalt für junge Mädchen, die wir aus Mangel an Theilnehmerinnen haben schließen müssen – wie kläglich ist das Alles?« (28). Much is said about the impoverished and insalubrious condition of the people; one of the hopes progressives invested in unification was relief of the poverty and backwardness of nineteenth-century Germany. Klemperer further declared morganatic marriage to be anachronistic.[14] But that is not so, either. In 1892 one of the daughters of the then prominent writer Wilhelm Jensen morganatically married the son of the duke of Saxe-Meiningen.[15] In general, Hedwig embittered the critics, who seem to have been as frustrated by her sexual recalcitrance as Prince von Roda himself. Even the faithful Karpeles protested that one could not empathize with her, a female counterpart to Oswald Stein in *Problematische Naturen*, and, apparently just not paying attention to characterization, he found it incomprehensible that she fled the

[9] Adolf Strodtmann, *Dichterprofile. Literaturbilder aus dem neunzehnten Jahrhundert* (Stuttgart, 1879), 1: 206.

[10] Alfred E. Goessl, »Die Darstellung des Adels in Prosaschriften Friedrich Spielhagens« (Diss. Tulane U, 1966), 109.

[11] Victor Klemperer, *Die Zeitromane Friedrich Spielhagens und ihre Wurzeln* (Weimar, 1913), 113.

[12] Wehler, *Deutsche Gesellschaftsgeschichte*, 3: 173.

[13] Fritz Martini, *Deutsche Literatur im bürgerlichen Realismus 1848–1898* (Stuttgart, 1964), 430.

[14] Klemperer, *Die Zeitromane Friedrich Spielhagens*, 115.

[15] Marie Jensen to Wilhelm and Berthe Raabe, March 13, 1892, Wilhelm Raabe, *Sämtliche Werke*, ed. Karl Hoppe et al. (Göttingen, (1960–94), *Ergänzungsband* 3: 464.

count.[16] Nor did Strodtmann distinguish himself by close reading when he reproached the »unnahbar spröde Eisjungfrau« for selling herself for »Rang und Reichthum an einen ungeliebten Mann.«[17] The irritable Klemperer castigated Hedwig's insincerity and found her chastity »widersinnig«; she merely torments the count and the doctor.[18]

For a different footing, we might begin by considering the title. It may be a small point, but it seems to me of significance that the title is not followed by an exclamation point, such as, for example, Friedrich Gerstäcker's *Nach Amerika!* The phrase does have such punctuation where it occurs in the text, but its implications are not obviously positive. Hedwig tells the count it has been his slogan since the Danish war: »Allzeit voran! Ob nun, was wir erobern wollen, eine feindliche Batterie ist, oder ein socialer Vortheil, oder ein schönes Weib – allzeit voran! Wir geben keinen Pardon, wir machen keine Concessionen, wir brechen ein Herz, das wir nicht beugen können.« But he will not break or bend her heart because of her love of freedom (126). Yet she tells the prince that she resents Stephanie, who could not make »sein stolzes Wort: Allzeit voran! zur Wahrheit ... nicht, wie jetzt, in dem engen und selbstischen Sinn seiner Parteigenossen, sondern in dem großen und edlen Sinn des Patrioten, der über seine Partei hinaus ein Vaterland hat« (307); Hedwig's implication being that she might have had such an influence with »die Ueberschwänglichkeit meiner Phantasie, der ungebändigte Thatendrang meiner Seele« (303). The count repeats the phrase when he is filled with hate at her resistance (442). When he is wounded at Gravelotte, the slogan evanesces, for his whole sense of self had been invested in warring against the French; now: »Allzeit voran! Das war jetzt vorbei für immer!« (457). There is a French version of the term, too, when a scheming baron incites the count to duel with the French marquis in disobedience to the policy of the king: »*en avant!*« (260).

The count is the man Hedwig loves, or might be able to, if it were not for his impatience with her democratic convictions, his contempt for the people he imagines riding as he does his horse (418, 442), his incarnation of everything about Prussia she has opposed. Their relationship is deftly symbolized in a scene when, on a walk together, they are attacked by a powerful buck in a place where the count has just said a brave and strong man could

[16] Gustav Karpeles, *Friedrich Spielhagen. Ein literarischer Essay* (Leipzig, 1889), 54–55.
[17] Strodtmann, *Dichterprofile*, 206.
[18] Klemperer, *Die Zeitromane Friedrich Spielhagens*, 114–15.

repel a whole regiment. The count, in attempting to protect her, is crushed against a rock ledge; the buck is shot by a forester who fortuitously comes by. Hedwig, thinking the count has given his life for her, cradles his head, but it turns out that only his right arm has been hurt, and afterward he is as peremptory toward her as before. This looks like standard fare, but there are several interesting details. Hedwig is not afraid of the buck, which she has known as »Hans« and regards as a friend; thus its hostility seems to be directed toward the count. It is not the count, strong though he may be, who subdues the raging buck, but the quasi-proletarian forester, one of Hedwig's good friends, who later hints to Dr. Horst that he would have preferred to shoot the count (98, 115–16). In addition, the laming of the count's arm prefigures the more serious crippling he suffers at Gravelotte.

Spielhagen's mode of »objective« narration, beginning *in medias res* without authorial explanation, allows such matters as Hedwig's inner relationship to the count to emerge gradually, as do the facts of her celibate marriage, though the signals are clear enough on a second reading of the novel. Similarly, our perception of the prince undergoes changes in the course of the narration. He seems at first to be depressed but well-meaning, frustrated at not being able to do more for his people. Unlike the count, he is courtly and considerate to the countess (91). His resistance to Prussia and Bismarck, his resentment at the events of 1866, seem at first consonant with the ethos of the novel (118). He is proud of a model farm he has overseen, which convinced a nobleman who had been skeptical of it (173). But he is trapped in an obsolete sense of self. Dr. Horst says he is not a statesman or politician; he is too high-strung and confuses the cause with the personal; his political aspirations are dismissed as »eine[] phantastische[] Laune« (208–09). The turning point in the narrative's evaluation of him may come when he orders Zeisel to arrange a gala birthday party to reinforce his conviction that his people truly love him. Parties almost always lead to disaster in Spielhagen's fiction, and this one, the preparations for which soon develop comic features, is no exception. During the preparations for it come the Prussian king's break with the French ambassador and the declaration of war, events that fill the people with Prussian enthusiasm. They fall away from the prince and celebrate the count, who knows how to do things like Bismarck (321), though their homage does not please the peevish count (423). Eventually the festival is overrun with undisciplined crowds and the pavilion burns down. In the meantime the prince has compromised himself with everyone, including Hedwig and Dr. Horst, by conspiring with the French. Opposition to Prussia is one thing, but disloyalty to the nation quite another. At the end he is a pathetic figure, weepy and suicidal, his hair turned white, pleading in vain for Hedwig's love. With a passionate speech, Hedwig tries to arouse him on his birthday to patriotism, but he replies only that he has never understood her (405).

The theme of the love of an older man for a young woman appears in a number of places in Spielhagen's writings; I cannot say exactly why. It is introduced early, in *Auf der Düne*, where Paul's observation of the twenty-year age difference between Gustav and Clementine is but a foreshadowing of the melancholy outcome: »ist und bleibt eine solche Ehe, wo ein Mädchen den Platz auf der Schulbank mit dem Ehrenplatze an dem Tisch eines Mannes, der den Jahren nach ihr Vater sein könnte, vertauscht, ein Wagstück« (2, 1: 202). As is customary with Spielhagen, the theme appears in variations.[19] The gentlest and ultimately most resigned version appears in *Quisisana*, his rewriting of Goethe's *Der Mann von fünfzig Jahren*. In some stories, such as *An der Heilquelle* and *Alles fließt*, the age difference in marriage is not that great but a good deal is made of it. In some situations elderly husbands are cuckolds, such as the pharmacist Siebold in *Faustulus*, whose wife is a sexual slave of the title figure; the elderly count whose young wife is loved by the narrator of *Mesmerismus*; and the pure fool Baron Astolf in *Susi*; in such cases, despite the acrid moralism, something of the comic buffoonery of Boccaccio's betrayed husbands attaches to them. Some old husbands are taken in order to be got rid of in the interest of a comfortable widowhood, such as the reactionary old Geheimrat von Dürieu married by Adele in *Frei geboren*. Sometimes the unequal unions thrive, such as that of Wollnow and Ottilie in *Was die Schwalbe sang* or Eilhardt and Stella in *Alles fließt*. Sometimes they are tragic, as in *Was will das werden?*, where Adele von Trümmnau can dissolve her white marriage to a neglectful roué thirty years older only at the price of turning over to him all her property (3, 4: 481, 486). But the worst of these liaisons is that between Prince von Roda and Hedwig, because it is grounded in unfulfillable expectations in one another that are in turn bound into a larger, constricting political and historical context. At the bottom of his fortunes the prince confesses, »daß ein alter Mann nicht um die Liebe eines jungen Mädchens werben darf und kann, ohne sich an ihr und an sich selbst zu versündigen« (2, 2: 402).

The political context is agonized and confusing, not only for the characters, I believe, but also for the author. Central to the consciousness of all the Germans except the prince is the patriotic aspiration for the unified na-

---

[19] It is possibly significant that two foreign novels in which Spielhagen was interested are formed around the theme: Alphonse Daudet's *Fromont jeune et Risler aîné* and »Julien Gordon's« *A Diplomat's Diary*.

tion. That Spielhagen is still within the mood of victory in the Franco-Prussian War and the founding of the Reich is indicated by his caricatures of the French emissaries, who are morally alien to the dialectic of opinion in which the German figures are involved. The Frenchmen are not only disingenuous and malevolent; they are also disloyal to one another. The Alsatian Rose/Rosel betrays the marquis for his own purposes, which turn out to be to create chaos and blunt the nationalist cause in the hope of instigating communist revolution (433–34); thus he is one of those »outside agitators« we hear about as explanations for dissidence to the present day. The marquis is fatuously vain with his monocle and courtly manners, certain of his irresistibility to Hedwig and of his superiority to the count with weapons, both convictions totally imaginary; he pretends to extol German poesy and the quaint tranquillity of the principality (159–61); he laughs when Rosel declares the name of the place is »Gerolstein« (180), doubtless an allusion to Eugène Sue; and he gloats that »diese dummen deutschen Bestien« will not be able to get rid of him (258). He courts Hedwig with allusions to Balzac's *Illusions perdues*, imagines himself playing a brilliant role in a novel, and daydreams »in bunten Schwärmen die tollfrechen Abenteuer aus dem Faublas« (171, 181, 250).[20] He and Rosel wonder what they are doing here in this paltry backwater that would be laughed at in Paris, but console themselves with the thought that no one need know; what is wanted is the propaganda value of being able to show support for France in a German land. These »französische Windhunde« cure Zeisel of any French sympathies he might have had (275). When the count is lying among the dead on the battlefield, he must drive off French corpse-robbers who have the appearance of hyenas (450). The bogey of the *Erbfeind*, a term Hedwig herself employs when reproaching the prince (309), is no less unproblematically intact here than it was in *Deutsche Pioniere* two years before.

The problem, however, is Prussia, its hegemonic ambitions, its militarism and brutality, unpromising for the realization of the ideal Germany for which people like Hedwig (and the author) hoped. The prince's chancellor says of the count's Prussian socialization: »Es ist ein wunderlich Ding, Ihr Herren, um das preußische Wesen. Das hat eine Schneide, der sich nichts abschleifen läßt, und eine Höflichkeit, vor der man sich in Acht nehmen mag« (52–53). Dr. Horst is suspected by the jealous, belligerent count of

---

[20] This last allusion is to the late eighteenth-century light novel *Les Amours du Chevalier de Faublas* by Jean-Baptiste Louvet de Couvray. It is sometimes remarkable what swarms in Spielhagen's own head. There is another pejorative allusion to Faublas in *Platt Land* (*AR* 2, 5: 116).

Hanoverian, »Welf« allegiances, but he refuses the letters from Welf sources that Rosel tries to deliver; Horst is merely personally grateful to the king of Hanover, who financed his medical studies (149). If he fought for Hanover at one time, he is no longer prepared to do so; at one point, Hedwig says of him that he once had sacrificed himself for a blind king and now does so for a prince who will not see (210–11).[21] The severely wounded count is rescued on the battlefield by Hanoverians, accompanied by Horst and Zeisel in Prussian and Saxon uniforms respectively (451), a clear demonstration of the desired subordination of particularist allegiances to the comprehensive nation. The count, on the other hand, is the incarnation of everything about Prussia that is feared and deplored. He is peremptory and harsh; he demands that Hedwig yield to him practically as a matter of right despite her unambiguous resistance, and despite the fact that he is married and about to be a father. He is militaristic, monarchist with a belief in divine right, class-proud, antidemocratic, and contemptuous of a capable, liberal bourgeois like Dr. Horst; the prince calls up a detailed vision of how meanly and oppressively the count will rule (312–13). When the count understands that the prince has formed treasonable connections, as a law unto himself he orders a series of arrests and practically occupies his own principality; when he proclaims secret tribunals, the prince reaches for his last resource of irony: »Ich kenne die preußische Milde, sagte er; sie hat sich noch stets bewährt« (408).

At the end Hedwig tries to draw the count into the spirit of friendship and reconciliation. She claims to be confident that he will get the idea, unlike the old prince (462), but his response is muted. For the count's spirit has been broken by his battlefield wound. This is not the kind of war wound that a veteran can wear through life like a medal for heroism. The experience is traumatic. Spielhagen takes some pains to describe the battlefield of Gravelotte as a scene not of glory but of horror. The count is pinned under his horse, crippled and in critical condition; the awareness of the termination of his military identity induces a deadly depression. He

---

21 The references to Georg V in the text are rather mild. He did attempt at one time to combat Prussia's absorption of Hanover by supporting Austria in 1866 and organizing propaganda from Paris, but was obliged to yield. The prince is said to be in a situation similar to that of Georg V (84). For these reasons, *Allzeit voran* has sometimes been associated with Hanover, where Spielhagen had experienced Georg V's tyranny at first hand, but the king, though blind, was much tougher and more stubborn than Prince von Roda, whose principality is much pettier.

feels that his situation is not heroic; he is merely missing in action like a marauder, and for the first time he asks himself whether the price of victory might not have been too high (448). His severely wounded servant, whom a week before the count had put under arrest, asks to be shot because a poor man will not be able to survive as a cripple, and he dies after dragging himself to bring the count a cup of water (445–46). The subsequent victory celebration, the commendation of the king, and the award of the Iron Cross in no way restore his spirits. It seems that the integration of the Prussian nobleman into the nation can be achieved only by crushing the violent and despotic Prussian characteristics out of him.

Perhaps we may sympathize to some extent with the critics who found that the characterization of Hedwig failed to realize consistent plausibility. But she is best regarded as an allegorical figure, for all that Spielhagen opposed allegory in theory (*NB*, 81); her inconsistency reflects the author's own uncertainty and qualms. At one point Zeisel wants her to play the role of Germania at the birthday celebration (*AR*, 3, 2: 235–36). At the end of the novel she is seen standing on a height,

> schlank und groß schier über Menschenmaß.
> Und jetzt hob sie die Arme, zum Gruß, zum Segen. Er [Horst] wußte es: es galt nicht ihm; es galt den Braven Allen, die mit ihm zogen in den heiligen Kampf für ein einiges und freies Vaterland. (468)

This is certainly a monumental figuration of Hedwig as Germania.[22] But there are several things to consider. Hedwig herself resists homage; when Zeisel calls her their good angel, she thinks gloomily: »So hat er mich tausendmal genannt, der alte Mann, aber es gibt keine guten Engel, nur böse Menschen« (291). In a scene a week after Gravelotte, thus about a week before the capture of Napoleon III and the siege of Paris, she is unsure whether the people will have the victory they deserve or will concede it to the exploiters (466–67), a concern that strikes a surprisingly prescient note at such an early date. With her departure it becomes irrevocable that, as Germania, she can bond herself neither to the decayed man of the old order, the hard man of the new order, or the soft, humane man of bourgeois moderation; she is, as yet, without a partner. It is surely not insignifi-

---

22 Göttsche, *Zeit im Roman*, 719–20, also points out the identification. In 1874, still susceptible to the nationalist mood, Spielhagen praised the allegorical representation of the Battle of Sedan by Anton von Werner (*AmSk*, 305–16). As with his literary criticism, his art criticism here shows him more limited in intelligence and imagination than his fiction.

cant that »Germania« comes from the lowest caste of the German people. But most significant are the just cited final words, an interpretation of her gesture by the lonely liberal. They are formulated after the victory, during the creation of the nation, and yet they still project the hope for unity and freedom into the future; the fight is yet to be undertaken. It has been said of the ending that »dessen Auseinandersetzung mit der preußischen Vorherrschaft in Deutschland in eine zwiespältige Apologie der Reichsgründung mündet,«[23] but I think »Apologie« is not quite the right word; there is too much doubt and apprehension in the final formulations. Spielhagen is beginning to beware of his wishes.

---

[23] Göttsche, *Zeit im Roman*, 718.

13. The Gift of the Danai: *Sturmflut*

> *Sturmflut*, deine wilden Wogen
> Sind bald wieder abgezogen;
> Vieler Milliarden Segen
> War sobald nicht wegzufegen. (*NG*, 218)

A half-dozen years into the Wilhelminian Reich, Spielhagen had reached a more confident understanding of it and a temporary degree of accommodation, as is evidenced by his novel *Sturmflut* of 1877. The better informed reader may be surprised by this last claim. *Sturmflut* has the reputation of a politically and socially critical novel, indeed, it has become a kind of Spielhagen trademark. It does have a critical dimension, but encapsulated in an ultimately hopeful outlook that, once the postunification crisis has been weathered, so to speak, the Germany for which liberal progressives of Spielhagen's type had hoped was coming into being. The relative confidence in a congruence of patriotism with the ideals of the liberal, humanistic tradition was not to endure. Since *Sturmflut* is, except among a few specialized observers, the last Spielhagen novel registered by literary history, its trademark status foreshortens and distorts the full arc of his career, suppressing almost a quarter of a century of further struggle for a just representation of the national condition.

The historical impetus to the novel is one of the most refined ironies known to modern European history. After its victory in the Franco-Prussian War, the newly constituted German Reich imposed upon the staggering French Republic, which succeeded the collapse of *its* Reich, among other burdens, a reparations indemnity of five billion gold francs, one billion to be paid by the end of 1871, and the rest by three years after ratification of the peace, that is, by March 2, 1874. The magnitude of the sum astonished not only the French; even the English gulped.[1] Spielhagen may have

---

[1]   Hans Herzfeld, *Deutschland und das geschlagene Frankreich 1871–1873. Friedensschluß Kriegsentschädigung Besatzungszeit* (Berlin, 1924), 15. Herzfeld's history is impelled by a strong resentment of the Versailles Treaty and a desire to show

thought the reparations fair play, despite the destabilizing consequences; several years later, in *Noblesse oblige*, he makes much of the contributions the French extorted from Hamburg in 1813. But the French, calling upon their own patriotism, oversubscribed loans floated to raise the funds.[2] The sudden monetary inflow into the still primitive and undergoverned German economy contributed, or appeared to contribute, to an orgy of speculation leading to a panic with enduring consequences that considerably deflated the euphoria of unification. One might think of the Spanish Empire, several times driven to bankruptcy by the influx of silver and gold from America.

It is not clear to me as an inexpert observer of these matters whether anyone at the time had the economic discernment to realize that this extorted gift of the Danai was an invisible Trojan Horse, although Alphonse de Rothschild gloated in retrospect that »Our 5 billions have cost them dear« and that the crash was »the nemesis after the hubris of Versailles.«[3] The historian Wilhelm Oncken called it in retrospect »das große nationale Unglück« that caught the Germans completely unprepared »um das ›Danaergeschenk‹ einigermaßen zu verdauen.« He added that the Germans knew early payment would be harmful but accepted it in the interest of peace.[4] An astute observer at the time might have been forgiven for suspecting the French of particularly perfidious guile. Indeed, it was Jules Favre, the negotiator with Bismarck of the Treaty of Frankfurt of May 1871, who proposed the remarkable sum, though at first without the loss of Alsace and Lorraine, and Adolphe Thiers, who was to lead the Republic, thought it bearable. Although the French attempted delay at first and at one point sought an extension of one year for the final payment, in the end they not only paid on time, but early, by September 1873, in their desire to be relieved of the occupation troops imposed to guarantee payment. This acceleration, it has been said, created »eine technisch unangenehme Lage« straining »die volkswirtschaftliche Aufnahmefähigkeit.«[5] Bismarck was ferociously impatient at any haggling or signs of delay, determined »to force

that Bismarck's policy was much less oppressive and more considerate of France's welfare than France's persecution of Germany after World War I. For modern accounts from contrasting vectors see Fritz Stern, *Gold and Iron: Bismarck, Bleichröder, and the Building of the German Empire* (New York, 1977), 143–56, and Niall Ferguson, *The World's Banker: The History of the House of Rothschild* (London, 1998), 705–37.

2   Allan Mitchell, *The German Influence in France after 1870: The Formation of the French Republic* (Chapel Hill, 1979), 25–26, 39.

3   Ferguson, *The World's Banker*, 735, 737.

the Thierist republic repeatedly into the stooped posture of an inferior«;[6] the ease with which the French met the obligation did not please him.[7] Despite the counsel of his banker Gerson Bleichröder (who actually assisted the French in raising the funds[8]), Bismarck was not notable for his grasp of economic matters; for all his powerful intelligence and shrewdness, he was fundamentally a back-country *Junker* who thought in terms of military force and power politics.

At the time the crisis appears to have been experienced but not fully understood; generally it was ascribed to the rapacious greed of the eventually notorious *Gründer* with their overwrought ambitions, their incompetent swindles, their watered stocks, their investment schemes guaranteed by the names of aristocrats and admirals who had no understanding of them. This was basically Spielhagen's view also.[9] Much of this activity was involved with railroad building, which in Prussia had been traditionally carried on by private rather than state enterprise. In the early 1870s »twenty-seven new private companies received concessions from the Prussian state. This spectacular boom of private railway enterprise in northern Germany now spurred a number of moral equivalents to the American ›robber barons‹ of the late nineteenth century.«[10] The notorious failure of the overextended

[4] Wilhelm Oncken, *Das Zeitalter des Kaisers Wilhelm. Allgemeine Geschichte in Einzeldarstellungen. Vierte Hauptabtheilung. Sechster Theil* (Berlin, 1890–92), 2: 552–53.

[5] Herzfeld, *Deutschland und das geschlagene Frankreich*, 15, 63, 65, 162, 167, 254, 263, 264. Herzfeld's view is that Bismarck tolerated this economic disturbance out of the goodness of his heart. Cf. Mitchell, *The German Influence in France*, 44: »In the autumn of 1872, Germany was already beginning to feel the first seriously negative repercussions of the postwar years.« Wehler, *Deutsche Gesellschaftsgeschichte*, 3: 98–100, shows that the effect of the French gold was greatly exaggerated, the increase in the money supply had begun before unification, and the crash started in Austria, then spread to the United States.

[6] Mitchell, *The German Influence in France*, 29.

[7] Herzfeld, *Deutschland und das geschlagene Frankreich*, 16.

[8] Mitchell, *The German Influence in France*, 39. Bleichröder was involved only at a beginning stage. The Paris Rothschilds were determined to shut him and all German bankers out, even the Frankfurt and Vienna Rothschilds (Ferguson, *The World's Banker*, 731, 734). Instead Bleichröder received the Iron Cross, second class (Stern, *Gold and Iron*, 156).

[9] Katherine Roper, *German Encounters with Modernity: Novels of Imperial Berlin* (New Jersey and London, 1991), 64, remarks of this that Ernst Schmidt's eulogy at the end of *Sturmflut* »propounds an idea that became deeply ingrained in German mythology: the crash of 1873 represented a moral judgment against the Germans, and their redemption would come only through their repentance of the greed that had led to it.«

[10] Allan Mitchell, *The Great Train Race: Railways and the Franco-German Rivalry, 1815–1914* (New York and Oxford, 2000), 50.

railroad entrepreneur Bethel Henry Strousberg in 1875 was doubtless one of the model events for Spielhagen's novel, which, however, takes place earlier, beginning in August 1872.[11] For it was Spielhagen's inspiration to associate the monetary flood with a meteorological one, a terrible tempest that struck Germany's Baltic coast in November of that year.

The novel begins on board a ship that runs aground because of the skipper's failure to take the advice of a merchant captain on board, Reinhold Schmidt. In a conversation with an aristocratic General von Werben and the local ministry president von Sanden, it emerges that they agree in their opposition to a plan to build a military harbor for the benefit of the Berlin-Sundin railroad; Reinhold tells of macrometeorological changes that will one day bring a flooding tempest to the area. The president is so impressed with Reinhold's technical competence that he offers him the post of pilot commander, putting him in charge of twenty-four pilots and other officials. Schmidt eventually accepts at the cost of his hopes for his advancement as a captain but out of patriotism, a sense of duty, and an instant attraction to the general's daughter, Else. In Berlin Reinhold visits his uncle Ernst, a marble manufacturer and embittered forty-eighter who lives in discord with his beautiful daughter Ferdinande, and, it emerges, his workmen; he has renounced his son Philipp, a *nouveau riche* railroad entrepreneur and partisan of the new order Uncle Ernst detests. Ferdinande, a pupil of the blithe and witty but socially unobservant sculptor Justus Anders, is in love with the general's son Ottomar, who is engaged to the trendy Wagnerian and Schopenhauerian enthusiast Carla von Wallbach and will be disinherited if he does not marry a noblewoman, while Justus forms a liaison with Else's cheery friend Marie (called Miete or Mieting) von Strummin. Else, who will also be disinherited if she does not marry a nobleman, is expected to wed Count Axel Golm of ancient lineage but cannot stand him. Carla comes to be lusted after by Golm, who must obtain the harbor construction concession, advantageous to his own property, to avoid bankruptcy; thus he is violently hostile to those who oppose the project, especially the plebeian Reinhold.

The general is estranged from his sister, Valerie von Warnow, because of her adulterous relationship with the irresistibly demonic Papal secretary Giraldi, who is plotting to obtain her wealth and the Warnow estate lo-

---

[11] On Strousberg as the model for Philipp Schmidt, see Bernd Neumann, »Friedrich Spielhagen: Sturmflut (1877). Die ›Gründerjahre‹ als die ›Signatur des Jahrhunderts,‹« *Romane und Erzählungen des Bürgerlichen Realismus. Neue Interpretationen,* ed. Horst Denkler (Stuttgart, 1980), 267.

cated on the harbor concession; if he can get Ottomar to marry Ferdinande, Valerie will be a half million richer. Giraldi sells the Warnow estate at a high price to Count Golm, who, however, is ultimately unable to make the payments on his loan because of the precipitate fall of stock investments, which also draws Ottomar into forging promissory notes in his father's name, causing Carla's brother to refuse a duel with him. The general sends his son a pistol in the expectation that he will restore his honor by taking his life but he flees with Ferdinande. The fall in the inflated stock price is precipitated by a fiery speech in the Reichstag by the liberal leader Eduard Lasker demanding the exposure of corruption in the award of railroad concessions. Philipp Schmidt is deeply into fraudulent business dealings; on the occasion of a grossly luxurious party on the day of Lasker's speech, at which Philipp has himself toasted and celebrated with fanfares, he is arrested, but he has planned ahead and manages his escape while locking the police officer in a room. He attempts to escape to Chile with his stolen money but is captured and takes his life.

As this plot machinery unspools, the tempest predicted by Reinhold rises, inundating the area and threatening everyone. Count Golm flees with Carla, whose erotic attraction to him is quenched by his display of selfishness and cowardice; they are rescued by Reinhold, who comports himself heroically. Ottomar and Ferdinande flee but are stalked by the jealous sculpture pupil Antonio, who may be – the narration is somewhat coy about it – the abandoned son of Giraldi and Valerie. Obsessed with Ferdinande, Antonio has been trying to murder Ottomar through much of the novel; Ferdinande receives the stab wound intended for Ottomar, who is killed by a falling tree in a last moment of unaccustomed bravery. Antonio and Giraldi get into a raging fight with one another and both drown. In the end Reinhold and Else marry, as do Justus and Mieting, both across class boundaries; the bereaved fathers, Uncle Ernst and the general, implacable enemies from the barricades of 1848, are reconciled.

Spielhagen was more voluble about the genesis of *Sturmflut* than of any other of his novels except *Problematische Naturen*; he wrote an essay entitled »Wie ich zu dem Helden von ›Sturmflut‹ kam.« But, as one can see from the essay's title, he is again caught in his obsessive dialectic of *Finder* and *Erfinder*, of estimating the relationship between model and fiction. »*I want a Hero*,« he said to himself, citing the opening line of Byron's *Don Juan,* not a problem for Homer or Cervantes *(NB,* 211–12). Soon afterward he found his hero in the Rügen pilot Friedrich Müller, a man who, after having been in office a couple of weeks, acquitted himself admirably during the flood in 1872 (214–16). Retrospectively Spielhagen worried whether he had abused the confidence of a man he never saw again (218).[12] He tells us he said to a lady friend: »ich möchte ein Bild der Verwüstung geben, welche der Milliardenunsegen in ökonomischer und sittlicher Beziehung über Deutschland gebracht hat« (219–20), adding that the idea of bringing the panic and the flood together had become an *idée fixe* even though the two events had nothing to do with one another and were half a year apart (220).[13] He thought of making his friend Lasker the hero of the novel, but considered that »ein Romanheld darf nicht zu aktiv sein, nicht an der Spitze der Phalanx marschieren; er absorbiert sonst alles Interesse« (220), a principle probably derived from Walter Scott. As was his custom, he explicated the title image in the text. Early on, the president links the flooding storm predicted by Schmidt to »eine Aufstauung von Fluten ..., die sich in einem ungeheuren Strom – einem Goldstrom, meine Damen – von Westen nach Osten ergossen haben« (*AR*, 1, 8: 70). Later he reminds Schmidt of this conversation:

> Nun *Ihre* Sturmflut, – ich hoffe zu Gott, sie wird nicht kommen; – aber, wenn sie käme, wie Sie prophezeit haben – ich würde sie für ein Gleichniß dessen nehmen, was über uns hereindroht, ja! für ein Zeichen des Himmels, ob wir vielleicht, aus unserem frevelhaften Taumel, aus unserm Schaum- und Traumleben erwachend, emporschreckend, uns den gleißenden Schein aus den Augen reiben, um – wie unser Fichte sagt, zu sehen, – »das, was ist.« (1, 9: 156)

As I mentioned earlier, this uncharacteristic employment of symbol, which seems rather contrary to Spielhagen's theoretical principles, reconciled the generally disdainful Martin Swales to this particular novel: »Die Sturmflut wird zur organisierenden Konstellation einer differenzierenden, breitspektrigen epischen Darstellung.«[14]

---

[12] Spielhagen's daughter gave a different account of how he derived the hero of the novel and other characters from life: Antonie Spielhagen, »Zum 80. Geburtstag Friedrich Spielhagens,« *Gartenlaube* [57] (1909), 167–68.

[13] The tempest occurred in November 1872, Lasker's speech exposing the collusion in railroad concession favors on February 7, 1873. Spielhagen (*NB*, 220) remembered the speech as having been delivered in May, possibly confusing it with another one in which Lasker criticized railroad free enterprise. For a review of Lasker's speeches, see Hermann Schierding, *Untersuchungen über die Romantechnik Friedrich Spielhagens. (Unter Benutzung unveröffentlichter Manuskripte)* (Borna-Leipzig: Noske, 1914), 39–40; for an account of the events, James Harris, *A Study in the Theory and Practice of German Liberalism: Eduard Lasker, 1829–1884* (Lanham, MD, New York, and London: UP of America, 1984), 93–95.

[14] Martin Swales, *Epochenbuch Realismus. Romane und Erzählungen* (Berlin, 1997), 106. Leo Löwenthal, *Erzählkunst und Gesellschaft. Die Gesellschaftsproblematik in der deutschen Literatur des 19. Jahrhunderts* (Neuwied and Berlin, 1971), 169, is unusual in disparaging the symbolic title as »kitschig.«

In truth it seems to me that much of Spielhagen's strongest writing is to
be found not only in the rising terror of the storm at the end of the novel,
which moves in overlapping sequences, a kind of narrative *Nebeneinander*,
from one set of beleaguered characters to another, but in all the settings of
the sea, including those of the opening chapters. This strength comes not
only from a realistic transformation of his own life experience but from his
enthusiasm for the shore environment and the seascape. The sea, he wrote,
was his first love and would be his last (*FuE*, 1: 34). Imagery of storms
and floods is commonly found in his texts. In several places »Sturmflut«
becomes a metaphor for the coming uprising of the people that, according to a prediction near the end of *Was will das werden?*, will punish both
the reactionaries and the liberals (*AR*, 3, 5: 450). Michelet's *La Mer*, which
Spielhagen had translated, contains a vivid description of a tempest lasting
six days and nights at Royan near the mouth of the Gironde.[15]

Whether he was as successful with the other part of the simile is less
certain. The crash and its effects naturally turn up in novels by others as
well. Spielhagen mulls the meaning of it in his discussion of his friend Karl
Frenzel's novel *Die Geschwister* (*AmSt*, 327–43). Fontane, some years later in
Frau Jenny Treibel, took note of the French gold:

> Als aber nach dem siebziger Kriege die Milliarden ins Land kamen und Grün-
> deranschauuungen selbst die nüchternsten Köpfe zu beherrschen anfingen, fand
> auch Kommerzienrat Treibel sein bis dahin in der Alten Jakobstraße gelegenes
> Wohnhaus ... nicht mehr zeit- und standesgemäß, und baute sich auf seinem
> Fabrikgrundstück eine modische Villa mit kleinem Vorder- und parkartigem
> Hintergarten.[16]

The gold itself is not much of a palpable presence in Spielhagen's novel,
and I, at any rate, find the financial machinations hard to follow, as I usually do in German novels, doubtless owing to my ignorance of such matters.
A tour de force is a series of juxtapositions: of Philipp Schmidt's elaborate
party with the worried financial conspirators buttonholing one another in
the vestibule, confounded by Lasker's speech; of the consternation Justus

---

[15] Jules Michelet, »La tempête d'Octobre 1861,« *La Mer*, 2nd ed. (Paris, 1861),
69–86.
[16] Theodor Fontane, *Frau Jenny Treibel, Sämtliche Werke*, ed. Edgar Gross, Kurt
Schreinert, et al. (Munich, 1959–75), 7: 15. Katherine Roper, »Imaging the
German Capital: Berlin Writers in the Two Unification Eras,« *1870/71–1898/90:
German Unifications and the Change of Literary Discourse*, ed. Walter Pape (Berlin
and New York, 1993), 187, points out that Karl Gutzkow's last novel, *Die neuen
Serapionsbrüder*, also deals with the crash. It was published, like *Sturmflut*, in
1877.

Anders causes by following Philipp's toast to the »Fürst-Reichskanzler ... mein Ideal; aber – ein unerreichbares!« with a second one to Lasker, seconded by the artists present (1, 9: 261, 263); of the police officer's effort to arrest Philipp as courteously as possible, allowing Philipp to outwit him and flee, with the collapse of the social event into general chaos as an objective correlative of the economic crash.[17] This is all, to be sure, rather melodramatic, a feature of the novel's tone that has been much complained of, and that is exaggerated by my own précis above, which cannot do justice to the texture of social interplay, satire, and comedy, or the passages of clever dialogue. The melodramatic effect is heightened by the calculated symmetry of poetic justice and swatches of sentimentality, especially in the figuration of the dying, angelic, exceedingly empathic blind girl, Cilli Kreisel, who may be descended from the blind young woman Eugenie Leiding in Wilhelm Raabe's failed second novel, *Ein Frühling*, but here seems rather crudely designed to tug at the reader's heartstrings.[18]

In any case, the respect occasionally shown to the novel has never been more than relative, and there has been a great deal of objection to it from that time to this. Fontane, in an unpublished review, complained that it was just random story-telling without regard to »die Wahrheit der Dinge« (which he, on the threshold of his own career as a novelist, apparently knew precisely), that it did not touch one soothingly or lift one in a conciliatory spirit above the quotidian as a novel should. He ranked the characters according to their correspondence to truth, declaring Giraldi »einfach ridikül.«[19] The demonic Catholic conspirator from darkest Italy

---

[17] Three years before *Sturmflut*, in Alphonse Daudet's *Fromont jeune et Risler aîné*, book 4, chapter 3, familiar to Spielhagen, the firm falls into bankruptcy while a party is being given; just as in Spielhagen's novel, there is dancing upstairs while the crisis emerges downstairs.

[18] A different view was expressed by Dolf Sternberger, who defended »Rührung,« today dissolved in general cynicism about motivation and sincerity; Cilli is »das einzige Wesen, über dem in jener fahlen Welt die Sonne machtvoll schien. Immerhin, hier schien sie«: Sternberger, *Panorama oder Ansichten vom 19. Jahrhundert* (Frankfurt am Main, 1974), 198; the allusion is to *AR*, 1, 8: 139. Dieter Kafitz, *Figurenkonstellation als Mittel der Wirklichkeitserfassung. Dargestellt an Romanen der zweiten Hälfte des 19. Jahrhunderts (Freytag · Spielhagen · Fontane · Raabe)* (Kronberg, 1978), 107–08, remarks more accurately that there is an incongruence of her ideals and her fate. Joachim Worthmann, *Probleme des Zeitromans. Studien zur Geschichte des deutschen Romans im 19. Jahrhundert* (Heidelberg, 1974), 111, uncharitably derives her from Jean Paul as »eine jener ätherischen Figuren von kindlicher Unschuld, die ... in die Trivialliteratur abgesunken sind«; presumably he is referring to the blind Liane in *Titan*.

[19] Fontane, »Friedrich Spielhagen. *Sturmflut*,« *Sämtliche Werke*, 21, pt. 2: 199–202. The editors in their annotation designate the novel as »den Höhepunkt seiner literarischen Entwicklung« and go on to say that »Fontanes Interesse an dem

was the most vulnerable object of criticism in the novel. Heinrich Hart, like Fontane, declared him ridiculous.[20] Klemperer, not unexpectedly, found him exaggerated and melodramatic, and the chapters in which he appears superfluous; Spielhagen's friend Strodtmann also thought the novel did not need him.[21] At the end of the nineteenth century a historian of the novel, who thought *Sturmflut* »einer der bedeutendsten Romanschöpfungen unserer Literatur,« found it damaged by »die etwas verbrauchte Figur des Jesuiten im Frack,« a type done better by Eugène Sue.[22] A modern critic has dismissed him as »bloße Intrigantengestalt, Theaterbösewicht.«[23] Only one lonely doctoral candidate in the past found the Giraldi plot unbelievable but not fatal to the novel, which she quite liked.[24]

Certainly, Giraldi is rather megalomanic; to Antonio he boasts: »Ich sage Dir, Knabe, daß Könige zittern, wenn sie fühlen, daß Gregorio Giraldi's Hand auf ihnen liegt; daß der heilige Vater in Rom selbst sich nur so lange unfehlbar weiß, als ich in seiner Nähe bin!« (120–21). This reference to Pius IX's declaration of Papal infallibility in 1870, so shocking to German Protestants and especially to liberals, gives us the clue, should we need one, to Giraldi's presence in the novel; he is an objective vindication of Bismarck's *Kulturkampf.* The connection is underscored by Giraldi's association with a half-blind *Exzellenz* who is said to cause the Antichrist Bismarck more trouble than the plenipotentiary of a great power (20, 30–36); his menacing behind-the-scenes power, at least in Giraldi's perhaps embellished account, may be intended to remind us of the all-powerful Grand Inquisitor in Schiller's *Don Carlos.* The cynical conspirator has been identified, rather deflatingly, as the wily Catholic politician Ludwig Windthorst.[25] The critics

---

Romancier S. nahm in der Folgezeit schnell und zusehends ab« (872). Here we see the familiar reception pattern both established and uncritically accepted.

[20] Heinrich Hart, »Friedrich Spielhagen und der deutsche Roman der Gegenwart,« in Heinrich and Julius Hart, *Kritische Waffengänge*, ed. Mark Boulby (New York and London, 1969), 60–61.

[21] Klemperer, *Die Zeitromane Friedrich Spielhagens*, 119–20; Strodtmann, *Dichterprofile*, 207.

[22] Hellmuth Mielke, *Der Deutsche Roman des 19. Jahrhunderts* (Berlin, 1898), 375–76. Giraldi is not a Jesuit but a layman in service to the Church. Klemperer makes the same error.

[23] Kafitz, *Figurenkonstellation*, 108.

[24] Elfriede Kloster, »Die Technik der Gesellschaftsszene in den Romanen Friedrich Spielhagens und Theodor Fontanes« (Diss. Frankfurt am Main, 1944), 62.

[25] Klemperer, *Die Zeitromane Friedrich Spielhagens*, 119; Schierding, *Untersuchungen über die Romantechnik*, 110. Hart, »Friedrich Spielhagen,« 43, asked why the author had masked Windthorst's identity when it was obvious. A reviewer in a Catholic periodical was naturally distressed: E-e [Emil Fritsche], »Sturmflut,« *Im Neuen Reich* 7, no. 1 (1877): 375.

have been right to find this episode superfluous; it has nothing to do with the analogy of storm and economic disruption, nor has the figure allegedly representing Windthorst any relevance to the plot. But my concern is that Spielhagen, by associating himself *e contrario*, through the bloodthirsty villainy of his Catholic figures, with the illiberal and ultimately failed policy of the *Kulturkampf,* appears to be adapting himself to the Bismarckian order, despite an inconsistency with the negative valence given to Philipp Schmidt's admiration of and identification with Bismarck. The unpersuasiveness of the Giraldi-Antonio-*Exzellenz* complex is a sign of its compromised function in the novel.

The complacency appears also in the static characterizations. Of all the figures, only the parvenu swindler Philipp exhibits much of a dynamic and ironic personality. Reinhold Schmidt is the perfect young German, strong, handsome, steady, competent, heroic when necessary, reliably loving. One would doubtless be pleased to know such a man, but as a fictional character he lacks dimension. It has been said that Reinhold's stability is disappointing to the reader, »robs the work of conflict and therefore of a vital energy,« and that he serves the author as »his own straight man.«[26] Else von Werben, who falls in love with Reinhold at first sight, is perfectly steadfast, perfectly indifferent to class considerations or to the loss of her wealth should she transgress them. The greedy and lubricious Count Golm, who, it emerges, has seduced and left pregnant the sister of an impoverished tenant on his property, is a perfect villain, and the incompetently conniving Ottomar von Werben a perfect upper-class weakling. There is a high degree of managed reconciliation, involving most of the characters except the impossible Golm: Reinhold Schmidt and the artist Justus Anders win the respect of their social superiors and marry the highborn Else von Werben and Mieting von Strummin respectively, after conventional complications, almost without hindrance; Ottomar von Werben and Ferdinande Schmidt are buried and mourned together as a sign of a union that should have been allowed. The former bitter enemies from the barricades of 1848, General von Werben and Ernst Schmidt, achieve a reconciliation with an ease that has made more than one observer suspicious.

This clearly programmatic development in the novel was early prefigured by a planned design of Anders for a war memorial depicting a reconciliation of figures modelled on General Werben and Ernst, who at that time angrily rejects the idea (1, 8: 126–33). Several features of the development

---

[26] Alexander Robinson Anderson, »Spielhagen's Problematical Heroes« (Diss. Brown University, 1962), 150–51.

are striking. One is that the reactionary, aristocratic general with his military bearing and rigid notions of caste appears to have a finer and more flexible character than the bourgeois liberal Ernst Schmidt. The general ultimately accepts the union of his daughter with Reinhold even though the name of Schmidt has been sullied by Philipp's conduct (1, 9: 332–33). The general's dispatch of a pistol with which he expects his shamed son to take his life may seem implausibly severe, but we will recall Spielhagen's admiration for military virtue. On the whole, the general seems to be the more gracious and forthcoming of the two; Ernst, on the other hand, is extremely rigid and, if anything, more insistent on class status and correctness than the general, beset as he is with implacable hatred of monarchy and nobility (1, 8: 369). It is perhaps understandable that Ernst has renounced the son who has abandoned bourgeois virtue for the sleazy ethics of the capitalist class; in fact, the shared condemnation of and mourning over their lost sons eventually joins the two fathers in brotherhood (1, 9: 342, 451).

But Ernst has also alienated his daughter Ferdinande by neglecting her emotionally and particularly by disrespecting her artistic ambitions as a pupil of the sculptor, creating a bitterness in her with which she eloquently reproaches him. As a manufacturer he is a harsh master. When his workers begin to organize against him (for which he oddly blames Bismarck, 1, 8: 155), he orders them all dismissed as socialists in one furious gesture; when his foreman refuses to dismiss the workers, he fires him also. The narrator's attitude toward this matter is unclear. Bismarck had not yet implemented his notorious *Sozialistengesetz* of the year following the novel, so that presumably is not an issue. The striking workers, whom Reinhold tries to mollify, are inflamed with brandy (250); the owners and the police make common cause against them. When the understandably distraught workers and poor people caught in the flood begin to riot and loot, they turn into the bestial mob conventional in portrayals of the subcivilized underclass at the time. On the other hand, when the loyal bookkeeper Kreisel, the father of the angelic Cilli, declares he must be dismissed also because he is a socialist, adding: »Ich halte auch den Communismus unter Umständen für gerecht« (257), Ernst pooh-poohs it; his renewed bond with Kreisel may be an indication that his attitude toward labor relations may become more gentle. All in all, however, this is the most critical portrayal of a traditional liberal figure in all of Spielhagen's fiction.

The reconciliation seems more canted toward the general's terms. Like much of the Prussian nobility, his family is not wealthy and has lived for military service (358), a positive valence for Spielhagen, as we have seen, a quite different sort of nobility from that of the rapacious *Junker* Golm.

For his part, the general yields on the inviolability of class boundaries and develops at last some sympathy for his wayward sister, in miserable thrall to Giraldi. He is forced by circumstances, by his son's shaming of him, to acknowledge Ernst's character, but he does so in terms that assimilate Ernst to nobility: »eine fürchterliche Stunde war's, als er sich so tief, so tief vor dem stolzen Plebejer demüthigen mußte, wenn der Mann selbst auch das Siegel des Adels, den die Natur verleiht und das Leben manchmal bestätigt, auf jener mächtigen Stirn, in jedem Zuge des schönen, ehrfurcht-heischenden Antlitzes trug« (1, 9: 334). But Ernst not only relaxes his class prejudice in their first approach to one another on a train in pursuit of their sons, he renounces much of the democratic and revolutionary conviction of his past. He regrets his Enlightenment skepticism that has led to contempt for the sacred law and to excessive individualism, and has concluded that »der Grundsatz schrankenloser Freiheit und absoluter Selbstbestimmung in seiner äußersten Consequenz schwächere Geister zu Abwegen führen kann,« though one might wonder who has ever held such principles (1, 9: 338, 340). Ernst's gratification at his son's suicide because it proves that he was not cowardly (458) clearly shows him cleaving to the general's military ethos.[27]

It is not surprising that the paradigmatic class reconciliation, morally and ideologically weighted as it is toward the aristocratic side, has made the novel appear to be canted toward the notorious conformation of the German middle class with the aristocracy.[28] Spielhagen, as is his custom, ends the novel with an oration, Ernst's eulogy at the funeral of Ottomar and Ferdinande. He asserts that there has been too much greed and selfishness, but the disaster proves that we must love one another (459); though not clearly indicated, the implication from his experience with the general as well as from the achieved marriages is that this love must transcend class boundaries. Ernst's prediction that the sun will shine again and there will be hope for the future indicates an acceptance of the Bismarckian Reich that he had earlier bitterly opposed: »Das walte der Gott der Wahrheit und der Liebe zu der Menschheit Ehre und des deutschen Namens Herrlichkeit!« (459).

This last utterance is a sign of what strikes me as one of the most salient features of this novel: an amelioration of Spielhagen's customary antireligious attitude. Catholicism, to be sure, remains irredeemable; the two Ital-

---

[27] Earlier in the novel, Reinhold has been very impressed by the general's cordial treatment of him, which in turn is owing to his service at Gravelotte and his battlefield promotion to reserve officer (1, 8: 334).

[28] See the now classical view of this matter in Ernest K. Bramsted, *Aristocracy and the Middle-Classes in Germany: Social Types in German Literature (1830–1900)* (Chicago, 1964), 237.

ians clearly abuse religion. Giraldi, when seducing Valerie away from her husband, had sworn

> bei St. Peter's Dom, von dessen Riesenkuppel aus dem blauen Himmel goldene Ströme niederrieselten, daß die Liebe dieses schönen nordischen Weibes das goldene Fußgestell werden solle seiner Macht, die er, der Laie, im Dienste St. Peter's, und doch frei, – frei, wie er hier, einem Adler gleich, über der Welt schwebte, – ausspannen wollte über die ganze Welt (412),

and he promises Antonio »glänzende, ecclatanteste, herzerquickende Rache an Deinem Feinde. Ich schwöre es Dir bei dem süßen Herzen Jesu und der allerheiligsten Jungfrau,« after which both cross themselves (240–41). But the German characters develop a more acceptable religious discourse, especially as the storm rises. Cilli, in an effort to persuade Ernst to reconcile with his daughter, adverts to Christ's forgiveness of his persecutors (317). One would think this not the right language to appeal to the old forty-eighter. But after Ferdinande employs cultic analogies to denounce his harshness, »zerbrochen hast Du meine Seele, – mein Herz, meine Seele, meine Liebe Deinem Stolz geopfert, hingeschlachtet – mitleidslos, wie ein fanatischer Priester die Lämmer hinwürgt an dem Altar seines Götzen« (319), Ernst blames God for persecuting him and asserts it is not our fault if »unser Wissen und unsere Weisheit Stückwerk ist,« then suspects that Cilli has been God's messenger (320); he accepts that she is when he declares: »ich glaube an einen Gott, Herr General, Demokrat und Republikaner wie ich bin« (339). At the end, the local pastor sends word he is too hoarse to give the eulogy at the funeral of Ottomar and Ferdinande. Von Strummin accuses him of not wanting to offend the count: »Die Pfarre von Golm, die ihm der Graf versprochen hat, steckt ihm in der Kehle!« (449), normal conduct for Spielhagen's clergymen. But no, reports Reinhold, more sympathetic than the old aristocratic blowhard, the pastor is truly unwell and worn out from bringing aid and consolation in the crisis (450). It is as though Spielhagen were correcting himself, adjusting his attitude toward religion and its representatives. Ferdinande's grave monument, meanwhile, is a Pietà she has modelled for Anders (450). Here we see, in small but precise compass, the peace the novel has made with the realities of the Reich.

It is, of course, true that *Sturmflut* contains a vehement critique of fraudulent speculation and the conspiracies of capitalists with greedy noblemen. But the mighty Lasker has put this evil out of the world and the future looks bright. Men like Reinhold will protect the nation and true lovers will transcend class barriers. I should like to show in what follows that Spielhagen did not remain in this position. To prefer this novel is to condescend to him, consigning him to a dubious literary rank. The very faults of the novel, its melodrama, its lengthy patches of sentimentality, can be attributed to its adjustment to the dominant discourse. This was not the best he could do nor the end of his searching. The class conflict continues, reconciliation remains elusive, and the truce with religion turns out to be temporary.

14. Rural Idiocy: *Platt Land, Uhlenhans*

> *Plattland!* ja, das Land ist flach,
> Stroh deckt noch das Katendach,
> Atmosphäre junkerlich
> Doch was wär' ich ohne dich? (*NG*, 218)

Spielhagen was a city man and an urban writer, notwithstanding his sometimes expressive seascapes and landscapes. The course of his personal life indicates this. The town of Stralsund, where he grew up, had in 1864 26,693 inhabitants, of whom 2,236 belonged to the military garrison. As I remarked earlier, Spielhagen regarded his home town as a social and cultural backwater; when it appears as »Sundin« in his fictions he never represents it with much affection or even distinctive detail, as though there were nothing there.[1] Bonn, with 19,996 in 1861, was smaller and he cared for it less. Leipzig, with 85,394 in 1864, was more like it, as was Hanover, only slightly smaller with 79,694, though even there his autobiographical account suggests a feeling of provinciality. Complaining of the tedium of being stranded overnight in Zug in Switzerland, he noted: »Wer in großen Städten zu leben gewohnt ist, kann sich kaum eine, oder vielmehr gar keine Vorstellung von dem Thun und Treiben der Leute in solchen kleinen Oertern machen. Es kommt ihm vor, als ob die Menschen vor langer Weile sterben müßten« (*AmSk*, 71).

But Berlin, where he moved permanently in October 1862 a few months after returning from Switzerland, in the following year registered 552,020 inhabitants and was one of the fastest growing cities in the world; by the time of his death it had reached about two million.[2] As the growing metropolis approached and surrounded him he indicated no pronounced annoyance; the electric lights, pneumatic post, and elevators that captured his attention

---

[1] In *Platt Land* Stralsund is mentioned (*AR*, 2, 5: 497) as the place of historical events alongside of the »Sundin« of the present.

[2] The figures for the 1860s are taken from *Allgemeine deutsche Real-Encyklopädie für die gebildeten Stände. Conversations-Lexikon,* 11th edn. (Leipzig, 1864–68).

could, of course, only be experienced in the city. In his stories set in spas and resorts, the guests, when they are not landed nobility, are city people. In the last phase there is a notable inclination to set stories in Berlin. In *Was will das werden?* the protagonist's whole hometown milieu is shifted to Berlin, and at the beginning of book VIII, chapter 9, he finds that fate is turning him into a »Großstädter« (*AR*, 3, 5: 274). The recently married Antoinette in *Frei geboren* feels liberated in Berlin:

> Die zum Teil unabsehbar langen Straßen; die weiten Plätze; die Pracht so vieler Gebäude; die Menge, das Gewimmel der Menschen – das alles mutete mich wundersam an. Hier pulste der Wille zum Leben mit einer leidenschaftlichen Kraft, für die ich einen Maßstab zu haben glaubte in der Lebensleidenschaft, die immer in mir gewesen sein mußte und mir jetzt nur zum Bewußtsein kam. Wie ein Geschöpf erst weiß, was es kann und vermag, wenn es in das ihm gemäße Element versetzt ist: ein Vogel, der dem Käfig entflohen ist und zum ersten Mal die Schwingen in der freien Luft regen darf. (*NF*, 7: 233)

Spielhagen's relatively few rural settings, on the other hand, tend to be backward and oppressive. I think this is because when he thought of the countryside – excepting Thuringia, which he always enjoyed – there came to mind the coast of Pomerania and the Baltic islands, especially Rügen, a landscape of agricultural estates governed by autocrats with few limitations on their arbitrariness and populated by tenants who, in Spielhagen's rendering, are often severely impoverished. As I mentioned earlier, he went out of his way to assert that he and his family had had nothing but pleasant personal experiences with the local aristocracy, probably, as I imagine, to certify that his notorious critique of them did not proceed from personal resentment but from »objective« portrayal of the more general social environment. In any case, two years after the relatively hopeful *Sturmflut*, set in his homeland, we get a much less encouraging account of life in the area in *Platt Land* (1879).

The title is a pun on the flatness of the land on the North German coast with its low islands and *Plattdeutsch* dialect, with which the protagonist, like the author himself, has difficulties; as always, the verbal connection is signaled in the text, this time, right at the beginning: »Hier in der Heimat der plattredenden Menschen ist man wirklich auf dem platten Lande!« (2, 5: 2; the Low German is mostly hinted at, rarely reproduced in the text). Set in 1844, the novel begins with the arrival of a young Thuringian baron, Gerhard von Vacha, in the Pomeranian countryside, where he hopes to learn more about agriculture because of his need to contribute to the support of his orphaned brothers, one a painter in Italy, one just completing his legal studies, one on his way to America. Gerhard's vaguely defined position on the estate of Moritz Zempin, a bluff, hospitable, vociferous liberal, has been mediated by an old friend, Anton Stude, who hangs around as Zempin's feckless factotum and has led Gerhard to believe he was to be the mentor of the son of the house, who, however, had been killed in an accident with a horse three years earlier. Stude describes the milieu as a pastoral with humorous features and a comfortable place to loaf, and at first it seems like a continuous party, with children and adults playing games and thirty, forty, fifty people from the neighborhood at table, but Gerhard will soon discover that the company is nothing like »die Gesellschaft, deren Harmlosigkeit und Gutmütigkeit ihm Stude so gerühmt« (133); indeed, his experiences grow increasingly bitter and eventually quite dreadful.

The rather long, typically complex novel is difficult to summarize conveniently for three reasons. First, the technique of »objective« narration binds the reader closely to Gerhard's consciousness; for the most part, we see and understand only what he does. It has been pointed out that when Gerhard is unsure, so is the narration; where he loses clear consciousness, the narration must be interrupted.[3] Thus the exposition is piecemeal and over long stretches rather opaque to the reader; an important part of the background exposition emerges only in the very last pages. One sees here as clearly as anywhere the perhaps more commercial than aesthetic advantage of »objective« narration for holding the reader's attention and generating suspense. Secondly, however, Gerhard, though a good, decent, even rather moralistic young man, is not an especially clever one. He is easily influenced, constantly changes his mind about his estimation of others, and sometimes makes misjudgments that are refuted in the next pages. His tendency to be emotionally overwhelmed to the point of several times wanting to flee the scene, along with the rapid succession of one true love after another, may remind one of Oswald Stein in *Problematische Naturen,* though Gerhard is more serious and inwardly stable.[4] Thirdly, the relations

---

[3] Andrea Fischbacher-Bosshardt, *Anfänge der modernen Erzählkunst. Untersuchungen zu Friedrich Spielhagens theoretischem und literarischem Werk* (Bern and Frankfurt am Main, 1988), 42. Karpeles, *Friedrich Spielhagen,* 65–66, had already noticed that Gerhard is never absent from the narration; Wilhelm Scherer's review, »Zur Technik der modernen Erzählung,« reprinted in *Kleine Schriften zur neueren Literatur, Kunst und Zeitgeschichte* (Berlin, 1893), 2: 166, also comments on the closeness to Gerhard.

[4] Scherer, »Zur Technik,« 164, was reminded of *Problematische Naturen,* especially at the beginning. Göttsche, *Zeit im Roman,* 702–03, has also noted this parallel, observing that Gerhard »trotz vorübergehender emotionaler Verunsicherung als die moralische Identifikationsfigur des Romans fungiert«; it may be that I see Gerhard as more buffeted by the brutal environment than Göttsche implies.

among the characters are largely determined by events in the past and in the previous generation, which have been kept secret and emerge only in segments that bewilder Gerhard and therefore the reader, so that the novel has something of the inner structure of a detective story. In what follows I shall try to rearrange the pieces to make them more manageable, while, as usual, leaving out a good deal.

Moritz Zempin, for all his apparent ebullience and generous political opinions, is gradually revealed as a beleaguered incompetent, deeply in debt; Gerhard realizes that Zempin's neighbors come to his table to eat up the interest owed them (149); the partying indicates more squander than hospitality and from the excessive drinking takes on the appearance of a bacchanal. Zempin is at odds with his dour, violent-tempered brother Johann on a neighboring farm; Johann rages against his brother, the forester Garloff, and the government but wins Gerhard's good opinion because he is a bird lover. Johann Zempin has two daughters, the dream-like beauty Maggie and the plainer, Cassandra-like Edith. Gerhard falls promptly in love with Maggie, embraces her in the forest, and gives her a ring; Zempin seems to encourage this connection and she at one point plays the role of Thekla in Schiller's *Wallenstein*: »Du darfst hier Keinem trauen, nur mir!« (137). But everyone warns him against her as a Loreley, especially a Baroness Basselitz, an ungrammatically speaking former goose girl who is ambitious to marry Maggie to her son Bogeslav, called Lasing, a balding milksop who looks like a turtle; it turns out that this is what Maggie has been plotting for all along. By that time Gerhard has transferred his love to the good sister Edith, who, it emerges, has a volume of *Wilhelm Meister* missing from the edition in Gerhard's home. At the same time Gerhard is besieged by Zempin's second wife, the cheery, voluble, and flirtatious Julie, who tries to turn Gerhard against Edith and makes every effort to seduce him. Stude calls her a Pandora's box with a false bottom (437). She finally manages to sleep with him while he supposes he is only having erotic dreams of her but he finds a bow from her dress in the morning. The parallel to Wilhelm Meister and Philine is the most specific of several allusions to Goethe's novel, eventually spelled out by Gerhard with a series of, as it seems to me, inaccurate correlations to the characters (487).

Hovering in the background is an elderly, obstructionist, apparently slow-witted subordinate called Vadder Deep; this may be a label name from English, for he turns out to be a deep plotter who has entangled the bankrupt Zempin in debt and buys up all the obligations, so that he becomes the owner of all the property, a fact that emerges while he is blandly waiting tables. The forester Garloff is an angry man, who, when in the army, stabbed an officer who had insulted him and was pardoned to ten years of fortress imprisonment because of his valor in battle. His pregnant daughter Anna believes she must marry the brutal, alcoholic *Oberinspektor* Klempe; she ends by drowning, Spielhagen's usual disposal method for desperate females. She is actually pregnant by Zempin, who, it emerges, has ravished women in the neighborhood from the Baroness Basselitz to trollops maintained for him by Vadder Deep. At the top of the social pyramid are the vaguely well-meaning, uncomprehending Count Ulrich Westen, who wishes to defend monarchism and conservatism against godless liberalism, and his countess, Alix, who lectures Gerhard on the need for aristocrats to stick together against peasant parvenus like the Zempins; she finds the rumor that he is to marry Maggie ridiculous.

The count is instrumental in the background story insofar as he is attempting to restore the reputation of a French officer, believed to have disappeared with the regimental funds in 1813; he had been wounded and trapped in the snow but rescued by a German friend, who translates *Wilhelm Meister* to him, astonishing him that the Germans could have such a wonderful book. This is the book that Gerhard found in Edith's possession, because the German was his grandfather, and it turns out that he and the Frenchman were murdered and robbed by the father of the Zempin brothers together with Vadder Deep, whose theft initially funded his plots, and Garloff.[5] Every effort is made to suppress this story, especially so that the criminal family background should not endanger Maggie's marriage to Lasing.[6] Vadder Deep succeeds in the short run – the count actually admires his business acumen and they share the desire to let bygones be bygones – but with poetic justice, he is killed by a falling stone while attempting to serve the count by digging up a megalithic grave, a project he had tried to pursue against Zempin's opposition. Zempin, despite his promiscuity, grows jealous of Gerhard and challenges him to a duel;

---

[5] He was once a rider with Schill's *Freikorps*, who excuses himself on the ground of hatred of French. He did not know the other man was German but would have hated him even more for associating with a French officer; nevertheless he has repented. I suspect in this ambiguous case some inner revision of Spielhagen's nationalistic affects, such as will come to the surface in *Noblesse oblige* three years later.

[6] It is psychologically interesting that Johann Zempin, who was twelve at the time, has repressed the traumatic memory, but sudden fires can trigger psychotic states in him during which he speaks French without having learned the language (185–89). Gerhard supplies an interpretation of Johann's condition that Edith finds »sehr scharfsinnig« but doubtful; it turns out to be quite wrong (189).

when Gerhard fires into the air Zempin aims directly at him, but is shot down by Garloff, who then takes his own life. At the end Gerhard is living happily with Edith in his Thuringian home while visitors tie up a whole list of plot threads.

The most remarkable aspect of the novel is the speed with which character and situation accelerate into catastrophe. At the beginning we might suppose that we are being led into a bucolic setting, possibly a version of *Dorfgeschichte*. Stude tells Gerhard that Jean Paul should have lived here (72–73). To be sure, Gerhard thinks his friend wasting away in this place, brooding to himself: »Man ißt nicht ungestraft Lotos mit den Lotophagen!« (74), possibly a variant of the line from Ottilie's diary in *Die Wahlverwandtschaften*: »Es wandelt niemand ungestraft unter Palmen.«[7] But at this point he is far from perceiving the potential for disaster in the situation, though on a second reading the signs of disorder begin to appear early on. The deterioration is externally accelerated by the partying and particularly by an elaborate festival that Stude, much like the factotum Zeisel in *Allzeit voran*, is obliged to organize. In that novel, as here and in numerous other narratives, such as *Sturmflut*, parties and celebrations catalyze quarrels and confrontations, often escalating to destructiveness and serious fighting. Already in part one of *Problematische Naturen* there are two catastrophic balls, in Chapters 22–27 and 58–60. Many years ago the »Verbindung von Fest und Katastrophe« in the novels was noted.[8] The escalation in strife is often associated with drinking. Shortly after arrival Gerhard finds himself rather offended by a party atmosphere in which men and women douse each other with water and which develops into a proper bacchanal: »in das Geschrei der Knechte, das Kreischen der Mägde mischte sich jetzt wütendes Gebell und langgezogenes Heulen der Meute, als ob die wilde Jagd hinter dem Bosket vorüberbrauste« (49), and later on Julie finds herself unable to serve supper because people are too busy drinking (325).

The evils of alcohol and the relationship of drink with dissoluteness are, of course, familiar themes in realist fiction. One might think of Gervaise's saint's day feast in Chapter 7 of Zola's *L'Assommoir*, which ends with

[7] Johann Wolfgang von Goethe, *Werke*, vol. 6, *Romane I*, ed. Benno von Wiese and Erich Trunz (Hamburg, 1958), 416.

[8] Kloster, »Die Technik der Gesellschaftsszene,« 110. Kloster notes, in addition to *Problematische Naturen* and *Platt Land*, *Die von Hohenstein, In Reih' und Glied, Was will das werden?, Noblesse oblige, Opfer, Ein neuer Pharao, Sonntagskind,* and *Frei geboren* (110–11). She adds that this »Verbindung« goes back to »eine uralte literarische Tradition« (120).

something like a riot in the street.[9] But, although Stude sermonizes on the terrible vice of drink and predicts that all on the estate will perish of it (354), I do not think that alcohol is the efficient cause of vice, violence, and degeneracy, as sometimes seems to be the case in Zola. Rather it dissolves the inhibiting veneer of civilization from the brutal and anarchic potential already present in the characters. The narrator of *Problematische Naturen* observes on a similar occasion: »Der dünne Firniß äußerlicher Cultur, aus welchem die ganze sogenannte Bildung dieser bevorrechteten Klasse bestand, begann von den Strömen Weines, die unaufhörlich flossen, in einer erschreckenden Weise heruntergespült zu werden, und die nackte, trostlos dürftige Natur kam überall zum Vorschein« (1, 1: 217). The *Hühnengräber* on the disputed property where the most disastrous outing takes place are as close to a symbol as Spielhagen is likely to get. That »bereits seit zwei Stunden ein Kriegsbeil nach dem andern ausgegraben wird« Stude ascribes to the spooks of »die alten hier begrabenen Berserker« (2, 5: 326), but a careful reading indicates that the revellers bring their berserk readiness with them. The count's determination to open the graves is thus an indication of his imprudence, and Vadder Deep's death while attempting to do so a form of recursive poetic justice.

The figuration of the reactionary count is an indication that Spielhagen is reverting to type in regard to class. The lower classes appear unruly and recalcitrant. Zempin complains that he brought Enlightenment with him from the university, trying to create free peasants on the basis of his reading of Goldsmith's *Deserted Village*, but no one will follow him (111–12). As for Zempin himself, he appears actually to justify the count's complaint that parvenus are trying to behave like aristocrats (244–45), for he conducts himself as a resentful, would-be tyrant, of whom Stude says that he hates the count »weil er für sein Leben gern selbst ein Graf wäre, oder ein Fürst, oder König« (439–40). In keeping with the positive impression Zempin makes in the early part of the novel, his political opinions appear acceptable, if somewhat vehemently expressed. No sooner has he met Gerhard than he praises the sacred sun of 1830, adding that he himself helped to build the barricades in Paris and including Gerhard in the somewhat extravagant locution: »die wahre Freimaurerei der Bildung, die wahre Demagogie ...

---

[9]   Frederick Brown, *Zola: A Life* (New York: 1995), 248, points out that, especially in the novels after 1871, there are »scenes in which Zola's mercurial characters gather for a banquet or ball that invariably disintegrates into a melee.« *L'Assommoir* was published in the same year as *Sturmflut*.

im Namen der wahren Dreieinigkeit und Dreiherrlichkeit: im Namen der Freiheit, der Gleichheit und Brüderlichkeit« (14–15). But Gerhard already finds him somewhat theatrical, and later, when Zempin denounces the ministry »bei dem himmelschreienden Not der schlesischen Weber, bei dem heiligen Trier'schen Rock-Skandal, bei den unglaublichen Bundes-Zuständen,« Gerhard is reminded of Mirabeau, but the magic Zempin had exerted on him has been obviated by what Gerhard has been learning about him (148). Much as in the case of Uncle Ernst in *Sturmflut*, the militant liberal is also deeply hostile to rebellious workers. To Gerhard he declares that humaneness is out of place in dealing with the »Gesindel« (395). But it is a little difficult to place the author in this matter, for Zempin makes this comment after an episode when Gerhard has tried to deal fairly with the grievances of casual workers over their food, whereupon they decide he is a pushover and start brawling again, obliging him to produce his pistols in order to show them who is boss (374–75). In any case, when Zempin is far along in his deterioration, he has a fierce confrontation with the workers; when his carriage is attacked by the *Oberinspektor* Klempe at the head of a drunken mob, the enraged giant nearly kills Klempe with his bare hands and smashes the others to the ground with a pitchfork. To be sure, the attackers, with their »brutalen Gesichter,« try to kill Gerhard as well, seriously wounding him (428–29).

In the matter of religion Spielhagen seems to be finding his way back to his fundamental position after his moment of accommodation in *Sturmflut*. When, early on, Zempin says that, having experienced »Tage, in denen der Baal der Tyrannei von seinem Piedestal der Lüge und Heuchelei gestürzt wird, wie ein thönern Gebild des Aberglaubens und der Pfafferei, der er ist,« he must believe only in a God of freedom and justice, Gerhard says simply: »Ich glaube an ihn« (14). Later, Gerhard has a moment of radical skepticism about the existence of God when he considers Anna Garloff's pathos; he prays for a sign of God's justice to restore his faith in man: »Wer soll noch an Menschenhoheit und Menschenwürde glauben, wie soll das Chaos nicht wiederkehren, wenn du deine Engel nicht schützen kannst!« (459–60). Thus he is trying to hang on to a kind of liberal, secularized faith, but throughout the novel one has the feeling that, for all the narrator's closeness to Gerhard's perspective, he is more naive and limited in perception than the narrator. Garloff, through his embittering experiences of class oppression, has given up belief in God except for the principle of an eye for an eye (505). The local pastor is not as bad as some in Spielhagen's works, more fool than knave; he does permit Garloff to bury his drowned daughter against regulations, but he does so because he wants everyone to keep mum; he is a trimmer, an evader, who babbles on about how lucky the Zempins are with an inheritance just at a time when their lives have fallen into total catastrophe (475, 480).

Given Spielhagen's views about the immediacy of models and situations, it is a little difficult to understand why he set this work thirty-five years in the past. It is possible that he was still hesitating to confront the new Reich critically and therefore located these wretched circumstances in his homeland back into the preunification past. Karpeles praised the novel as »ein gut Stück der Kulturgeschichte Pommerns in der neuen Zeit, ein Werk von historischer Bedeutung.«[10] But there is nothing in the novel to indicate a contrast with the present; the concluding *Happy-End,* to use the German term, is no more than a tying up of narrative strands and furthermore, unlike in *Sturmflut,* it is removed from the geographical setting of the novel out of Pomerania into Gerhard's Thuringian homeland. Otto Brahm asserted of *Uhlenhans,* which is set even further back into the past, in 1835, that »Spielhagen, der Dichter des Modernen, bleibt modern selbst da, wo er uns in die Vergangenheit ein gutes Stück rückwärts führt,« holding to the present even when he seems to want to flee it.[11] Perhaps the critical and desolate tone held the reader's attention more than the chronological setting.

Uhlenhans (1884) is set a decade earlier in a similar locale, but less space will be devoted to it because, although it reinforces Spielhagen's bleak view of rural conditions, it falls back into some of his less attractive narrative habits. The title figure, Baron Hans von Prohn, a large, unkempt man of thirty, is struggling to maintain an estate on the island of Rügen against a sea of troubles, most of which emanate from his own family. His grandfather had wasted the substance of the estate; his grandmother has married a Frenchified former Swedish diplomat, named, as elsewhere, Lindblad, a malicious, degenerate intriguer with a gambling habit; although Hans lives in an outbuilding in order to leave the main house to the old couple, Lindblad resents him bitterly for being kept on an allowance, especially as he feels hopelessly déclassé among the rustic boors. Uhlenhans,

---

[10] Karpeles, *Friedrich Spielhagen*, 64. Much of Karpeles's writing indicates an enthusiasm for the new Reich on the part of the Jewish critic and literary historian. See my essay, »Rückwirkende Assimilation. Betrachtungen zu den Heine-Studien von Karl Emil Franzos und Gustav Karpeles,« *Von Franzos zu Canetti: Jüdische Autoren aus Österreich. Neue Studien,* ed. Mark H. Gelber, Hans Otto Horch, and Sigurd Paul Scheichl (Tübingen, 1996), 163–88.

[11] Otto Brahm, [review of *Uhlenhans*], *Deutsche Rundschau* 38 (1884): 309.

Low German for »Eulenhans,« is so called because he is blind in one eye that remains open like an owl's. It emerges that, in his boyhood, it was shot out by his brother Gustav, who was jealous of Hans's superiority with the crossbow. Hans, however, has never wavered in his love for his brother, for he is a modern version of the traditional figure of the pure fool, striving to be a good man, kind and faithful to all, thinking the best of everyone, consequently scorned, ill-used, and betrayed on all sides. He is secretly in love with a poor relation, Hertha, who, he knows, loves the handsomer and more dashing Gustav. He, however, had disappeared to escape his debts and Hertha is supposed to be engaged to his bosom friend Count Axel Grieben, a hard-drinking gambler at odds with his father over money; it soon emerges, however, that Hertha wants nothing to do with him.

At the beginning of the novel Gustav returns, apparently on a mission from King Ludwig I of Bavaria to the Prince of Oldenburg, whose daughter is to marry Ludwig's son, King Otto of Greece.[12] Furthermore, Gustav has brought with him a Greek wife, the stunningly beautiful Isäa, one of Spielhagen's most ruthless *femmes fatales*, accompanied by their neglected child, Eua, and a violent old harridan named Zoë, who hates Gustav and is an ally of a vengeful Greek named Valianos, who regards himself as Isäa's husband and lurks in the background, stalking the couple. Isäa is the daughter of an imprisoned smuggler named Kolokotronis, who happens, with one of Spielhagen's patented coincidences, to share the name of the revered Greek patriot Theodoros Kolokotronis (1770–1843), here elevated to the rank of prince, also imprisoned, but possibly a candidate for amnesty. Gustav passes her off as the daughter of the latter, so that she is revered as not only a belle but also a princess. Gustav, however, seems to regret his association with her and to regard his marriage as dissolvable, as he ardently woos Hertha, who, in order to escape from her own susceptibility to him, engages herself to Hans, a move from which she soon recoils in repugnance. Isäa, meanwhile, learning that Gustav is not as rich as she thought he was, imagines herself as the sovereign of these barbarians and bewitches all the

---

[12] It is not clear to me whether there is a dimension of political criticism in the allusions to Otto's reign in Greece, which, as readers of the novel were likely to remember, ended in ignominy and revolution. The letter exposing Gustav, to which we shall come presently, observes: »Hat sich doch in München ... selbst der allerdings etwas phantastische König täuschen lassen, und dem ›liebenswürdigen Rugier,‹ mit einer delikatesten Mission betraut, zu der man an solcher Stelle nur allerprobte Personen erwählt!« (*AR*, 2, 7: 355). In the circumstances this seems a rather devastating comment on Ludwig I.

men except Hans, especially the elderly Prince Prora, who gives her a decorated carriage he had intended for his wife, and Axel, to whom she offers a reward of sex if he will flee with her, even though she regards him as a »blonder deutscher Dummkopf« (2, 7: 307). Axel's father wants him to marry Comtesse Ulrike Uselin, a twenty-five-year old beauty with a dowry of half a million, but she refuses him as she has all suitors; once she proposed to Hans, but he refused her, being able to love only Hertha.

Axel, it emerges, has impregnated Hans's former flame Hanne Prebrow, daughter of a dissolute tenant; Hans rescues her from drowning herself and for his pains is reputed to be the father, partly through Hanne's own guile, a rumor that estranges Hertha further from him. A friend of Hans, Carlo von Lilien, foster son of the prince, turns up with a letter exposing Gustav's deception; Hans, devastated, disappears for a time, arousing Gustav's hope that Hans has killed himself, solving all the brother's problems. When he thinks: »meinetwegen hätte er überhaupt nicht geboren zu werden brauchen; das wäre das einfachste gewesen« (358), he reminds one of Schiller's Franz Moor. Since Hans has given Gustav the key to the drawer containing the proceeds from a successful rye harvest, telling him to take what he needs, he steals several thousand talers. A party organized by Gustav ends in a shooting in which he attacks Hans but is killed by Valianos; Hans, wounded in his good eye, is arrested for the crime. Although Isäa flees to London with Axel, she marries not him – his guilt in regard to Hanne has been revealed – but a duke nicknamed for his habits »Lovelace.« Carlo marries Ulrike. Hertha has discovered Hans's goodness and has learned to love him, but it is too late; he frees her from her promise, and when a mob of workers, made rebellious by Hans's kindness to them, attempt to liberate him by violence from the jail, he faces them down, saying the law, whether good or bad, must be respected; his innocence having been established in a letter from Isäa, he is freed, but all the time he is in pain from his wound, from which he dies on the steps of the jail, saying that Hertha's love would have been too much happiness for him.

Substantial parts of the novel are examples of the reader's sense of *déjà lu* of which Spielhagen's critics often complained. The married Gustav's erotically inflamed courting of Hertha reminds one of the married count's erotically inflamed courting of Hedwig in *Allzeit voran*. The conspiratorial, overwrought, ultimately bloodthirsty Greeks are counterparts to the Italians in *Sturmflut*; Valianos, in fact, has sworn on the Virgin to kill Isäa, her child, and her seducer if she does not return to him in twenty-four hours (312). The malicious, ungrateful, and potentially rebellious workers are by now recognizable. The unscrupulous Isäa's flight to London with a lover repeats that of Nanni in *Angela* and prefigures that of Lili Israel in *Was will das werden?* We have already seen the secret seduction and abandonment of a poor girl by a depraved nobleman in *Sturmflut* and *Platt Land*. The »bacchantische[ ] Lust« (410) at the party leading to violence and catastrophe is by now familiar. So is our author's susceptibility to manipulative sentimentality, here in the figuration of the pure fool Hans, scorned, misunderstood, and abused by everyone as he strives to be loving, kindly, and self-denying, recognized in his moral excellence only at the moment of his death. He wants to improve his property for the benefit of those who live on and near it (216); he is happy to the point of singing at the thought that his treacherous brother and vixen of a sister-in-law will live together with him in the manor house (224). At the very beginning of the novel he has donated a cow to help out a tenant, who therefore holds him in low regard (4); Gustav nearly laughs in Hans's face when he proposes to give a party, for Gustav has already begun the arrangements for one (223); Hertha has a nightmare after she has impulsively engaged herself to Hans in which he comes upon her as a big, one-eyed dog, embraces her while weeping, then turns into Gustav, for whom Hertha still yearns (116–17). While at the end Carlo declares: »Noch nie war er jemand begegnet, der seinem Ideal eines guten Menschen so durchaus entsprochen hätte,« Hans reproaches himself for his poverty of spirit (451–53). One may be inclined to think that an author who creates such a figure is feeling sorry for himself.

Two aspects of the novel indicate some movement. One is Gustav's self-estimate as a man of imagination, superior to rural yokels, starting with Hans, and maliciously contemptuous of Axel, who is supposed to be his friend and coconspirator. He supposes, quite wrongly, that Hans in his philistine sluggishness regards his »Phantasie, Herz, Verstand, Geist« (111) as faults. As his situation becomes ever more perilous, he takes courage from his superiority: »Was wissen diese Menschen, die keine Phantasie haben, von unsereinem!« (357). We have seen something like this before in Malte von Zehren of *Hammer und Amboß*, who has become a criminal while imagining himself an aristocratic robber baron, more a figure of romance than of history. But Gustav puts greater stress on his superiority as a creator of fictions, that is, the lies that he tells and then opportunistically revises with a quickness of mind that he admires in himself. In a moment when he is about to be caught, he thrills himself with the prospect of »die furchtbarste Lüge, im Vergleich zu der alles, was er je in seinem Leben und was er noch eben gelogen, Kinderspiel war« (252). The caricatured parallel to the artistic creator of fictions is plain enough. It frustrates Gustav, to be sure, that his excellence in this regard must remain secret; he several times fantasizes about how amazed the others would be if they only knew. There is a perverse authorial irony in this exploration of the porous boundary between fiction and lying, not least because the irredeemably wicked Gustav radiates more energy and more of a certain kind of creativity than anyone else in the novel. The self-formed and self-regarding man or woman whose real or imagined superiority to the common run of human beings conduces to ruthlessness and evil will appear in several permutations in Spielhagen's later writing.

Another hint at the future is the deepened cynicism of tone. Everyone except Hans and his friend Carlo is self-seeking, mean-spirited, and disloyal; even Hertha exhibits no small degree of vanity and selfishness, possibly the reason why the author does not allow a union with Hans, despite her belated recognition of his true character, to culminate in a *Happy-End.* Spielhagen's familiar satire of the upper classes is acquiring a more derisive edge. An example is the festival given by the amorous prince, in which he believes he is able to provide particular pleasure to Isäa by announcing with a toast to her that King Otto, upon reaching his majority, has amnestied her »father,« the patriotic hero. The prince arranges a fireworks display with flaming letters spelling »Hellas,« »Theodor Kolokotronis,« »Liberator liberatus,« and »Isaea« (283–84); Gustav, of course, has been laughing up his sleeve, imagining what fun it would be to tell them all how deluded they are (277). The irony that a sovereign German prince can admire revolutionary patriotism in someone else's country is perhaps lurking under the surface. Spielhagen does not end this novel, as had been his custom, with a spirited oration hopeful of the future; he has only the dying Hans urge: »Seid gut! seid Menschen! (467). This prospect seems to be receding in a process of which Spielhagen may not yet have been fully aware in his conscious mind.

15. What Now?
Was will das werden? Ein neuer Pharao

The fading of Spielhagen's literary reputation in the 1880s did not depress his industriousness; he soldiered on with a doggedness that might even be regarded as a form of heroism, or at least of fidelity to purpose. His later works include large, ambitious novels, reworking and revising his characteristic themes. Among them is an elaborate first-person *Bildungsroman*, *Was will das werden?* of 1887, which, along with *Problematische Naturen* and *In Reih' und Glied*, is one of his three longest works, each running to over a thousand pages. The title, alluded to in the text, as was his custom, is taken from Acts 2: 12, where the Apostles are amazed by the miracle of Pentecost. The King James version – »What meaneth this?« – does not capture the future-oriented thrust of the German rendering. But Spielhagen's employment of the allusion is ironic, for the biblical moment is optimistic, leading to Peter's prophecy of the outpouring of the Holy Spirit, when »your young men shall see visions, and your old men shall dream dreams« (2: 17), while the tone of the novel is conflicted and its future dimension uncertain; Spielhagen has become more radically insecure in the Reich.[1] As at Pentecost, people speak in tongues, but they do not understand one another and come to little accord. In an attempt to gain control over the characteristic complexity of the novel, I shall begin with a survey of the constellation of main characters.

---

[1] Franz Rhöse, *Konflikt und Versöhnung. Untersuchungen zur Theorie des Romans von Hegel bis zum Naturalismus* (Stuttgart, 1978), 203, remarks correctly that the title already reflects »eine Unsicherheit, die auch nach all den Debatten und Diskussionen in neun Büchern am Schluß nicht gewichen ist, es sei denn, man wollte das alte Fortschrittspathos als Lösung anerkennen.« Spielhagen had already alluded to the phrase in his diary from Switzerland: »Wie soll das werden? fragten wir mit dem Apostel« (*AmSk*, 70). Later, in *Herrin*, he has the Jewish physician, Geheimrat Lombard, when distressed about his daughter, sigh the phrase from the New Testament »hundertmal«: he then prays »fromm zu dem Gott seiner Väter« (*NF*, 4: 361). This seems incongruent, perhaps a moment of authorial inattention. In *Opfer*, Wilfried von Falkenburg, bewildered by his stress with his fiancée, thinks to himself: »Wie soll dies werden?« (6: 63).

The narrator, almost seventeen in 1870, believes that his name is Lothar Lorenz and that he is the son of Peter Lorenz, a poor, kindly carpenter who makes coffins and suffers from another of Spielhagen's white marriages with Katharina, a stunning beauty, who is cold and aloof, refusing to her son all the love for which he helplessly yearns. There are two unfriendly older stepbrothers: Otto, a lethargic wounded war veteran who becomes an apprentice carpenter, and the rather mean August, an apprentice locksmith who joins the cavalry but deserts to Switzerland and the French in what he takes to be the revolutionary cause. Among the neighbors are a bluff, good-humored drayman, Hopp, who drives the hearse with Lorenz's coffins, with his pretty daughter Christine, and the crass Jewish merchant Isidor Israel, known as I. I., whose gentler and weaker son, Emil, is one of Lothar's schoolfriends, while Emil's sister Jettchen, a skinny, hook-nosed, shy pianist, secretly loves Lothar. Other schoolmates are two aristocrats, Astolf and Ulrich von Vogtriz; Astolf remains consistently one of Lothar's enemies, but he is protected by the physically powerful and emotionally complicated Ulrich, whom Lothar calls »Schlagododro« after the giant in Immermann's *Tulifäntchen*, forming a friendship beset over the years with many stresses and ultimate antagonism. Schlagododro later has an affair with Christine Hopp but abandons her for class reasons. The Vogtriz boys had a cousin, Ernst, but he has been killed in an accident with a horse. His father, Major Egbert von Vogtriz, takes an interest in Lothar, who seems to resemble the deceased boy and who impresses the major with manners and education surprising in a carpenter's son; Lothar, for his part, develops an almost idolatrous admiration for the major (see Chapter 7). He has a daughter, the coquettish beauty Ellinor, who in the course of the novel is supposed to marry Astolf but has no intention of doing so. Another school friend of sorts is the pale, elegant, contemptuously intellectual Adalbert von Werin, who lives in poverty with an odd, obsessive mother and an unsmiling but intelligent sister Maria, her countenance paralyzed by a stroke when her father, accused of irregularities as a tax official, shot himself. While Schlagododro detests Adalbert, he likes Maria, but she distrusts his character and his allegiances, especially as she is, like her brother, a political and religious progressive, not to mention that Schlagododro also courts Ellinor.

Slithering through the novel is a sinister character named Weissfisch, who initially appears as a theater director. After the carpenter has died, Lorenz is at loose ends, trying to write a drama about Thomas Münzer. He has been lamed in his right arm when he runs into Adalbert's sword when attempting to protect him from an attack by an enraged Schlagododro, incidentally, to his frustration, keeping him out of military service in the

Franco-Prussian War. Weissfisch gets him an acting job with a Jewish director who has renamed himself Joseph Lamarque. But Weissfisch is actually the agent of the reigning duke, who has charged him with bringing Lothar to him as a protégé. In character, this duke is kin to the flighty, neurotic king of *In Reih' und Glied*, estranged from his duchess, claiming to wish he were not a ruler, professing sterile liberal sentiments, even a devotion to Social Democracy, and asserting collegiality with Lothar as a writer, unsuccessfully attempting to extract praise for his own poems.[2] Lothar develops a warm association with the duke's daughter, Adele von Trümmnau, who desires, against her father's wishes, to divorce her worthless husband, an absent, gambling diplomat, with whom she lives in yet another white marriage, in order to marry a Russian count, Alexei von Pahlen, a proscribed radical conspirator.

Behind this constellation of characters lies a complex of hidden family relationships and other connections reaching well back into the past. In the first place, Peter Lorenz is not Lothar's father but his stepfather. He came from a family of poor nailsmiths – there is a family tradition in a woodcut of an ancestor torn by dogs for poaching – and, having apprenticed as a stone carver, became a successful sculptor, but, when he marries his landlady's slatternly daughter to preserve her from degradation as a model, he fails in his art, for an artist needs purity in his house. Always having thought of princes as »gräßliche Wüteriche« (*AR*, 3, 4: 105), he joined the revolution of 1848, where he lost a finger and was captured by the then Lieutenant Vogtriz, learned carpentry in prison, and escaped. His wife having divorced him when he was in prison and then having died, he married the abandoned Katharina Frank out of pity for her and her child; she, having become an introverted Catholic, could be grateful but not loving to her husband and forgot motherhood. We shall skip the rest of his story of Lothar's origin, as it is evidently a red herring leading away from the truth. The mother, it turns out much later, is the daughter of a Vogtriz who went to America and made a rich marriage; the orphaned, headstrong girl ran away, eventually falling in love with a strolling actor, who is paid off

2   Kuno Francke, *Weltbürgertum in der deutschen Literatur von Herder bis Nietzsche* (Berlin, 1928), 113–14 associates the duke with the liberal-minded and musically talented Duke Ernst II of Saxe-Coburg, whom Goessl, »Die Darstellung des Adels,« 91, n. 49, later associated with the duke in *Hans und Grete*. Such identifications seem insecure to me. But when we hear that the duke is jealous of the theater success of the neighboring ruler (*AR* 3, 4: 469), one is surely invited to think of Georg II, duke of Saxe-Meiningen, who sponsored one of the most admired theater troupes in Germany.

and eventually shoots himself; she is now being sought as the millionaire heiress of her grandfather, »Arabella Vogtritz« (sic, 507). It appears that she wandered back to Germany as an American actress named Miss Wilson, in which character the duke fell in love with her, but, when he refused to divorce his unloved duchess and marry her, she attempted to drown herself and their child, but was rescued by a miller. It is after these events that she encountered Peter Lorenz. Thus Lothar's mother is a Vogtriz, whose wealth, evidently, has attracted the Catholic Church in the person of a priest who attempts to manage her and balk Lothar, and his father is the duke, accounting for his persistent desire to draw Lothar to him; later he learns that the duke intended to give him a baronial title (3, 5: 103–04). As he begins to grasp that Adele von Trümmnau is his half sister, his erotic attraction to her is dampened if not wholly suppressed. Thus once again we have a situation in which an apparent plebeian has secret noble and even princely family connections.

However, the motif is handled differently here. First of all, the secrets are not secret for long; by at least the middle of the novel they are evident to the reader. They also come to be evident to almost everyone else; it is Lothar who attempts to keep them secret in order to protect his mother's reputation and also to escape the uncertain enticements offered by the duke, whom, for his mother's sake, he is bound to despise, and he is repeatedly nonplussed when he discovers that others already know his true identity; they, in turn, are in various ways puzzled at his refusal to take advantage of his status and potential wealth. His reason is his determination to maintain his class loyalty; at his stepfather's death he has sworn an oath of fidelity to the poor and the abandoned (3, 4: 312). Thus he attempts to flee the duke to South America, leading to the Zolaesque scenes in the underworld of the Hamburg docks to which I called attention in Chapter 10, but, with one of Spielhagen's patented coincidences, Lothar encounters there his stepbrother August, in flight as a deserter, and sacrifices his ticket to allow August to escape while he himself is pursued by the duke's agent, Weissfisch. Five years later, after having failed, or become disgusted by, his theatrical experience, he determines to become a worker, apprenticing himself, despite his lame arm, to his stepbrother Otto, a struggling carpenter of window frames, who is poorly skilled, dejected, and somewhat indolent, insisting that no success is possible until the Social Democrats take over. Lothar tries to manage Otto's affairs as best he can. His acquaintances are bewildered by his determination to remain a *Handwerker*; Ellinor, when he rubs her nose in it, finds it shocking and calls him »unritterlich,« to which he replies, in his effort to impose class identity on himself: »Ich bin auch, Gott sei Dank, kein Ritter, gnädiges Fräulein« (3, 5: 178–79).[3] Only at the end, when his mother's wealth has been lost in the collapse of the Israels' bank and he has determined, after the orchestrated failure of his *Thomas Münzer*, to give his literary vocation one more try, does he have a full reconciliation with his mother and can marry Ellinor, daughter of his father's quondam enemy, now Colonel Vogtriz.

This reconciliation is different from that of the former enemies from 1848, Ernst Schmidt and General von Werben in *Sturmflut*, each giving some ground to the other in mutual tolerance, for Vogtriz has been drawn entirely away from his aristocratic and monarchist commitments into a liberal, even radical activism. He becomes associated with the nihilists Pahlen (now disguised as »Capt. Edgar Smith«) and Adalbert; there is a melodramatic scene when all three are arrested, whereupon Adalbert shoots himself (403–04). Vogtriz is attacked as a traitor in the newspapers and is scorned by his family, especially his nephew Schlagododro; eventually he escapes to Switzerland with Pahlen. Thus the bourgeois is not assimilated to the aristocracy; the aristocrat is assimilated to the radical left. This is an indication of the altered political tone in the novel, to which we shall come shortly.

The first-person *Bildungsroman* sometimes suggests an autobiographical element, as in the case, for example, of Gottfried Keller's *Der grüne Heinrich*. However, *Was will das werden?* appeared when its author was fifty-eight years old; although the final version of Keller's novel appeared when he was sixty, he began it at thirty-one. Spielhagen's narrator is about a generation younger than the author; nevertheless, he seems to replicate some of his author's experiences, especially acting in the theater and making his commitment to a literary vocation dependent on the success or failure of one work.[4] The first-person form relieves Spielhagen of all the strictures of objective narration.[5] The narrator can indulge in foreshadowing, often in an ominous tone. Lothar is repeatedly critical of his youthful naïveté. While not as scathingly self-contemptuous as Keller's narrator, he can sometimes grow sardonic. He tells us that his idealistic ear was pained and outraged when I. I. spoke openly of money; he laughs at the praise of something so

---

[3] Spielhagen does not seem to foreground a political and class distinction between *Handwerker* and *Arbeiter*, which had become significant at the time. This may be an indication of a movement toward the left end of the liberal spectrum.

[4] Roper, *German Encounters with Modernity*, 79, observes how Lothar successively rehearses Spielhagen's own dilemmas.

[5] For a comment on the autobiographical element and a survey of the authorial intrusions, see Fischbacher-Bosshardt, *Anfänge der modernen Erzählkunst*, 132–35.

contemptible as money and tells I. I. that he hopes for a world in which there is no money and all men can be free (3, 4: 135). He recalls this moment sardonically when he wishes he had some, at a time when he accepts employment from I. I. to accompany a delivery of his profiteering army supplies as his only way to get to the war. This connection gets more convoluted when a dubious, anti-Semitic journalist named Streben pays Lothar surprising sums for his poems, with which he wants to repay I. I.'s charity, only to discover that the money came secretly from Jettchen; thus he is paying I. I. with his own money (411). This is just an example of Lothar's struggles for subsistence that belong to the *Bildungsroman* experiences, but, as is often the case in the post-Goethean *Bildungsroman*, they are experiences of disillusionment abrading the idealistic faith that impelled the pursuit of self-formation in the first place.[6] As he mulls the incongruity of his admiration for Vogtriz, the man who fired on and arrested his stepfather, he asks himself: »So taugt doch wohl diese Ordnung nicht ganz? So ist doch etwas faul in diesem Staat?« (3, 5: 56). In fact, Lothar's course through his youth is marked by insecurity, labile emotion, uncertainty, and a sequence of unfulfilled purposes.

The critics have found much to object to in the novel. There has been complaint of the implausibility of the character of Lorenz's mother;[7] that the coldness and hostility of a mother toward her son can occur in real life I can certify from personal experience, but her account of her vengeful motives and the process of reconciliation with Lothar may not easily persuade the reader. One critic has characterized this rather sudden development as kitsch.[8] But when critics complain that the novel offers nothing new, no vision of totality or clear structure of hope, »no comforting words about the German future,«[9] it seems to me that they fail to appreciate how Spielhagen alters the import of similar materials under the pressure of his

---

[6] Göttsche, *Zeit im Roman*, 52, places Spielhagen into a development in which the *Bildungsroman* (or *Individualroman*) and the *Zeitroman* intersect. But one might add that it is just the engagement with contemporary history that decomposes the initial optimism of the *Bildungsroman*, as Raabe's *Abu Telfan*, mentioned by Göttsche in this connection, indicates. Lothar himself observes: »Wenn es den Menschen so schwer gemacht wird, zur Meisterschaft im Leben zu gelangen, darf man sich wundern, daß es so viele Stümper gibt?« (*AR*, 3, 5: 180).

[7] Klemperer, *Die Zeitromane Friedrich Spielhagens*, 129; Goessl, »Die Darstellung des Adels,« 160.

[8] Henrike Lamers, *Held oder Welt? Zum Romanwerk Friedrich Spielhagens* (Bonn, 1991), 139–40.

[9] Klemperer, *Die Zeitromane Friedrich Spielhagens*, 137; Lamers, *Held oder Welt?*, 99, Anderson, »Spielhagen's Problematical Heroes,« 154.

environment. Fritz Martini was closer to understanding when he observed that the confused form of the novel reflects the state of affairs at the time with its diluted, insubstantial aesthetic idealism.[10] In some ways Spielhagen has recovered some of the firm positions that seemed to become insecure in the first years of the Reich, for example, concerning religion. The conniving priest who tries to maintain control of Lothar's mother may be another stock figure out of the *Kulturkampf,* but the representation of the Protestant pastor, Renner, returns to Spielhagen's attitude toward religion when Lothar causes a scandal, especially among his upper-class connections, by refusing, out of loyalty to his stepfather, to be confirmed. Renner reflects a current development as a propagator of Christian Socialism, into which he seduces among others the journeyman carpenter with whom Lothar attempts to work to improve his stepbrother's affairs. Renner has been identified with the Prussian court theologian Adolf Stoecker.[11] Like Stoecker, he attempts to exploit anti-Semitism in order to lure the resentful victims of the social order from Social Democracy, shifting the blame for oppression from the dominant order onto the Jews. Lothar's resistance to Renner is a motif that runs through much of the novel, even though the treatment of the Jews is one its most disappointing features, as I discussed in Chapter 8 above.

The theme of the aristocracy has become, if anything, more intricate. The self-pitying duke expatiates on his concern for the poor and his desire to rule justly, but Lothar learns how destitute and oppressed the duke's own subjects are and is told by his rescuer, the miller, how the duke, by diverting water from the millrace, is forcing local people to emigrate to America (3, 4: 525–27, 540–46). Vogtriz, who wishes to find his way to progressive commitments and grieves that he has twice fired on the people, once on the barricades of 1848, then again in quelling a riot protesting Israel's urban development with its displacement and unemployment of workers, must abandon his class identity. One who cannot do this is Schlagododro, who is virtually a tragic figure, for despite his capacity for love and friendship, especially toward Lothar, he cannot in the long run tolerate Lothar's refusal of allegiance to monarchy and aristocracy, so that they become enemies de-

<hr />

[10] Martini, *Deutsche Literatur im bürgerlichen Realismus,* 431. Martini places the time of the action in the mid–1880s, but Roper, *German Encounters with Modernity,* 89, n. 33, has rightly corrected him, dating the second volume in the late 1870s.

[11] Victor Klemperer, »Die Juden in Spielhagens Werken. (Eine Studie zu seinem achtzigsten Geburtstag),« *Allgemeine Zeitung des Judentums* 78 (1908/09), 104: »ein meisterliches Stöcker-Porträt.«

spite themselves. Schlagododro's exploitative treatment of Christine exhibits conventional habits of his class. I commented in Chapter 6 on the perceived incongruity of his effort to study economics. Accompanying Schlagododro's prejudices is a streak of anti-Semitism, so that it is doubtless meant as ironic that he is mortally wounded in a duel with the Jewish Lamarque, who, as an actor, is even more skilled in weapons than the aristocrat.

A feature of the novel that may annoy the reader is the lengthy space devoted to political debate, which seems to bring the narration virtually to a halt for a good many pages toward the end. But these clotted passages, though artistically clumsy, reflect a crisis in political allegiance in Spielhagen's perspective. The basic premise is the decline of the liberalism that fueled the enthusiasm for national unity in the first place, a development stressed by all historians of this period. It is explicitly articulated by Lothar's teacher and encourager, Professor von Hunnius: »Es geht mit dem Liberalismus abwärts.... Es ist das Schicksal aller Mittelparteien in Zeiten, wie die unsre, wo die Gemüter in einer Weise erregt sind, daß ihnen nur das Extremste genügt.« Liberalism is being ground up between »Staatssozialismus,« that is, Bismarck's tactical occupation of social welfare policies, and »der Sozialismus *sans phrase*« (3, 5: 348). Hunnius himself presents the reader with some interpretive difficulties. Previously such liberal mentors have been sources of supportive wisdom for Spielhagen's protagonists. But Hunnius, who has become a busy politician, a member of both the *Landtag* and the *Reichstag*, appears as an opportunist who advises accommodation to the middle ground; although an old forty-eighter, he has given up republicanism as mistaken and claims to have found a better way to national unity (3, 4: 85). Furthermore, he is infected by the anti-Semitism that pervades the novel's atmosphere, blaming liberalism's decline also on its association with Jews (3, 5: 348–50). He looks, therefore, like a symptom of the decline of idealism in the political climate of the Reich. Yet he is a significant support to Lothar, defending him when his forthrightness gets him in trouble in school, combatting and defeating in an election the odious Pastor Renner, offering sobering advice on Lothar's effort to write his Münzer drama. He is, I think, a transitional figure, a type of which Spielhagen cannot yet let go but which already exhibits symptoms of obsolescence.

Bismarckian policy and Social Democracy are not the only extremes beleaguering liberalism. Militant French egalitarianism, represented by Lothar's hapless stepbrother August, is not taken seriously and is rejected as treasonable while Christian Socialism is little more than a device of the dominant order to dupe the working class. But much of the sometimes wearying political debate in the novel concerns »nihilism,« represented by

Pahlen, a coconspirator of the Russian terrorist Sergei Nechaev (28, spelled »Netschajeff«), and the imperiously austere Schopenhauerian Adalbert von Werin. The question of whether the term is correctly understood in the novel or whether it has any intelligible meaning need not concern us. In Pahlen's debates with Hunnius nihilism is characterized by a replacement of socialist dependence on the unreliable and uneducated masses with an insistence that the existing order can only be violently overthrown from above by culturally advanced activists who will gain the support of noble officials, of the upper ten thousand, and of military officers; thus Pahlen and Adalbert cultivate Colonel Vogtriz, though Lothar suspects them of suppressed disdain for him as a naive humanitarian. Pahlen shocks Lothar by advising him to get his mother's millions, identify himself as a Vogtriz, and, metaphorically, I believe, take the colonel prisoner (134). Spielhagen is certainly not advocating this authoritarian radicalism, which appears in the debates as abstract and *weltfremd*. Adalbert, who, with his posture of caustic superiority, impresses the young Lothar and serves his *Bildung* by articulating unconventional ideas, retains the intellectualized contemptuousness of a bright but arrested adolescent and ends in philosophical despair. But Count Pahlen, for all that he seems somewhat woolly-minded, remains a sympathetic figure down to his ultimate exile to Switzerland. The space that Spielhagen gives to this option is an indication of the insecurity of location that has befallen him despite Hunnius's concluding rhetoric.

The insecurity is evident also in the open-endedness of the novel that has made some critics uneasy. It lacks the full closure customary especially in the first-person *Bildungsroman*, written, one presumes, from a point of retrospective stability. Two matters in particular are left unresolved. One is the uncertainty as to whether Lothar's gamble on his literary vocation with one more decisive effort actually succeeds. Since he has written this account of himself, perhaps we are to conclude that he has become a *Dichter*, but this is nowhere made explicit. Nor is the literary quality of his drama about Thomas Münzer entirely clear. It is all too evidently impelled by ideological purpose, like Lothar's provocative sonnets critical of Bismarck (210–13); it is likely that the Münzer drama is meant to recall Lassalle's drama *Franz von Sickingen* (1859), much criticized by Marx and Engels.[12] The entanglement

---

[12] See Peter Demetz, *Marx, Engels and the Poets: Origins of Marxist Literary Criticism*, tr. Jeffrey L. Sammons (Chicago and London, 1967), 107–15. In the novel, however, it is the semicultured duke who recommends that Lothar read Lassalle, »ein profunder Kopf« (*AR*, 3, 4: 444). Since the duke has just spoken of the Peasants' Wars, this may actually be an oblique allusion to *Franz von Sickingen*.

of Lothar's drama in various opportunistic contexts makes it hard to evaluate. His own recollection that he began it with the conviction that »Vater Apollon würde dem Tapferen gnädig sein!« (3, 4: 402) is clearly self-ironic. His mentor Hunnius finds it promising but immature and advises him to lay it aside and take up the sword of activism (413–15). Lothar has trouble getting it staged, and when Lamarque puts it on for one performance, it is panned by the critics, possibly a Jewish conspiracy, for only the Jewish director Lamarque is praised, although Pastor Renner dictates one of the hostile reviews; eventually Lamarque brings it back to a provincial stage with some success (3, 5: 350–51, 369–70, 442–43). On the whole, this seems like a tossup; some promise, but no clear assurance of literary success, and with this we are left; we do not know what it will become.

The other unresolved question, perhaps the most surprising turn in the novel for the constant reader of Spielhagen, is Lothar's marriage to Ellinor. Up to now Spielhagen's protagonist, if he is successful in love, has ultimately married what might be called, without disparagement, the good girl. But Lothar's inconstant attraction to the auburn-haired Ellinor looks like one of those impermanent infatuations through which Spielhagen's protagonists often pass, although those who mean well by him keep insisting that they belong together. She is not exactly a *femme fatale*, but she is portrayed as a coquette and perhaps something of a man-killer in the decisive way she repels Schlagododro as well as Astolf, whom her family presses her to marry. As a teenager she laughs »über junkerliche Scherze« that make Lothar's blood boil, and she matures into a »vollendete Weltdame,« not usually a positive characterization (3, 4: 268–9; 5: 173). Schlagododro, who is rough but not stupid, thinks she and his brother Astolf deserve one another and doubts that she is capable of love (246–47). Her father looks upon her with disappointment, recalling her as conceited and coquettish at age ten and regarding her as the logical daughter of the wife he regrets having married (275). When she rejects Astolf, Lothar finds her frivolously playacting (299–300). She does declare her love to him, and they have a curious, innocent relationship like Adam and Eve, »was der Engländer ›flirtation‹ nennt« (326–27); with her father's fall, she is reconciled to him and attacked with him in the newspapers as an emancipated woman associating with Social Democrats, though even then Lothar doubts her steadfastness, always conscious of her shock when she learns that he is an artisan (433–35, 328–29). That his mother proposes to employ her in a school for disadvantaged children in order to cure her »Vornehmheit« (386) may strike the reader as uncertainly promising. Just before Ellinor and Lothar fall into one another's arms at last he is still worrying that his love for her is »ein schönes Irrlicht,«

that she will never understand his sense of purpose, and that she lacks the »köstliche Selbstlosigkeit« of his half sister Adele (436). It is true that with this alliance Lothar not only becomes a kind of son to his imagined, ideal father Vogtriz, but also reenters his family heritage (I make him and Ellinor out to be second cousins; Lothar is, as always, shocked when he discovers that she already knew they were related [300]). But the ground of this union seems much shakier than that of concluding marriages in earlier novels; once again we do not know what it will become.

Two years later, *Ein neuer Pharao* (1889) indicates Spielhagen's further dissociation from the Reich. The sequence of biblical titles clearly indicates this, as Roper has noted.[13] The reference, of course, is to Exodus 1: 8: »Now there arose up a new king over Egypt, which knew not Joseph,« leading, in the short run, at any rate, to bondage and oppression. As usual, the thematic reference is explicitly articulated in the text (3, 3: 133, 523, 529). While the publication of the novel in 1889 might suggest that the new pharaoh was Kaiser Wilhelm II,[14] who began his inauspicious reign in the preceding year, the occurrence of two assassination attempts on Kaiser Wilhelm I along with other internal evidence dates the action of the novel in the spring and summer of 1878; thus it is in chronological sequence to *Was will das werden?* The new pharaoh might be thought of as Bismarck, but is more generally the Wilhelminian order as a whole.

The plot of the novel is formed by the calamitous intersection of two already dysfunctional families. The one is that of Geheimrat Johann Fürchtegott von Ilicius, member of the Reichstag and speculator, who has evolved from a radical to a reactionary and is said to have been one of the founders of the *Neue Preußische Zeitung*, universally known from the Iron Cross on its masthead as the *Kreuzzeitung*, and thus having aided Bismarck's career. His second wife, a Baroness von Alden, née Countess Uttenhoven, had divorced her first husband, a liberal forty-eighter, when he was condemned to death. Ilicius is divorced from his first wife, whom he simply abandoned in order to marry the noblewoman; he has since been ennobled

---

[13] The titles »suggest a fundamental change in Spielhagen's outlook during the three years [accepting Henning's date of 1886 for the earlier novel] separating their publication. A world of fermentation and open possibilities in the first has been replaced in the second by oppression and rigidity. The two novels form a progression from hope for the unfinished revolution to near despair«: Roper, *German Encounters with Modernity*, 76.

[14] Asserted by Volker Neuhaus, »Friedrich Spielhagen – Critic of Bismarck's Empire,« *1870/71 – 1989/90: German Unifications and the Change of Literary Discourse*, ed. Walter Pape (Berlin and New York, 1993), 141.

himself. His children are Herbert, twenty-six, a junior legal official; Stephanie, twenty-four, an amiable but quite stupid woman who is married to Baron Egon von Scharfeck, an idler and gambler eventually said to be one or two hundred thousand marks in debt, while she carries on a possibly adulterous affair with Count Axel von Karlsburg, friend of her brother Reginald, a twenty-three-year-old officer; and Ada, eighteen or nineteen, a negligible beauty known dismissively as »das Blumengesicht« (83). In the house is also Baroness Marie von Alden, nearly twenty-nine, daughter of the wife's first marriage, a perfect Cinderella of liberal sentiments who is expected to manage the household but whose practical concerns bring her the scorn of her half siblings and the bitter criticism of her irresponsible and profligate mother. She has tried to escape the family by becoming a nurse but this breach of class constraints has been thwarted. The narration is closest to her consciousness; something has already been said of her in Chapter 10. Outside the family is Hartmut Selk, son of Ilicius by his first marriage, whose mother took her maiden name so as not to be of any trouble. Originally a bright and capable boy sent to the university by his father, his involvement with the Social Democrats brought him a jail term of a year and a half, causing him to be summarily expelled from the family. Inwardly a vengeful radical, he is attempting to live by his wits, a not inconsiderable resource that he eventually overestimates.

At the outset of the novel both Marie and Selk seek employment with the newly arrived American family of James Curtis, Marie unsuccessfully as governess, Selk successfully as Curtis's secretary and factotum. Something has been said of this family in Chapter 9. Curtis is an apparently wealthy businessman who is propagating an investment scheme in a Wichita-Choktaw railroad, which the bright, now nihilistic Selk promptly recognizes as a swindle and which he aids in the hope of entrapping his father and causing chaos generally. We learn in time that Curtis was once a slave dealer who went to the gold rush, where he killed white, black, and Indian men, in fact, eating one of the dead Indians, an experience that has caused the condition of his apparently boorish but actually mentally ill wife, the only person to whom he shows any tenderness. His relations are poor with his children, Ralph, thirty-one, an ailing, gentle professor of German at Columbia University, and Anne, nineteen, a stunning, athletic beauty burning with a vivid heroic ambition for which she can find no outlet. Also in the family is an older companion to the children, Charles Smith, a slender, white-haired German and former forty-eighter, whom Curtis first met in the gold fields, where he tried to be a hermit, then later in New York. He had been an abolitionist, for which he had been nearly lynched, had been wounded in the Civil War, and had tried to found a school for orphans and children that was destroyed by »[z]elotische Pfaffen, denen er nicht bibelgläubig genug war« (108); poor and ill, he was taken as a tutor into the Curtis household. Although he had sworn never to return to Germany, he has done so for the sake of Ralph. Smith, as becomes evident to the reader and successively to the characters, is the former Baron Hartmut von Alden and therefore Marie's father. Thus we once again have a secret family relationship, though an attentive second reading reveals unmistakable indications of it from an early point. It turns out that Hartmut Selk was actually named for him, for he had been a friend of the quondam liberal Ilicius, who betrayed him by stealing his wife.

Even by Spielhagen's standards, family and erotic relationships in this novel are malevolent and sometimes ferocious. The brothers Herbert and Reginald hate each other[15] and both are contemptuous of their sisters, especially the feckless Stephanie; all more or less ignore Marie, not least because she has no money. Stephanie wants to divorce Egon; they have a three-year-old child whom nobody, mother, father, nor grandmother, wants. As the Ilicius fortunes decline, Axel offers to pay Egon's debts, thus, in effect, as Herbert recognizes, buying Stephanie. Reginald, less out of chivalry to his sister than concern for the family honor, kills Axel, now faithless to her, in a duel, and she and Egon can be forced back into their marriage. The brutally egotistical Curtis, indifferent to his son's illness and dying, is hated by his daughter; his deranged wife longs for a way to get rid of Smith. Selk virtually stalks Marie, who had cared for his blind mother when she was dying; she, however, has been put off by his coldness to his mother and rejects him as heartless, thus fueling his already vengeful sense of having been ill-used in life. Herbert is tough and mean, the very picture of the new man of the Reich, but he does stay focused on the main issues and strives to keep the family affairs in some kind of order. Reginald, who is believed to be engaged to a Lotte Blumenhagen, falls hopelessly in love with the ravishing republican Anne, who scornfully rejects him for his conventionally medieval views on class, monarchy, and Jews. Ralph appears to be attracted by the vacuous coquette Ada, which Marie, fighting down what she regards

---

[15] The view of Anderson, »Spielhagen's Problematical Heroes,« 160, that »Reginald and Herbert« are »indistinguishable« is one of many examples of inattentive reading. Reginald is less competent but also softer than Herbert; when Anne definitively rejects him, he weeps; even when he is reconciled to marriage with his promised fiancée he weeps at night (270–71, 420–21). One cannot imagine this of Herbert.

as her unworthy jealousy, can hardly believe. Actually Ralph turns out to love Marie, but the frail young man dies despite her nursing care.

However, all these emotional entanglements are put in the shade by the passion of Anne, who translates her vigorous American republicanism into scorn for the Germans' unemancipated women, police-state atmosphere, worship of the Kaiser, and lack of initiative. Since women can do nothing effectual by themselves, she longs for a kind of superhero, a powerful conqueror beyond good and evil bringing the apocalypse of the petty, fettered, self-interested society, to whom she can be a self-sacrificing partner by his side or at his feet. She finds this hero, incongruously enough, in Selk. She accurately recognizes in him the destructive potential and nihilistic instincts of frustrated ambition and vengeful resentment. She gives herself to him sexually and attempts to inspire him to some genuinely bold act. But in her fervor she overestimates his exceptionality; Marie rightly warns her that he is just like the other young men of today that she scorns and that he will drop her when he discovers her father is not as rich as he thought (483–84). As one of her acts of aggression she goes on a shopping spree, her father's credit acknowledged by obsequious merchants, buying lavishly expensive objects that shock Marie in their extravagance (in one genuinely funny moment, Reginald, who is seeking her, memorizes the word »shopping« he has heard in connection with her, looks it up in an English-German dictionary, and successfully finds her in Gerson's department store [208]). But in order to aid Selk, she sells all her valuables, including her horse and tackle, in an equally frantic spree. Selk likes the sexual conquest well enough, but otherwise he comes to find Anne's zeal more than a little strenuous; in fact, her effect on him of reducing him to just another shallow opportunist of the age is not without a degree of bleak comedy. When she declares to Marie that Selk is a giant who will conquer weaklings, she resembles »einer zornigen Löwin« (347), but Selk himself comes to feel in her presence like a zookeeper who knows he will one day be torn to pieces by the lioness he had always controlled (382). Upon the second assassination attempt on the Kaiser and the report that the assassin has been killed, Anne is exalted by the thought that Selk has at last performed the great symbolic deed and sacrificed himself to inspire the people to rise up, but then is disgusted to see that the people in their love of the Kaiser abhor the assassin; she then finds Selk quite alive, rifling her father's cash box. She knocks him down with her horsewhip, gives all her money to Smith, and commits suicide.

The fastidious reader may well feel that Spielhagen has gone off the rails here, if not passing worse judgments of sensationalism or even meretriciousness.[16] Selk is not alone in concluding that Anne has gone completely crazy, and the reader may feel a little craziness in the author as well. But there continues to be something perversely magnetic about Anne. All her wildness in the idiom of freedom and emancipation discharges an erotic panache. She has the blue-black hair and lithe form of Spielhagen's most admired female figures (86). Marie's embrace of Anne generates another of his moments of same-sex erotic *frisson*, not, however, reciprocated this time: »Nun weinte sie laut auf, ihre Arme um den schlanken jungen Leib, der da vor ihr ruhte, schlingend; ihr Gesicht an den Busen drückend, dessen herrliche Formen das feine Nachthemd kaum verhüllte. Aber ihre Umarmung wurde nicht erwidert....« (485). Anne is too far gone in a condition »in welchem die Süße der Wollust mit der Bitterkeit des Todes buhlt« (486). It is not improbable that Spielhagen himself was a repressed Victorian in whom a more emancipated eroticism struggled, and that he knew it. Furthermore, Anne's mad exaltation is a symptom of the by now almost paralyzing frustration with political and social conditions.

The political message of the novel seems to me blurred and possibly confused. Smith's position is, for the most part, clear: the new pharaoh knows not Joseph; the idealism of the generation of 1848 is no longer effective: »der deutsche Idealismus ist das Salz der Erde. Wenn dieses Salz dumm wird, womit soll man salzen?« (139). This phrase had already been employed by Professor Willy in *Was will das werden?* when he mourns the necessity of the war with his beloved France that will stop the source of intellectual and aesthetic refreshment for many years (3, 4: 335–36). Marie has recognized that Smith is »aus einer andern Welt, einer andern Zeit – einer Welt und Zeit, die noch in dem Menschen den Menschen suchten und zu schätzen wußten; für die es sich nicht immer nur um Aeußerlichkeiten, gesellschaftliche Beziehungen und Rücksichten, um Mein und Dein handelte!« (3, 3: 56). He cannot adapt to the new Germany; he will return to America, taking Marie with him. The opinion of critics that Spielhagen just rejects the present in a immobile attachment to the ideals of 1848 seems to me mistaken; rather there is now a sense of the irrelevance of allegiance

---

[16] If the redoubled assassination attempts seem sensationalistic, the effect belongs to the times rather than to the literary representation: J. W. Burrow, *The Crisis of Reason*, 195, recalls of the Russian nihilists: »Between 1881 and 1911 their bag of victims included three ministers, a prime minister, a brace of generals, a grand duke and a tsar,« and of the non-Russians: »a king of Italy, an Empress of Austria, a Spanish Prime Minister and Presidents of France and the United States.«

to 1848.[17] In the final oration of the sort with which Spielhagen likes to end his novels Smith modifies his position somewhat, saying that the republican dream of 1848 was impossible, for the *Kaisertum* is suited to the Germanic spirit, more so than Caesarism to the French (526). He warns of the radicalism under the surface, not only of the working class; people will not need the naturalistic novel to teach them how miserable everything is (527). He ends by saying that perhaps a new pharaoh may come who will know of the »Joseph der Humanität und des Idealismus« (529). If this is a hopeful gesture in the direction of the young Wilhelm II, Spielhagen was soon to be disabused of such notions; anyway, Smith would have been more likely thinking of Friedrich III. Some of this seems rather muddled, but it is associated with an outburst against modern literature by the »American minister« in opposition to a young *Privatdozent*:

> Jene Litteratur, die Sie befürworten: die realistische, oder, wie sie sich selbst mit Vorliebe nennt: die naturalistische, – deren Hauptvertreter in Frankreich Zola, im skandinavischen Norden Ibsen, in Rußland sagen wir: Dostojewski – ist, – ich glaube, Sie werden mir das zugeben, – durch und durch radikal, ultraradikal, wie nach meiner Ansicht, noch nie die Litteratur.... Die Liebe, wie unsre Dichter sie bis jetzt besungen haben, ein kindisches Märchen! die Familie ein Lügenrattennest! ideale Strebungen ein Sport der Thoren, oder eine Maske, hinter der sich die Selbstsucht bequem verbirgt! das gesellschaftliche Dekorum Sand in die Augen für die Naiven! der Staat eine Institution, erfunden von den Klugen und Mächtigen zur bequemen Ausbeutung der Dummen und Machtlosen! (331–32)

He goes on to say that either the authors believe this, then they should abandon literature for the revolution, or if not, they are only striving for an aesthetic effect.

This minister must be, as was pointed out in Chapter 9, none other than Bayard Taylor, American minister in Berlin from May to December 1878 (another indication for dating the action of the novel), with whom Spielhagen was almost certainly acquainted.[18] It is not obvious what we are

---

[17] Klemperer, *Die Zeitromane Friedrich Spielhagens*, 139–40; Goessl, »Die Darstellung des Adels,« 176. Smith can be blinded by his preoccupations; he welcomes the petty schemer Selk »als Waffenbruder, möchte ich sagen, in dem Kampfe des Idealismus gegen eine Welt, die jenseits und diesseits des Ozeans in wüstem Materialismus schon versunken ist, oder zu versinken droht,« causing Selk to say to himself: »Dies wird immer besser« (407–08). Politics is being absorbed by rhetoric on all sides.

[18] Taylor had a copy of *Problematische Naturen* in his personal library; he shared with Spielhagen, who was a prominent translator of Taylor's admired poems, acquaintances with Duke Ernst II, the crown prince, and Auerbach, who pronounced Taylor's funeral oration. See John T. Krumpelmann, *Bayard Taylor and German Letters* (Hamburg:, 1959), 214, 160–61, 154–58.

to think of this, for the debate continues indecisively, and the minister gets red in the face and out of breath, though that may be owing to his ailing condition. He is not much respected by some of the characters, though when Curtis declares him an ass one must consider the source (150, 152). One might suppose the profoundly conventional, asexual, and antifeminist Taylor a writer not altogether congenial to Spielhagen, though he did certify »the eternal laws of Art.«[19] But here he is seconded by none other than Ralph, the American professor of German, who expresses his dismay at the bookstore windows full of foreign works with which the Germans are abandoning their own values: »Als die Vorzüge deutscher Poesie erschienen aber uns Amerikanern immer die Innerlichkeit, die aus dem tiefsten Herzensgrunde schöpft, und der ideale Schwung, der sich hoch über die gemeine Wirklichkeit der Dinge erhebt« (335).[20] We shall not detain ourselves here on the uncertain ground of Spielhagen's problems with Naturalism and contemporary literature, except to note how evidently his very novel is beginning to approach the characteristics censured by the American minister.

The literary debate seems to lead away from the political ground of balked democracy to one about Joseph's idealism versus the new pharaoh's materialism. Smith is opposed by another old forty-eighter, Dr. Brunn, who is a remake of Hunnius in *Was will das werden?*, having made his peace with the new order. It may be ominous to learn that he was a member of the delegation from the Frankfurt parliament that offered the imperial crown to Friedrich Wilhelm IV (135). Perhaps he was never a republican, thinks Smith, and perhaps he did not vote for the abolition of the nobility, while Smith had renounced his »mit tausend Freuden« (136). Brunn defends Bismarck's steady purpose of providing money for army and internal peace, »Tabaksmonopol und Sozialistengesetz«; the national liberals will have to give up their »Velleitäten.« He advises Smith to abandon his *Illusions perdues* and open a new chapter. Smith, he says, is an idealist, which is good and necessary, but »wir in das Land des echten Idealismus nur durch die heutige

---

[19] Paul C. Wermuth, *Bayard Taylor* (New York, 1973), 164. I have not found that the sentiments ascribed to Taylor in the novel appeared in print, although he might have said such things in conversation.

[20] I have no way of knowing whether Spielhagen was aware that just such propagation of the great German culture was the gospel of American *Germanistik* in those times. See Richard Spuler, »*Germanistik*« *in America: The Reception of German Classicism, 1870–1905* (Stuttgart, 1982). This was about the time when Spielhagen was becoming acquainted with Hjalmar Hjorth Boyesen, like Ralph an American professor of German (see Chapter 9). Taylor was a »nonresident« professor at Cornell, lecturing intermittently on German literature. The Cornell professor Boyesen »named Taylor as his mentor« (Krumpelmann, *Bayard Taylor*, 55).

Wüste des Realismus gelangen können« (274–77). Smith, for his part, says he does not see how Brunn can stand

> diesen prahlerischen, säbelrassenden Chauvinismus; diese Loyalität, die sich Friedrich Wilhelm IV. Wort zum Wahlspruch genommen zu haben scheint, und sich in ihrer byzantinischen Uebertreibung erst recht schön dünkt; diesen krassen Materialismus, der jeder idealen Wallung hohnvoll ein Schnippchen schlägt; dieses Strebertum bei Jung und Alt, dem der Erfolg alles ist, es mögen die Mittel sein, wie sie wollen. Das ist mein Deutschland nicht. (367)

Since Brunn is maneuvered onto the side of the materialistic present, it is perhaps meant ironically that at the end he warns Smith that he doesn't belong in America, where materialism is worse, but in idealistic Germany (528).[21]

The stress on the materialist threat to idealism indicates a shift of focus from concerns about political structures to the fear of commercialism, less an anticapitalist affect than an anxiety about greed engulfing personal relations and the public atmosphere, threatening to become, Smith fears, »die Signatur der ganzen modernen Menschheit« (406). Indeed, at one point he warns that the spread of »das alte Manchestertum« will lead »zu einem Weltenbrande« among the unhappy and anxious peoples, thus appearing to predict World War I (137). Herbert, unimpressed by Selk's pretense of altruism, tells him: »Heutzutage thut niemand etwas umsonst, auch nicht ein Gemütsmensch« (452). This is the pure voice of the new pharaoh, but the threat is largely American, generating, as I pointed out in Chapter 9, a convoluted antinomy with the image of an America setting a standard of freedom, in, for example, the relations of the sexes, as Anne keeps insisting, that the Germans are far from reaching. Since Spielhagen had no direct experience of America, the contradictions belong to the well-attested *image*, as the French have it, of the foreign other.

But there is another discourse that may be disturbing to the modern reader at least: that of race. Anne impresses a party in the Ilicius house by singing »Niggerlieder« with which she outclasses the untalented singing of the »Blumengesicht« Ada (92–94). The term is in no way pejorative; the narrator makes clear that these songs associate Anne with sympathy for the

---

21 It does not seem to characterize Brunn very positively that, as mentioned in Chapter 10, he advises Marie against nursing as a task »*contra naturam*« for »ein junges blühendes Mädchen« (328). Apart from the general women's issue, to address Marie, who at twenty-nine was in danger of becoming an old maid, as a blooming maiden seems either dull-witted or disrespectful.

oppressed and burdened, although the more mannerly Ralph calls them »Negerlieder« (103). In one place Anne, in order to demonstrate to Selk her repudiation of her slave-dealing father, tells him of one of her »Niggerlieder« about a father who sells his mixed-race daughter into slavery, which, she adds, Longfellow made into a ballad, the same poem, as I pointed out in Chapter 9, that is cited verbatim in *Die schönen Amerikanerinnen*.[22] Anne tells Reginald that only one with Negro blood can understand the songs, then declares that she has a black ancestor, thrusting her fingernails at him (214–17; Spielhagen evidently still believed in this old misconception). This is clearly an aggressive antiracist move, designed to shock Reginald's prejudices, among them his anti-Semitism. But when she rejects Reginald the spots on her nails seem to turn black as ebony: »Ein abergläubischer Schauder durchrieselte ihn, als ob er im Begriff gewesen wäre, seine Seele an eine Teufelin zu verkaufen, und ein glücklichster Zufall hätte ihn nur noch eben aus dem Höllenfeuer gerettet, an dem er sich schon die Finger versengt« (271). Since this is a stage of Anne's transformation into a virago, the reader may sense a certain slippage here on the narrator's part into a racist discourse that was gaining ground at the time the novel was written. Chargeable to Marie's consciousness, but perhaps also to the author's, is her recognition that the gleam in Anne's eye was like Ralph's: »Geschwister beide in dem gährenden Blut, das von dem Urgroßvater, dem Neger, her durch ihre Adern rollte.... [D]aß in dem blühenden Körper ein Dämon hauste, groß und wild und unbezähmbar, wie der Samum, der Afrikas Flammenstirn umsaust« (482).

Striking in the novel is not only the viciousness in personal relations but the breakdown of poetic justice. Ilicius, to be sure, gets an ironic comeuppance. Having failed to perceive Bismarck's tactics, he comes to be on the *right* of the chancellor; when he makes a speech in the Reichstag against the Socialists not in harmony with Bismarck's current policy, he is summarily dismissed, a blatant act of ingratitude worthy of the new pharaoh.[23] Since this event occurs simultaneously with his ruin by Curtis's investment scheme, he is crippled in a stroke, leaving thoroughly modern Herbert in charge of the family. As he says:

---

[22] Longfellow is mentioned several times in the text. Ada is proud that Ralph has given her a luxury edition of Longfellow's poems, though she asks him to recite Poe's »Raven« (228); given Spielhagen's relative evaluation of Longfellow and Poe, perhaps this choice is meant to cast doubt on her sensibility.

[23] »Clearly referring to May 1878, when Bismarck's first anti-socialist legislation was defeated after brief debate, this episode makes Ilicius the scapegoat«: Roper, *German Encounters with Modernity*, 84.

Wir sind die Herren – von Gottes- und Rechtswegen, weil wir die Zeit verstehen, unser staatsmännisches Metier verstehen; weil wir die Kraft gehabt haben, aus uns den [Bismarck] hervorgehen zu lassen, der es in dem Metier zur höchsten Meisterschaft gebracht und eine Schule gemacht hat, in die freilich Dummköpfe nicht gehören, in der aber kluge Köpfe es auch zur Meisterschaft bringen können. Bringen müssen. Laßt nur noch so ein fünf, ein zwei Jahre vielleicht nur ins Land gehen, und man wird von Herbert Ilicius zu reden haben! (458)

Curtis, however, escapes completely, abandoning his family except for his curiously beloved wife. He will not return to America, where he sold off all of his property in anticipation of the crash (presumably the Panic of 1873), and he is confident that the stupid Germans will provide him with enough »Kleingeld« to allow him to live a couple of comfortable years on the Continent (472). Herbert is promoted and becomes engaged to his boss's daughter; the disgraced Egon has a prospect of returning to the officer corps, his honor rescued by Reginald's killing of Axel in a duel, for which Reginald presumably will suffer two months of confinement and then marry the once rejected Lotte Blumenhagen; »das Blumengesicht« can marry her once neglected admirer now that he has inherited his aunt's fortune. The cynical marriages with which the novel concludes look like a parody of a *Happy-End* (518–20). Of the best human beings, Ralph has died and Marie and her father flee into exile. The rhetoric of optimism has diminished to a small voice; the new pharaoh appears to be victorious. Klemperer, in his intact patriotism before World War I, deplored the survival of evil and decided that Spielhagen just did not understand his times;[24] in retrospect we may think better of his powers of observation.

---

[24] Klemperer, *Die Zeitromane Friedrich Spielhagens*, 140–41. Zinken, *Der Roman als Zeitdokument*, 22, on the other hand, was sufficiently impressed by the apparent prediction of World War I to praise »wie realitätsnah und hellsichtig Friedrich Spielhagen seine Zeit beschreibt.«

16. Giving Up: *Sonntagskind, Stumme des Himmels*

> Und dürften also weiter leben, einsam
> Und glücklich eines in des andern Liebe! –
> Wie lange? scherzte ich. – So lange, Liebster,
> Wie du mich liebst. Du kannst doch lange lieben? –
> Ja, ewig, Herz. Und du? –
> Sie lehnte fester
> Sich nur auf meinen Arm, doch sagte nichts....
>
> (»Am Strande,« *G*, 153–54)

The incipient incongruence of patriotic, idealistic hope with oppressive, disappointing reality detectable in *Was will das werden?* and *Ein neuer Pharao* exerts a substantial influence on the next major novel, *Sonntagskind* of 1893. For one thing, the melancholy tone has deepened, approaching the tragic; the uncertain outlook for the future figured in the uncertainly promising marriage of Lothar Lorenz now becomes bleaker. Even the title itself bears an irony not employed in this way by Spielhagen previously. A »Sonntagskind« in traditional German usage is blessed with good fortune, like the child »born on the Sabbath-day« in the English rhyme, »brave and bonny, and good and gay.«[1] But the aspiring writer Justus Arnold, though he achieves a more evident success than Lothar Lorenz, is battered by misfortune and ultimately betrayed in his deepest longings. More curiously, perhaps, the novel is more allusively literary than its predecessors, even exhibiting in places a kind of elementary intertextuality. One would suppose that a self-consciously literary manner of narration would be a violation of principles of objectivity since it calls attention to authorial management and voice, possibly a sign that the grip of Spielhagen's obsessions in this regard is loosening along with his confidence in his animating convictions. The most evident device in this regard is the employment and application to themselves by Justus and his beloved Isabel of *Märchen* motifs, however,

---

[1] There are several versions of this rhyme; this one is cited from *Harper's Weekly* of 1887 in John Bartlett, *Familiar Quotations*, 11th edn., ed. Christopher Morley and Louella D. Everett (Garden City, 1944), 956.

not in a premonitory or allegorical way, but antithetically to real-life experience, thus underlining the now starkly perceived dichotomy between the poetically imagined ideal and the world as it is. Spielhagen had not done this since the beginning of his career, when he inserted an obliquely emblematic *Märchen* into *Clara Vere* (*AR*, 2, 1: 17–23). A ballad in ottava rima entitled »Sonntagskind« presents itself almost uniquely among his poems as a *Märchen*, in which the protagonist goes into the forest, finds fairies in a mist, falls in love with one despite the warning that »[w]er sich Feeenliebe erkoren / Ist hier und ewig verloren« and is found dead in the morning (*G*, 168–71). However, even as a boy Justus knows that there are no witches and fairies in the forest, no utopian worlds, as in his books (*NF*, 1: 2–3); his *Märchen* is consciously constructed fiction. Let us begin, then, with a gradually developed version of it, called »Das Märchen von dem Oger, der Fee und dem jungen Jäger« (127), which the rather precocious sixteen-year-old Justus recites – it is not yet written down – to a group of the characters sheltering from a rainstorm.

A hunter, Hubert, calls in the forest for the fairy Maiennacht, who can only be seen on a Sunday. She calls him »Sonntagskind« – in older legend the Sunday's child was also able to see spirits – and postpones him for a year, putting a ring on his finger that will not come off, so that he is estranged from other girls, though he cannot remember what the fairy looked like. After a year, she takes the ring, but she has been reported for dancing with a human. Now bad times come; the king of the spirits threatens to turn her into a lemur. She tells of an ogre who eats the tops of fir trees while his laborers cut them down. The rest are burned to keep the workers poor so that they freeze and starve; Maiennacht's power to protect the forest is reduced and she will die with it. While she can save herself by marrying the ogre's handsome son, she prefers death because he is evil to the poor. The laborers come the next day to cut down the forest. The ogre offers a deal; he will save ten trees a day if Maiennacht will dance with his son. If she does not, she will be locked into the steel tower of a castle. Hubert finds the castle, which is surrounded by a pyre of burning trees. The ogre is choking on a treetop, so Hubert pretends to be a doctor; his son, who is hoping for his father's key so he can get to Maiennacht, tells Hubert that if he does not cure the ogre, he will be burned alive, which Hubert, with fairy-tale logic, finds natural; if he does succeed, he will also be burned, but killed first. Hubert tricks the ogre into killing himself, the prince grasps the key, they fight while the workers, who hate the prince, watch. Hubert kills the prince with the hundred-pound key, saving the fairy while the workers burn the castle. Hubert takes Maiennacht to a hermit in the forest, who marries them, but she sickens, having become human for love of him. The spirit king forgives her and lets her dissolve into the ether like a fairy. Now there are two endings: Hubert dies in one and becomes a hermit in the other.

Those who hear this lose no time in solving it as an allegory. The ogre is identified with Count Waldburg, who here, in a place called Eisenhammer in Prussian Poland on the Russian border, despoils the forest for a cellulose factory while oppressing his workers. His son Armand, one of Spielhagen's typically worthless aristocratic youths, is enraged by the implications of the story and conceives a violent hatred of Justus, the son of a poor forester. Maiennacht is identified with the stunningly beautiful, fourteen-year-old orphan Isabel, with whom Justus is intensely in love; he is determined to serve her selflessly, for example, by doing her schoolwork. She is reputed to be the daughter of the local priest, Pietrek Szonfalla; this is a rumor, confirmed only very late in the novel,[2] at first spread by Anna, his housekeeper, if that is what she is, one of the most sinister of Spielhagen's domestics, who hates Justus and intrigues against him at intervals, eventually becoming the servant of Isabel, whom she robs. The slovenly, alcoholic Szonfalla, despondent in the ruin of his life and memories of an aesthetic ambition to live like a cardinal, who has been exiled to this remote place by the prince-bishop as a punishment, is one of Spielhagen's most positively drawn clerics in his capacity for love and kindness. He is removed from office by the authorities in Breslau and replaced with a real priest, mean, arrogant, and censorious, who promptly disgusts the workers. Isabel adopts the terms of the *Märchen*, persistently referring to Justus as »Sonntagskind« and to herself as »Maiennnacht.« The main thread of the longish novel follows Justus's imperishable love for Isabel and the manner in which their relationship evolves consistently and inconsistently with the *Märchen*. Isabel has been sent to the manor, the castle of the *Märchen*, to live with the ogres.[3]

Justus is first called »Sonntagskind« by his deeply loving mother, who attempts to relieve the family's poverty with laborious embroidery supplied to a dubious Polish Jew named Löb, to whom Justus was to have been apprenticed if the family could come up with enough money. The father is initially unloving to his wife and harsh to his son; he is embittered by class

---

[2]   When she refers to herself for the first time as »Isabel Szonfalla« and still later to »meinem — nun gut! — meinem Vater« (*NF*, 1: 360, 428).

[3]   The German word is both cases is *Schloß*, which creates a little difficulty for English usage, as the *Schloß* of a nobleman in modern times is more likely to be a manor house than what we would call a castle.

resentments that have cost him several positions until he has been driven to this far corner of the Reich. He is particularly obsessed with the notion that he is the unacknowledged son of a duke. Thus again we have the motif of secret descent from the nobility, but here it is disengaged because it may be only a delusion and it has, in any case, no further consequence. However, Justus wins his father's affection with his own act of class resistance. At a festival he is made to play the horn; the count offers him gold pieces, but his father refuses to allow him to accept them, enraging the count and jeopardizing the father's job. But Justus, who had meant to play only for Isabel, sticks up for his father and later goes to the manor to appeal for him. Although it is Isabel who actually achieves the father's reprieve, the count, like all men in the novel, being infatuated with her, Justus's act of solidarity and courage releases the father's love for his son and wife, improving the family situation. However, the father has been ignoring Löb's smuggling activities and when, with his new conscientiousness, he attempts to enforce the law, Löb has him killed; the mother dies around the same time.

The count, impressed with Justus's well-spoken manner (like Vogtriz with Lothar), invites him to the manor to be Armand's companion. Justus declines on the grounds that his father would not permit it, impressing the count as insolent. Eventually he is persuaded, although he is unable to do the incorrigible Armand any good, who, jealous about Isabel and enraged by the *Märchen*, reverses it by instigating a fight with Justus and wounding him with a heavy key. While the count pays his medical costs and the burial costs of his father, Justus cannot return to the manor. But he has made other acquaintances there, among them the count's daughter, Sibylle, a pale, ailing, pious woman, who loves the protagonist silently and forlornly through much of the novel, rather like Jettchen Israel in *Was will das werden?* Isabel impishly recommends that Justus marry Sibylle, but, though he remains friends with her, like any decent Spielhagen character he is not attracted by her religiosity. Also in the household is a clever English governess, Edith Brown, who tries to present herself to Isabel as a warning example: an originally well-born beauty with whom all men were in love, she was arrogant and heartless until she was orphaned and impoverished; too undereducated for good positions, she became a governess, causing various melodramatic episodes with her coquetry and need for admiration; Isabel, who claims not to know what a coquette is, remains undistracted from her desire to have many admirers. Edith is in love with and eventually marries the household physician, Dr. Eberhard.

In the count's employ is a factory director, Körner, a gruff, opinionated man who nevertheless tries to persuade his employer to improve labor relations by building workers' housing. The count is impervious to such notions and, later in the novel, Körner breaks with him. More important for Justus is Körner's wife Eve (or Eva; the spelling varies), a competent, forthright, intelligent woman who is the daughter of a literary scholar, Professor Richter. She comes to be a critical but encouraging reader of Justus's writing efforts, once endeavoring to direct his attention to poetic motifs close at hand with Emerson's poem »Apology« »in einer, wie ich glaube, leidlichen Übersetzung« (in fact Spielhagen's own, 293–94),[4] eventually mediating Justus to her father's attention. The relationship between Justus and Frau Körner increases in intimacy, evolving in time to first names and the employment of *du*, and develops an amorous undercurrent that is only indirectly expressed. She implies an alternative, intellectual and comprehending, to the long unattainable Isabel. Though not beautiful, Eve is pleasing, has a good figure, and is lithe and strong, unlike the jumpy Isabel or the tired Sibylle (123). These are features elsewhere found in Spielhagen's admired women, and, in fact, Isabel, despite her irresistible magnetism, with her blonde hair and brown eyes (3, 6) may not entirely correspond to the author's ideal of feminine beauty, though her black brows (357) suggest she is a composite. In the long run, at any rate, Justus is not to be deflected from his *Minnedienst* to her.

After some delay, Justus obtains a position in the packing department of the factory, gradually acquiring experience in all departments while learning about alienating mechanized work and the demoralization of the workers, whose spirits are killed by vice and drinking. He goes to live in the attic of a worker, Christian Anders, a convinced, studious Social Democrat who recommends to Justus the writings of Lassalle, »des braven Mannes Heiliger.« Anders agrees that the count, one of the worst of the ogres, is at fault, eating not trees but people: »ich meine diese ganze kapitalistische Wirtschaft, die Millionen von Menschen vertiert, damit ein paar Tausende menschlich leben können« (220). This rather Marxian language is more explicit than it has been before in Spielhagen's fiction, and Anders earlier makes the interesting point that the factory is a good thing because it produces the paper that will end the *Märchen* by bringing workers the learning that will enable them to overthrow the ogres (80–81). This almost Brechtian idea is an indication that *Sonntagskind* has an immediately contemporary setting. It is so close to its own time that the dates are coded: a letter of Isabel to Justus is dated »188*,« one of Eve to her father »189*,« thus directly contiguous with the novel's publication date (312, 346).

---

[4] *The Works of Ralph Waldo Emerson* (Philadelphia, 1906), 6: 172–73.

Anders has a daughter, Marthe, who is a year and a half older than Justus but represents another contrast to Isabel, of whom she is jealously disapproving. But she also disapproves of Justus's way of life, especially the effort of the well-spoken, literate forester's son to become a worker. For the proletarian girl wants to get out of the proletarian milieu. She is skeptical of her father's doctrines as encouraging laziness and passivity, does not want to be married to her local beau, one Stanik Stolarzeck, and be beaten by him, but pursues a career as a nurse, at which she succeeds with the assistance of Dr. Eberhard, who gets her a position in the *Charité*, eventually we see her as a private nurse to the disabled Countess Sibylle. She is outside the *Märchen*, a sensible woman always ready with good advice, thus a briefly considered pragmatic but not really compelling alternative for Justus. For her part, she is gnawed by frustration, musing bitterly near the end of the novel that even killing Isabel would not do any good (571).

Anders has a second wife, the black-eyed, broad-cheeked Albinka, who, being Polish, is naturally libidinous and amoral; she scorns her careworn husband and his stupid socialist books. Here we have the most desolate extreme of Spielhagen's motif of the love of an older man for a younger woman. Albinka lusts for Justus and, supposing Marthe absent, falls upon him, successfully arousing him for a moment, but Marthe discovers them, whereupon Albinka attacks her with a knife; Justus, protecting her, is stabbed in the hand. This is obviously a reprise of the laming of Lothar in *Was will das werden?* with a similarly deflective effect, for Justus is no longer able to work on the factory floor. He obtains a more sedentary, secretarial position in *Oberdirektor* Körner's office; it is a tedious job but it keeps Justus afloat while he works at his writing. The job is mediated by Eve, bringing them closer together. Albinka, having been seduced by Stanik, ends her life with one of Spielhagen's now familiar drownings.

Around this time Isabel becomes engaged to a Baron von Schönau, whose acquaintance she had made in the manor. She says she would naturally have preferred to marry Justus, but he is too young and too poor, adding that, like Don Carlos, whom she has seen acted on the stage, he has »nicht einmal etwas ›für die Unsterblichkeit gethan‹« (241). Of course she does not love Schönau, who seems to be an innocuous, well-meaning fellow, but a poor manager of his own affairs and a gambler, whose depletion of his wealth Isabel does nothing to prevent. She makes fun of his first and last poetic image, that he would have married her if she had fallen to earth from a star (243, a reference to her illegitimate birth). They travel about from one city and resort to another, from which »Maiennacht« intermittently sends her »Sonntagskind« letters complaining of her boredom with high society and Justus's neglect of her. When the baron's health fails, Isabel must care for him, whether she likes it or not, for three years. Justus, already persuaded that she cannot love him, is now persuaded that he has finally lost her, but is in no way dislodged from his fidelity. He enters upon a period of life detailed in a lengthy »Tagebuch eines Einsamen« (259), much of which is concerned with his efforts to write a novella or novel under the advice of Eve and her father. When, during a strike, Anders, who has called for a workers' uprising against the ogres, is shot by Körner, Justus feels he can no longer work for him and takes a job assisting Professor Richter in Berlin. The Körners follow them there – as is repeatedly the case in Spielhagen's late fiction, there is a movement of characters toward Berlin – for Körner has lost his job in a quarrel with the miserly count, who wants a ruined manor restored for Armand at impossibly low cost. This project follows upon Armand's settlement of a huge gambling debt by marriage to a Jewish millionairess, Fräulein Seligmann, who has renamed herself Christine. She, though thin and unprepossessing, is a compliant and would-be loving woman who is treated by Armand with the utmost contempt and brutality; Sibylle and Isabel befriend her when she wants a divorce, but Edith is unsympathetic, saying that Christine's troubles are her own fault because she just wanted to be a countess. Christine drowns in a suspect ice-skating accident.

Edith's bitterness has to do with her problem about Isabel, who has reappeared as a widow, smoking cigarettes and praising Wagner, a full-fledged *femme fatale*, with whom all men, including Edith's husband, become infatuated; Edith comes to wish her dead but realizes that Eberhard will love her beyond the grave; she weeps in despair as she realizes she has met her master in power over men (562). By then Isabel has married a both ecstatic and uneasy Justus. That this achievement of longed-for bliss occurs 160 pages before the end of the novel will seem ominous to the reader familiar with the Tolstoyan convention that happy families do not nourish fiction, and so it turns out. Isabel is now acculturated to high society and relentless admiration, for all her complaints of boredom and of men as nasty, stupid nuisances; Justus must understand that she is not going to be »eine ehrbare Frau Försterin,« going so far as to suggest that he revive his father's chimera of »prinzliche Abstammung« (524, 428). Even before the marriage Justus gets entangled in a duel with one of her foppish admirers. Another of the lovelorn is a new character, an ebullient lawyer named Siegfried Sandor, who keeps a photograph of Isabel on his desk, declares that if he were blessed as Justus he would fling a ring of Polykrates into the sea every morning and that he only refrains from shooting himself not to burden Justus, but will shoot him if he is unable to be happy in his marriage (497–98, 438, 542).

Indeed, the marriage brings difficulties; he finds he cannot afford what she regards as her modest requirements for servants, fine furniture, and a carriage, and so must accept the indignity of invading her inheritance from the baron. He is exasperated by her insistence on entertaining socialites of no interest to him while his old friends withdraw, as Sandor says, like »die amerikanischen Indianer vor den in ihre heimischen Wälder und Pairrien [sic] nachdrängenden Blaßgesichtern« (514–15); she, in turn, objects to Justus's refusal of sociability. Worst of all, Isabel, who appeared to share the *Märchen* spirit with Justus, turns out to be actively opposed to and jealous of his literary vocation, which is now beginning to yield some modest success; in fact he receives a letter from the court telling him that the duke of his original homeland admires his works, deplores his legal troubles with his novel, hopes that Justus knows the duke's own literary efforts, with unintended irony regrets that Justus's father had been driven out of the country, and offers him a sinecure as court librarian with a title of *Hofrat*, a prospect that cheers Isabel briefly; a photo of His Highness is included (579–81). She wants him to give up writing and devote himself exclusively to her. What has developed unexpectedly is a conflict between beauty and poesy. Immediately after the marriage ceremony Justus begins to worry about the compatibility of poesy and love; even Goethe's bond with Frau von Stein did not endure, and, although he is not fit to tie Goethe's shoe, »ein Dichter bin ich doch auch.« But might he not »aus ihrer Küsse Süßigkeit Lethe trinken und des Vaterlandes vergessen, der Freunde und des Berufes strenger Pflicht?« (444). The wise, moribund Sibylle gently speaks of a fairy-tale figure who loved beauty more than poesy »und in den Wogen der Schönheit versank seine Poesie,« expressing the hope that Justus will overcome this condition (522–23).

If I understand the novel correctly, Dr. Eberhard is mistaken to say that Isabel is »die verkörperte Poesie« (403); beauty is identified with aesthetic elegance, which is further associated with wealth; poesy with an idealistic, obligating public vocation. If this is the case, it seems like a revision, even a dichotomization, of the original concept of *Dichtung* derived from the *Goethezeit* that impelled Spielhagen's theoretical convictions. While the increasingly sorrowful Justus spends more and more time away from home, Isabel begins to despair at the evident impossibility of the situation and secretly wishes to die; even before the marriage she has given Dr. Eberhard a letter to be handed to Justus after her death. She will not attempt suicide but allows herself to become pregnant in awareness that childbirth would be dangerous to her. While the grieving Dr. Eberhard struggles to insist that she will recover, she takes longer to die than Puccini's Mimi three years later, desolating not only Justus but all her other worshippers. She makes him promise not to marry Sibylle or Marthe (570), and he assures her in her last moments that a man who loved her could never love a second time. As she dies, he promises to make his Maiennacht immortal in his poetic realm, »das noch viel größer und mächtiger und herrlicher ist als das der Ogers« (597), but the last sound heard is that of the »Ogerknechte« demanding to be admitted in order to carry off Isabel's corpse (598).

In Chapter 11 I commented on this novel's rewriting of Dumas's detested *Affaire Clémenceau* and the extent to which it was nevertheless under the influence of its French ancestor. No doubt Spielhagen was concerned to elevate the level of conventional decency. Isabel, for all her erotically charged frivolity and coquetry, is never adulterous (though she claims she had a predisposition to wickedness from which she had been preserved by Edith's warning, 354), and the partly subliminal attraction between Justus and Eve would never cross into impropriety. Nevertheless, Isabel, in her very frankness, so winsome in itself, about her weaknesses, her instinctive playacting, her need for admiration and indulgence, seems to be puppetized by determinants beyond the reach of her will, nor are the men who fall under her spell any more responsible: »Was konnten die Armen dafür, daß Isabels Augen so wundersam glänzten? was konnte Isabel dafür, daß sie unwiderstehlich war?« (501).[5] To be sure, readers are not likely to have caught this twenty-five-year-old parallel, but another even older one might have struck one or another: the pattern of a third-person narrative interrupted by a long, first-person diary insert, then continuing in the third person, in uncertain consonance with the author's theoretical principles, recalls the first version of Gottfried Keller's *Der grüne Heinrich*, which also ends in tragic failure of aspirations, though in that case of art rather than love.

Otherwise there is a good deal of literary allusiveness that goes beyond the conventional tag lines of *Bildung*. For example, Isabel, writing to Justus from the manor about her conquests, asks, insincerely, I think, if Sibylle is the fairy in the *Märchen*: »Das wäre dann freilich für mich eine *illusion*

---

5 Earlier, Justus has mused about determinants: »Denn schließlich sind es doch die Verhältnisse, die den Menschen machen.... Wie kann der einzelne gesund sein, so lange die Verhältnisse ungesund sind?... Gewiß, unsere modernen Realisten haben recht, wenn sie in der Erklärung ihrer Menschen wieder und immer wieder den Hauptaccent auf das ›Milieu‹ legen, in welchem der Betreffende aufwuchs und lebt«; but then he wonders how very different people can emerge from the same milieu (301).

perdue« (199); she is reading the governess's copy of Balzac even though she has been told it is not a book for her. Reading French novels is never a good sign, and Justus has a more elevated taste; he asks Marthe to recover from the manor his copy of Scott's *Quentin Durward* (202). Probably the reader is expected to remember that the chivalrous and preternaturally fortunate Quentin woos and wins a Countess Isabelle, and there may be a further ironic contrast with the recurrent feeling of the star-crossed Sunday's child that he lacks sufficient heroism to contend with the ogres. Given Spielhagen's unfriendly view of Ibsen, it is no doubt ominous when, in anticipation of the marriage, Isabel rents an expensive »Puppenheim« (429), though by stretching a point one might venture a comparison of the relationship of Justus and Isabel with that of Torvald and Nora, though with Spielhagen more favoring the husband. Isabel remarks that the realists have shown marriage to be »ein trauriges, dunkles Kapitel,« giving as an example Tolstoy's recently published *Kreutzer Sonata*. Justus predictably dismisses it as »ein schiefes, überspanntes und nicht einmal ehrliches Buch« (396), whatever that may mean.[6]

Yet the skepticism about marriage recurs in *Sonntagskind*, is shared by Justus in places, and seems borne out by the course of his longed-for union, along with other rocky marriages, such as Armand's or Eberhard's.[7] It may not be inappropriate to observe that the narrator of the detested *Affaire Clémenceau* concludes that marriage is »un acte absurde,«[8] especially since *The Kreutzer Sonata* is *also* the confession of a man so exasperated by his faith-

---

[6] In 1895 Spielhagen wrote an open letter to Tolstoy, protesting that his pacifist absolutism had led a follower into personal disaster (*AW*, 205–16). Tolstoy took note of it but unsurprisingly held to his own view; see Henning, *Friedrich Spielhagen*, 232–33, n. 116.

[7] Justus's own mother had scorned an early lover, who, while dying, sounds a little like Luise in Schiller's *Kabale und Liebe* when he hopes that »wir uns wiedersehen da, wo keine Ehen geschlossen werden« (14). Eve warns Justus that ideal and reality are two very different things: »Das gebe nichts als Konfusion und Unglück, wovon man sich überzeugen könne, wenn man einen Blick in die Ehen, besonders die jungen werfe« (314). Isabel chides Eberhard for believing in happiness, indicating, incidentally, that she is not completely besotted by Wagner: »Ich halte mit Ihrer gütigen Erlaubnis diesen Glauben für eine Thorheit und Elsas: ›Es giebt ein Glück, das ohne Reu‹ schon deshalb für einen Nonsens, weil selbstverständlich ein reuevolles Glück kein Glück sein würde« (422). When assuring Edith that Eberhard will get over his infatuation, Isabel asserts that women are loved because they want to be: »Ob das eine Heirat zur Folge hat, oder haben kann – es ist eins, wie das andere .... die Liebe der Männer gar nicht aus dem Herzen kommt, sondern nur aus einem Gemisch von Sinnlichkeit und Phantasie« (506–07).

[8] Alexandre Dumas fils, *Affaire Clémenceau. Mémoire de l'accusé* (Paris, [1909]), 65. See Chapter 11.

less wife that he stabs her to death. While facing the possibility of death in a duel, Justus recalls a »Gedicht seines Lieblingsdichters Robert Browning,« in which a lover is stabbed by »die Bravi« just after his ecstatic kiss with his beloved, asking only that she not allow her golden hair to be soiled with his blood (410). The poem is obviously the dramatic romance »In a Gondola,« later printed in full in *Mesmerismus*, as I pointed out in Chapter 9. Justus smiles at the recollection, perhaps in wry comparison of his feelings with Browning's impossibly elevated and cryptically ethereal tone.

Stylistically, there are passages of syntactically fragmentary indirect discourse (e.g., 166–68) of a sort not seen before. There is also an unusual hint of symbolism. When Justus and Isabel are honeymooning on the north shore, she is frightened by the repeated appearance of a ship with black sails. There is nothing ominous about this ship; it is but a vessel for passenger transport around the island, but Isabel decides it is a ghost ship that will leave them stranded with the demons that menace them. Justus, who knows perfectly well that the ship is innocuous, is unable to repel the image; when Isabel is failing, he feels that his happiness has fallen into its ghostly shadow (450–51; 501). Spielhagen is still careful not to integrate symbol into narrative; it remains a psychological construction of the characters. Nevertheless it calls attention to itself because of his customary avoidance of such devices.

Justus is shown to advance further in his literary career than Spielhagen's previous author figures. The novel over which he long labors with the advice of Eve and her father is accepted for publication for a small but welcome honorarium if Justus will shorten it (303). Isabel, who asserts her confidence that she is its heroine, expects that it will help her forget the »grausame Prosa« of her upper-class life (313). But he determines to write his next novel or novella on the »Milieu, wie unsere Realisten sagen, und vor dem ich von Tag zu Tag mehr Respekt bekomme« (307). As I mentioned in Chapter 11, Körner scorns the portrayal of the mining milieu in *Germinal* (307–08), but since it is he who shoots down the striking worker Anders, his judgment may be discredited in retrospect. Justus may also be emancipating himself from Professor Richter's dismissal of the new realism. It is possible that Richter represents Spielhagen's older critical self. But it is also possible that his critique of Justus's first novel is a self-criticism on Spielhagen's part: of disproportional pacing, unrealistic characterization, and especially the unnatural consequences of his »im übrigen löblichen Methode, den Leser mit seinen subjektiven Ansichten zu verschonen und zu demselben nur durch seine Personen zu sprechen, die sich durch ihre Handlungen und Reden selbst erklären mögen« and »seine Neigung zum Sentimentalen und Pathetischen« (289). Later Isabel says that »Deine Menschen durchschnittlich zu gut, viel zu gut sind: zu groß denkend, zu edel empfindend, zu konsequent handelnd, nebenbei auch teilweise zu geistreich. Sie sprechen alle wie Du« (395); the latter criticism was often made of Spielhagen. We see Justus drawing upon his most recent working-class experiences, for he struggles for a catastrophe to bring the fictional »Anders« to a tragic end (his actual tragic end having not yet occurred), and calls upon Weber's *Freischütz*: »Samiel hilf!« (316). This operatic gesture reminds us that Justus's high-minded aspirations are constantly accompanied by a deprecating self-irony. By the time he is around twenty-six he has published three novellas that get him into a crossfire of criticism from chattering academics (344–45). His next novel, almost completed at the time of the duel, is eventually accepted for serialization in several newspapers, doubtless in Spielhagen's experience a sign of success (409, 427). This novel is confiscated by the prosecutor's office, taking it off the Christmas season market and forcing Justus into a costly court case, though he is ably represented by Sandor (553–55); he regards this confrontation as his last battle against »die Ogerherrschaft« (575). The episode may draw on Spielhagen's memories of the prosecution of *Angela* (see Chapter 10); however, here the charge is not of lewdness but of incitement to political unrest.[9] This significant transformation implies a sociopolitical thrust to Justus's otherwise undescribed novel. He also has problems with the staging of a drama about the events of 1812–13 because it treats French atrocities drastically at a time when the authorities are concerned not to wound »die bekanntlich leicht verletztliche gallische Empfindlichkeit« (496). The performance is sabotaged by an actress who has failed to seduce the immovably monogamous Justus. This work sounds like Spielhagen's own drama of 1891, *In eiserner Zeit,* which is based on *Noblesse oblige*; I do not know whether he had comparable difficulties with it.[10]

---

9   The book is charged with the »Paragraphen hundertdreißig und hunderteinund-dreißig,« which in the hands of the prosecution are »sehr elastisch« (554). §130 threatens with fine or imprisonment anyone who threatens the public peace by inciting »verschiedene Klassen der Bevölkerung zu Gewaltthätigkeiten gegen einander«; §131 threatens with the same punishments anyone who publicly calls »Staatseinrichtungen oder Anordnungen der Obrigkeit« into contempt by false or distorted facts (which may, evidently, be fictional). E. Lundberg, *Strafgesetzbuch für das Deutsche Reich vom 15. Mai 1871* (Leipzig, [1880]), 39, 40. We do not learn how Justus's case came out.

10 Henning, *Friedrich Spielhagen,* 175. Spielhagen's drama, however, like the novel, takes place a year later, in 1813–14. In a letter to Paul Heyse of January 8, 1891, Fontane numbered Spielhagen among »die gefürchtesten Theaterquängler, die nicht müde werden, mit ihren ältesten Ladenhütern den Direktionen beschwerlich zu fallen«: *Briefe,* ed. Walter Keitel and Helmuth Nürnberger (Munich, 1976–94),

While the recurrent, by now familiar debates about literature in the novel appear to turn on resistance to modern realism and Naturalism, what we can make out of Justus's evolution as a writer suggests that he is moving more in that direction. Such movement is already suggested when Justus, worried about his obligations in an impending strike, wishes that he had »eine Faser der herkulischen Kraft, die Zolas Muskeln schwellt, wenn es gilt, einen Augiasstall zu räumen« (321). But his sorrowful experience of the incompatibility of beauty and poesy in his marriage has the disconcerting effect of persuading him of the incompatibility of poesy and reality, obliging a retreat into an autonomous realm of literature. Calling, he claims, on Goethe, he asserts

> daß sich ... die ephemere Schönheit in das Reich der Poesie und Kunst, wo sie ewig ist, hinüberretten müsse. Das ist in meinen Augen das Kreditiv und der Adelsbrief der Poesie und Kunst – unter der ich deshalb ein für allemal die idealistische verstehe: die Poesie und Kunst der Homer, Sophokles, Shakespeare, Goethe und Schiller – der Phidias, Praxiteles, Michel Angelo und Raphael – daß sie der aus dem wirklichen Leben fliehenden Schönheit die Arme öffnet und ihr ein Heim bereitet in ihrem ewigen Reich. Und so meine ich, es ist mit der Schönheit und der Poesie, wie mit der Lessingschen Wahrheit, die Gott in der einen Hand hält und in der anderen das Streben nach Wahrheit. Wer möchte nicht zur Wahrheit gelangen, zumal wenn er ein Lessing ist? und doch bittet er um das Streben nach Wahrheit. Und wer, wenn er zwischen der Schönheit und der Poesie die Wahl hätte, würde nicht –
> Ganz ergebenst um die Schönheit gebeten haben, unterbrach ihn Sandor. (490–91)

This is met by a strange laugh from Isabel, who immediately has a seizure of the illness that will eventually end her life. Justus repeats this view when he muses that he has failed to combat the misery of the workers (521–22). To me these shifting discourses about literature indicate a continuing uneasiness about the relationship of poesy and reality. Against Justus's temptation into an autonomous realm one must set the novel itself, which in its political and social aspects is in touch with the Naturalist mode if not completely pledged to it. Thus, though Justus is more stabilized in his literary career than Lothar Lorenz, there is still uncertainty on his horizon, quite apart from the desolating and disillusioning emotional experience he has suffered.

4: 86. Yet in 1875 Fontane had reviewed *Liebe für Liebe* as a great success in a sold-out house with good expectations for the future, although, with a malicious barb typical of him, he concluded that it would triumph until it »bei eintretender Ernüchterung, an seinem Fehler stirbt«: Theodor Fontane, *Sämtliche Werke. Aufsätze, Kritiken, Erinnerungen*, ed. Walter Keitel and Helmuth Nürnberger (Munich, 1968–86), 2: 212.

Sonntagskind does not seem to have much captured the attention of scholars and interpreters, but I think, for what such evaluations may be worth, that it is, on the whole, Spielhagen's best novel, not least because of its more relaxed acceptance of its own literariness.

The next novel, *Stumme des Himmels* of 1895, will concern us somewhat less, for though it contains Spielhagen's customary class stresses, it otherwise has less of a political and public dimension. It is perhaps for this reason that is set back in 1868, before the founding of the Reich.[11] But in its tragic tone it reinforces the author's melancholy sense of life's futility. The tone is set by the title, not likely to be easily recognized by the reader but identified, as usual, in the text (2: 235–36). It is a reference to Jean Paul's *Vorschule der Ästhetik*:

> Es gibt Menschen, welche – ausgestattet mit höherem Sinn als das kräftige Talent, aber mit schwächerer Kraft – in eine heiliger offne Seele den großen Weltgeist, es sei im äußern Leben oder im innern des Dichtens und Denkens, aufnehmen, welche treu an ihm, wie das zarte Weib am starken Manne, das Gemeine verschmähend, hängen und bleiben, und welche doch, wenn sie ihre Liebe aussprechen wollen, mit gebrochnen, verworrenen Sprachorganen sich quälen und etwas anderes sagen, als sie wollen.... Es sind – wenn nach den Indiern die Tiere die Stumme der Erde sind – die *Stummen* des Himmels.[12]

In particular, a skepticism about love and marriage continues from *Sonntagskind*.

The novel begins on the island of Norderney, where Baron Ulrich von Randow is bored in the third week of a four-week vacation, trying to fill up his time with hunting. There he meets Eleonore Ritter, a good-looking, bright, well-traveled orphaned woman of quality background who has recently returned from four years as a governess with a noble family in England; she makes watercolors and, as it turns out later, writes sketches.[13]

---

11 The date is nowhere given but is clear from the protagonist's service in the »böhmisch-österreichischen Feldzug[ ] vor zwei Jahren« (*NF*, 2: 42). Other datable references hold to this time precisely.

12 Jean Paul, *Werke*, ed. Norbert Miller (Munich, 1960–63): 5:52. To this Spielhagen added a reminiscence from Goethe: »denen kein Gott gab zu sagen, was sie leiden« (*NF*, 2: 236). The neoliberal Dr. Brunn in *Ein neuer Pharao* and Major von Vogtriz in *Was will das werden?* had already cited the allusion to Jean Paul (*AR*, 3: 3: 129; 3, 5: 209).

13 Ulrich has not traveled but has been pleased by a book that was not learned but made one feel one was breathing Egyptian air; Eleonore guesses it was Curtis's *Nile Notes of an* [sic] *Howadji* (41), which Spielhagen had translated at the beginning of his career. This is the first of several self-references of the author, a device he had previously used only sparingly when at all.

Ulrich rescues her from a sandstorm, and when two women drown in their bathing facility – Ulrich has wrested the helm from a captain who fears a fine if he goes too near the women's area – he panics at the thought that one of them might have been Eleonore. They fall in love, embrace, and kiss. This is all very nice, except for one thing: Ulrich has a wife and three children. In fact, it is his depression over his domestic situation that has caused his unobservant doctor to send him on this holiday, but to no avail. The twenty-nine-year-old Hertha is a fine wife, efficient and loyal; indeed, she urges him to take as much time as he needs to recuperate. But she is earthbound, normal, domestic, emotionally undemonstrative except when frightened; she has not kept pace with her husband in the acquisition of *Bildung*. For his part, Ulrich is displaced. As a younger son, he expected to enter an intellectual course of life – he broods over a neglected Aristotle commentary – but his older brother died in a riding accident, making him the estate owner and thrusting him, as it were, into rural idiocy (his doctor tells Hertha Ulrich is suffering from »die Einförmigkeit des Landlebens« [*NF*, 2: 226]); he can barely think about the rye harvest that is now pressing, leaving it to his wife and his employees to manage. Eleonore, not wishing to harm Hertha, disappears, leaving a letter that makes Ulrich feel ill used, even though he had been intending to abandon her. As we get to know Ulrich better, we see that he is a deeply self-oriented personality, blundering from one emotional crisis to another and feeling betrayed when he is balked.

Thus it is the old story, one might say. Spielhagen engineers his version by bringing his characters into a tight knot with one another through a series of coincidences. On a train to Berlin, Eleonore encounters an elegant, blond young man with a coronet on his luggage and his cuff links, Count Guido Wendelin. This is a new sort of aristocrat in Spielhagen's fiction: a kind, considerate, unassuming, English-toned gentleman in the literal sense of the term. Of course he falls in love with Eleonore, but the experienced reader will guess that the soft, bland man with a deep sense of his own insufficiency is not going to get the girl. It emerges, however, that he is a neighbor of Ulrich in Farther Pomerania; his great praise of Ulrich's person and character makes Eleonore very uncomfortable. She visits her aunt, a *Geheimrätin* who has come upon hard times and tries to maintain a boarding-house, uncertainly occupied by a Chilean, a Japanese, and a Russian, all M.D.'s sent by their governments and all, of course, becoming infatuated with Eleonore. The most important of these, Gregor Borykine, is another of Spielhagen's Russian nihilists; he must flee the police (the jealous Japanese marquis having denounced him) and leave his papers with Eleonore.

Although he gets some of her sketches published in Petersburg, she has mixed feelings about him; she finds him vital, adventurous, large-spirited, but also tyrannical, bossy, and committed to unreal purposes. However, he speaks to what she misunderstands as a certain nihilism in herself that is nothing more than her vigorous desire for emancipation, for Eleonore is one of Spielhagen's most decidedly feminist characters. She is deeply envious when she learns that Borykine's sister, Wera, is a student in Zurich, and is frustrated that this is not possible for a German woman.[14]

She answers an advertisement in the *Kreuzzeitung* (perhaps an ominous sign) from a *Generalin* von Arnfeld seeking a governess with good English skills. This position thickens the plot considerably, because the Arnfeld estate is not only near Ulrich's and Guido's; the *Generalin* is Hertha's mother by her first, demeaning marriage for money to a despised bourgeois when she was an impoverished baroness, leaving her with a corresponding dislike of her oldest daughter. She also disdains her daughter Clementine, a plain but once active woman lamed in a fall from a tree, who first appears as a kind of passive Cinderella somewhat like Sibylle in *Sonntagskind* but turns out to have a rather roguish perception of her social environment. She had been hopelessly in love with Ulrich, becoming deathly ill when she observes him embracing Eleonore. The mother is desperately trying to marry the youngest daughter, the pretty and coquettish Kittie, to Guido to repair the family fortunes. In fact, Eleonore's role is to teach Kittie English to make her more attractive to Guido, a purpose with no hope of success, for Guido desperately desires to marry Eleonore. In this he is supported by his mother, an elegant Norwegian of royal descent who tries to impress Eleonore with a parable of resignation. She had been in love with a musician but renounced him because he was betrothed to her best friend, who is now her housekeeper; instead she married a good-hearted, mediocre count from whom she has the good-hearted, mediocre son.[15] She adds that one who lusts for happiness is a slave (320–21).

---

14 The University of Zurich »began admitting women to regular study in the later 1860s«: James C. Albisetti: *Schooling German Girls and Women: Secondary and Higher Education in the Nineteenth Century* (Princeton, 1988), 123. *Meyers Großes Konversations-Lexikon*, 6th edn. (Leipzig and Vienna, 1902–09), 7: 44, sub »Frauenstudium,« gives the date specifically as 1867, thus precisely a year before the action of the novel. Albisetti points out that there were so many Russian radical women at Zurich that in 1873 the Czarist government ordered them to return home or face permanent exile and that German women were sometimes afraid to go there for fear of encountering »nihilists« (126–27, 135).

15 The artist is named Hjalmar and the fiancée Brita. This looks like a gesture of homage to Spielhagen's Norwegian-American protégé Boyesen, whose »Story of an

The details of the plot machinery operating out of this situation may be left to the interested reader. Suffice it to say that Eleonore, deeply in love with Ulrich but unwilling to destroy his marriage or harm the innocent Hertha, agrees to marry Guido, though she is horrified at the thought of intimate relations with a man she does not love. Borykine in Swiss exile, outraged at this violation of principle, writes to her to say that she must not do it and sends her Wera with false passports and papers to conduct her to Petersburg, where he will rescue her. Eleonore is rightly skeptical of Borykine's judgment and so, it turns out, is Wera, who regards herself as a remorseless revolutionary, while her brother, whom she has not informed of her true, evidently hopeless mission, is a »sentimentaler Phantast« (439). Hertha is bewildered at Ulrich, who wanders about, ignores his children, thinks of traveling alone to Italy and Greece to reach higher regions without being fettered by family, and refuses sexual relations with her, until a local judge, a former suitor of Hertha's, tells her that he saw Ulrich and Eleonore together on Norderney, catching him a lie. He finds her at the edge of a lake without the courage to drown herself, and out of pity partly reconciles with her, even offering to take her to Italy for her *Bildung*, though he remains deeply miserable. At a water festival of the landed gentry – another opportunity to elaborate on the fatuousness and decay of the nobility – Eleonore must be rowed to the deathbed of Clementine, whose illness her mother ignores. On her way to Guido's mother to break her engagement, Eleonore must stay at a hotel other than the one she had expected and, by accident, encounters Ulrich. They have a night of love, but in the morning Eleonore has gone out in a boat and vanished; Ulrich, diving into the water, also vanishes. The boatman, who has not wept in sixty years, does so here (462), as no doubt we should also.

Indeed, *Stumme des Himmels* is a tearful work in which there is much weeping and death-wish by Ulrich, Eleonore, Hertha, Guido, Clementine, and others; it drifts dangerously into sentimental melodrama and has a good deal of the appearance of magazine fiction. But, apart from the continued tone of melancholy, punctuated, as in much of the late work, with sardonic social comedy, and the reiterated skepticism about marriage as unnatural

Outcast« he translated, after the main character, as »Glitzer-Brita« (see Chapter 9). Boyesen died on October 4, 1895, so that it is possible if unlikely that the reference is meant to be a memorial. Whether the name on the false passport Wera brings to Eleonore, Grace Claribel Gordon (429), is a hidden allusion to »Julien Gordon,« also translated by Spielhagen, I am unable to decide. That the »Reseda« is Eleonore's favorite flower (32) in a novel published between Gordon's *Mademoiselle Réséda* and Spielhagen's translation of it might be a temptation to a more adventurous interpreter than I.

and love as delusion, there are other features that might bear attention. No other work of Spielhagen's has such a pronounced English orientation. English seems to be the prestigious language; characters use it with one another. For example:

> *Shocking!* murmelte er.
> *Why, dear count,* sagte Eleonore gelassen; *she is the mistress, and I am used to be treated as a governess.*
> *But you shouldn't,* sprudelte er. *I can't stand it. And I have a great mind to tell that – that woman –* (312).

There is much reference to English-language literature. Ulrich shows himself cosmopolitan and up-to-date when he refers in his thoughts to a recently published novel, *No Thoroughfare* (89).[16] Fine distinctions are made: Guido prefers Thackeray to Dickens, perhaps a sign of undeveloped taste, for his mother thinks Dickens the greater writer but prefers Byron and Shakespeare to both, as does Eleonore (170). Eleonore has given Borykine *David Copperfield* to read, and he, not knowing what will become of him in Zurich exile, takes heart from Mr. Micawber (163). Clementine's taste is also certified in her liking for English literature, especially Byron and Browning; when she was recovering from her accident her pastor orally translated *The Vicar of Wakefield* for her, then taught her to read English in four weeks (188–90). Eleonore is beguiled by the English style of Guido's surroundings, which might compensate her for *Entsagung*, while he supposes that one of the handsome men in England must be her lover (302, 293). That Frau Arnfeld and Kittie know no English devalues them. It looks to me as though Spielhagen here is straining away from the disappointing Reich to an imagined, alternative, more promising national culture.

The novel continues from *Sonntagskind* a tendency to a more literary execution, along with further tentative probes into symbol and leitmotif. At the beginning, when Ulrich is still puzzled by his depression, and just before he first sees Eleonore, gulls fly over him with a hollow laugh, plunging him into a panic attack. After he meets her, he dreams of flying for the first time since he was a boy (27); the juxtaposition of the two images seems ominous. Eleonore's aunt is characterized at both the narrative and the dialogue level as having an »altmodisches Herz,« while Guido has a standing, all-purpose adverb, »selbstverständlich« (passim). The parallelisms and evident organiza-

---

[16] This is doubtless the mystery written by Wilkie Collins with the collaboration of Charles Dickens for the Christmas issue of *All the Year Round* in 1867. See Andrew Gasson, *Wilkie Collins: An Illustrated Guide* (Oxford and New York, 1998), 115–17. One notices again the precision of dating.

tion of plot may strike the reader as artificial, but certainly seem like something of a departure from the theoretical principles on which Spielhagen still was insisting. The, even for him, exceptional degree of coincidence in the management of the plot is not just a narrative convenience but is recuperated recursively at the level of narration. Early on, Ulrich broods, with a narrative irony detectable only in retrospect, that he has grown old into a life »in dem kein Zufall vorkommt! Niemals!« (34). Eleonore, who has earlier asserted that there is »auf ihn [Zufall] kein Verlaß« (33), later speaks of »der Zufall – wenn es ein Zufall war« that has brought her together with Ulrich, and, later, she and Guido of gratitude to the »Zufall« that has brought *them* together (94, 309), this time in mutual, strained refusal of perception. All this reiteration on more than one level implies, I think, that, whatever Ulrich and Eleonore may feel subjectively, their great love is not one of Wagnerian inevitability, but just one of those things that can happen to people in an accidental concatenation of circumstances, leading to »kein Ausweg,« as Ulrich correctly renders the meaning of the title *No Thoroughfare* (89). At one point he realizes that he has the same feelings for Eleonore that he had for an earlier inamorata, and concludes that, if love can be sequential, the institution of marriage is nonsense (253–54).

Despite the attentiveness with which Spielhagen maintains the action of the novel in 1868, in some ways its tone and posture is more of its time of publication. Eleonore's pronounced feminism seems to belong more to the last quarter of the nineteenth century than to the 1860s. »Du weißt,« she writes to Ulrich, »ich denke sehr frei, viel freier, als man uns Frauenzimmern gemeiniglich zu denken erlaubt, ja, auch freier als der Durchschnitt der Männer« (94). The erotic aspect, often lurking just under the surface, is here more pronounced and explicit; Ulrich is not insignificantly attracted to Eleonore's body as it is revealed by her storm-soaked clothes, while she is very conscious of her body when imagining marriage to the unloved Guido. At one point she feels she would yield to Ulrich if he would ride away with her, until the pale image of Hertha intervenes (277). While her intense effort to submerge desire in duty might remind us of the otherwise unadmired George Eliot, she is far from a paragon of sentimental virtue. Though she is touched by the story of Guido's mother, she decides afterwards that the countess's resignation was cowardly, only possible without true love; »ihr Verstand größer war als ihr Herz,« she broke the musician's genius and only told the story to get her to marry her mediocre son (326–27). Eleonore is proud and self-willed, and at one point, she permits herself a scornful outburst addressing the helpless Hertha in the third person: »Daß es der pure blöde Zufall [!] war, der sie in den Besitz brachte; daß, hätte der

Mann vor zehn Jahren die Nebenbuhlerin gesehen und gekannt, diese heute an der Stelle stehen würde, wo die andre steht ... solche frevlen Gedanken muß man sich natürlich aus dem Sinn schlagen« (401). When she receives a reconciling and forgiving letter from Hertha, Eleonore breaks out in bitterness at her unsuitability to Ulrich:

> ... brav, ehrlich, gerecht, – soweit sich die Gerechtigkeit mit der üblichen naiven Selbstliebe verträgt – ein Muster von einer Frau, wie man sie lange vergeblich suchen mußte. Und doch! und doch! armer, armer Ulrich! Warum sie, die jeden andern glücklich machen konnte! Nein, du beste aller Frauen, das bringst du nicht fertig: es wird nicht kommen, wird nicht besser werden; es wird so bleiben, wie es war. Mein armer, armer, geliebter Ulrich! was magst du in diesen Tagen gelitten haben! was magst du leiden! (426)

But it would be a mistake to see this as a case of two people made for each other separated by circumstance and convention. As we can see from this passage, Ulrich maintains his hold on Eleonore partly through a persistent emotional theatricality; at one point he wants to kill Eleonore and cover her with kisses while hoping for a duel with the inoffensive Guido (279–80, 282). He never makes as much of an effort as she does to achieve resignation and act with due consideration for the people around him, beginning with his family; as is often the case with Spielhagen, the man is weaker than the woman. The now familiar undercurrent of skepticism about love and marriage raises a doubt about the utopian perfection of a union of Ulrich and Eleonore. Spielhagen allows himself a quite strange moment near the end of the novel, when Ulrich and Eleonore yield to the consummation of their love. After having sworn fidelity to their love for one another: »Ihre trunkenen Blicke schwammen ineinander, und ihre Seelen küßten sich, während ihre Gedanken weit auseinander irrten.« What the narrator means here is that she is already thinking of ending her life, but the sudden access of divergent thoughts at the moment of longed-for union is jolting. Ulrich does not notice her thought, only that it »den Glanz ihrer Augen erhöhte, um ihre Lippen ein Lächeln zaubernd, tödlich-schön, wie das der Medusa« (454). This seems like a *fin-de-siècle* simile, reminding one perhaps more of Klimt than of any mid-century image.[17] The effect is even more pronounced in those works in which tragedy and pathos yield to satire and brittle comedy, to which we shall turn in the next chapter.

---

[17] Spielhagen seems to make an uncharacteristic slip in his sense of time when he has Borykine write in opposing Eleonore's marriage: »*Fin-de-siècle* Menschen, die ihre Sache auf nichts gestellt haben, wie Sie, dürfen sich solchen Luxus nicht mehr gewähren« (427), a locution that does not seem appropriate to 1868.

17. Refuge in Satire and Decadence:
Alles fließt, Susi, Faustulus, Herrin

Every one of Spielhagen's narrative works is included in his collected editions, such as those employed for this study, with one exception: the novella *Alles fließt*, which originally appeared together with *Mesmerismus* in 1897 (*MAF*). *Mesmerismus* was taken into the collected editions (*NF,* 5) but *Alles fließt* was not. It was, however, published between *AR* and *NF* by Reclam in 1903. I have no explanation for this curious idiosyncrasy. Did the Staackmann firm dislike it and decline to take it into the collected edition? But Staackmann published it in the first place.[1] Did Spielhagen himself not wish to feature it? Why, then, did it appear with Reclam? Was it a special arrangement for some purpose of his own? One might be reminded of Wilhelm Raabe's insistence on publishing *Zum wilden Mann*, against all opposition, as the two-thousandth volume of Reclam's *Universalbibliothek*.[2] Perhaps if one day we obtain systematic access to Spielhagen's correspondence we shall find an answer to this question. I will try to show, however, that the absence of this text in such canon as there may be is significant and deplorable.

The story, which takes place in an unnamed provincial capital in the immediate present, begins with a festive occasion attended by three old friends in their forties, Emerich, a violinist and conductor, director of the conservatory, with his wife Regine, whose birthday it is; Arnold, a writer and literary

---

[1] Spielhagen had published in several firms but when Ludwig Staackmann founded his own around 1870, Spielhagen, who had known him for some years, became permanently his exclusive house author. The firm survived the founder's death in 1897. See Henning, *Friedrich Spielhagen,* 74, 85. What relations were like after that I do not know. Three years after Spielhagen's death, Karl Kraus directed one of his patented polemics against the authors of the firm, »Die Staackmänner,« as providers of paltry *Heimatliteratur* for railway travelers: *Literatur und Lüge* (Vienna, 1929), 318–25. Since Kraus professes not to read their novels, or any novels, he comments instead on the authors' photographs. Spielhagen is not mentioned.

[2] See Jeffrey L. Sammons, *Wilhelm Raabe: The Fiction of the Alternative Community* (Princeton, 1987), 231. *Alles fließt* was printed in the Reclam format; although the *Gesamtverzeichnis* lists it as No. 4270 of the *Universal-Bibliothek,* the copy I saw did not have a series number. Other texts in the series were *Die Dorfkokette* (sic; 4100) and *Was die Schwalbe sang* (4138), both in 1900.

professor at the Polytechnic with his wife Astrid; and Eilhardt, a painter and director of the Academy with his wife Stella. Emerich, whose garrulousness in toasting is feared, not least by his wife, is a man of invincible cheerfulness and bonhomie, who refers to his marriage as »eine unendliche Melodie« (*MAF*, 265). Regine, in turn, though she knows nothing about music – possibly an advantage for spousal harmony, as we shall see – is nevertheless convinced that her husband is a genius. The other two, four-year-old marriages are not in such splendid condition. Both Arnold and Eilhardt have married younger protégées; Astrid, who is of Danish origin, admired Arnold's writing and translated his novellas, while Stella was Eilhardt's painting pupil. But now both wives have evolved beyond their husbands' tutelage and aesthetic principles, Astrid writing as a modern Naturalist and Stella painting in the Impressionist mode. The husbands feel betrayed. Astrid, Arnold complains, has not evolved to »meinen größeren dichterischen Zwecken« (158), while Stella adheres to Millet and Henri Rousseau (172). The wives feel misunderstood and scornful of their husbands' work. Astrid refuses to praise Arnold's novella (157); Stella is persuaded that »die Malerei noch andere Zwecke habe, als den Philister in seinem faulen Frieden mit sich selbst und der Welt zu bestärken« (172). Consequently both are encouraged and courted by younger men, Astrid by Alfred, a writer in the new style, and Stella by Willibald, a handsome, somewhat caddish painter with Parisian manners. A hostile chorus in the background is formed by two defenders of the eternal values, Dr. Mädler »von der höheren Töchterschule« (230) and Professor Bimstein of the Art Academy.

Astrid has already published a novel anonymously, but now wishes to publish another, *Wenn Frauen Mut hätten*, under her own name, although her husband has asked her not to publish it all. She leaves the details to Alfred because she does not bother with the mechanics of publishing. Through a mix-up that is unclear but blamed on Alfred, the book appears under her husband's name, Astolf Arnold. Alfred tries to explain that the publisher might not have known Arnold could not have written such a book because publishers read very little and just react to names (207). Astrid is, of course, enraged, and when Arnold learns of it, he is mortified. Meanwhile, Stella's paintings have been refused for an exhibition even though her husband, who had, of course, disqualified himself from directly participating on the jury, retained his influence. According to the unctuous Willibald, Eilhardt said that his wife had yet to become an artist. Willibald, who had assured her of success, now claims to have warned her of the unacceptability of »die drei Kinderleichen mit der sich im Todeskampf windenden Mutter,« adding: »die *vérité*, die *vérité vraie* – das ist das rote Tuch für diese Ochsen«

(216). Stella has painted a portrait of Willibald, who decides to wreak vengeance by smuggling it into the exhibit under her husband's name, which he is able to do because the catalogue is printed in Alfred's firm. Now Eilhardt is the object of a scandal.

Thus the quarrel between the old and the new has generated a perfect catastrophe. With a further twist on Spielhagen's theme of the older man with a younger wife, Eilhardt and Arnold regret their marriages: »Was hatten wir alten Kerls die jungen Mädels zu heiraten!« (261). They regard their marriages as ruined and plan to leave their wives. Alfred reminds Astrid of her Scandinavian modern background; she has not grown up »unter der grauenhaften ästhetischen Depression des Goethe-Schiller-Fetischismus« but surrounded by »die lebensvollen Gestalten eines Ibsen, Björnson, Arne Garborg« and secretly reading »Dostojewskis Raskolnikow« (151). She looks down on Stella because she has no »Nora-Blut« in her veins (193). Willibald, sexually attracted by Stella though uncomfortably aware that he is acting out a dissembling role, urges her to flee with him to Paris, holding up particularly as a model the emancipated writer Marie Baskirtscheff, last lover of the artist Bastien Lepage.[3] Stella, though aware of the absurdity of a married woman with children running off with a character like Willibald, is nevertheless aroused.

However, in this crisis, some half-formed alternatives begin to emerge. Eilhardt twice ventures the opinion that aesthetic differences have nothing to do with love (153, 161). More importantly, the husbands develop a lurking respect for their wives' achievements. Eilhardt says to Arnold of the portrait of Willibald:

> Das Bild ist nämlich gut; man kann's sogar ausgezeichnet nennen. Du mußt dich freilich ... nicht unmittelbar davorstellen. Da siehst du nur Kleckse: graue, blaue, rote. Aber wenn du in die nötige Entfernung trittst ... mit dieser Kühnheit, dieser Sicherheit – Alter, ich sage dir: da kriegt man unwillkürlich einen heidenmäßigen Respekt vor solchem donnermäßigen Können. Und freut sich im stillen, daß das

---

[3] On these allusions, see Hubert Ohl, »Spielhagens Spätwerk und das Fin de Siècle. Figuren und Motive,« »*Realismus?*« *Zur deutschen Prosa-Literatur des 19. Jahrhunderts*, ed. Norbert Oellers and Hartmut Steinecke, *Zeitschrift für Deutsche Philologie*, Sonderheft, 120 (2001): 187–88, 195 n. 35. Marie Bashkirtseff (1858–84), as she is customarily spelled, was an ambitious Russian painter in Paris who died young, leaving a diary that was a sensation when published four years later. The painter Jules Bastien-Lepage (1848–84) was an older friend, not a lover. See Colette Cosnier, *Marie Bashkirtseff. Un portrait sans retouches* (Paris, 1985). Spielhagen criticized her as a phenomenon of modern excess in his late lecture on Goethe and in a rhymed aphorism jibed at her (spelled »Baskirtzeff«) for her self-promotion (*NB*, 87; *NG*, 142).

Bild auf der Ausstellung ist, auf der es von Banalitäten wimmelt, über die man weder lachen noch weinen kann. (254–55)

In other words, Eilhardt has learned how to look at an Impressionist painting. Arnold, for his part, says of Astrid's book: »Ich möchte es und ich könnte es nicht geschrieben haben ..., aber ein bedeutendes Buch ist und bleibt es« (261). But they cannot tell their wives these things because it would look like flattery. Astrid begins a letter: »Lieber Arnold. Ich kann dies Leben nicht länger ertragen. Ich – «, but the words »verlasse dich« will not come out of her pen; she did not know that she was a coward (266–67). When Stella comes weeping hysterically over Willibald's invitation to accompany her to Paris, Astrid tells her that she is ungrateful for Eilhardt's kindness, and then she begins to muse that perhaps her hard-line Naturalism does not help the poor and burdened, that the world needs an art that points to the ideal and the sublime, a thought that brings her to a reconsideration of Arnold:

Ich habe seine Bücher wieder gelesen. Es können nicht alle zu den Gewaltigen gehören, deren Schritt, die spätgeborenen Enkel erschütternd, durch die marmornen Hallen der Zeit dröhnt – zu ihnen gehört er nicht. Nein. Aber welche helle Freude an allem, was gut und schön ist! Welch herzliches Verlangen, diese Freude in dem Busen der Leser zu entfachen! Welch edler Zorn gegen das Schlechte und Gemeine! Welch inniges Mitleid noch mit dem Gefallenen, dem man so gern Mahadöh sein möchte, ihn mit feurigen Armen zum Himmel emporzuheben! (274–75)

Stella thinks Astrid has gone crazy; the passage sounds like an apologia on Spielhagen's own behalf and, more worrisomely, seems to suggest a conversion from Ibsenism to Spielhagenism. But this is not quite what is happening, as we shall see presently.

After various farcical complications, everyone converges at the railroad station, Regine, tipped off by a tipsy Emerich, having warned Astrid and Stella that their husbands are leaving for Paris. Willibald, who has skeptically purchased a ticket for Stella, is not surprised when she does not join him. As he observes Stella embracing Eilhardt, Astrid holding Arnold's hands, and Regine straightening Emerich's tie, he comments to himself: »Das reine Rütli! *Sauve qui peut!*« (282). But this reconciliation scene is not the end of the story. A year later we find Dr. Mädler and Professor Bimstein complaining that Eilhardt has not resigned his position or even divorced his wife, while Arnold and Astrid have published a book together with six novellas, alternating authorship and style:

hier die alte Goethesche Schule mit ihren zarten Konturen: ihrer über Gute und Böse mildlächelnden Ironie; ihrem *horreur* vor dem Gemeinen und Häßlichen; ihrer durchsichtigen Sprache; ihren Perioden, die Zeit haben, in harmonischer Gliederung tönend zu verrollen. Dort die neue: derb zufahrend, mit plumper Faust Menschen und Dinge packend; ohne Scheu vor dem Schmutz, den sie gierig aufwühlt; in der Sucht, wahr zu erscheinen, die fortströmende Rede in naturalistische Brocken zerkrümelnd. Und – es klingt wie Blasphemie – als Motto des Buches das Lessingsche: »Nur muß der eine nicht den andern mäkeln. Nur muß der Knorr den Knubben hübsch vertragen.« Ich erlaube mir, diese Sorte von Verträglichkeit verächtlich zu finden. (290)[4]

Mädler and Bimstein determine to denounce these provocations in the critical press, but anonymously, so as not to get into trouble. For their part, Arnold, Astrid, Eilhardt, and Stella have been invited by Alfred, Willibald, and »einem namhaften Pariser Schriftsteller« (Zola?) to join them in a journal of the arts to appear in both German and French with the title *Pantarhei*, meaning, as Arnold pedantically explains, »alles fließt« (293), indicating the flow and change of aesthetic modes.[5]

This, for some reason, partly suppressed text is very remarkable for several reasons. In the first place, it is quite funny, doubtless the most comic of all of Spielhagen's works.[6] The snippy dialogue indicates the combat of all against all that has become the hallmark of his social representations. Eilhardt and Arnold quarrel over which of their arts is more complex; Astrid scorns Stella's emotionality, lack of domestic skills, and noisy children; Willibald, though apparently making common cause with Alfred, is privately certain that he will have no success with the »Eisberg Astrid,«

---

4 The motto is slightly misquoted from Lessing's *Nathan der Weise*, II, 5, appropriately for the novella's theme of tolerance.

5 Spielhagen titled the introduction to NB »ΠΑΝΤΑ PEI.« Ohl, »Spielhagens Spätwerk,« 197, makes the point that the essay is more conservative than the novella. Still, Spielhagen concedes that Naturalism, as meeting a readiness of the times, has a right to exist and that »man Kunst und Kunstanschauungen seiner Zeit, wie die Jahreszeiten, wie das Wetter des Tages, mit dem nötigen Gleichmut hinzunehmen hat« (*NB*, 11, 13).

6 The comic tone is a minor feature of Spielhagen's œuvre but is certainly present and increases in the late work as it becomes permeated with satire and sarcasm. He himself wrote that the paired novellas *Mesmerismus* and *Alles fließt* »scheinen mir bedeutsam für den Pathetiker und für den Humoristen, die vielleicht zu gleichen Teilen ursprünglich in meiner Veranlagung stecken, nur das in dem Drang des Lebens und Schaffens der erstere viel öfter und ausgiebiger zum Wort gekommen als der letztere«: Ella Mensch, »Erinnerungen an Friedrich Spielhagen,« *Westermanns Monatshefte* 110 (1911): 359. Fontane professed to admire both: »Tragik und Phantastik hüben, Genre und Ironie drüben, aber in einem sind sie sich doch gleich, in einer großen Modernität nach Stoff wie Behandlung«: to Spielhagen, January 28, 1897, Fontane, *Briefe*, 4: 632.

while Alfred thinks him horribly arrogant and hopes Stella will drop him (181–82); a theater director who appears to agree with Mädler and Bimstein about the horrors of the modern and is pleased that they are not allowed into his royal theater thinks privately of them, when they fail to appreciate his parting bon mot: »Die Sorte verdirbt einem doch immer die schönsten Nüancen« (244). There are a number of cultural and literary pleasantries. When Astrid tells how Arnold walked out of the house when her book appeared, Stella enthusiastically imagines he has *slammed the door* and is not a dishrag like Ibsen's Torvald; Arnold has closed the door quietly, but Stella is still excited that she does have, contrary to Astrid's claim, »Nora-Blut« in her veins (196–97). When Alfred tries to find words to declare his love to Astrid, he quotes Gretchen – not Goethe's but Gounod's – until he notices that his gloves do not match (211), and when Willibald runs out of phrases in his letter urging Stella to flee with him, he covers himself with an allusion to the race of men who, according to Heine's poem, die of love: »Die Asra machen nicht viel Worte« (269). Eilhardt and Arnold plan, literally, to take »französischen Abschied« and to send telegrams »an die verlassenen Ariadnen« (265). But, as Ohl says: »Man sollte über den lustspielhaften Elementen dieser kleinen Geschichte ihren Ernst nicht verkennen.«[7] There is a good deal of feminist assertion, encapsulated in the comic discourse, to be sure, but nevertheless pungent. Willibald describes to Alfred »die Geschichte von Stellas künstlerischer Emancipation, nebenbei *mutatis mutandis* von tausend Frauenemancipationen« (172) – the first time, I surmised in Chapter 10, that this term appears in Spielhagen's fiction. Stella herself cries: »Die moderne Europäerin ist keine indianische Squaw« (197), and startles the usually self-possessed Astrid by suggesting that they swap husbands (191).

Any reader must be struck by the conspicuous symmetry of the structure: the characters, events, and narrative devices mirror one another. The effect is highlighted by the characters' attempt to deny symmetry. Astrid denies that her purely business-like and principled relationship to Alfred is anything like Stella's to Willibald, beguiled as she is by his youth and good looks (189, 270); Arnold similarly claims that his case oddly resembles Eilhardt's, except that »zwischen mir und Astrid kein Wesen in Fleisch und Blut steht, wie zwischen dir und Stella, sondern nur ein Princip« (259). The symmetry is redoubled when both couples converge at the railroad station, and closes in a circle with a friendly gathering of the three couples as in

---

7   Ohl, »Spielhagens Spätwerk,« 197.

the opening scene. Such artifice seems incompatible with the theory of narrative objectivity, for it calls attention to authorial management.[8] Beyond this there are a number of apparently recursive musings, as in Arnold's self-defense: »In der Dichtkunst giebt es sehr verschiedene Höhengrade, und man kann von niemand verlangen und erwarten, er werde, oder vermöge höher zu steigen, als seine Kräfte ihn tragen« (158). But he does evolve, to Bimstein's annoyance: Arnold, who previously had written »nur Jambendramen ..., die man dreimal und nie wieder bringen konnte, und ... Romane, die jede Mutter ihrer Tochter getrost in die Hand geben durfte,« now under Astrid's influence writes novels that exceed the French and the Russians (241). In fact, Mädler's and Bimstein's grumblings look like stuffy parodies of Spielhagen's own often reiterated principles, and it may be a wistful confession on the author's part when he has Bimstein speak of writers »die vor dreißig oder mehr Jahren einen ganz guten Klang hatten. Nur daß sie heute nicht mehr ziehen« (287). In any case, it seems that the flood of the new can no longer be stanched. The theater director complains that his wife, an actress not allowed to perform since her marriage, exercises her mind with »Tolstoi, Maupassant, Dostojewski, Flaubert, Zola, Bourget – wer kann alle die Namen behalten!« (240). That the cosmopolitan journal the characters intend to found will oppose all »Principienreiterei« (293) is truly a concession on Spielhagen's part. With these gestures he clearly separates himself from the company of those traditionally oriented writers with whom he had earlier identified himself.[9] No comprehensive account of Spielhagen can be fair without taking into consideration the gestures of toleration and acceptance of the modern in *Alles fließt*.

---

8   Fontane said in his letter: »Bei Novelle 2 [*Alles fließt*] hat mich die virtuose Behandlung der Parallelen und in diesen hinwiederum die Herausarbeitung der Gegensätze ganz besonders gefesselt«: *Briefe*, 4: 632. It is possible that he is noticing a degree of convergence with his own artistic standards.

9   Christa Müller-Donges, *Das Novellenwerk Friedrich Spielhagens in seiner Entwicklung zwischen 1851 und 1899* (Marburg, 1970), 101, aptly contrasts Paul Heyse's *Marienkind* (1891), in which a painter who has erred into Naturalism and a girl deluded into aspiring to be a nun are cured by love into normality, in part under the mentorship of an elder who teases the painter sarcastically about the absurdity of choosing ugly subjects for art. The painter and the girl declare themselves in the *Alte Pinakothek* amidst the traditional art works, where they will not be discovered because the other painters »meiden seit einigen Jahren diese Räume«: Paul Heyse, *Gesammelte Werke* (Berlin, 1872–1914): 27: 151. A later painting of his wife and child is scorned because it exhibits no »Schmutz« (159). Striking here is not only Heyse's obtuseness, but the contempt in which impoverished people are held, not only as motifs: »ein blödsinniges Bauernkind in einem schmutzigen Hemde«; »Ihre kleine charakteristische Cretine auf dem Brunnentrog« (65, 69).

However, this humorous tone is not the only one Spielhagen developed as he edged toward *fin-de-siècle* decadence. An unexpectedly confrontational, sardonic denial of readerly expectations had already appeared in his novella *Susi* two years earlier, in 1895. Susi is a beautiful young baroness, talented in singing and painting, in a small dukedom that is now of doubtful importance under the constitutional arrangements of the Reich, and married to Baron Astolf von Wachta, a landowner of old family and sometime advisor to Duke Heinrich, a friend from student days. Astolf is amazed by his good fortune at having married Susi, who, however, is annoyed by his bluff loudness and bored to death by her »insipiden Ehe mit ihrem idealen Schlagododro« (*NF*, 3: 274). She is one of Spielhagen's patented *femmes fatales*, with whom everyone is infatuated, including the duke, his totally amoral, financially dependent factotum, Odo von Brenken, and a young painter, Fritz Sommer. Trolling for a main chance, Susi allows herself to be seduced by the duke, musing on the possibility of a morganatic marriage, notwithstanding that she is already married and the duke has a duchess, unattractive and ailing though she may be. This situation requires the disposal of the duke's previous, fading mistress, a singer who does not, however, go quietly, and partly through her machinations along with a couple of Spielhagenish coincidences, Astolf discovers his wife's infidelity. Actually, he discovers her with Brenken, but the latter makes a speedy decision – »Am Ende ist sich doch jeder selbst der nächste« – to give up his master (357). Astolf, horribly disillusioned that his wife is »eine Dirne« (375), becomes nearly insane with emotional devastation; he feels he cannot challenge the duke: »Von seinem Landesherrn kann man keine Satisfaktion fordern« (376). He thinks of arranging a secret suicide, then of killing Susi, from which he is prevented by a memory of Dumas's *Affaire Clémenceau*, which had disgusted Spielhagen thirty years before (380). Yet he thirsts for revenge: »Ja, Rache! Rache! Rache« (378). Meanwhile, the duke, who is in a political situation in which he wants the reliable Astolf as his minister, hopes things can be smoothed over when they meet at a hunt. Astolf approaches him with drawn sword, but, in a truly spectacular coincidence, the duke is attacked by a boar and Astolf gives his life driving the animal off; he is now celebrated with allusions to the self-sacrificing hero Froben in Kleist's *Prinz Friedrich von Homburg* (400), although opposition newspapers drop broad hints that something else was going on. Brenken, analyzing the situation, concludes that Susi and the duke are through, even though the duchess has meanwhile died in childbirth. Brenken explains to her that her reputation is damaged and that a baroness cannot have a duke as a lover; only a circus rider or an actress can do that, not a lady; with an allusion to Schiller's *Don Carlos*, he says that she will have to return to her father »fern von Madrid« (404, 403).

This précis will not appear either very elevating or very original. Indeed, we find here some familiar character types, but strikingly diminished. The duke is one of Spielhagen's familiar rulers: passionate but unstable, wanting to be both a lord and a good fellow, blaming everyone but himself for his misfortunes, and dabbling in culture: he debates with young Sommer about a sketch of Susi by Franz Lenbach, bores courtiers, who have heard it all before, with a tour of his collection of art and antiquities, and invites Brenken into his carriage with an allusion to »mein verstorbener Freund Berthold Auerbach« (233). But he also chafes at the limitations of a duo-decimal »Serenissimus« (240) in the modern Reich. When Brenken enrages the duke with quite just and wise criticism, he is ready to sign Brenken's death warrant (236). He muses that the old days, when one could just have a husband ambushed, »waren leider nicht mehr ... hier war er hilflos wie der letzte seiner Unterthanen« (314) and he finds himself at the crisis beset with »für einen regierenden Herrn geradezu unleidlichen Sorgen und Kümmernissen« (373). These are nonsensical imaginings for an anachronism who has to worry about his rights being challenged by the opposition in the *Landtag* (318). In the matter of Susi, he also must submit with gritted teeth to the chastisement of the royal prince, who contributes to the termination of the affair.[10]

Spielhagen's type of pure fool might be said to begin with Gotthold Weber in *Was die Schwalbe sang*, whose self-effacing sacrifice might have amazed even Dickens, though he remains a competent hero, which one can no longer say of the hapless Uhlenhans, while Astolf, for all that he has earned a doctorate (251), seems still further diminished; although he is the only moral and honorable person in the story, his extreme obliviousness, his »lammherzige Gutmütigkeit« (364) might arouse even the reader's impatience, and his demonstrative love for Susi certainly irritates her. With a narration that shifts in and out of the characters' consciousness, switching between direct and indirect discourse, it is not clear whether we should put on the narrator's or Susi's account the observation that »[e]s war vielleicht etwas Neufundländermäßiges in dem Ausdruck von Astolfs Wiedersehens-

---

[10] Again one wonders whether this relatively informal, gracious, and astute figure might suggest Crown Prince Friedrich. If so, it would place the action of the novella in the mid–1880s, between the death of Auerbach in 1882 and the accession and death of Friedrich III in 1888. The references to Lenbach, at that time at the height of his celebrity, would support such dating.

freude« (315). He thinks of moving away to assist Susi's ill father in administration, thinking he will be doing her a favor, while she is horrified at being immured in the forests on the Russian border with no company but »den hypochondrischen Papa, der nicht den kleinsten Spaß verstand, und stupide Krautjunker, die nach dem Pferdestall rochen« (276–77). Alternatively, even after he has received a letter from the vengeful singer exposing Susi's infidelity, he considers accepting the duke's offer to make him chief minister, imagining how his dear wife will look the first time she is addressed as »Exzellenz« and telling himself that her noble love has made him into a man (348). When he is pleased at the thought that the duke might be in love with Susi because it will purify him from his degrading relationship with his mistress and compensate him for his ugly duchess, »denn das reinigt, das läutert; das wird ihm geben, woran es ihm bis jetzt fehlt: den Ernst der Lebensführung, die Kraft der Entsagung, den Ekel vor allem Gemeinen, die Anbetung von allem, was edel, schön und groß ist; das wird ihm zu einem Manne machen,« we might find ourselves, against our better judgment, agreeing with Susi: »Ist es menschenmöglich, daß man so dumm sein kann? ... Wenn einer so leicht hinter's Licht zu führen ist, wo bleibt denn da der Spaß?« (246–47). Brenken, for his part, is confident that Astolf is a man stupid enough to keep his word; again one might think of Schiller, this time of *Kabale und Liebe*, III, 1, where Wurm explains to his courtly master the unheard-of bourgeois morality of keeping one's word (359). The story's corrosive decadence decomposes Spielhagen's idealism at the narrative level.

As for Brenken, we have earlier seen types of the impecunious factotum and hanger-on of an establishment, such as the fairly harmless Zeisel in *Allzeit voran* and Stude in *Platt Land*, or the much less harmless Weissfisch in *Was will das werden?*, but Brenken is an extreme case of the willful denial of conscience. All his considerable courtliness, cleverness, and perceptivity is directed toward his own welfare, and successfully so. His survival amazes the duke, who cannot understand why Astolf has not shot him: »Es war positiv unheimlich, einen Menschen zu sehen, mit einem Menschen zu sprechen, der, nach dem natürlichen Verlauf der Dinge, gar nicht mehr leben konnte« (372). To be sure, serving the duke in the matter of Susi puts stress on Brenken's principled absence of principle: »Von der lästigen Gepflogenheit, sich moralische Vorwürfe zu machen, war er für gewöhnlich nicht geplagt; in diesem Augenblick kam er sich sehr erbärmlich vor, nannte sich einen ganz gemeinen Schuft. Was anders war er denn, als ein Kuppler?« (296). But this scruple is generated by his own lust for Susi and his worry how he must appear in her eyes – an unnecessary concern, for Brenken suits Susi just fine:

Aber sie fand – heut mit ganz besonderer Genugthuung –, daß kein Spiel so bös war, für das der Mann nicht eine gute Miene gehabt, und keine Sache so uneben, die er nicht glatt gemacht hätte. Die Moral sei eine Erfindung von Spießbürgern für Spießbürger, und in diesem Falle würde selbst das tugendsamste Spießbürgerauge keine Unmoralität entdecken können. Auch nicht die Spur davon. (323)

At the end, she says complacently to him:

Wissen Sie, Brenken, Sie sind doch *entre nous* ein furchtbares *mauvais sujet.*
Sehr schmeichelhaft, erwiderte Brenken. Ich nehme an, daß Sie unter einem *mauvais sujet* einen Mann verstehen, der absolut kein Vorurteil hat; den schlechterdings nichts imponiert; der entschlossen ist, sich das Leben, soweit es geht, ganz nach seinem Geschmack einrichten – *enfin*: einen Menschen, der genau so ist, wie er sein muß, wenn Sie ihn heiraten sollen. (406)

For his part, Brenken wonders if Astolf will strangle the witch: »Verdient hätte sie's. Schade wär's aber doch« (359). All the same he would be glad to be »der Besitzer einer gewissen Perle ..., die, wenn sie gleich schon einen und den andern Schatz geziert, in seinen Augen wenigstens, an Wert nicht das mindeste eingebüßt hatte« (364). At the end his former friends cut him because of the scandal, but the last sentence, in the place where Spielhagen normally puts his moral, reads: »Mit einer Susi und ihrer Million – das müßte doch wunderlich zugehen, wenn man in zwei Jahren oder so nicht wieder obenauf wäre!« (409).

Thus they would seem well matched, though a rational observer might wonder why either one would think it in any way safe to be mated with the other. The ultimate *femme fatale* Susi resembles Isabel in *Sonntagskind* in her playacting and incapacity to love, but she has none of Isabel's endearing characteristics, her poetic sensibility or her ingenuousness. She is a relentless schemer, a heartless prevaricator, indifferent alike to her father, her husband, and her infant child (»von Babys sieht eines aus wie das andere, schreit eines wie das andere« [281]); at the end she regrets that Astolf did not kill her lover, the duke (405). By all Victorian standards we should abhor her, but do we? There is something indomitable about her – »ich fürchte mich nie« (220), she says early on, and this sin of pride never attracts the retribution that literary convention requires – and for all her wickedness, she can be a comic figure. The duchess, who, like everyone else, loves her, nevertheless so bores her with her charitable projects and proposals to combat Social Democracy by compelling the poor to Lutheran prayer in their homes that Susi thinks of meowing like a cat, or throwing down her embroidery and dancing a tarantella (256). Like Isabel, she is exasperated by the passion she herself incites in men: »Warum nur diese Männer immer vor einem auf den

Knieen herumrutschen müssen?« (362). In the midst of the *fin-de-siècle* she was accepted as true to life.[11]

Quite un-Victorian is the attitude toward love, which, as Susi thinks, is »überhaupt Unsinn!« (304). Except for the unworldly Astolf, all passion is sexual. Susi denies sex to her husband or grants it, as circumstances indicate, in the latter case despite a promise of fidelity to the duke (248–49, 316). The rejected mistress offers sex to a gardener boy in order to employ him as a spy and go-between (328). As for Brenken, though he has thrown love overboard with all other prejudices, his nerves nevertheless vibrate in Susi's presence (324). The duke is so passionate and sexually enthusiastic that she finds him tedious and absurd (304–05, 314–15). From the outset she is determined to master him: »Wer von ihr gekostet hatte, der sollte sich ewige Sklaverei daran gegessen haben« (257). She seems to have acquired some of the sexual indifference and self-control of Zola's Nana. In fact, when Brenken arranges for her to have access to a villa on the ducal property, she weighs the implications, for she has read too many French novels not to know what that means (329). The thought has occurred to me that *Susi* might be a parody of what Spielhagen supposed a French novel to be.[12] But in its refusal of the closure of poetic justice it might remind one also of a systematic affront to reader expectation such as Mark Twain's paired *Story of the Bad Little Boy* and *Story of the Good Little Boy.* Perhaps critics today might make an effort to get over their aversion to *Susi.*[13]

These figures seem to indicate an endemic deterioration of character in Reich society, a new kind of person, ruthless, amoral, bloated with arrogance and conceit, meanly fallen from the great German potential of the *Goethezeit.* That this was indeed Spielhagen's concern is indicated by two short novels that address the problem in its male and female forms. The male case is that of *Faustulus* (1898), which Fontane, unexpectedly, professed

---

[11] Mielke, *Der Deutsche Roman des neunzehnten Jahrhunderts,* 426: »eine seiner lebenswahrsten Frauenfiguren.«

[12] In connection with Baron Astolf, one might think of similar figures in the novels of Daudet known to Spielhagen: the kindly, elderly, goodhearted, duped Risler in his relation to his scornful wife Sidonie, who trysts with his partner in *Fromont jeune et Risler aîné,* or the kind, simple, bear of a cuckolded husband to whom the protagonist is apprenticed in *Jack.*

[13] Goessl, »Die Darstellung des Adels,« 199, asserts that it »erhebt sich kaum über das Niveau [sic] eines Zeitungsromans,« although it is hard to imagine a family newspaper of the time printing it; Müller-Donges, *Das Novellenwerk Friedrich Spielhagens,* 21, numbers it among »sieben künstlerisch völlige unzulängliche« novellas too poor to discuss.

to admire.[14] The title character is a prominent small-town physician named Arno; oddly, we never learn whether this is his first or last name. He aspires to an amoral ruthlessness wholly incongruent with his resources of mind and character. Deriving his personality from a hard, struggling childhood and youth, he claims to have two souls in his breast, »eine Poeten- und eine Medizinerseele« (4: 170–74), he is struggling to compete with Goethe by composing a drama *Faustulus*, apparently unaware that the very form of the word is a diminutive, he scorns Goethe's Faust as a weak moralist inferior to Mephisto and stupid enough to believe in the devil.[15] Arno's dramatic character, an alleged portrait of himself as a ruthless Roman, will take responsibility for himself, accept his good and evil dreams in a work that will be »verdammt viel wahrer« than Goethe's; he will be noble, sensitive, and violent, capable of all crimes, as Goethe said of himself, not mediocre in virtue and vice like Faust (30–32, 75–76). Arno knows that the terrible secret of being and loneliness is a sphinx more terrifying than the *Erdgeist*, »die Fratze, vor der Goethes armseliger Faust zusammenbricht« (50). He considers himself a ladies' man, »was Goethe einen frauenhaft gesinnten Menschen nennt«; Faustulus with his qualities of imagination does not need to look into a magic mirror to see naked Helenas (62, 74).

Arno seduces the wife of an apothecary, another of the hapless older husbands, driving her to morphine addiction and eventually to a mental institution, and then a coastal pilot's daughter, Stine, who has picked up some nursing knowledge from her uncle, a disrespected *Heilgehilfe*, therefore sarcastically titled »Kollege« by Arno. At first he scorns her despite her efficiency, as was pointed out in Chapter 10, where her sad end was discussed. He is pleased when he feels that she fears him: »Faustulusnaturen müssen gefürchtet, wollen gefürchtet sein« (94). But Arno has overestimated his toughness; visions of the drowned Stine appear to him nightly, even as he works heroically in the typhus epidemic. Experimenting with the vision out of psychological interest does not help; he diagnoses himself as mad; *now* he can know love for her (225–26). Feeling entrapped by his artful fiancée,

---

[14] In a letter to Spielhagen of November 22, 1897, Fontane praised it in detail, placing it in the first rank of all he knows since *Sturmflut*. *Briefe*, 4: 676–77. Is it permissible to suspect this effusion of good will a little?

[15] As for the two souls, Arno appears to be a better doctor than poet, even though he scorns his profession as accidental and petty. In fact, he is shown several times to be competent, he works conscientiously in the typhus epidemic, on which he is an acknowledged, published expert, and shortly before the catastrophe he is offered the directorship of a Berlin hospital and a university professorship. Might poetic aspiration be a form of wicked hubris?

he denounces himself as an »unentschlossener, elender Feigling« (223) and begins to think of a suicide of his own, putting himself, after an elaborate wedding eve party and one last vision implying forgiveness, into a situation to be knifed by a more successful Valentin, an uncouth fisherman who had courted Stine and whom Arno had scorned as »der greuliche Fischmensch« (142 and passim). The parody, the tone of which is harsh and grim, without a touch of the humor Spielhagen often otherwise employs, is not directed against Goethe. Arno is clearly not without talent; a drama of his is accepted and performed by the great Eduard Devrient (223–23), but he is constantly aware of his poetic inferiority to Goethe. His notion that Goethe was great but Faust a fool and that he, Arno, is bringing out the heroic soul that Goethe did not know he had (228–29) appears as a pathetic delusion when one contemplates Arno's character and conduct. Moreover, it is likely that Spielhagen had Nietzsche in mind here as a modern antipode to Goethe. In the final monologue of Arno's drama, which we are obliged to read as he recites it just before he is murdered, Faustulus addresses himself to Christ as his enemy, the redeemer of slaves, beggars, and petty people who corrodes heroism with hypocritical meekness (231–32; the poem appears as one of Spielhagen's own in *NG*, 48–49). These Nietzschean echoes are clearly disparaged by being associated with a man like Arno.[16]

The female case of the new ruthlessness is Rebekka Lombard in *Herrin* (1899, set in 1886), who has named herself Becky after Thackeray's Becky Sharp (261). A twenty-five-year-old beauty with Spielhagen's customary lithe, strong figure and blue-black hair (405), she is the daughter of a wealthy Jewish physician and *Geheimrat* who has acquired part of a Pomeranian estate belonging to the counts of Bassedow. Becky is extremely accomplished, an artistic and intellectual Spinozist who speaks Latin and French, has studied history, philosophy, and science, and, to her father's discomfort, has published a pamphlet on Jewishness in Zurich, where she has earned a Ph.D. *summa cum laude*, since the M.D. was too easy; she

---

[16] Mielke, *Der Deutsche Roman des 19. Jahrhunderts*, 426, noted that *Faustulus*, along with *Selbstgerecht* (1896), was written against Nietzsche's revaluation of moral values. For some reason *Faustulus* is set back in 1854 (61), so that Arno cannot be responding to Nietzsche, but the tone of the narration belongs to what is increasingly recognized as Spielhagen's *fin-de-siècle* phase. In a late satirical sonnet, the »Übermenschen« are mocked for »[i]hr Hauptgeschäft: die Umwertung der Dinge«; see also a satirical reference to Zarathustra, whose thought today's groundlings do not grasp (*NG*, 124, 192). On reflection, I am far from sure that I have got to the bottom of *Faustulus*, which may be Spielhagen's strangest and most private work. Others may be able to get farther with it.

almost married another of Spielhagen's Russian nihilists, who despaired at being turned down and was hanged a year later in Moscow (261–62).[17] She has now mastered agriculture, which takes her, like Italian, two months to learn (263), for no other reason than to govern the estate. For Becky is obsessed with a queenly desire to rule, to be master. She also wants the rest of the estate with its manor house. In a modern idiom, we could say that she wants to have it all. It strikes her that the obvious route to these goals is to marry the count.

The current count, Kurt, is absent at the beginning the story; he has been travelling aimlessly, and when he returns he appears as quite a melancholy young man. He thinks of himself not as a landowner but as a soldier. He has served a hereditary prince on intimate terms, but when his brother-in-arms succeeds to his dukedom, he seems to forget any obligations to Kurt, becoming preoccupied with other matters.[18] Furthermore, he can no longer afford to travel, for the substance of the estate was wasted by a profligate father, the reason the larger part of it is in the hands of a Jew, a circumstance that fills him with particular bitterness. He can hardly afford the necessary repairs on the dilapidated manor house. He is incensed when he learns that his neighbor's daughter, whom he imagines as fat, ugly, and

---

[17] Ohl, »Spielhagens Spätwerk,« 186, n. 24, complains that his chronological precision has failed him with Becky's claim, »in Zürich liefen Frauenzimmer zu Dutzenden herum, die alle Doktoren waren« (262), that this could not be true of the 1880s, only of the late 90s when the novel was written, and that Ricarda Huch was the first German woman to earn a doctorate in Zurich in 1905. However, while Becky may be expressing herself hyperbolically, Albisetti, *Schooling German Girls and Women*, 137–38, reports women degree recipients in the 1880s, whereas Huch began studying in 1887. Two German women had earned M.D.'s in 1875 and 1876 (125). Spielhagen, in fact, was personally acquainted with an early example: Dr. Ella Mensch, who corresponded with him for some years from Darmstadt and met him in the 1890s; she had, according to the *Gesamtverzeichnis des deutschsprachigen Schrifttums*, completed a Zurich dissertation on doublets in modern German in 1886. See Mensch, ed., *Er lebt noch immer! Ein Spielhagen-Brevier* (Leipzig, 1929), 18.

[18] As usual, it is unclear whether we are to make an identification here. Later a letter from the duke to the count is signed »Ernst Ludwig« (455), suggesting the grand duke of Hesse (1868–1918) who succeeded to his throne in 1892 and began to found a well-known theater center and artists' colony right at the time of the publication of *Herrin*. Although the historical Ernst Ludwig, like any member of a ruling house, rose through the ranks from lieutenant to general and, at least in principle, commanded his own regiments, his biographer has said that »die militärische Laufbahn mit Beförderungen und Ernennungen im Leben Ernst Ludwigs eine untergeordnete Bedeutung hatte«: Manfred Knodt, *Ernst Ludwig Großherzog von Hessen und bei Rhein. Sein Leben und seine Zeit* (Darmstadt, 1978), 52. This does not sound much like Kurt's intrepid superior.

vulgar, has been copying a madonna in his chapel. However, he is obliged to acknowledge Lombard's gentlemanliness and, ashamed at his own un-gentlemanly rudeness, get over his suspicion at his neighbor's claim that he would like to see the property restored to its original owner. Depressed and brain-fevered, Kurt collapses while wandering about in a storm, to be rescued by Becky in her carriage. He is dangerously ill, but he is treated by the capable Lombard and naturally, though against his instincts and preju-dices, falls hopelessly in love with the beauteous Becky, who, her father thinks, has frightened death away in league with demons (365). Normally such a marriage would be advantageous: Becky approaching the altitude of her imagined self as countess and »Großgrundbesitzerin« (289), Kurt repair-ing his fortunes and reuniting the property. For Becky there is no question that they will marry; she wills it. She does not love him – like many of Spielhagen's later female characters, she does not believe in love – and wishes Kurt were intellectually a little more cultured, nor is she physically attracted to him, but not repelled either, so that is all right (393–95). But, as we gradually learn, there is no hope of such an alliance.

In the first place there is a large cultural gap between the military man and the overachieving bluestocking. It appears, as so often with Spielhagen, in connection with literary matters. Kurt, trying to find something to read that does not offend him, like Rousseau or the memoirs of the Duchess d'Abrantès, or bore him like *Dichtung und Wahrheit* with all those »Ab-schweifungen über Malerei, Litteratur und sonstigen Kram« and immoral stories of Gretchen and Friederike (341), comes across novels of Scott, which he reads with genuine interest (in German; his English is weak, never a good sign); in *Ivanhoe* he begins to make identifications with his own situ-ation, contrasting in particular his disappointing experience with the duke to Ivanhoe's relationship with King Richard. This is an interesting and ef-fective device, for, as we follow Kurt's reading practice and his subsequent construction of parallels, we get a sense of the limitations of his mind and imagination, which apply also to his conventionally reactionary social and political views, sharply contrasting to Becky's radicalism. Since he does not know he is a character in a Spielhagen fiction, he is later amazed at the name coincidence between Rebecca of York and Rebekka Lombard, not to speak of the nursing of the wounded hero. But he cannot relate to the modern literary world in which Becky is at home. He is bored with an hour-long discussion about Ibsen, of whom he has never seen or read a line but has heard »er sei ein völlig verdrehter Knopf [sic?] und bodenlos unmoralisch dazu.« Who cares whether *The Wild Duck* is progressive or regressive? In his frustration Kurt gets into a rage: »Nicht die blasse Bohne verstand er von dem ganzen Kram« (445–46). Becky, for her part, was an intimate of the same Marie Baskirtscheff who served as a model for Stella in *Alles fließt*, from whom she has particularly learned the importance of maintaining strict control over sensuality in order not to be enslaved (424), while men are too trivial to enslave: »welcher Mann ist denn wert, daß man ihn unterjocht! Wie oft habe ich das Thema mit Marie durchgesprochen!« Men are themselves slaves of sensuality, vanity, prejudice, class, and office (442–43).[19]

Yet after recalling such principles, she finds herself, to her annoyance, lusting for Kurt (425, 443–44). Furthermore, once Kurt and Becky are betrothed, aristocratic class practice quickly obstructs her ambition to shine. In one telling scene, Becky, who supposes herself to be »eine vollendete Reiterin« (458), is downgraded by Kurt, and, in fact, she fails to jump a ditch successfully because she has lost her temper; she must be literally pulled off her high horse by Kurt, after which they do not speak to one another (466–67). Even worse is the deflating experience of gaining access to society. Previously no one in the neighborhood has visited the Lombards because they are Jews: »schade doch, daß sich anständigerweise mit der Person nicht verkehren läßt« (369). Now she is admissible, but only as an appendage; it is Kurt who is seen as the important person.

Jewishness, however, is the difference that brings the crisis. Everyone expects Becky to convert; why would she not? Kurt himself assures a friend that a Count Bassedow will never marry a Jewess (462). She, of course, has no idea of doing such a thing; she is not a believer in God at all, as she has shown in her published pamphlet; to convert to Christianity would be childish and a violation of her autonomy (473). Just at this time the neglectful duke reemerges with a invitation to Kurt to be a poorly paid *Oberhofmarschall* of his little principality. The duke has heard about Becky; of course she will be baptized, then there will be no difficulty about her; one is, after all, Christian but also tolerant (454–55). When Kurt shows Becky this letter, her rage knows no bounds. Is not an *Oberhofmarschall* a servant, she taunts, »der oberste Bediente an einem fürstlichen Hofe? So was wie *Majordomo* in England? *Maître d'Hôtel* in Frankreich?« (471). Kurt has

---

[19] It seems likely that Spielhagen was acquainted with Hugo von Hofmannsthal's review of Marie Bashkirtseff's journal (1887): »Das Tagebuch eines jungen Mädchens. ›Journal de Marie Bashkirtseff,‹« *Gesammelte Werke. Reden und Aufsätze I 1891–1913*, ed. Bernd Schoeller with Rudolf Hirsch (Frankfurt am Main, 1979), 163–68, where Spielhagen could have read: »ein durstiges und belebendes Verlangen nach Macht, nach irgendeiner Herrschaft und Königlichkeit.... ›Ah, si j'étais reine!‹« (166). See Ohl, »Spielhagens Spätwerk,« 188.

difficulty maintaining his composure at this, concluding that he must break with her; when he tells her that he will write about her to his father, she explodes: »Ich habe Sie steigen lassen – da waren Sie etwas. Da wollte sogar ein Herzog Sie zum Bedienten haben. Jetzt lasse ich Sie fallen. Jetzt sind Sie wieder, was Sie vorher waren! nichts! nichts! nichts!« (474). She must be committed to a madhouse, where she dies of a stroke.

There are a number of not uninteresting ancillary characters and sub-plots in this story with which one could spend some time, but there can be no doubt that its main design is to amalgamate the theme of the *femme fatale* with that of the ruthless, tyrannical Wilhelminian personality. One of the important secondary figures, the young Jewish Professor Rehfeld, whom Lombard wanted Becky to marry and who has married Becky's plainer and more ordinary friend Ännchen, remarks that pride is the illness of the times and fills the madhouses (439). A modern scholar has had no difficulty observing that Becky is Faustulus's sister.[20] The tragic conflict of the story is one of hyperbolic modern hubris with the suffocating conventions of class. Ohl has said of Becky's »Begabungen« that »deren Häufung nicht frei von Unwahrscheinlichkeit ist.«[21] Indeed it is not; the implausible characterization indicates a movement into the surreal, a sign, it seems to me, that the reality with which Spielhagen was confronted can no longer be accommodated by the discourse of realism as he understood it.

However, in retrospect one might wonder whether Spielhagen was well advised to conflate issues of social psychology with those of Jewishness. Ohl's judgment that there can be »selbstverständlich keine Rede davon ..., der Altliberale Spielhagen sei vielleicht doch ein verkappter Antisemit gewesen« seems to me underestimate the problem somewhat.[22] It is true that the main thrust of the ethos of the story is the acceptance of Jews as fellow human beings. Becky ironically paraphrases a line (658) from Schiller's *Wallensteins Lager*: »Juden sind so zu sagen auch Menschen« (464). At the end of the story two successful mixed marriages occur without much commotion: Reh-feld's with Ännchen and that of the son of Becky's mentor Frau Krafft with a Jewish girl. Kurt must learn to distinguish the Jew Lombard from »the Jews« and recognize his fine, generous character; at the end, as he tells the duke, he properly refuses Lombard's offer to continue to support him as a son-in-law but will leave Lombard his manor house in his will (490).

---

20 Müller-Donges, *Das Novellenwerk Friedrich Spielhagens*, 124.
21 Ohl, »Spielhagens Spätwerk,« 186.
22 Ohl, »Spielhagens Spätwerk,« 191. He adds: »oder hinge doch wenigstens einem reaktionären Frauenbild an,« which I think fair enough.

However, Kurt has had other experiences with »the Jews.« The sum received for the property was lost in the failure of a Jewish bank, and, although the bankers honorably shot themselves, he still thought: »Es war schon ein Vergnügen eigener Art, sich mit Juden in Geschäfte einzulassen« (295). Peters, the only manservant Kurt can afford, is deeply disapproving not only of the liaison with Becky but of his having to do with Jews at all; even in his illness it is not right for a count to be in a Jewish house (389–90). Peters's wife also knows »the Jews« from experience, warning her husband that he cannot prevent the count from marrying »die Jüdsche« and that he had better try to be nice: »Lehre du mich die Jüdschen kennen! Die sind so hart wie Flintenstein. Wenn einer sechs Jahre lang Köchin bei Kommerzienrats Schmalbach gewesen ist, dann kennt er das. Verstehst du?« (399). There is a particular problem with Frau Krafft. The widow of a man who died after only a week as director of a girls' school, she has worked as a housekeeper to put her son through the university. She is one of those well-mannered, stable, middle-aged women who appear variously in Spielhagen's texts as dispensers of good sense and emotional support. But she does have something of a problem with »the Jews.« She warns Ännchen not to admire Becky so much; she is not »gut, was wir Christenmenschen so nennen« (279). She explains that it is harder for Jews to be good without the model of Christ; since they are mistreated they lack »Menschenliebe« and think only of themselves. To be sure, she is only judging Becky here; she knows that Christ was a Jew and, as for Lombard, he »ist ein wirklich guter Mensch, wenn er auch seine Tochter verzieht und die Mucke hat – du lieber Gott, unsere Mucken haben wir alle! – daß er partout ein Jude sein will« (280). When Ännchen later thinks that Becky and the count must marry, Frau Krafft laughs uproariously (325), but when she sees the matter is serious, she works to separate them, foreseeing disaster, for, though Becky is as prideful as Lucifer and the count, like all men, has no idea of reality or of Becky's inability to love, she will not master him (426–27, 441). In all of this she is, of course, right, but an uneasiness about Becky's Jewishness seems to have something to do with it; she is at first shocked at the appearance of the daughter of a Jewish lawyer her son will marry, though gets to like her (431–32), and is annoyed that Ännchen accepts the Jewish Rehfeld without consulting her (436). Ännchen's mother dismisses Lombard to her husband, a rising psychiatrist, as rich because Jewish, a »Finanzgenie,« and when he counters that Lombard is a physician of genius, she says her husband could be twice the genius and still would not be a millionaire (258).[23]

---

[23] This is the first psychiatrist in Spielhagen's works and, I should think, one of the

None of this is too serious, but the question is to what extent the reader is left with an identification of Becky's relentlessly ambitious personality with Jewishness as such, as his biographer assumed: »Ein besonderes Relief erhält die Dichtung dadurch, daß Becky Jüdin ist und so die Rassenfrage in den Konflikt hineinspielt.«[24] Becky herself makes such an identification; she wants to assume the qualities ascribed to Jews, »daß sie schrecklich von sich eingenommen, über die Maßen eitel, ruhmsüchtig und was dergleichen löbliche Eigenschaften mehr sind. Ich meine löblich aber ganz ernsthaft« (260). Kurt says of her death that it freed her »vom dem Fluch des Trotzes gegen Gott, der ja ihre Krankheit war,« though it is clear that he has made no effort to understand her thinking, declining to read her pamphlet (488). In her delirium she appears as the queen she aspired to be:

einen weiten wallenden, purpurroten Abendmantel über den Schulter; um den Kopf, als Turban, ein großes Stück Goldgaze geschlungen, aus dem das blauschwarze Haar in dicken ungleichen Strähnen herabfließt; den nackten Hals, die nackten Arme mit Ketten und Spangen behangen; in der Hand einen mächtigen Fächer von weißen Straußenfedern, mit dem sie sich majestätisch Kühlung zufächelte; das lodernde Feuer des Wahnsinns in den großen schwarzen Augen; das entsetzliche Lächeln des Wahnsinns um die üppigen Lippen:
   Du kennst mich nicht, gute Frau. Ich sehe es an deinen erstaunten Blicken; ich bin die hochberühmte Königin von Saba, die da kam aus Arabien, Salomo, den großen König von Juda, zu versuchen mit Rätseln, die er alle löste – alle! (484)

This apparition may remind us of the fantasized identities of Else Lasker-Schüler, whose career was beginning around this time. But in context it melds the ambitiousness turned to madness with the voluptuousness of the *belle juive* into a distinctly »oriental« image. In 1899 the recent memory of failed anti-Semitic politics, though perhaps somewhat faded, ought to have been sufficiently present to suggest to Spielhagen the need for more precision in these matters.

---

earliest in German literature. His mentor Lombard says he is the best in Germany (267). He can read Becky's character from her appearance, as she acknowledges (359–60, 362). When describing his encounter with him after Becky's confinement, Kurt wonders whether he spells »Psychiater« correctly (486).

[24] Henning, *Friedrich Spielhagen*, 173.

18. Final Melancholy:
Opfer, Frei geboren

In February 1900 Spielhagen turned seventy-one years old. According to literary-historical convention, he had long since declined into insignificance. Nevertheless, he had mustered his forces for two more ambitious novels that move his familiar themes forward into what he regarded, sorrowfully, as the spirit of the present; whether or not he realized they would be his last works, he achieved with them a final reckoning with the society of the Reich at the close of the nineteenth century.[1] Furthermore, he experimented with something he had not attempted before: novels linked by shared characters and overlapping family fates. In numerous places in his œuvre there are recurring character types and sometimes recurring characters, but the realism of interlocked family and social histories on the model of Balzac and Zola is a new departure. Somewhat oddly, the first novel to appear is set later than the second; nevertheless, Spielhagen chose to publish them in reverse narrative order, as they appear in his collected editions.

The first of them, *Opfer*, appears to take place in 1893.[2] The protagonist, Count Wilfried von Falkenburg, is on the threshold of a devastating crisis in his life that will explode within a few days, though at first he senses only an inchoate uneasiness. Brother of a reigning prince, Dagobert, he is an unemployed *Assessor* with no money of his own, but with a rich aunt, Adele von Dürieu, who adores him and maintains an open account for him at the bank of the Jewish Bielefelders. He is expected to become a landowner and is engaged to a vivacious beauty, his cousin Ebba von Falkenburg, »das

---

[1] It has been pointed out that the two novels attracted more attention at the time than the reception history would indicate, but were rarely mentioned in later »Gesamtwürdigungen.« Although *Opfer* was criticized, *Frei geboren* received »fast ausschließlich lobende Kritik«: Lamers, *Held oder Welt?*, 162–63, 178.

[2] The chic Ebba von Falkenburg has read Paul Bourget's *Cosmopolis* (*NF*, 6: 54), published in 1893. Shortly thereafter her admirer Count Lessberg remarks: »Der Mann ohne Halm und Ar läßt Majestät ja nicht zur Ruhe kommen« (58), a reference to the chancellor Leo von Caprivi, who in 1893 got into a confrontation in the *Reichstag* with the agrarians; they disdained him because he was not a rich landowner. See Wehler, *Deutsche Gesellschaftsgeschichte*, 3: 1006.

schneidigste Mädel, das wir zur Zeit in Berlin haben« (*NF* 6: 11), as her adoring brother Falko declares. A jealous rival speaks of »ihren großen, lebenshungrigen Augen und ihrem rotblonden Männerfischerinhaar« (195). The narrative tone toward the haughty, self-centered, worldly Ebba is so uniformly hostile that the reader cannot suppose Wilfried will ever marry her. At first she presses for marriage, as the wife of an estate owner, not »Frau Assessor,« then is shocked when she discovers that he actually means to manage his estate, obliging her to live in rural idiocy (54–55).[3] Later, when she has become engaged to the swaggering, smug Count Lessberg, to whom she is better suited, »Wilfried hatte das schöne Mädchen kaum je so schön gesehen; aber von dem Zauber, mit dem sie ihn einst umsponnen, verspürte er nichts« (367).

Two critical events, one pathetic, the other comic, at least on the surface of things, that, among other effects, estrange him from Ebba, take place in close succession to one other. The first is Wilfried's encounter with the proletarian Schulz family. This begins when he tries to help the injured boy Fritz, who is rudely treated as a vagabond by a police officer until he realizes Wilfried's class standing and becomes obsequious. Wilfried gets Fritz into the care of a Dr. Brandt, whose wife, an active Social Democrat, is another of Spielhagen's rational, competent middle-aged women. The Zolaesque Schulz family consists of the father, an unemployed and alcoholic table-setter, thus below the status of waiter; a pretentious mother who was once a servant in the Falkenburg household; a daughter, Elise, who became a factory worker but through bad company has sunk to prostitution, from which Wilfried tries to rescue her; another daughter who is very ill and dies shortly; a son Hermann, who, having been driven out by his father's hatred, works as a bank clerk; and the beautiful dark-eyed Lotte, a milliner, with whom Wilfried falls helplessly in love. Wilfried's involvement with her and her family draws him into a Social Democratic milieu to which he makes every effort to adapt. At a party rally he makes a speech that causes the police to break up the meeting when he refers to Samson bringing down the temple, and they threaten him with prosecution under §130.[4] For in the meantime he has become estranged from his class through a breach with his aunt.

Adele, though good-hearted, is a little dotty, and what she is mainly dotty about is Goethe, whom she has taken up as compensation for dissatisfac-

3   Adele's adviser remarks that today rural life has become »etwas Prosaisches« and marked chiefly by bankruptcies (116).
4   See above, Chapter 16, n. 9.

tions in her life. She maintains a salon in which Goethe worship is required, giving an opportunity for a good deal of fustian posturing. She bestows a kiss on a copy of *Faust*, which she keeps in a velvet case and from which she quotes out of context (116); complicity with the presumably *goethefest* reader is achieved with incessant quoting of Goethean tags as a form of wisdom literature applicable to all circumstances. An aged general, Max von Frötstedt, who enjoys special prestige because he once actually saw Goethe in person, reports a dream in which he explained the *Goethe-Gesellschaft* to the great man himself, who did not approve of it, having hoped instead for a »Tempel einer wahrhaft humanen, weltbürgerlichen Literatur« (130). The heresy offends a professor, who defends the *Goethe-Gesellschaft*, declaring, with one more of the innumerable textual allusions, that the dream did not reflect Goethe's spirit but »des alten Herrn eigener Geist« (132).[5]

Wilfried commits a faux pas by defending the old general's dream and by arguing that Goethe's spirit is best honored by concern for the disadvantaged. Goethe, he asserts, was a mirror of the eighteenth century. »Für einen Dichter des neunzehnten, meine ich, sollte der Heroenkultus ein überwundener Standpunkt sein«; the modern writer must reflect the ideas of his own time as they emerge from the mind and heart of the people, whose representatives today offer them only »eine archaistische Weltanschauung und Geschichtsschreibung« (138). This speech is not a model of clarity, but it is perceived as radical in motive; as Adele's sinister servant insinuates to her, »das kommt alles von der Sozialdemokratie« (142). Adele is devastated, persuaded that Wilfried has turned traitor against her; she is even more shocked when she is told that he has said things that one can read in the *Vorwärts*. Wilfried regrets his outburst but the breach is hard to heal. Adele demands an apology that he feels he cannot make; he tries unsuccessfully to jolly her by exhibiting his own *Goethefestigkeit* with a quote from *Tasso* (185). Adele mourns the failure of her salon, the last of its kind in Berlin, with which she is said to have hoped to surpass the »*bureaux d'esprit* der Herz, der Rahel, Fanny Lewald, und wie die *Bas bleus* von ehemals alle heißen« (150). She changes her will with a quote from *Die Wahlverwandtschaften*, declaring that her allegiance to Goethe is thicker than blood (184–85); an ill-willed aristocratic lady induces her to cut off Wilfried's bank credit with an apocryphal quote, »Frisch gewagt ist halb gewonnen, sagt der Meister« (269).

---

[5] In a critical distich, »Goethomanen,« Spielhagen glossed what he supposed would have been Goethe's distaste at the development: »Anders nicht ist es: der Deutsche, zum Dogma macht er sich alles – / Heiliger Goethe, wie klar sahst du voraus dein Geschick!« (*NG*, 206).

Wilfried is at first incapable of grasping the seriousness of this quarrel. He cannot believe that a difference of opinion about Goethe could disrupt relations of love and loyalty because he does not realize the extent to which the *Bildung* of which he himself is a possessor is understood as one of the pillars of the social order. How can a Social Democrat, the aristocratic lady insinuates to Adele in order to undermine Wilfried, have the right understanding, or any understanding, of Goethe (266)? But the withdrawal of support is actually advantageous to him, because it helps him to realize how wasteful and luxurious his life has been and motivates him to jettison the surplus. His marriage to his haughty fiancée is no longer possible. One might say that a dose of genuine Goethean renunciation has followed upon emancipation from the falsity of the Goethe cult. A reconciliation does occur, partly mediated by the good impression Lotte makes upon Adele as Clärchen to Wilfried's Egmont, but it comes too late.

Wilfried, it emerges, has many enemies owing to his pattern of non-conforming attitudes, to which others are more sensitive than he is himself. Among these enemies is Count Lessberg, who envies him Ebba and successfully alienates her from him. Another is Frau von Haida, recently widowed from a unloved husband whom she married because Wilfried had rejected her advances. She is determined to win him or destroy him, whichever comes first, employing for the purpose a new lover, Major von Bronowski, who hates Wilfried for both literary and personal reasons. Having already sent Wilfried transparently anonymous verses satirizing Ebba,[6] at one of Spielhagen's ominous parties she has an actor recite a poem tweaking Wilfried as a »putziger Salonsocialist« (311). This jibe sits painfully because of its at least partial plausibility and turns out, in fact, to have fatal consequences.[7] Wilfried, having sold off all his valuables, obtains a job at 250 marks a month in the office of Adele's legal adviser, *Justizrat* Werner, who, exclaiming »Heiliger Bebel!« (375), regards Wilfried's conduct as completely nonsensical and promises to be a nasty boss, presumably to cure him. But when an announcement of Wilfried's engagement to Lotte is

---

6   The poem begins: »Komtesse bin ich vom reinsten Blut, / Ich zähle achtzehn der Jahre; / Wie steht so schneidig von Gerson der Hut / Zu meinem rotblonden Haare!« and hinting that after her marriage she will be free to have affairs (153–54). Spielhagen, who did not like to waste texts, had included a version of it among his own poems, beginning: »Freifräulein bin ich von echtem Blut,« and leaving out the allusions to F[alko] and W[ilfried] intelligible only from the novel (*NG*, 105–06).

7   This sonnet, too, had appeared with somewhat different wording, without the term »putziger Salonsocialist,« in *NG*, 123.

published, Werner is so incredulously outraged that he fires Wilfried. The whole Schulz family is now under police surveillance because Hermann, who has mutated from Social Democracy via Nietzsche to nihilism, has absconded from the bank with what Arthur Bielefelder assures the public is one hundred thousand marks but is variously reported as a million or a million and a half. Lotte loves Wilfried but increasingly doubts whether they actually can marry. Around this time a message comes from Schulz's long-lost brother, who emigrated to America forty years ago; now having found prosperity, he wants to help his family and invites them to live with him. Schulz imagines the proverbial rich uncle from America to be worth millions, which will relieve him from having a Social Democratic fool like Wilfried as a son-in-law; when the brother sends him a mere $1,000 and offers a relatively modest life on a farm, Schulz feels downright betrayed, but Lotte is determined to get the family to America, and does. She writes Wilfried a loving letter of farewell, which he, characteristically for Spielhagen's males, resents as a sign she did not truly love him. He is beset by melancholy and, when Bronowski insults him by muttering »Salonsocialist« (474) on the street, Wilfried accepts the necessity of a duel with the superior marksman, in which he is mortally wounded.

Much in this novel will seem familiar. The critique of the nobility proceeds apace.[8] The aristocrats try to deflect Wilfried from his path. »Wie verpicht sie alle darauf sind,« Wilfried thinks at one point, »mich zu einem Schuft zu machen!« (415). The affable but profligate gambler Falko is anxious that Wilfried not break with his sister so that he can continue to sponge off him as Adele's heir presumptive, causing Wilfried to think to himself: »das war nun das moralische Rückgrat dieser Leute, die sich einredeten, die unzerbrechliche Stütze von Thron und Altar zu sein!« (211). Falko finds himself obliged to marry the daughter of the banker Bielefelder; he does not want a Jewess for a wife – one result is that he is relegated to a provincial regiment – but what can one do? As for Wilfried and Lotte, marriages across class boundaries are no longer as achievable as they appeared to be in *Sturmflut*. Spielhagen, to be sure, will have known of the tragic dimension of this theme from Berthold Auerbach's *Die Frau Professorin* (1846) and perhaps also from Gottfried Keller's rewriting of it, »Regine,« included in *Das Sinngedicht* in 1881, though in *Opfer* the class gap is wider,

---

8   When »[e]in vierschrötiger Bürger« bumps into Falko without asking pardon, making him very angry – »Man ist bei Gott seines Lebens nicht sicher vor der verdammten Krapüle« (8–9) – one may be inclined to think of Arthur Schnitzler's *Leutnant Gustl*, written in the year *Opfer* was published.

actually impossible to bridge, as Lotte perceives more clearly than Wilfried, thus more like that in Fontane's determinedly untragic *Irrungen Wirrungen*, published in book form in 1888. Of all of Spielhagen's upper-class figures, Wilfried is the most earnestly introspective, the most sincerely desirous of getting his life on a moral footing: »Nach einem Leben, wert, gelebt zu werden« (66). The underlying theme of both his assertions at Adele's Goethe evening and his oration at the party rally is »justice.« It is a commentary on the social situation in the Reich that everyone understands this term to imply revolution and class war.

The attitude toward religion undergoes a variation. Through Frau Brandt Wilfried makes the acquaintance of Pastor Römer and his serious, untidy wife. Römer is a Christian socialist; since he is determined to bring a pragmatic gospel to the working class, he is not permitted to have a position in the church.[9] There can be no doubt of Römer's good intentions of selfless service to the poor, but Wilfried does not like him or his purposes. Even charity is suspect when it is involved with religious faith. Still, when, before the duel, Wilfried divides the 60,000 marks he has obtained from the sale of his belongings, he leaves a third of it to Römer (the remainder is divided between Frau Brandt and the care of the hospitalized prostitute Elise Schulz, 484). But the Christian alternative to Social Democracy seems not admissible to the ethos of the novel.

Practically everyone attempts to dissuade Wilfried from casting his lot with the working class, Adele by cutting off his funds; Falko by appealing to class loyalty so that Wilfried can continue to be an easy source of loans; Lotte by repeatedly insisting that he should stop helping her family because he is only enabling its pathologies, while her father confidently awaits Wilfried's reconciliation with his aunt, for he has no use for a son-in-law »der für den ›Vorwärts‹ schreibe und in socialdemokratischen Versammlungen Mumpitz rede, über den alle Welt lache«; *Justizrat* Werner by firing him when his engagement to Lotte is announced (426, 410). Werner dismisses Social Democracy as »Unsinn von A bis Z,« just as Falko claims to be certain Wilfried cannot be serious about it, and a legal official, an old acquaintance who is trying to find a way to avoid Wilfried's prosecution, assures him that no one can believe in Social Democracy, not even Wilfried

---

9 This form of Christian socialism is not to be confused with the reactionary and anti-Semitic *Christsoziale Partei* that began to emerge in the late 1870s, associated with Adolf Stoecker and represented by Pastor Renner in *Was will das werden?*, on which see Wehler, *Deutsche Gesellschaftsgeschichte*, 3: 921–22. It is more like a Protestant version of the worker-priest movement in France.

himself (397, 323, 329). Even the landlady in the poor apartment he takes objects to a count associating with the Schulzes and is sure he will reconcile with his aunt rather than marry the »Puppe von Tochter mit den schwarzen Rattifalli-Mausifalliaugen« (401). The many friends who visit him when he is dying take a dim view of his killer Bronowski, for no one could have taken Wilfried's »socialdemokratische[ ] Eskapade« seriously; they excuse it as »Extravaganz eines geistreichen Kopfes« (486–87).

The most eloquent dissuader is Wilfried's kind and intelligent brother, Prince Dagobert; as a liberal member of the upper house he is sympathetic to Wilfried's commitments, but believes he can serve better if he maintains his position in society and his financial independence. Dagobert has a hidden motive; his heart is not healthy and he expects that Wilfried may have to be the guardian of his children. In a letter after this dialogue, his wife, against Dagobert's orders, warns Wilfried of her husband's condition, adding that both are confident that »mein geliebter Schwager Wilfried, der *gentleman born and bred*, hat ein für allemal mit den Socialdemocraten nichts zu schaffen« (359), and after Dagobert has died, Wilfried finds that he is one of the executors of the estate and foster parent of the children, which he takes as a sign that his brother wanted to teach him »*noblesse oblige*,« giving him a responsibility that is feasible for a count with Aunt Adele's millions but »undurchführbar für den Socialdemokraten« (452).

Wilfried himself, with the zeal of a convert, turns out to be too extreme for the Party; not only does he get the meeting broken up by the police with his speech; when he attempts to publish in the *Vorwärts*, the editor tells him that he would get them all arrested; he tones Wilfried's writing down, leaving out what he, like authors everywhere, regards as the best parts. In fact, Social Democracy itself seems to be undergoing a domestication. Hermann Schulz, after the suicidal *acte gratuit* of his theft, sends Wilfried a letter in which he takes the familiar nihilist line that only the powerful, leading the sheep-like masses, can bring about revolution, adding that Social Democracy is »jetzt nichts weiter als der verschämte linkeste Flügel der kapitalistischen Wirtschaft« (482). Hermann is an extremist, but Dagobert also says that Social Democracy is evolving from a revolutionary to a reform party (353), and old General von Frötstedt predicts that in the event of war the Social Democrats will fight »trotz ihrer internationalen Republik wacker wie die Leute von *anno* dreizehn für Gott, König und Vaterland« (419), rather impressive foresight for the 1890s.

For all this novel's curiosity about Social Democracy, it seems that Frötstedt represents the cultural past for which Spielhagen still mourns. Earlier he claims to be an old, radical revolutionary because he belongs to a generation that carried not only Goethe and Schiller, Homer and Horace in their backpacks, but also »die Romantiker! Der herrliche Achim von Arnim! Der noch viel herrlichere Kleist! Das war mein Mann. Vor seinem Prinzen von Homburg, seiner Hermannsschlacht, ziehe ich den Hut« (178). This allusion to the Romantics is unusual for Spielhagen, though one notices that the general specifically names the most politically confrontational of Kleist's dramas. Frötstedt claims to have heard from Ernst von Pfuel the anecdote about Kleist weeping hysterically at the death of his own Penthesilea.[10] This was a kind of faith (one supposes, in the power of the imagination) that has died in the social class in which it once lived but has now found its way »in das arme, ungebildete Volk.... Das Reich, von dem sie träumen, an dessen Kommen sie festiglich glauben, ist ein anderes, noch mächtigeres, größeres, wenn es gleich auch von dieser Welt, erst recht von dieser Welt ist« (179). Thus the oldest character in the novel claims the proletariat as the true successor to the *Goethezeit* in a way that might have been expressed, with some adjustment in vocabulary, in the rhetoric of the bygone German Democratic Republic.

Whether or not the novel presents Social Democracy as viable and adequate to the requirements of justice, the basic difficulty, as is customary with Spielhagen, lies in the incompatibility of the socialized upper-class consciousness with the lower-class environment. Wilfried, after all, does not like being crowded by smelly, ordinary people or bumped on the third-class tram the militantly populist Pastor Römer makes him take (24–25, 229–30). When he first encounters Fritz Schulz he feels that he knows no more of the lives of such people than of the Hottentots (29). Frau Brandt, trying to separate him from Lotte, causes him to doubt that he will be able to live without taste, beauty, and grace (219–20). When a delicate Fritz is released from the hospital and Wilfried says »er gleicht einem der Engelknaben auf einem präraphaelitischen Bilde,« Lotte has no idea what he is talking about (427). Wilfried feels he must attend a Social Democratic »Sommerfest,« a prospect about which Lotte, as though she had read about catastrophic

---

[10] Spielhagen probably has this anecdote from Varnhagen von Ense. See Helmut Sembdner, ed., *Heinrich von Kleists Lebensspuren. Dokumente und Berichte von Zeitgenossen* (Frankfurt am Main, 1984), 154. However, it could have been a family tradition. Pfuel was a swimming enthusiast, and, according to Henning, *Friedrich Spielhagen*, 2, he was associated with Spielhagen's father in the establishment of Magdeburg's first swimming pool (this must have been before Spielhagen was born). I am not sure the anecdote actually makes Frötstedt's (or Spielhagen's) point. Both Pfuel and Varnhagen make cameo appearances in *Noblesse oblige* (*AR*, 3, 2: 239).

outings and parties in Spielhagen's earlier works, has serious and justified misgivings, for despite putting the best face on it Wilfried is out of place and uncomfortable, making Lotte uncomfortable as well. This is the place where, as usual, the title motif comes up: count or not, in order to prove that he is not a »Salonsocialist,« he must bring the sacrifice of his participation (429). But what is the benefit? Wilfried's attempted *Opfer* alters nothing in the world except for bringing much unhappiness. When he contemplates his death in the duel, he asks himself what he is dying for:

> Glaubte ich ehrlich an mein sociales Programm, was wäre mir der Hohn eines frechen Junkers? Aber der Frechling hat recht: Zum Volke gehöre ich nicht – das verbieten mir die verwöhnten Nerven; zu den Aristokraten nicht – das geht gegen mein besseres Gewissen. So läuft der Riß, der in der Gesellschaft klafft, mitten durch meine arme Seele wie durch das wankelmütiges Herz. (483–84)

Thus the whole novel appears as a chronicle of wasted time, or, at least, whatever is evolving and generating in society is taking place in a realm to which a man like Wilfried, for all his sterling qualities, cannot find his way.[11]

During a lavish, electrically lit party at the home of Arthur Bielefelder – again a prelude to disaster, as Hermann Schulz's huge embezzlement is beginning to be felt – Wilfried asks to visit Arthur's invalided mother, Antoinette, and does so despite Arthur's attempts to prevent him. When he kisses her hand, she says: »Immer galant! Ja, das haben wir so im Blut« (303), for she is a born Baroness von Kesselbrook. She claims to have achieved freedom and resignation because her husband and children do not love her, but she felicitates Wilfried for being truthful, getting out of dependence, and finding his way to his true self (305–06). Later we hear of her death and the hypocritical obituary obscuring her life (457). Earlier there has been an account of the young Antoinette with two other beauties, the sisters Adele and Carola von Reckeberg (111–15). Adele has married an old, rich Huguenot, Dürieu, whose death has enabled her to devote her wealth to Wilfried; Carola a prince struggling with his indebted estate of Falkenburg, thus becoming the mother of Dagobert and Wilfried; Antoinette the Jewish banker Philipp Bielefelder. *Frei geboren* tells how these things came about, especially the last.

---

[11] Cf. Kafitz, *Figurenkonstellation als Mittel der Wirklichkeitserfassung*, 117: »Das liberale Programm früherer Romane Spielhagens ist ersetzt durch einen ethischen Sozialismus; im ganzen überwiegt aber ein pessimistischer Grundzug, der auch seine Wirksamkeit relativiert. ›Opfer‹ endet in äußerster Hoffnungslosigkeit.« Yet there still may be a flicker of hope under the surface.

This novel begins with a preface in which the author says that the story of Antoinette's life was to have been »eine Episode meines Romans ›Opfer‹« (*NF*, 7: iii). But now that he has come into possession of the papers in which she dictated the story of her life, shortly after which she died of causes unknown to the author after becoming totally impoverished by the collapse of the bank, he is able to publish this memorial to the great-hearted dispenser of charity. The absorption of the author's voice into the fiction, though, of course, not unknown to realism in general, is unprecedented in Spielhagen's writing and another sign of the loosening of the narrative conventions he imposed upon himself. Also unprecedented, except for the memoir of the imperiled virtue of the young Mrs. Durham read by Sven in *In der zwölften Stunde* and the encapsulated narrator of *Die Dorfcoquette*, is the employment of a first-person female narrator, a daring and difficult task for a nineteenth-century male author. The only other example by a major German writer I know of is Wilhelm Raabe's *Im Siegeskranze* (1866). Antoinette, a fifty-two or fifty-three-year-old invalid, dictates her memoir to a faithful companion, interpolating diary materials from earlier phases of her life.[12]

The memoir is divided into books corresponding to the periods of her life. An orphaned noblewoman with little money of her own, Antoinette is put into a cloister school, a place that she loves, largely owing to the kindly, tolerant principal, *chère Maman* (17), but also because of her love of learning. There she meets Adele and Carola. Early on Antoinette observes: »ich war von jeher eine leidlich ehrliche Seele, die freilich eine bedenkliche Neigung hatte, mit andern streng ins Gericht zu gehen, aber sich selbst nicht schonte, wenn die Reihe an sie kam« (7), and this strictness of judgment is soon evident, for the others do not meet her standards. Antoinette is more hostile to Adele than the narrator of *Opfer*, where she appears as deluded and conceited but essentially good-hearted, rather than, as here, dangerously idiotic. In Antoinette's view she is a prevaricator and a conformist, social-climbing snob who allows herself to be influenced by the deceased principal's successor, the bigoted Sister Ambrosia. Antoinette loves Carola better, with a bit of a same-sex crush, but eventually concludes that she is

---

[12] Antoinette at first appears to have been born in 1841, as she was ten years old when her father was killed in a riding accident in 1851 (9, 12). According to the preface, she completed the dictation a month before her death, which followed immediately upon the collapse of the Bielefelder bank, thus in 1893 (iii). However, the first entry in her diary, begun when she was sixteen, is in May 1856 (21), which would make her birth year 1840.

stupid and allowed herself to be sold to the prince. Antoinette's sister Lida is a goose who marries a commonplace officer whose gambling debts and financial crises drain Antoinette's small fortune.

For Lida's marriage Antoinette is given permission to travel to what is for some reason called »D...f am Rhein« (34) to visit a miserly aunt who tries to marry her off to a would-be aesthete; Antoinette resists this plot but when she returns to the cloister she encounters Sister Ambrosia, who is hostile to Antoinette's free-thinking ways, treating her as a horrible example to others. After a quarrel, precipitated in part by her lack of reverence for Carola's high-class marriage, Antoinette leaves the school and moves into the house of her favorite teacher, a *Gymnasium* »professor« named Resber, from whom she hopes for advanced tutoring and teacher training. Resber, it turns out, is a frustrated, low-born intellectual and academic in shabby circumstances, too poor to be a *Privatdozent*, chained to his hated school and his paltry, narrow-spirited wife with missing teeth, dirty blonde hair, and similar daughter. Antoinette is too inexperienced to understand what is going on here. She tries to be friendly to the wife and daughter, whose oppressed condition arouses her sympathy, but they regard her with relentless hostility. A gentlemanly officer named von Gernot, who had served under Antoinette's father, adroitly helps her to understand that she has acquired the reputation, circulated by Sister Ambrosia, of being Resber's lover and thus a fallen woman. Antoinette determines to distance herself from him, but, after at first acrimoniously shutting himself off, he makes desperate love to her; she must flee to Düsseldorf.

At beginning of Book II, she learns that Resber has drowned, causing her, naturally, deep distress. At a loss for what to do, she finds in the newspaper an advertisement seeking a companion for an elderly couple. The consequence of this is that she is taken into the house of the wealthy Jewish businessman Samuel Bielefelder. At first this situation seems like paradise; the elder Bielefelders are kind, unpretentious people, if a little too religious for Antoinette's taste, though Samuel tries to guide her to his liberating idol Spinoza. The next generation is less charming. In Chapter 8 I have discussed the progressive deterioration of character in this Jewish family, so I will try to be brief here. The one son, Arthur, is an exclusively mercantile spirit who lives in an embattled marriage with a beautiful and haughty, Anglicized Jewess renamed »Jane Lilifield« from Rebekka Lilienfeld. She had wanted to marry his brother Philipp, but when they had a breach she married Arthur out of spite and treats him with scorn. After some hesitation, Antoinette marries Philipp. This marriage, though necessary to the whole enterprise of the two novels, seems somewhat undermotivated by the author. Philipp is rich – according to Arthur, owing to luck rather than business ability – and handsome; he is in parliament as a representative of the *Fortschrittspartei*. Whatever his other faults may be, he is not parsimonious. When Lida needs five thousand talers to keep her husband from being dismissed from the army in his latest debt crisis, Philipp advances the sum without hesitation.

Thus Antoinette feels ominously obligated, even when Samuel Bielefelder assumes the debt. Still, a little patience would have been wise; when Samuel Bielefelder dies, he leaves no money to his sons on the grounds that they are richer than he is, but after two millions of charitable bequests, he leaves Antoinette property worth a million (305–07). Antoinette does not love Philipp and seems sometimes not even to like him very much, but she is one of those many Spielhagen women, especially in the later work, who have ceased to believe that love is necessary or even desirable for marriage. This marriage turns out to be desolately bleak. Philipp's very mother warns Antoinette not to marry him: »Seine *ruling passion* ist Eitelkeit – meinetwegen Ehrgeiz«; he is just compensating for Jewishness with business and politics; all he lacks now is »eine unzweifelhaft christliche Frau,« to which she adds jokingly: »Ich denke gar nicht an Sie! Ich meine Ihre kaiserliche Hoheit, die Prinzeß Fatme von Fez und Marokko« (209), but she is not joking. At the beginning of Book III, Philipp says of himself: »der Jude ist entweder hart, wie Flintstein, oder weich, wie eine Molluske« (223); Antoinette at first thinks he is both, but in fact he is neither. He is not hard but affectless and selfish, not soft but weak, evasive, and indecisive. Like many of Spielhagen's women, Antoinette comes to find men in general »verächtlich« and »stumpfsinnig« (152, 386); she concludes that there are no knights except in the female imagination, just »Durchschnittsmänner« (161).

He allows her full freedom, which she believes suits her best. She becomes an admired hostess and presides over a salon attended by leading politicians, identified in the text by their initials.[13] Adele, to be sure, is

---

[13] The initials are expanded by Heinrich Spiero, *Geschichte des deutschen Romans* (Berlin, 1950), 323: »Leopold von Hoverbeck, Max von Forckenbeck, Franz Ziegler, Karl Twesten, Hans Bernhard Oppenheim, Eduard Lasker, und Wilhelm Löbe-Calbe [sic].« See also Zinken, *Der Roman als Zeitdokument*, 57. Wilhelm Löwe-Calbe (1814–86) was a forty-eighter returned from exile to become a representative of the *Fortschrittspartei*, whose fiftieth birthday in 1864 Spielhagen had celebrated with a poem in hexameters (*G*, 243–46). The most impressive speech in the salon is given by »B. A.« (*NF*, 7: 241), no doubt Berthold Auerbach, who at that time would have been forty-eight years old. It is likely that many of the other initials of persons in these scenes are identifiable.

offended that Antoinette has given up her noble title, will have children with Jewish blood, has lost her sense of authority, and has the reputation of consorting with rebels and nihilists, but Antoinette sticks to her guns, saying that she never allows matters of faith to interfere with freethinking, thinks nothing of divine right, is opposed to the existence of an aristocratic caste, and would rather live in a republic than a monarchy (243–49). When an addled forty-eighter, a count returned from exile in England and America, proposing to analyze air to prove life after death, is shot in a duel by a democratic journalist in love with her, she gets the reputation of a coquette who pursues »Männerfischerei« as sport, allowed by her husband to run wild (262). Philipp ignores the whole event; he seems unaware that she already has a reputation as a »Männerfischerin« (253) because she goes out riding with men, Philipp having proved to be an incapable horseman.

She bears him two sons, Arthur and Leonor, but, with that indifference to children characteristic of many of Spielhagen's women, and not only of the negatively valued ones,[14] she does not love them because they resemble Philipp in appearance and, in time, in unfeeling, mercantile character. Arthur in particular resembles the uncle he is named for, »der mir immer als der unerfreuliche Typ seiner Rasse gegolten hatte« (312). By Book IV Antoinette feels an emptiness in herself unrelieved by her lively social activities: »Die Welt nennt das ›femme incomprise‹ – ein spöttisches Wort, das sein leichtfertiges Gespinst so oft über einen Abgrund von Jammer breitet!« (319).

The consequence of this situation is a readiness for another man. When traveling by herself to Italy she meets a stranger who accompanies her to Dresden. Nothing comes of this – she is travelling with an older woman as a companion – but it is a prelude to an episode that was »der Höhepunkt und die Quintessenz meines Daseins« (325). The same von Gernot who had warned Antoinette about Resber, now a lieutenant colonel on the General Staff, wants to introduce one of Resber's former pupils, Count Roderich Werneck, as an admirer of hers. At a huge party (!), convened to celebrate a portrait of Antoinette by the then prestigious painter Gustav Richter, she

---

[14] This observation has been made of Fontane also: »Genauer zu untersuchen wäre die Rolle von Kindern in Fontanes Romanen.... Zu beobachten ist ... ein hoher Grad an Beziehungslosigkeit zwischen Mutter und Kind(ern), was sich nicht nur aus der Tatsache erklärt, daß die Erziehung der Kinder den Kindermädchen und Gouvernanten/Hauslehrern überlassen wurde«: Anja Restenberger, *Effi Briest: Historische Realität und literarische Fiktion in den Werken von Fontane, Spielhagen, Hochhuth, Brückner und Keuler* (Frankfurt am Main, Berlin, and Bern, 2001), 160, n. 166.

meets Werneck at last. Having repeatedly asserted that what she wanted most was a real man, she immediately feels that she has now found him. In one of the few comic moments in this melancholy tale, Philipp urges Antoinette to encourage him because there are too few aristocrats among their guests and »ein Graf ist immer ein netter Schmuck für eine bürgerliche Gesellschaft« (338–39). Spielhagen handles this relationship with Fontanesque discretion, but it may be that Antoinette and Werneck do not become intimate, for he must first go to active service and she says later that she had intended to belong to him fully after the war (388). However, he dies on the victorious field of Gravelotte. She takes this to be the extinction of her last hope, while at the same time mulling the evidence that the liaison would not have succeeded any better than any other; he has shown signs of religious belief, which shocks her and would have led to a split; in retrospect she thinks his attractiveness to her only sensual; and, perhaps worst of all, like many of Spielhagen's men, he shows symptoms of timidity, worrying about his career or the resistance of his parents to a divorced woman.

What she says she had found as »der unausdenkbar köstliche, nie wiederkehrende Silberblick meines Lebens« (337) turns out in the course of her own narration to be illusory. She decides she can love only herself and learn to be alone, busying herself with charitable work only to avoid despair, for she knows it is but a drop on the hot stone of poverty and suffering. As an interesting consequence of her frustrated adultery, she tries to be friendlier to her husband and children, though with indifferent success, and when she becomes pregnant again, she is horrified, ashamed to have betrayed her lover by having sex with her husband (375). During her pregnancy she discovers Philipp and Jane in an embrace. This will come as no surprise to the attentive reader, for the narrative has dropped numerous hints. An actress Philipp had seduced and abandoned had already come to Antoinette's attention; she obliges him, against his will, to give her an annual pension and takes the opportunity to extract a promise from him in regard to Jane, naturally to no effect (274–77). Upon discovering him with Jane, Antoinette falls down the stairs, crippling herself; there have been no events in her life in the eighteen years of invalidism and her »sogenannten Ehe« (386) since. She likes her prematurely born daughter Else a little, despite her empty head; it is she, as we recall from *Opfer*, who will trade wealth for class standing by marrying the desperate Falko von Falkenburg. Antoinette is more hesitant about Jane's daughter Chlotilde because of a suspicion that she is actually Philipp's child. Chlotilde also figured in *Opfer* as a languid beauty with the leitmotif of a tired smile, about whom Wilfried has the »grauenhafter Gedanke« that she resembles Ebba, »ein bißchen stark ins Jüdische transponiert« (6: 26). In one of the more frequent comic moments in that novel, Else and Chlotilde practically flip a coin to decide which will take Falko and which a Baron von Rentlow, though Chlotilde would much prefer Wilfried, with whom she is madly in love; perhaps she can have both (277).

The title of *Frei geboren* refers not to Antoinette's birth but to the religious independence she retains throughout.[15] The novel contains Spielhagen's most sensitive psychological portrayal. The memoir operates on several levels, a present self critically evaluating the naïveté of the past self in the diaries, correcting and probing the true motives of her adult self, and yet exposing areas of incomplete self-knowledge. The reader sees more clearly than she her obduracy of uncompromising pride and self-will, the degree to which her withholding of love relates to the lovelessness from which she suffers in her life, or the possibility that her sexual primness (punctuated by bursts of desire) or her denial of companionship might have driven Philipp into Jane's arms. Her ambition to dominate and rule the reader may find only relatively more moderate and better bred than Becky's in *Herrin*. Yet these faults in no way diminish her stature or her claim upon the reader's sympathy. For example, of her contempt for Carola's marriage to the prince she remarks retrospectively: »hochmütige Pharisäerin, die ich war« (7: 65). The critics who regularly complain that Spielhagen's characters are black-and-white types lacking internal differentiation should take another look at this novel.

A particularly interesting feature of it is the relatively advanced treatment of dreams. As an example among several, right at the beginning she has a dream of her experience in Resber's house in which they exchange roles, she as the demanding lover, he as the calm rejecter of her advances; when she awakes sobbing, she tries to put »die Dinge, die der Traum, so zu sagen, auf den Kopf gestellt, wieder auf die Füße,« wondering whether she had in fact actually loved Resber and observing: »Wie selten sind wir uns über unser seelisches Verhältnis zu einer andern Person völlig klar!« (4). Dreams, she concludes, reveal suppressed reality, but it ought to be possible to work out the meaning, even though »es durch diese Restauration nicht schöner wird« (5). Later she has an obvious puberty dream, when, in Adele's manor house, she encounters an officer whom at first she thinks is her father but turns out to behave like a lover; to this dream she ascribes knowledge of the relation-

---

[15]   The inner narrator of *Selbstgerecht* speaks of religion, also apropos of an aristocrat, as a »System, das ... freigeborene Menschen in Sklavenketten schlägt« (*NF*, 5: 158).

ship of a woman to a man, causing her crush on Carola to fade (30–31). In this connection Hubert Ohl has commented on »Spielhagens außerordentliche Witterung für geistige Strömungen, die gleichsam ›in der Luft liegen,‹« and, quoting Antoinette's self-analysis of her dream about Resber, reminds us that Freud's *Traumdeutung* appeared in that same year of 1900.[16]

The novel is about as feminist in spirit as one can ask of a German male writer at the end of the nineteenth century. One of Antoinette's resentments of Sister Ambrosia is that she teaches that women belong in the home and causes Adele to become enthusiastic about »das ›Ewig Weibliche‹« (28), a first symptom of what will become her deformed »Goethe-Manie« (32–33), but as Antoinette's miseries accumulate, she finds herself paraphrasing Iphigenie: »eine Bestätigung der uralten Weisheit, daß der Frauen Schicksal beklagenswert ist« (376). Musing in a somewhat self-exculpatory way on her decision to marry Philipp, she observes:

> wie die Dinge damals lagen, wo die Frauenemanzipation, von der heute so viel geredet wird und für die manches geschieht, erst eine nur hier und da scheu aufgeworfene Frage war, – ein Mädchen, das den Eingang zu einem Leben suchte, in welchem es seine Kraft, siegend oder untergehend, erproben und bethätigen konnte, fand keinen andern als die Heirat. (160)

The orphaned and homeless baroness makes her way initially by seeking and obtaining a job. Like other women in Spielhagen's fiction, she resents the limitations put on a girl's education and sees no reason why she cannot study and learn as well as a boy. She chafes at not being allowed to read Goethe, and she tells Resber, who agrees with her: »Ich weiß, ich könnte ebenso gut Latein und Griechisch, Mathematik und all das lernen, wie die Knaben« (27). In her Berlin salon, she begins to play a political role because her judgment is admired, except by Philipp, who, against her advice, resigns from the Prussian parliament, confident of winning a seat in the North German *Reichstag*, which he fails to do because his party drops him (316–17). The politicians call her »eine Seherin, eine Sibylle,« but she thinks she would prefer deeds to giving advice (284). When she hears Bismarck speak, she comes to hate him less, admiring his irony and choice of words; he comes to look like the true man she is seeking, calling to mind Napoleon saying to Goethe: »*vous êtes un homme*« (283, misremembering the anecdote a little), but Bismarck is displaced by her next candidate for »the man,« Lassalle, who dismisses Bismarck, to her agreement, as »ein unphilosophischer Kopf und bloßer Empiriker« (292).

---

16 Ohl, »Spielhagens Spätwerk,« 191–92

But Lassalle does not make the cut either; he talks all the time, paying no attention to anything she might have to say, and then makes a pass at her, breaking it off when he senses her unmistakable resistance. »Es geht nicht an,« she concludes, »Prophet und Don Juan in einer Person sein zu wollen; die Menschheit zur Freiheit führen zu wollen, während man selbst der Sklave seiner Begierden bleibt« (314). When she attends his trial for sedition in January 1863 (as the only woman present, incidentally), she gets into conversation with »der Schriftsteller S.,« who says he believed in Lassalle fourteen years ago but no more; he was then too young to recognize him as a »Phraseur und Poseur« who does not live, as Goethe said, »in der Burg der Leute, denen es nur um die Sache zu thun«; everything turns on his own coquettish person (296–98). There is nothing to prevent us from identifying »der Schriftsteller S.« with Spielhagen himself;[17] fourteen years takes us back roughly to Lassalle's trial in Cologne in 1848 for the theft of the Hatzfeldt cassette, which Spielhagen attended, and the acquittal in the Düsseldorf trial in 1849. The writer's retrospective view of Lassalle seems consistent with Spielhagen's.[18] Antoinette is surprised that S. does not mention Lassalle's Jewishness (298), which has so strongly impressed her; it will be recalled that the figures modelled on Lassalle in *Die von Hohenstein* and *In Reih' und Glied* were not Jewish. If this identification is correct, it would be a remarkable evasion of narrative objectivity's intention of excluding the author's voice; Antoinette's judgment, »Ich finde dies Urteil des Herrn S. zu hart; aber ganz unwahr möchte ich es auch nicht nennen« (298), would then appear as an ironic, if relativized, recursive self-criticism.

Of course, Spielhagen, as was his custom, used the novel as a vehicle for his political ruminations. In one place he has Antoinette express what may be his most optimistic sense of the future at this time:

> der Weg, auf den der gewaltige Mann [Bismarck] uns gedrängt hat, [ist] nur scheinbar ein falscher, in Wahrheit nur eine ganz unvermeidliche Krümmung des durchaus richtigen.... Daß wir erst gründliche Materialisten werden, gesteigertes Streber- und Junkertum, den Imperialismus und seinen greulichen Begleiter: den Byzantismus in den Kauf nehmen mußten, bevor sich der Deutsche auf sein Bestes, auf das was ihm den Vorrang unter allen Nationen garantiert: seinen hochherzigen, weltbürgerlichen Idealismus wieder besinnen und aus dem Traumland von früher in sonnenhelle Wirklichkeit hinüberretten konnte. (315)

---

[17] Klemperer, *Die Zeitromane Friedrich Spielhagens,* 171, did so, although he misread the abbreviation as »Schriftsteller Sp.« Klemperer's hostile and obtuse condemnation of the novel is otherwise of no use for the purposes pursued here.

[18] See Adolf Schumacher, *Ferdinand Lassalle As a Novelistic Subject of Friedrich Spielhagen* (Diss. U of Pennsylvania, 1910), 9: »essentially a repetition of what Spielhagen says about Lassalle in his autobiography.«

Later on, however, she thinks, like Spielhagen, »wollen die Reichen, Satten durchaus nicht hören, mögen sie fühlen; mag die soziale Revolution sie lehren, was in dem verruchten, ihnen so bequemen Schlendrian des *laissez faire, lassez passer* nun und nimmer würden,« and she declares herself a Social Democrat (374). In fact, in her thinking she unknowingly anticipates *Sturmflut*: she observes bitterly that, while there is no public welfare for the poor, »feierte die durch den Milliardenunsegen der Kriegsentschädigung entfachte Gründungswut ihre wüsten Orgien .... ein durch die ungeheuerste Erschütterung bis zu seinem Grunde erregtes Meer aufgewühlte Schlammmassen an das Ufer warf.« For this her lover died? (373–74)

At the end, Antoinette expresses a totally pessimistic view of the human condition. All the great men, from Solomon and Alexander to Frederick the Great, Voltaire, Napoleon, and Bismarck, have learned of the vanity of all things, the futility of governing slaves, and the ingratitude of the world; even Christ could not be certain that another one attempting to turn »Heloten der Sünde zu freien Tugendmenschen« would not be crucified again. Thus only art and philosophy remain, but they do not save us; they just provide some relief, expand the walls of our prison in the imagination. There is no truth behind the veil of philosophy but that we all die; the individual is but an easily replaced cog in the great machine; life is aleatory; mankind will come to an end: »So denn wären wir glücklich – oder unglücklich, wie man will – bei unsrer Monadenexistenz angelangt, bei unserem lieben Ich – dem verschämten Fichtes, dem brutalen Max Stirners – über das wir es nicht hinaus bringen, wir mögen uns stellen und drehen und wenden, wie wir wollen« (394–97).

As we know, it is impermissible to identify the opinions of fictional characters with those of the author. But it was always Spielhagen's custom to formulate his »message« fairly explicitly in his concluding pages, and, although there may be a space between the still creative author and Antoinette's dispirited depression, she may nevertheless express a mood of the author at the end of his career. »In diesem letzten Roman,« Henrike Lamers concludes, »rekapituliert er noch einmal seine eigenen Gedanken, um am Ende, wohl ungewollt, ganz von ihnen abzurücken.«[19] If so, it would explain

---

[19] Lamers, *Held oder Welt?*, 187. According to Henning, *Friedrich Spielhagen*, 154, Spielhagen wrote the novel in the state of grief following upon the death of his wife, to which circumstance the final peroration may be ascribed. Perhaps Samuel Bielefelder's inconsolable grief at the death of his wife reflects Spielhagen's own feelings, though probably not his return to religion in the hope of finding her in the other world (*NF*, 7: 266–68, 302–03).

why he reversed the chronological order of the novels and put *Frei geboren* last, making Antoinette's despairing capitulation his *envoi* to his readership, for whom it may not have been congenial. She recommends resignation and acceptance:

> Geben wir das thörichte Verlangen auf, mehr sein zu wollen; aber wollen wir, was wir sind, auch ganz sein: unser Sein zur höchstmöglichen Energie steigern! Nicht im Sinne Nietzsches, dessen »blonde Bestie« ernsthaft zu nehmen, ich mich nicht entschließen kann, wohl aber in dem von Spinozas *Suum esse conservare* [a phrase she has learned from old Samuel Bielefelder, 212], dessen letztes feinstes Produkt »der freie Mensch« ist, (397)

just as she understands herself to be free-born. But this is a very different tone from the critical but conciliatory acceptance of the political and social world found in the writer who had far overtaken Spielhagen in the favor of the public, Theodor Fontane. The following chapter will attempt to shed some light on this difference.

19. Spielhagen's Version of *Effi Briest*: *Zum Zeitvertreib*

> Der Zeitvertreib, das ist die Sünde!
> Das ist der Tod! der Tod!
> Fanny Lewald, »In Ragaz« (1880)

Coincidence plays a large, perhaps obtrusive role in Spielhagen's plotting, as critics have often complained. It may seem like laziness, purely for the author's convenience, a kind of disrespect for the implied contract between author and reader. The problem begins early, in *Problematische Naturen*, and was deplored early.[1] Spielhagen alludes to coincidence in ways that may suggest an uneasy conscience. He tried to give himself permission in his theoretical writings. Coincidence must not be accidental but meaningful: »daß für ihn [the hero] kein sinnloser Zufall, sondern nur ein sinnreicher existiert« (*BT*, 183), a formulation that places the management of coincidence on the authorial level. In an essay entitled »Wahrscheinlichkeit in der Dichtung,« he declares: »Auch der realistische Dichter, behaupte ich, muß sich auf Tritt und Schritt des Unwahrscheinlichen bedienen, um zu seinem Ziele zu gelangen, ja um nur überhaupt aus der Stelle zu kommen« (*AmSt*, 73). In the fictional texts he will comment on the device recursively, as at such a juncture in *Angela*: »Ein Zufall – freilich«; the more or less anonymous but Spielhagen-like writer who narrates *Die schönen Amerikanerinnen* comments at one point: »Sonderbar, sagte ich, während ich mich auf mein hartes Lager streckte, höchst sonderbar! wenn ich das in eine Novelle brächte, sie würden sagen: wie übertrieben! wie unwahrscheinlich! welche Versetzung der Bescheidenheit der Natur!« (*AR*, 2, 6: 156; 2, 4: 208-09). In *Problematische Naturen*, the unscrupulous Timm declares blithely at such a juncture:

---

[1] »Leider nimmt auch der Zufall als gefälliger Arrangeur in Spielhagens Romanen ein zu breites Feld ein«: Schierding, *Untersuchungen über die Romantechnik Friedrich Spielhagens*, 63; »Da die notwendigen Informationsträger bisher nicht eingeführt waren und gleichermaßen zufällig wie stereotyp eingesetzt werden, leidet die Romanqualität«: Fischbacher-Bosshardt, *Anfänge der modernen Erzählkunst*, 105.

> Ich gebe zu, der Zufall ist ganz wunderbar, der Euch nach so vielen Jahren zum
> ersten Male, ohne daß Ihr von Eurer gegenseitigen hochverehrlichen Existenz
> auch nur eine Ahnung habt, an diesem Orte und zu dieser Stunde zusammen-
> bringt; aber was ist's denn weiter? ich habe allen Respect vor dem Zufall, denn er
> hat mir schon oft im Leben aus der Patsche geholfen, wenn's mit allem Verstand
> der Verständigen Matthäi am letzten war. (1, 5: 440)

One might say this of the author Spielhagen himself. When a child dies at
the author's convenience in *Selbstgerecht*, he has his narrator mull whether
there is such a thing as fate or nemesis, only to wave the thought away with
the consideration that a mindless diphtheria epidemic has carried the boy
off (*NF*, 5: 143). By *Opfer*, Spielhagen is prepared to absorb *Zufall* onto the
narrative level; when Wilfried runs into Elise Schutz for the second time,
we hear in indirect discourse: »Wunderlich, daß er dem armen Geschöpf
so bald wieder begegnen mußte; aber er hatte ja heute schon so viel des
Wunderlichen, Außerordentlichen erlebt, da mochte er dies zu dem übrigen
zählen« (6: 101). On another such occasion, Frau Brandt remarks: »Wollte
das einer in einen Roman bringen, die Leser würden die Köpfe schütteln,
die wenigstens, denen das Wunder nicht der Menschheit bester Teil ist.
Und doch geht alles mit völlig natürlichen Dingen zu. Es bleibt eben ewig
wahr: *truth is stranger than fiction*.« (165).

It is no doubt unintentionally ironic that Spielhagen, in his essay on
Fontane's *Effi Briest*, criticizes improbable coincidence in regard to the
fortuitous discovery of Crampas's letters to Effi (*NB*, 108-10),[2] for between
Spielhagen and Fontane a coincidence will emerge over which »die Leser
würden die Köpfe schütteln« if encountered in fiction. It happened fortuitously that in 1897 Spielhagen published a short novel, *Zum Zeitvertreib*,
based on the scandal of 1886 in the Ardenne family that was the source
of *Effi Briest*. However, this piquant parallel has not been helpful to Spielhagen's reputation; on the contrary, it has particularly stimulated disdain
for him. That the Schlagododro Spielhagen should have blundered onto
the delicate and refined ground of the beatified Theodor has been perceived
as virtually a sacrilege. A quarter of a century ago it was observed: »In der
heutigen Fontane-Renaissance nimmt sich ein Spielhagen recht antiquiert
aus und scheint nur durch ›Ausgrabungsarbeiten‹ von Literaturhistorikern

---

2   This was a sore point with Fontane, who had worried about motivating the
    discovery of the letters. See Thomas Tyrell, »Theodor Fontanes ›Effi Briest‹ und
    Friedrich Spielhagens ›Zum Zeitvertreib‹: Zwei Dichtungen zu einer Wirklichkeit«
    (Diss. Rice University, 1986), 115.

neben dem Quader Fontane auch zum Vorschein zu gelangen.«[3] It became customary to dismiss *Zum Zeitvertreib* a priori, sometimes, it would appear, sight unseen. One can read from the distant past that *Zum Zeitvertreib* is »eins seiner schwächeren Werke« or from closer to our own time that it lies »ohne Zweifel jenseits der Grenzen des noch Interpretierbaren.«[4] The biographer of Else von Ardenne declares that, while *Effi Briest* is »eine Sternstunde der deutschen Literatur,« of Spielhagen's novel »wird nicht lange die Rede sein.«[5]

Hans Werner Seiffert cites the judgment of Helene Herrmann that it is a »ganz minderwertige Novelle« and then adds that »es Spielhagen mehr darum zu gehen scheint, das Ereignis des Gesellschaftsskandals zu kolportieren,« a defamatory judgment for which there are no grounds.[6] Yet Ohl supports him: »Der Eindruck des Kolportagehaften bei Spielhagen entsteht letztlich durch die am Drama orientierte, vermeintliche ›Objektivität‹ der Darstellung, die sich kommentierender Erzählereingriffe oder bildhafter Vorausdeutungen weithin enthält«; thus Fontane is more »modern,«[7] which seems odd, since at this time Fontane generally supported Spielhagen's principle of objectivity. On having heard what I suspect to have been his lecture to the *Goethe-Gesellschaft* on Goethe and epic poesy, Fontane wrote:

> Nicht minder als hinsichtlich dieser Frage bin ich in bezug auf die Technik des Romans mit Ihnen in Übereinstimmung. Was mich aufrichtig freut. Das Hineinreden des Schriftstellers ist fast immer vom Übel, mindestens überflüssig. Und was überflüssig ist, ist falsch.

Then, characteristically, he backs off from Spielhagen's rigor in the matter: »Allerdings wird es mitunter schwer festzustellen sein, wo das Hineinreden beginnt. Der Schriftsteller muß doch auch, als *er*, eine Menge tun und

---

3   Gregor H. Pompen, »Dichtung und Wahrheit – Spielhagen auf den Spuren Fontanes,« *Festgabe des Deutschen Instituts der Universität Nijmegen. Paul B. Wessels zum 65. Geburtstag,* ed. Hans Pörnbacher (Nijmegen, 1974), 112. Pompen is interested only in Spielhagen's critical essay, paying no attention to *Zum Zeitvertreib.*

4   Schierding, *Untersuchungen über die Romantechnik Friedrich Spielhagens,* 84; Jürgen Kolbe, *Goethes »Wahlverwandtschaften« und der Roman des 19. Jahrhunderts* (Stuttgart, Berlin, Cologne, and Mainz, 1968), 149, where at the same time Kolbe urges a comparison of the two texts (n. 70).

5   Manfred Franke, *Leben und Roman der Elisabeth von Ardenne, Fontanes »Effi Briest«* (Düsseldorf, 1994), 68.

6   Hans Werner Seiffert, »Fontanes ›Effi Briest‹ und Spielhagens ›Zum Zeitvertreib‹ – Zeugnisse und Materialien,« *Studien zur neueren deutschen Literatur,* ed. Seiffert (Berlin, 1964), 258, 267. Tyrell, »Theodor Fontanes ›Effi Briest‹ und Friedrich Spielhagens 'Zum Zeitvertreib,'« 95, rightly finds this charge »so ungerecht, daß sie eine Entgegnung kaum verdient.«

7   Ohl, »Spielhagens Spätwerk,« 180, 179.

sagen.«[8] In recent years there has been more attention to the comparison, but, despite an appeal some time ago,[9] there remains an unwillingness to credit Spielhagen with much literary achievement, as though that would detract from Fontane's stature, to read the text with anything like the attentiveness normally applied to *Effi Briest*, or to contextualize it in the evolution of the latter phase of his career.

Why it took him so long to react to the motif is unclear.[10] Like Fontane, Spielhagen had some acquaintance with the Ardennes, largely, it seems, through the household of Carl Robert and Emma Lessing, publishers of the *Vossische Zeitung*. In fact, Spielhagen's association with Elisabeth (Else) von Ardenne was much closer. He had known her and exchanged cordial letters with her in the years before the crisis in her marriage. The lively tone of the letters suggests that he was attracted to her, perhaps a reason why he always mentions his wife. One would think this relationship would have created a particular difficulty for him in view of his (inconsistent) principle that fictional figures should have models in personal acquaintance, as was the case with all but one in *Problematische Naturen* (*FuE*, 2: 414-15; cf. characteristic tergiversations, *AW*, 106-07). It seems retrospectively ironic that, in a letter to Else, he praised himself for having held to this principle in *Platt Land*: »In dem Roman ist fast keine Gestalt, die ich nicht persönlich genau gekannt.... So ist beispielsweise die extravagante Figur der Baronin getreu nach dem Leben gezeichnet, so getreu – bis in die krause Ausdrucksweise hinein – daß ich ob dieser indiscreten Treue nachträglich einige gelinde Gewissensbisse verspüre.«[11] Thus he explained sheepishly to Fontane that with the »model« of the Baroness von Ardenne »hatte ich

---

[8] To Spielhagen, February 15, 1896, Fontane, *Briefe*, 4: 533; see also the half-apology for *Die Poggenpuhls*, November 24, 1896, 4: 615. On Fontane's gradual convergence with the principle, see David Turner, »Marginalien und Handschriftliches zum Thema: Fontane und Spielhagens Theorie der ›Objektivität,‹« *Fontane-Blätter* 1 (1968-69), 265-81.

[9] Kafitz, *Figurenkonstellation als Mittel der Wirklichkeitserfassung*, 121: »politische Intentionen ... fordern aber eine Betrachtungsweise, die sich auf den Argumentations- und Ausdruckshorizont des Gegenstandes einläßt.«

[10] The novella was first published in installments in *Dies Blatt gehört der Hausfrau*. Spielhagen to Fontane, February 20, 1896, Walter Schafarschik, *Erläuterungen und Dokumente. Theodor Fontane. Effi Briest* (Stuttgart, 1972), 92. The book publication dates make it appear that the texts were farther in part in time than they were. *Effi Briest* appeared in *Deutsche Rundschau* from October 1894 to March 1895, the book version in 1895, dated 1896. The periodical publication of *Zum Zeitvertreib* ran from 1895 to 1896; the book appeared in 1896, dated 1897.

[11] Spielhagen to Else, Baroness von Ardenne, December 12, 1878, Seiffert, »Fontanes ›Effi Briest‹ und Spielhagens ›Zum Zeitvertreib,‹« 288.

fortwährend mit der Gefahr zu kämpfen, all zu deutlich zu werden und so die pflichtschuldige Diskretion zu verletzten. Die Sache lag für mich um so schlimmer, als ich – mein Plan brachte es so mit sich – dem Charakter der Heldin unedle Züge beimischen mußte, von denen das Original nach meiner Überzeugung frei war und ist.«[12] One might ask then: why make use of the »model« at all? In my opinion, this is one of the many instances that indicate the irrelevance of Spielhagen's theoretical worries to his practice. *Zum Zeitvertreib* has no more to do with the specifics of the Ardenne case than *Effi Briest*. Considerable effort has been expended on measuring the differences between both stories and what we know of the actual event. These comparisons are not without interest but contribute little to our understanding of the texts.

The novel is briskly narrated, covering a period of about two months, from the first of October to the second of December.[13] The main characters are three married couples: Elimar Meerheim, a modest army captain, and his exceptionally pretty and good-humored but clueless wife Adele; Viktor von Sorbitz, an *Assessor* with fierce ambition for a position as *Regierungsrat*, and his stunningly beautiful wife Klotilde, a bored mother who is another dark-haired *femme fatale*; and Albrecht Winter, a schoolteacher who has risen from subproletarian origins with literary hopes, and his loyal, loving, but plain and socially not very presentable wife Klara, daughter of a village tailor and mother of his three children. None of these marriages is in particularly good condition. Best off appears to be Elimar, the most amiable and thoughtful of the figures, but he married Adele, widely regarded as a goose, even though he had once been in love with Klotilde. She now regrets this and believes that she and Elimar still belong together. She has married Viktor »aus Ärger« and now must tell herself: »mein Gott, der Ärger macht blind!« (*NF*, 3: 84). They live with one another on a war footing but as allies in the social world, since Klotilde is prepared to support Viktor's promotion by flirting with his superiors. Viktor is a brutal egotist, one of Spielhagen's new men of the Reich. Albrecht is a pitiable case. Burdened with conspicuous manly beauty and a small amount of literary talent, he suffers under his drudgery in the school while longing for the grace and dignity of better society.[14]

---

12 To Fontane, February 23, 1896, Schafarschik, *Erläuterungen und Dokumente*, 94.

13 Tyrell, »Theodor Fontanes ›Effi Briest‹ und Friedrich Spielhagens ›Zum Zeitvertreib,‹« 66. Tyrell finds some internal inconsistencies in the chronology (97, n. 6).

14 On the deterioration of Albrecht's standing in the reader's perception, see Jürgen Viering, »›In welcher Welt der schauderhaften Widersprüche leben wir!‹ Überle-

The plot is simple and abrupt. The restless Klotilde spots the handsome, elegantly dressed Albrecht in a tram; later she encounters him at a party (!) at *Ministerialrat* Sudenburgs, whose daughter Stephanie, on Klotilde's suggestion, invites Albrecht to direct a performance to celebrate her father's sixtieth birthday. One of the plays he proposes is »die Dramatisierung einer Novelle, die ich vor ein paar Jahren veröffentlichte, und von der ich nicht sagen könnte, daß sie ein großes Publikum gefunden hat« (62-63); the experienced reader will recognize here another of Spielhagen's recursive ironies, for the story is clearly his own *Das Skelet im Hause*.[15] At the performance Albrecht and Klotilde have their first kiss. The further development of the affair is a comedy of errors, with furtive meetings in carriages and trite letters left in general delivery under their pet names of »Ballade« and »Siegfried« (149). They finally have a rendezvous in a compartment of a restaurant, which is so shabby that Klotilde, who has grown weary of Albrecht's demanding self-pity – he is worried about missing a meeting at school – leaves him to go home alone. She decides to make peace with Viktor, but it is icy and the ride home is slow. She is preceded by a detective whom Viktor, with misgivings, has hired at the urging of his friend von Fernau.[16] Having been told of the rendezvous, Viktor leaves his home, challenges the inexperienced Albrecht to a duel, and shoots him down. During the comings and goings of those preparing the terms of the duel, Spielhagen, with harsh irony, has Klara elated at the supposition that these distinguished gentlemen are about to invite Albrecht to a university professorship. In the last scene, she comes screaming to Klotilde, demanding her husband back, attacking her physically, and then cursing her: »Kokettieren und grimassieren und buhlen sie nur so weiter – seien Sie sicher, mein Fluch begleitet Sie auf Tritt und Schritt!« (211). Good, ineffectual Elimar tries to calm everyone, but the last image is of Klotilde's sobs mixed with hysterical laughter (212).

---

gungen zum ›Zeitroman‹ bei Fontane und Spielhagen am Beispiel von Fontanes *Effi Briest* und Spielhagens *Zum Zeitvertreib*,« *Literatur und Sprache im historischen Prozeß. Vorträge des Deutschen Germanistentages Aachen 1982*, ed. Thomas Cramer (Tübingen, 1983), 1: 331-32.

[15] Albrecht goes on to say: »Seltsamerweise aber ist der Stoff schon wiederholt Bühnenschriftstellern anziehend genug erschienen, den Versuch zu wagen, ihn zu einem Drama umzugestalten. Diese Versuche sind leider sämtlich mißglückt« (63). The *Gesamtverzeichnis* lists one such effort by Karl Pauli, *Das Skelett* [sic] *im Hause. Lustspiel in 1 Akt nach Friedrich Spielhagen*, in the series *Kleines Theater* (Paderborn, 1893).

[16] If the publication of the novella »vor ein paar Jahren« (63) is to be taken literally, this would date the action of the story around 1880, though the employment of a private detective may suggest a somewhat later time; it is a rather new idea for Germany, as Fernau remarks: a Londoner or Parisian would have thought of it at once, unlike the Germans, who are »schwerfällig« (132).

So far the reader may feel that Spielhagen has once again reached into the limited population of his casting department. We have seen before the brutal aristocrat and the devouring *femme fatale*, as well as the disappointed husband whose wife has not evolved to his level of *Bildung* and savoir-faire as far back as *Die von Hohenstein*, where the clever but plain wife is named Clärchen, and in *Stumme des Himmels*. However, in those cases, although the wife is treated with sympathy and understanding, the discontent and frustrated potential of the husband is made somewhat more congenial to the reader. Here, however, the perspective is canted the other way. Klara is a fine woman and the real victim of the tragedy, while Albrecht is a caricature of a frustrated, dissatisfied, vain, ultimately sterile and small-calibre *Bildungsbürger*, though he rises to a degree of contrition and self-knowledge in his farewell letters. This shift in evaluation of man and wife, though not drastic, is important and has been missed by the critics.

Albrecht is a success in his own sphere, admired by his pupils and colleagues and talented enough to write entertainments that please the undemanding audience at the Sudenburgs, where he can »unter diesen Dilettanten als ein durchgebildeter Künstler erscheinen« (79).[17] But, somewhat like Resber in *Frei geboren*, he is not satisfied with the position to which he has risen from his origins as a Harz miner's orphaned son who had been a goose boy and shepherd until the pastor took him in (25). He is in the process of publishing an academic treatise, aspiring to the university professorship, but above all, he wants his dramas performed at the Royal Theater. To this end he shows himself prepared to permit any censorship of his text and lets the theater manager lead him around by the nose by inviting him to submit his play and then stalling him. He allows himself to be captivated by Klotilde, even though he occasionally would like to strangle »das schöne Weib, das so zum Zeitvertreib ihre Circekünste an ihn übte« (80); later he thinks that only her class status makes her different from a courtesan (144-45). Elimar, from the time he sees Klotilde beguiling Albrecht, has worried about the outcome; a man from the lower class is wax »in den Händen einer gefallsüchtigen, keineswegs übrig gewissenhaften aristokratischen

---

17   In Franke, *Leben und Roman der Elisabeth von Ardenne*, 120-21, there is a photo of Else and her lover Hartwich costumed for a tableau. While the amateur dramatics might make one think of *Effi Briest*, the rehearsal scene with its aesthetic squabble reminds me particularly of a comparable one in Ludwig Tieck's *Der junge Tischlermeister*, where, however, adultery turns out to be a positive experience of *Bildung*. Unfortunately, Spielhagen denied ever having read Tieck (*FuE*, 2: 299, 340).

Dame«; Viktor may give his wife too much freedom, but »an seiner Ehre durfte man dem alten Korpsburschen und Reservelieutenant nicht rühren! und mit dem Schulmeister würde er verzweifelt kurzen Prozeß machen!« (75). Albrecht's vows of love consist of subliterary clichés. He tries to imitate the insincere cunning characteristic of social discourse, when he praises to Klotilde the »Damen Ihres Kreises« he actually disdains as »Repräsentantinnen der feinsten Bildung, des exquisitesten Kunstsinnes« (90), not fooling her for a moment. For her part, she sees herself theatrically, as Maria Stuart to Albrecht's Rizzio, with Fernau as »Boswell« (sic, 26), doubtless not considering, as the reader is perhaps intended to remember, that Rizzio got himself murdered. Later the enraged Viktor tries to remember something from *Maria Stuart* but in his *Halbbildung* identifies Albrecht with Mortimer (195). When Klotilde surveys Albrecht from a distance, »sie sah dann mit unheimlicher Klarheit seine Schwächen: seine Eitelkeit und Selbstgefälligkeit; seine pompöse Weise, zu gehen und zu stehen, durch die doch immer der pedantische Schulmeister blickte; sein krampfhaftes Bemühen, durch nichts an seine plebejische Abkunft zu erinnern, um gerade das Gegenteil von dem hervorzubringen, was er erzielte«; it is tasteless to be interested in such a man (82-83).

Spielhagen, as is his wont, expresses the erotic excitement between them more explicitly and passionately than Fontane ever does, but it leads to no actual intimacy, and, in fact, seems to have little to do with the other person. Klotilde is attempting to relieve her dissatisfaction and boredom; Albrecht is beguiled by entry into a higher, more elegant class, thinking that, if he could win Klotilde, it would be his »Adelsdiplom« (33). The erotic, while highlighted, is also mocked; Klotilde finds her own desire for Albrecht »positiv lächerlich« (43). Albrecht, like so many of Spielhagen's males, develops sexual timidity; he is frightened at the thought of *chambres garnies* he has heard of, rentable by the hour (153). At no point do Albrecht and Klotilde actually seem to like one another. Since there is no consummation of the relationship, Albrecht's death in the duel appears completely unnecessary, piteous rather than tragic. When he is challenged by Viktor, he knows at once that he is lost. He had »kaum je eine Pistole in der Hand gehabt und ganz gewiß keine abgeschossen,« while »seinem Gegner schon von der Universität her der Ruf eines unfehlbar sichern Schützen gefolgt war« (198-99). For Viktor the bourgeois Albrecht is barely *satisfaktionsfähig*; he agrees with Fernau when he grumbles: »Nächstens werden wir noch unsere Schneider mit Einladungen begehren…. Man sollte in solche Stellungen Bürgerliche nie gelangen lassen« (187). This is unintentionally comic insofar as Viktor's title is a recent one conferred for his father's military service, as

Klotilde, descended »aus uralt freiherrlichem Geschlecht,« derisively observes (24, 114). In fact, Viktor *von* Sorbitz is hardly less of a bourgeois parvenu than Albrecht is, or would like to be.[18]

Let us stipulate once and for all the aesthetic superiority of Fontane's finesse and delicacy, as Spielhagen himself did, perhaps diplomatically; assuming that Fontane knew the Ardennes less well, he conceded: »So konnten Sie sich freilich leichter von der Erdenschwere der Wirklichkeit befreien, die meinem Roman, fürchte ich, anhaftet.«[19] But we may still note some points of comparison. There is, first of all, one of Spielhagen's ominous party scenes, to which Albrecht has been invited because the Sudenburgs hope to employ him as mentor for the lazy son of the house, »die richtige Berliner Treibhauspflanze ... bis er den Jungen nach Prima gelotst hat« (32). Albrecht reacts to this imposition with an enraged outburst, in his thoughts only, of course, of Social Democratic execration of the aristocracy: »Den Fuß muß man ihnen auf den steifen Nacken setzen; ihre Herrlichkeit vor die Füße werfen – ihre freche, zusammengelogene und gestohlene, brutale Herrlichkeit! Ah, ein Luther! ein Luther!« (32). This has a comic effect in view of Albrecht's yearning for entrée into just that society; perhaps the more encomiastic than derogatory word »Herrlichkeit« is meant to give him away. While not as catastrophic as some of Spielhagen's gatherings, the party is nevertheless a source of mischief as the first stage of erotic attraction and Albrecht's involvement, owing to his reputation as a *Literat*, in the ominous sixtieth-birthday celebration. His disabling ambiguity appears after he overestimates the importance of the success of his salon performances on that occasion, in a phrase that lies on the boundary of authorial narration and indirect discourse: »er hätte hineinjauchzen mögen in diese geschminkte Maskerade der oberen Zehntausend« (107-08). The patient depiction of social gatherings and dinner parties, along with commentary before and after, is a well-known feature of Fontane's narrative technique. But Spielhagen's use of such scenes stands in sharp contrast to Fontane's

---

18 Ardenne's title was of Belgian origin and therefore of inferior value until he arranged to have a Prussian barony conferred on him in 1873: Franke, *Leben und Roman der Elisabeth von Ardenne*, 30.

19 To Fontane, February 23, 1896, Gotthold Erler, »Die Ardenne-Affäre bei Fontane und Spielhagen,« *Fontane-Blätter: Sonderheft* (1869): *Zur Entstehungs- und Wirkungsgeschichte Fontanescher Romane*, 66. Viering, »»In welcher Welt der schauderhaften Widersprüche,‹« though sympathetic to Spielhagen on ideological grounds, nevertheless agrees that ideological considerations are irrelevant to literary value and acknowledges Fontane's aesthetic surplus (338-39, 343).

»Gesellschaftsritual« von »Dîner und Landpartie« and what has been called the »Katastrophenlosigkeit« of his scenes of hospitality.[20]

The conciliatory humor to which both Fontane and Spielhagen laid theoretical claim has in the latter's case, as we have seen, long since been abraded by his experience of the Reich. This difference emerges in conversation, with which I would submit Spielhagen is no less skilled than Fontane, but the tone is very different; while Fontane's is civil, often humorous, or, in the case of Innstetten, rather stiff but nevertheless refined and gentlemanly, Spielhagen's is snippy and sarcastic, indicative of the war of all against all characteristic of his representation of social life. Fontane's characters are, for the most part, reasonably respectful of one another on the surface; Spielhagen's are backbiting, resentful, and inclined to mockery. For example, one of the young officers, ogling the beautiful Adele, gushes: »Diese lachenden, blauen Augen, diese lustig blitzenden, weißen Zähne, dies fröhliche Geplauder – wahrhaftig, das wirkt wie eine Oase auf den verschmachtenden Wanderer in der Wüste« (17). This remark gets repeated, and from now on Adele is known among the blades as the »oasis.« During the preparations for the sixtieth-birthday celebration, a comically ferocious dispute breaks out between a professor and an artist. The professor wants to use Wilhelm von Kaulbach's Goethe illustrations as models for tableaux; the artist stalks out after calling Kaulbach a mannered charlatan (52-54). The hidden joke here is that the »Prachtausgabe des Bruckmannschen Albums der Goetheschen Frauengestalten« the professor displays must be one of those to which Spielhagen provided the commentary.[21] The tone Klotilde and Viktor employ with one another bears no resemblance to the subdued noncommunication in the Innstetten home; at one point Klotilde demands

---

[20] Peter Demetz, *Formen des Realismus: Theodor Fontane. Kritische Untersuchungen* (Munich, 1964), 137-45; Kloster, »Die Technik der Gesellschaftsszene,« 177.

[21] Beginning in 1864, Spielhagen appended to photographic reproductions of Kaulbach's famous, internationally circulated Goethe illustrations popular commentaries that were often reprinted in various formats. In the introduction to *Goethe's Frauengestalten nach Originalzeichnungen von W. v. Kaulbach* (Munich, n. d.), Spielhagen elevates Kaulbach to equal standing with Goethe: »hier hat ein König einem andern König zu bauen gegeben« (no p. n.). My copy of this is a luxury quarto; the corresponding octavo, *Goethe-Gallerie. Nach Original-Cartons von Wilhelm v. Kaulbach* (Munich and Berlin, n. d.), has the same illustrations in a slightly different order with similar but revised texts. The commentaries are uncritically laudatory, transpose Kaulbach's drawings into narrative, and show a side of Spielhagen within the taste of his time. Whether in *Zum Zeitvertreib* he is making fun of himself and his earlier enthusiasm or characterizing the young, modern artist as a fool I cannot decide.

a divorce, which Viktor refuses on grounds of appearances; she counters that children are better off when unsuited parents separate and that if he were a man he would not hold on to a wife who so clearly says she wants to be freed; in the end she denies him sex and locks her door on him (115-16). But Viktor thinks his marriage no worse than that of his colleagues and allows himself to be consoled by his »friend« Fernau: »Lieber Sorbitz, wer lernt diese *fin-de-siècle*-Frauen aus? Es ist da alles Nerven, Idiosynkrasien, Illusionen *perdues* oder *à perdre*, falsche Appetite – was weiß ich« (129).

Spielhagen alternates between the brittle, devious social language in dialogue »in diesem Kreise mit der wunderbaren Akustik und seinen hundert gierigen Späheraugen« (85), in which events are subject to impudent commentary, and indirect discourse, which in Viktor's case reveals his fundamental callousness but in Klotilde's an inner uncertainty and unclear yearning for something different; the tentative steps she takes in her inner life toward self-awareness and her consciousness of the disregard in which she is held as a woman make her seem less of a vamp and more deserving of pity. Destabilized by her attraction to the more cultivated Albrecht, she comes to recognize the people of her own circle as

Herdentiere, die sich zum Verwechseln ähnlich sahen; alle dieselben Manieren hatten! dieselben abgebrauchten Phrasen gedankenlos herunterplapperten! und von denen keiner einen Schritt wagte, es wäre denn irgend ein Leithammel vorausgesprungen, worauf sie sämtlich in stupider Hast nach derselben Seite drängten! (83)

To Albrecht she mounts the same complaint about the tedious trivialization of women and the pettiness of men that we have heard elsewhere:

Es bringt mich oft an den Rand der Verzweiflung. Ich könnte ein Verbrechen begehen, wenn ich sicher wäre, es rettete mich auf ein paar Tage, ein paar Stunden nur aus diesem Sumpf, in dem ich ersticke. Ihr Männer freilich! O ja, ich glaube schon, daß Ihr Euch nicht langweilt! Da ist Euer Beruf, da ist der Sport, das Spiel, *la femme*! Da sind die Dummheiten, die Ihr ungestraft begehen könnt, oder meinetwegen auch gestraft, und die dann jedenfalls noch viel interessanter und pikanter werden. Aber wir! Puppen habe ich vorhin gesagt; und dabei bleibe ich: dressierte Puppen; dressiert von Euch und für Euch, die Ihr mit uns spielt und uns in den Winkel werft, wenn Ihr Euch satt gespielt habt. (93)

All will agree that we are not likely to hear this rebellious language from Fontane's Effi, who only remarks in passing that Innstetten did not know how to love. Towards the end, Klotilde comes in her private thoughts to sympathize with Victor's wrath and determines, too late, to make peace with him (178).

The difference from Fontane emerges in the constellation of characters as well. One may think of his gentle, melancholy apothecary Gieshübler, who hopelessly, resignedly, and loyally worships Effi. His counterpart in *Zum Zeitvertreib* is the worldly travel writer Fernau, who figures as Viktor's friend but persistently courts Klotilde. Viktor seeks advice from him, but, since Fernau desires to exacerbate the crisis in the hope that Klotilde will fall to him, he inflames Viktor's class resentment and recommends to him the employment of a detective, thereby indirectly bringing the duel about. Albrecht could not be more unlike the nonchalant, blasé Crampas.

The respective duels (in Spielhagen's case, only reported) bring us to the most curious point of coincidence between the two texts. To the famous dialogue between Innstetten and Wüllersdorf, in which it is established that, at least for men who have been socialized as they have been, the duel, no matter how dubious in principle and, in this case, pointless, is an imperative that cannot be evaded, there corresponds Viktor's consultation with Elimar, who is appalled and tries to talk Viktor out of it. Elimar distinguishes dictates of social honor, under which »wir in Rom wie die Römer thun [müssen],« even if »wir in ihr die bare Unvernunft sehen,« from matters of personal honor that do not have to be exhibited to the public (191-92). Like Innstetten, however, Viktor replies that the matter is already potentially public. Elimar despairs: »Mein Gott, in welcher Welt der schauderhaften Widersprüche leben wir! Da ist eine Gesellschaft, vor der wir innerlich keinen Respekt haben.... Ein Weib, das der Mann, der trotzdem den Stein aufhebt, geliebt hat! Und das so liebenswert ist!« (193). This perhaps unintended reference to Elimar's earlier involvement with Klotilde annoys Viktor; he obliges Elimar to feel he is defending a position he would not take in his own case. To himself Viktor muses that he will have to take the matter to his military commander, »ein schneidiger Herr, der in Ehrensachen keinen Spaß verstand. Dem sollte Elimar mit seinem sentimentalen Wischiwaschi gekommen sein!« (194).

Again the contrast with Fontane is noteworthy. The exchange between Innstetten and Wüllersdorf is strictly man-to-man; it is unthinkable that Wüllersdorf should have an emotional attachment to Effi. The duel situation is tragic, a clash of imperatives that the participants believe must be resolved in a lethal rather than a humane way, though they both know the difference. In terms of social status, Innstetten and Crampas are comparable, if not exactly equals; Crampas accepts the duel and his own loss of life as appropriate to the code. Viktor, on the other hand, in no way shares Elimar's moral reservations. The duel in *Zum Zeitvertreib* is a form of, to be sure, illegal but nevertheless tolerated murder; the inexperienced Albrecht is the equivalent of an unarmed man. Viktor, unlike Innstetten, has no qualms about shooting him down, before or after.

Elimar's horrified reaction may well express Spielhagen's own opinion of the dueling ethos at this time; the most decent man in the story, he is also ineffectual, without any moral leverage. Humanitarian liberalism has become impotent in the Reich, while Albrecht is a victim of his own ambition to rise in class standing, forcing him into a dueling ethos for which he has no competence.[22] Before going off to his commander, Viktor »strich mit der Taschenbürste den Schnurrbart rechts und links aufwärts« (195); this gesture, referring unmistakably to the style of Kaiser Wilhelm, may remind us of Heinrich Mann's *Der Untertan*, begun a decade later.[23] Spielhagen warned Fontane, perhaps not without a bit of an edgy claim on behalf of his own, less conciliatory realism, not to have the book read to him: »Der Roman in seiner *gewollten* satirischen Herbheit und rücksichtslosen Herausbildung aller, auch der grausamsten Konsequenzen ist keine Lektüre, wenn man den Sprudel im Leibe hat und mit aller Welt gut Freund sein möchte.«[24]

The unwillingness to perceive *Zum Zeitvertreib* on its own terms began with Fontane himself, who sent Spielhagen a bizarre critique:

> Der Roman unterstützt, gewiß sehr ungewollt, die alte Anschauung, daß es drei Sorten Menschen gibt: Schwarze, Weiße und – Prinzen. Der Adel spielt hier die Prinzenrolle und zeigt sich uns nicht bloß in den diesem Prinzentum entsprechenden Prätensionen, sondern – und das ist das etwas Bedrückliche – beweist uns auch, daß diese Prätensionen im wesentlichen berechtigt sind.... Durch das Hervorkehren dieser Dinge nährt man nur jene Überheblichkeitsgefühle, die man ausrotten möchte.[25]

---

[22] This may be another sign of Spielhagen's alienation from the national liberal majority. Ute Frevert, *Ehrenmänner. Das Duell in der bürgerlichen Gesellschaft* (Munich, 1991), 98-99, observes: »Das kritische Potential, das das Bürgertum des Vormärz gerade wegen seines zivilen Charakters noch ausgezeichnet hatte, war in dem Maße verschwunden, wie sich die Söhne und Enkel dieser Bürger aktiv und passiv mit dem Militärsystem verbanden und sich dessen Normen und Verhaltenskodizes zu eigen machten.... Zeitgenossen, die an der Antinomie beider Ehrbegriffe [zwischen militärischer und bürgerlicher Ehre] festhielten, rückten zunehmend an den linken Rand des Meinungsspektrums, von wo aus sie die bürgerlichen Deserteure an deren ursprüngliche Glaubenssätze erinnerten und ihren Abfall mit erbitterten Schärfe attackierten.« She points out, 120, 132, that bourgeois politicians could not bring themselves to oppose the dueling ethos, so that the only opponents were the Social Democrats, a further indication of Spielhagen's convergence with Social Democracy.

[23] Cf. Restenberger, *Effi Briest: Historisch Realität*, 91: »narzißtische Selbstverliebtheit und militärisches Preußentum.«

[24] To Fontane, May 28, 1896, Erler, »Die Ardenne-Affäre,« 67.

[25] Fontane to Spielhagen, August 25, 1896, *Briefe*, 4: 586. It is not without significance that, although Fontane appeared to respond collegially to Spielhagen's essay

Spielhagen, so long scolded for his *Adelshaß*, must have stared when he read this and wondered what in his text could have appeared to condone class arrogance. It can only be ascribable to Fontane's sacred-cow status that critics feel obliged to support him in this view.[26] Two more recent studies replicate this attitude. While they pay more attention to *Zum Zeitvertreib* than their predecessors, they both make it clear, perhaps understandably, that Fontane's novel is their main interest[27] and therefore they suffer from a lack of familiarity with Spielhagen's œuvre. One hesitates to urge a complete reading of it on anyone, but when Tyrell declares that Spielhagen knows no mixed characters, writes only about himself, wrote only one first-person novel, or has only male heroes, or Restenberger that Spielhagen punishes Klotilde in order to support »die männliche Leserschaft in ihrem Selbstverständnis als Männer und in ihrem Machtanspruch über Frauen« and that, unlike Fontane, he regards adultery as a threat to the social order, one may feel that a wider acquaintance would have been helpful.[28] Tyrell's worst moment comes when he declares Albrecht, notwithstanding his faults, to be a victimized hero: »Wir, die Leser, mögen freilich (mit Fontane) an Albrecht Anderes auszusetzen haben, ich glaube aber, daß es Spielhagens Absicht war,

---

on *Die Wahlverwandtschaften* and *Effi Briest*, the evidence is that he hindered its publication in the *Deutsche Rundschau* by damning it with faint praise to Julius Rodenberg in a letter of February 18, 1896 (535), while assuring Spielhagen two days later that he tried to support it (536-37). Whether Spielhagen, in turn, meant to tweak *Effi Briest* a bit when he has the clueless count in *Herrin* puzzle over Becky's initials with »Ein weites Feld!« (*NF*, 4: 298), I would not venture to guess.

26   See, for example, Ohl, »Spielhagens Spätwerk,« 181. Tyrell, »Theodor Fontanes ›Effi Briest‹ und Friedrich Spielhagens ›Zum Zeitvertreib,‹« 103, rightly says that Spielhagen goes much farther than Fontane in his criticism of the aristocracy. Restenberger, *Effi Briest: Historische Realität*, 102 and passim, criticizes Tyrell for his view of Fontane's conservatism as conformed, on the whole, to the social ethos of the Reich, but I hold with Tyrell on this point.

27   Tyrell, »Theodor Fontanes ›Effi Briest‹ und Friedrich Spielhagens ›Zum Zeitvertreib,‹« 7, 9, n. 19: »Unser besonderes Interesse gilt hier Fontanes Roman,« rather than Spielhagen's, which is »ein geschickt konstruiertes, durchaus sauber gemachtes Werk, dem aber alles abgeht, was auf eine weitergehende Beschäftigung mit ihm Anspruch erheben könnte.« Restenberger indicates no interest in other works of Spielhagen except for his novel theory, while she is clearly well read in Fontane and mounts a detailed comparison with *L'Adultera*.

28   Tyrell, »Theodor Fontanes ›Effi Briest‹ und Friedrich Spielhagens ›Zum Zeitvertreib,‹« 104, 151; Restenberger, *Effi Briest: Historische Realität*, 198-99; cf. 250. In this and related matters Restenberger would have benefited from spending less time on radical feminist theory and more on Spielhagen's works, especially *Frei geboren*. Why could one not as well claim that Fontane punishes Effi for her adultery by having her ostracized, grow pale, and die young?

in Albrecht einfach einen herrlichen Menschen (zugleich ein Selbstbildnis!) zu geben, der hauptsächlich an der Schlechtheit der Welt zugrunde ging.«[29] This I believe to be quite impossible; if, as Tyrell suggests, Albrecht's ambivalence toward the aristocracy »spiegelt eine gleiche Ambivalenz bei Spielhagen wider, wie denn Albrecht überhaupt sehr viel von seinem Schöpfer in sich trägt,« it is a recursive and ironic self-criticism of the author.[30]

Restenberger gets into her worst difficulty in a contradiction between her determination to accept Fontane's critique that Spielhagen was insufficiently critical of the aristocracy and her insistence that *Zum Zeitvertreib* has not endured in contrast to *Effi Briest* because Spielhagen's preoccupation with class conflict has come to be of no interest, since the aristocracy is no longer with us.[31] Apart from the gross presentism of the evaluative principle, the argument gives too much credit to Fontane's critique, no less obtuse than Spielhagen's of *Effi Briest*, which she measures not in context but against her own interpretation, the beneficiary of a hundred years of refined critical scrutiny. Like many critics she insists that Spielhagen maintains a typological, black-and-white characterization, but when she says he condemns Klotilde without any understanding for her situation or claims of Klotilde herself that »[b]edingungslos akzeptiert sie den Warencharakter ihrer Ehe wie der Ehe allgemein,« she is not sensitive to the undertones I have tried to point out, and her criticism that Fontane makes Innstetten »zu einem menschlicheren, vielschichtigeren Charakter als Spielhagens Viktor«[32] is un-

---

29 Tyrell, »Theodor Fontanes ›Effi Briest‹ und Friedrich Spielhagens ›Zum Zeitvertreib,‹« 104.

30 Tyrell, »Theodor Fontanes ›Effi Briest‹ und Friedrich Spielhagens ›Zum Zeitvertreib,‹« 70. Restenberger, *Effi Briest: Historische Realität*, 99-100, declares that Albrecht must be the hero according to the theoretical plan she believes structures the novel; earlier, however, she has said that Elimar »zum eigentlichen Held und zur Identifikationsfigur der Geschichte stilisiert wird« (84). Given Elimar's ineffectuality, I doubt that this can be right, either. Rather than considering that Spielhagen might be in control of his characterization, she charges it to his incompetence that »Albrecht Winters Empfindungen wirken, so wie sie Spielhagen ausdrückt, lächerlich« (205; see also 230). Like many others, Restenberger is too fixated on Spielhagen's theory and inattentive to its late deterioration.

31 Restenberger, *Effi Briest: Historische Realität*, 97-98, 189, 193, 200, 257. She asserts: »Seine lebenslängliche Abneigung gegen standesrechtliche Privilegien des Adels rührt von diesem Kontakt mit dem Pommerschen Adel her« (71), when he tells us the opposite in *FuE*, 1: 197-98.

32 Restenberger, *Effi Briest: Historische Realität*, 190, 100, 194, 191. She misspells Innstetten's name as »Instetten« throughout, even when quoting primary and secondary text. This is not unusual; Viering, »›In welcher Welt der schauderhaften Widersprüche,‹« does so also. In return, Restenberger spells Viering as »Vierig« throughout as well as turning Glenn A. Guidry into »Guidry A. Glenn« (137, n. 120, and in the bibliography).

fairly derived from a digressive orientation on the real Ardenne case, for the more reasonable comparison would be with the characterization of Albrecht, unclearly seen through the lens of Fontane's critique.[33]

The temptation to employ the two texts for a comparison between Spielhagen and Fontane is irresistible. But the record shows that insisting upon the comparison reinforces prejudices about Spielhagen, impeding insight into the particulars of his writing and its literary-historical location. Restenberger may be right, as she repeatedly insists, that Spielhagen puts more individual blame on his characters than the all-comprehending and all-forgiving Fontane, but whether this difference is owing to Fontane's greater sensitivity to social determinants is, I think, more debatable.[34] Fontane's social critique of Wilhelminian society remains mild, at least on the discursive surface, and is absorbed into a recognizably aesthetic tragic tone. Spielhagen's tone, typically for the late work, is one of punishing satire, as Fontane acknowledged, of a dangerous environment in which comical and stupid events are potentially lethal. Which view of the Reich would we now say was more perceptive and relevant to the future?

---

[33] The acceptance of Fontane's rejection of Albrecht as a »Schwachmatikus« (*Briefe*, 4: 586) while complaining of one-dimensional characters refuses to perceive or, at any rate, grant any validity to Spielhagen's intended meaning.

[34] Restenberger, *Effi Briest: Historische Realität*, 48, 201. The equation of Fontane's allegedly deeper social sensitivity with »allgemein menschliche Anliegen« transcending his own time, »die Verklärung der historisch-gesellschaftlichen Wirklichkeit durch die Poesie zu einer Kunstwirklichkeit« moving the reader to identification (204, 205, 206) seems to me forced.

Epilogue. Spielhagen and Raabe: A Counterfactual Speculation

One might suppose that an essay on the relationship of Friedrich Spielhagen and Wilhelm Raabe would be extremely brief: there was none. Raabe mentions or alludes to Spielhagen rarely and with curt disdain. So far as I can see, Spielhagen, whom Fontane professed to admire for his breadth of reading,[1] never mentions Raabe in all his many pages of literary criticism and theory. In 1897 Spielhagen wrote an omnibus critique, »Streifblicke über den heutigen deutschen Roman«; he discusses Rosegger, Georg von Omteda, Fontane, Johannes Richard zur Megede, Clara Sudermann, Konrad Telmann, Otto Ernst, and Marie von Ebner-Eschenbach (*NB*, 135–69). In this list, part of which will send one to one's oldest *Dichterlexikon*, there is no place for Raabe. One would seem obliged to conclude that the two writers simply took no notice of one another. But in the literary-historical circumstances this is implausible. Rather, the mutual silence has an eloquence of its own. It invites speculation without, one must admit, much evidentiary help from the factual record. Despite a claim that there are few significant parallels in their lives and careers,[2] there are actually quite a number of a sort that ought to have led to a certain collegiality.

Spielhagen and Raabe were both North German Protestants who eschewed religious belief, Spielhagen more militantly. Both began as national liberals with an orientation on *Vormärz* idealism and hopes for a unified, strong, humane, and cultivated Germany that were disappointed by developments in the Reich. Spielhagen was two years and nine months older. His birthplace of Magdeburg was the town in which Raabe for four years

---

[1] »Ich bewundere nicht nur, was Sie schreiben, sondern auch, was Sie lesen«: to Spielhagen, October 11, 1897, *Briefe*, 4: 670.

[2] Gabriele Henkel, *Studien zur Privatbibliothek Wilhelm Raabes. Vom »wirklichen Autor«, von Zeitgenossen und »ächten Dichtern«* (Braunschweig, 1997), 115: »in der Tat sind wenige Parallelitäten zwischen dem poetischen Realisten Raabe und dem Romantheoretiker und Verfasser Romane Spielhagen auszumachen, will man nicht allzu bemüht vermeintliche biographische oder weltanschauliche Gemeinsamkeiten konstatieren.« The comment is directed against a brief suggestion of parallels by Hans Martin Schultz, *Raabe-Schriften. Eine systematische Zusammenstellung* (Wolfenbüttel, 1931), 135.

pondered apprenticeship to a book dealer. The North German coast that was Spielhagen's boyhood environment was the homeland of Raabe's most intimate friend, Wilhelm Jensen. Both attended universities without taking a degree, though for different reasons. Spielhagen took longer to find his way to his vocation. It is true that his first novella, *Clara Vere*, appeared one year after Raabe's debut, *Die Chronik der Sperlingsgasse*, but as Spielhagen well knew, his early novellas could not lay the foundation of a literary career. Not until four years later did he achieve his decisive breakthrough with *Problematische Naturen*, but thereafter their careers maintained a comparable productivity and similar tempo. Both lived relatively uneventful and apparently scandal-free bourgeois domestic lives. Both settled in cities, Raabe for forty years in Braunschweig, Spielhagen for nearly forty-nine years in Berlin. Dirk Göttsche sees them converging to a form of modernity in their last decade: »Im Spätwerk Spielhagens ist in den neunziger Jahren beispielsweise ein analoges Abrücken vom großen Zeit- und Gesellschaftsroman zu beobachten.«[3] In another place, Göttsche rightly, in my view, cites *Alles fließt* as a sign of this convergence, while arguing that »Struktur und Poetologie der Novelle wagen sich keinen Schritt über den bürgerlichen Realismus hinaus« in comparison to Raabe's *fin-de-siècle* challenge to conventions of realism in the fragmentary *Altershausen*.[4] The last novel Raabe published, *Hastenbeck*, appeared in 1899; Spielhagen published his two last novels, *Opfer* and *Frei geboren*, in the following year. Raabe worked on a novel fragment, *Altershausen*, breaking it off in 1902. In the following year Spielhagen published his last book, *Am Wege*, containing autobiographical and critical essays. The writing careers of both men had come to an end. Like Raabe, Spielhagen hated old age and dying, as is evident from many of his late poems. He outlived Raabe by a little less than three months.

They shared acquaintances, for example, with Berthold Auerbach, Spielhagen more intensely, and with Paul Heyse. Both had somewhat brittle relationships with Theodor Fontane, superficially courteous and collegial, under the surface uneasy and suspicious. Both rejected Freytag, whom Raabe dismissed scornfully as »der Hochgelahrte Magister und Hofrath Herr Gustavus Freytag«[5] while Spielhagen acidly remarked: »verzichte ich

---

[3] Göttsche, *Zeit im Roman*, 26.
[4] Dirk Göttsche, *Zeitreflexion und Zeitkritik im Werk Wilhelm Raabes* (Würzburg, 2000), 170–71. The point is fairly taken as far as it goes, but needs to be pursued on a broader base of late texts. Lamers, *Held oder Welt?*, 198, found it possible to assert: »Radikaler noch als die späten Werke Raabes und Fontanes formuliert Spielhagen die Verzweiflung über die absolute Sinnlosigkeit der allgemeinen wie der individuellen Existenz.«

gern auf einen Beweis *a priori*, daß der Verfasser von Soll und Haben und der Problematischen Naturen niemals einander anziehen konnten« (*FuE*, 2: 338–39).[6] Three years after Otto Janke in Berlin published *Problematische Naturen*, he became one of Raabe's many publishers with *Der Hungerpastor*. Both published extensively in *Westermanns Illustrirte Deutsche Monatshefte*.

Here, however, we begin to come to significant differences. Raabe was determined to focus his energies on and make his living from the writing of fiction exclusively, publishing little else except an occasional poem; he wrote one insignificant book review and no general commentary on literature, and he declined all opportunities for participation in literary life such as editorships. This was unusual in his time; the shape of Spielhagen's career was more conventional. He wrote in all genres, publishing two volumes of poetry as well as dramas that he tried to get performed, and, of course, the huge corpus of theory and criticism. He took on several editing positions in his younger days and later edited or coedited *Westermanns* for nearly six years, from October 1878 to September 1884.[7] During this time Raabe serialized five novels or novellas in *Westermanns*: *Alte Nester* (1879), *Das Horn von Wanza* (1880–81), *Fabian und Sebastian* (1881–82), *Prinzessin Fisch* (1882–83), and *Villa Schönow* (1884). There were also several unsigned notices of his books. He seems to have bypassed Spielhagen by dealing with Karpeles, Glaser, or the publisher Georg Westermann directly.

---

5 To Edmund and Elisabeth Hoefer, May 9, 1881, Wilhelm Raabe, *Sämtliche Werke*, ed. Karl Hoppe et al. (Göttingen, 1960–94), Ergänzungsband 2: 223. This edition will hereinafter be cited in parentheses as *BA* with volume and page number; E = Ergänzungsband.

6 The feeling was mutual. In the preceding year, Freytag wrote to his future third wife in a letter of December 1, 1889, about Spielhagen: »Es ist mir lieb, daß er erzählt, ich hätte ihn schlecht behandelt. Aber das ist sicher nicht wegen seiner Recension geschehen, sondern seiner selbst wegen.« Gustav Freytag, *Briefe an seine Gattin,* ed. Hermance Strakosch-Freytag and Curt L. Walter-van der Bleek (Berlin, 1912), 361.

7 Spielhagen is listed as editor from October 1878 to March 1879; after that no editor is named on the title page. He was a replacement for Adolf Glaser, who had been suspended owing to his involvement in a homosexual scandal; Raabe noted the change in his diary (Henkel, *Studien zur Privatbibliothek*, 116). Gustav Karpeles seems to have been Spielhagen's coeditor until 1882. Henkel, 117, says that Spielhagen greatly praised *Alte Nester*, but her source, Karl Heim, »Wilhelm Raabe und das Publikum,« (Diss. Tübingen, 1953), 104, indicates that it was Karpeles who did so. For details, see Eckhardt Meyer-Krentler, *»Unterm Strich.« Literarischer Markt, Trivialität und Romankunst in Raabes »Der Lar«* (Paderborn, Munich, Vienna, and Zurich, 1986), 90–91. Meyer-Krentler says that Glaser silently displaced Karpeles in 1882 and Spielhagen in 1884 (83), and indicates that up to then it had been Karpeles who vigorously encouraged Raabe (90–91).

There can be little doubt that Raabe avoided Spielhagen systematically. I mentioned in Chapter 3 that he did not send a contribution to the Festschrift for Spielhagen's seventieth birthday, even though Karpeles requested one from him more than once.[8] In that earlier chapter I also mentioned that Spielhagen's books are found in Raabe's library, but it is not known in every case whether Raabe actually acquired the books in question or they were added later by the family.[9] Nevertheless, at least in the early phase of Spielhagen's career in the 1860s Raabe seems to have kept some track of him, noting his novels and newspaper articles in his diary.[10]

Almost all of Raabe's private comments are unfriendly. In Chapter 3 I called attention to the most often cited of them, that Spielhagen had been reported in a newspaper to have declared himself a »Dichter-Journalist,«[11] and tried to show that this claim, which has never been documented, was most improbable. However, the phrase indicates that Raabe shared with Heinrich Hart and many critics afterwards the view that Spielhagen was an inartistic writer absorbed in tendentiousness. In a late interview (1901) Raabe is quoted as having seen in Spielhagen »die ›Agitationen eines freisinnigen Parteimannes‹« (*BA*, E 4: 138). Raabe was also apparently entertained by the episode of the prosecution of *Angela* and encouraged Eduard Engel in his jesting:

Auf das Höchste gespannt bin ich auf den zweiten Tag Ihrer Verhandlungen in Sachen des großen Prozesses Angela. Machen Sie den armen Spielhagen nur nicht

---

8 Wilhelm Fehse, *Wilhelm Raabe. Sein Leben und seine Werke* (Braunschweig, 1937), 595. Raabe noted the event in his diary (Henkel, *Studien zur Privatbibliothek*, 122).

9 According to Dorothea Bänsch, »Die Bibliothek Wilhelm Raabes nach Sachgebieten geordnet,« *Jahrbuch der Raabe-Gesellschaft* (1970): 112, Raabe wrote his name in Spielhagen's *Sämmtliche Werke*, revised edition (Berlin: Janke, n.d.). Henkel, *Studien zur Privatbibliothek*, 115, dates this edition as 1866–67, which seems to be a confusion with the earlier *Gesammelte Werke*; the *Sämmtliche Werke* were published, according to the *Gesamtverzeichnis*, in 1871, then were taken over by Staackmann. Henkel adds that Raabe indicated it was a gift of the publisher (121), thus distancing himself from it. The volumes of *Problematische Naturen* and *Durch Nacht zum Licht* have the name of Raabe's sister Emilie; one of *Deutsche Pioniere* in a later edition of 1907 is indicated by Bänsch as not known to have belonged to Raabe.

10 Henkel, *Studien zur Privatbibliothek*, 115. As he noted in the diary on September 7, 1879, he also spotted in the *Berliner Tageblatt* Spielhagen's eulogy of the publisher Georg Westermann and sent it to Glaser on September 13 (117 and n. 451). The eulogy was appended to an obituary article, »*In Memoriam*!« in *Westermanns* 48 (April-September 1880), 23–24.

11 To Paul Heyse, March 2, 1875, *BA*, E 2: 183.

12 To Engel, July 4, 1881, *BA*, E 2: 231.

zu nervös! Haben Sie sich schon an Mademoiselle de Maupin von Th. Gautier erinnert? Sie finden eine ganz ähnliche Scene darin wie in dem deutschen Buch; aber der Franzos hat doch anders gemalt wie der Deutsche in seiner unüberwindlichen Schämigkeit.[12]

Spielhagen was notorious for his nervousness, but it seems a little hard for a writer frequently criticized for erotic explicitness, as in the *Angela* case, to be charged with prudishness, especially by a writer as relatively reticent in such matters as Raabe. One wonders whether he had actually read *Angela*; to be sure, it would not have raised his estimate of his colleague. Only near the end of his life did he soften sufficiently to acknowledge a shared fate with Spielhagen among writers who had been left behind by the literary development: »uns Alte, die Heyse, die Spielhagen, die Raabe, die schon längst zu Boden liegen sollten!«[13] If it is somewhat dismissive to speak of Spielhagen in the plural, Raabe includes himself in the locution.

Digs are found also in the fictional texts. In *Deutscher Adel*, the weary lending-library proprietor Achtermann, who struggles to meet the fickle taste of his clientele – »Blech, Gold und Talmi« – is seen replacing on his shelves »»Auf der Höhe‹ – dritter Band; – ›Problematische Naturen‹« (*BA*, 13: 210–11). Neither author is named, but, despite Raabe's friendly personal attitude toward Auerbach, the pairing indicates that he did not think much more of him as a writer, possibly in consideration of the fact that Spielhagen vigorously propagated him. Rather cheekier is the device of having Achtermann's pal, Wedehop, count among his translations »Michelets Buch über die Weiber« (231), which, of course, Spielhagen had translated.[14] Still cheekier is the passage in *Kloster Lugau* where a character swears: »Bei Mylitta (hier ja nicht Melitta!), der zweifellosesten weiblichen Gottheit der Vergangenheit« (*BA*, 19: 25). The commentators have not noticed the disrespectful reference to Melitta von Berkow in *Problematische Naturen*, but readers at the time, even in 1894, are likely to have done so.

Thus Raabe did not ignore Spielhagen, but he certainly refused him good will. Reasons for this are not too difficult to imagine. In general it cannot be said that Raabe maintained a very generous spirit toward his fellow writers. He was not above jealousy and resentment, in large part from

---

13 To Robert Lange, July 25, 1909, *BA*, E 2: 492.
14 Henkel, *Studien zur Privatbibliothek*, 120, calls attention to the passages in *Deutscher Adel*. A further suggestion (121), that the characterization of Wendeline Cruse in *Im alten Eisen*, »hier habe es mit einem vollkommen ungebrochenen Lebensmut und einem durchaus unproblematischen Charakter zu tun« (*BA*, 16: 377), refers to *Problematische Naturen*, I find less compelling.

his bitterness at the disproportion between what he rightly regarded as his achievement and his struggles to gain a public and financial ease. Once he wrote plaintively to the more successful Jensen and his wife: »Sagt einmal wißt Ihr gar kein Mittel um die Leute zu bewegen, meine Bücher zu kaufen?«[15] The sight of Spielhagen's prosperity from his writing must have been galling to Raabe as it was annoying to Fontane, who heard

> »Spielhagen erhält hundert Thaler für den Bogen.«... Ja, diese Summe *kann* er kriegen.... Spielhagen ... läßt seine Romane in der Regel vorher in zwei großen Zeitungen *gleichzeitig* drucken, in Wien und in New-York, oder in Köln und Baltimore.... [S]o dürfen Sie nicht vergessen, daß Spielhagen neben mir ein Heros ist ... daß er, neben Auerbach, der angesehenste deutsche Romanschriftsteller der Gegenwart ist, während ich in allem nur so mitschwimme.[16]

There is bound to be a difference in prosperity between a writer who opens his career with a major best seller, as Spielhagen did, and one who begins with a *succès d'estime* like Raabe's *Chronik der Sperlingsgasse*. Still, Spielhagen, like Raabe, had occasion to complain that Germans will not buy books:

> Für Bücher geben hin mein schönes Geld!
> Eh' ich das thue, hole mich der Henker!
> Der Deutsche sagt's; d'rum nennt in aller Welt
> Sein Volk man das der Dichter und der Denker. (*NG*, 146)

Much like Raabe, Spielhagen despaired of maintaining a popular readership, as literature can survive only for the dwindling »*happy few*« of exquisite culture (*NB*, 5; English in the original). It is possible that Raabe's reported view of Spielhagen as a liberal agitator suggests some political estrangement, for he was certainly willing to go much farther in the direction of Social Democracy, but I think a detailed examination of their evolving attitude toward the Reich would show them not very far apart. There was also a difference between them in career strategy. Spielhagen's constant need to explain himself, to put his person before the public, contrasts starkly with Raabe's belief that reticence was a value in an author, criticizing even Theodor Storm for excessive self-promotion.[17]

However, the main difficulty between them was certainly Spielhagen's vigorously propagated theory of narrative objectivity, which must have seemed to Raabe a systematic repudiation of his experimental narrative

---

[15] Raabe to Marie and Wilhelm Jensen, February 15, 1874, *BA*, E 3: 214.
[16] Fontane, *Briefe*, 2: 403. See Tyrell, »Theodor Fontanes ›Effi Briest‹ und Friedrich Spielhagens' ›Zum Zeitvertreib‹« 3.
[17] To Edmund Sträter, March 24, 1890, *BA*, E 2: 278.

modes.[18] Raabe's foregrounding of a narrator, whom the readers of those days probably did not often distinguish from the author, is a prominent feature of his writing that has drawn a vast amount of comment. At times one may get the feeling that he is protesting directly against Spielhagen, for example, in his often quoted aphorism: »Ein echter Dichter sagt *Ich!*«[19] In that same *Deutscher Adel* where the lending-library proprietor grapples with *Problematische Naturen*, Raabe engages in one of his patented, ironic appropriations of the dissatisfactions of an imputed reader: »Es hat sich überhaupt schon auf diesen ersten Seiten unseres Berichtes eine Erzählungsweise eingeschlichen, die uns durchaus nicht gefallen kann!« (*BA*, 13: 184). Such examples could be multiplied ad infinitum. Spielhagen's dialectic of finding and inventing was strongly shifted by Raabe in favor of the imagination. In the most fantastic of his tales, *Vom alten Proteus*, he takes the occasion to allude to the Schillerian half brother haunting Spielhagen:

> Der Narr rechnet nach Jahren, der Kluge nach Tagen, der Weise nach Minuten, und wir, die wir das alles durcheinander sind, wir nehmen den Hut vom Nagel und machen einen Spaziergang durch den Aprilabend. Nicht dick und fett mit den Gefühlen eines Philisters, der das fetteste Schwein in der Gemeinde geschlachtet hat; auch nicht mit den Gefühlen des Genius, der da sagt: »Heute habe ich aber mal wieder das Dasein von hundert Individualitäten in meiner eigenen durchgekostet, und theatrum mundi mag nun meinetwegen einfallen!« – sondern ganz schmächtig und bescheiden, als des hohen Dichters entfernter armer Vetter oder vielmehr Halbbruder, wie die Ästhetiken sagen, der den Tag über wieder einmal saß und allerhand Rauchbilder des Lebens auf den Teller kritzelte. (*BA*, 12: 238)

A page later appears one of Raabe's most often cited slogans: »Unsere tägliche Selbsttäuschung gib uns heute!« (239).

Spielhagen, who flinched at the opening sentence of Goethe's *Die Wahlverwandtschaften*, might conceivably have regarded Raabe's writing, if he read much of it, as an artillery barrage of defiance to his convictions that could only be met by silence. Hans-Jürgen Schrader has suggested that Raabe intentionally confronted Spielhagen's theoretical prescriptions:

> Gegen jeden Punkt dieser Forderungen hat Raabe durch jeden seiner Erzähltexte aus der Braunschweiger Zeit unaufhörlich opponiert: gegen das vollständige

---

[18] Many observers have easily come to this conclusion. See, for example, Hans Kolbe, *Wilhelm Raabe. Vom Entwicklungs- zum Desillusionsierungsroman* (Berlin, 1981), 87–92; Werner Fuld, *Wilhelm Raabe. Eine Biographie* (Munich, 1993), 263–64, 302–03.

[19] Karl Hoppe, »Aphorismen Raabes chronologisch geordnet,« *Jahrbuch der Raabe-Gesellschaft* (1960): 105.

Verschwinden des Erzählers aus dem Erzählten, gegen eine Konzentration auf »Action,« die umweg- und atemlos vom ersten bis zum letzten Wort durchlaufen sollte, vor allem gegen jede Illusionierung des Lesers, als sei das hier Berichtete Wirklichkeit oder als gäbe es überhaupt, wie dies ein scheinbar objektives Erzählen glauben machen will, eine eindeutige, objektiv erkennbare Wirklichkeit.

He goes so far to suggest that *Alte Nester*, with its garrulous, intrusive narrator, was directed specifically against Spielhagen as the new editor of *Westermanns*.[20] On the other hand, Spielhagen, conceivably, might have regarded Raabe's narrative modes as disqualifying him as a *Dichter*, simply not to be credited as such. In this he would not have been alone, for many critics, however they might have admired him for other reasons, were positive that he had no idea how to tell stories and charged him for decades with »Jean-Paulian manner.«[21] If this was Spielhagen's reaction, then we would have a situation in which two contemporary writers not only disapproved of each other; each will have denied that the other was admissible to the aesthetic realm of literature. Such a result would be a telling commentary on the literary and critical atmosphere of Germany in the second half of the nineteenth century.

Suppose, however, contrary to the evidence adduced so far, that one of the writers might be imagined to have watched the other closely, to have competed with him with echoes, with corresponding forms and situations, with shared perspectives and locutions. What might we turn up if we were determined to find it? One might surmise that the gentle young blind woman Eugenie Leiding, who appears in *Ein Frühling* in 1857 (a less successful second novel like Spielhagen's second, *Die von Hohenstein*) reappears twenty years later as the saintly blind girl Cilli in *Sturmflut* (see my comment on this in Chapter 13). The short novel *In der zwölften Stunde*, first published in 1862, features a poor and ill dancer who nevertheless must continue to dance for the sake of her child (*AR*, 2, 1: 451) and may remind us of the poor dancer Rosalie in *Die Chronik der Sperlingsgasse* (*BA*, 1: 36, 50–52). Raabe set as a motto to *Der Hungerpastor* a quotation from Sophocles's *Antigone*: »Nicht mitzuhasssen, mitzulieben bin ich da!« (*BA*, 6:

[20] Hans-Jürgen Schrader, »Gedichtete Dichtungstheorie im Werk Raabes. Exemplifiziert an ›Alte Nester,‹« *Jahrbuch der Raabe-Gesellschaft* (1989): 23–24. While Schrader makes some pertinent points about digression, exposure of the machinery of narration, repetitiousness, and diffuseness, etc. in *Alte Nester*, it is not the most telling example because it is a first-person novel, a form that in Spielhagen's scheme was largely exempt from his narratological strictures.
[21] See Sammons, *Wilhelm Raabe*, 40, 154–55.

5). The book version was published in March 1864 (493). Rose in *Röschen vom Hofe*, written in the following year, is made to say: »Ich habe mir oft in diesen Tagen das schöne Wort der Antigone wiederholt, mit welchem sie den Vorwürfen des rauhen Kreon in stolzer Demuth entgegentritt: Nicht mitzuhassen, mitzulieben bin ich da« (*AR*, 2, 1: 598). The lines appear somewhat altered in a sonnet: »Auch ich ward nicht geboren, mitzuhassen, / Nur mitzulieben« (*G*, 20).

In 1866, Raabe undertook the very unusual experiment of employing a first-person female narrator in *Im Siegeskranze*; Spielhagen did the same, thirty-four years later, in *Frei geboren*. In *Deutscher Adel* (1880), already so useful for our purposes (and originally published in *Westermanns* just before Spielhagen took it on), we find Wedehop, who was credited with Spielhagen's translation of Michelet's *La Femme*, characterized as »dieses nach Paragraph zehn im zweiten Programm der Vorschule der Ästhetik *passive Genie*« (*BA*, 13: 237). The reference is to the same section and practically the same page of Jean Paul's work from which Spielhagen, fifteen years later, would take the title of *Stumme des Himmels* (see Chapter 16). At the beginning of *Alte Nester*, book version also in 1880, the narrator Fritz Langreuter tells how his father, a tax official, had been murdered by salt smugglers (*BA*, 14: 9). In *Sonntagskind*, thirteen years later, Justus Arnold's father, a forester, is killed by smugglers when he tries to enforce the law on them; Justus thinks: »Es war nicht der erste Forst- oder Steuerbeamte, der ihrer Rache zum Opfer gefallen war« (*NF*, 1: 186). In *Zum Zeitvertreib*, Albrecht kisses Klotilde, as he supposes, with »kaum einen Tropfen von Sinnlichkeit.... Es wäre denn eine Sinnlichkeit gewesen, wie sie Götter empfinden mögen, in deren Adern statt des Blutes Ichor fließt« (3: 148). Since Albrecht's emotions seem to be more derivative than distinctive, might he not be recalling the motif of the ichor that flows in the veins of the elevated figures in Raabe's novella *Frau Salome*, originally published in *Westermanns* in 1875 and in the *Krähenfelder Geschichten* in 1879? In *Unruhige Gäste* (book version 1886), one of the positive characters is a carpenter, the »Gentleman-Sozialist« Spörenwagen (*BA*, 16: 251), who shapes a coffin; a year later, the stepfather of Lothar Lorenz in *Was will das werden?* is a kindly carpenter who makes coffins.[22] Lorenz himself ends as a »gelehrte[r] Handwerker« (*AR*, 3, 5: 435). *Das Odfeld* (book version 1889) contains a scene, notoriously resistant to interpretation, of a fight between swarms of ravens in the sky (*BA*, 17: 26–32);

---

[22] That »Spörenwagen« practically rhymes with »Spielhagen« must be counted as a coincidence, given Raabe's attitudes.

nine years later, the would-be Faustulus has a sexually charged dream in which huge clouds of black crows fly over, cawing, »und dann wirbelten jedesmal die Krähenwolken wie toll durcheinander, indem eine Krähe mit ihren Krallen die Krallen der andern packte« (*NF*, 4: 38), an echo that is striking because of the rarity of the image.[23]

The common feature of all these examples is that Spielhagen's text is later than Raabe's. One or two hints that I might have ventured of motifs going in the other direction are a good deal more tenuous than these. Are we then entitled to construct a Spielhagen who, far from ignoring Raabe, scanned him closely and let himself be influenced by what he found? That would be tempting but, I fear, not *wissenschaftlich*. Textual parallels are notoriously easy to find in large corpuses of writing, especially when they belong to the same age and cultural environment. For example, it might catch one's attention that Velten Andres in *Die Akten des Vogelsangs* wishes himself »ein friedliches Ende auf Salas y Gomez« (*BA*, 19: 260–61; the motif is repeated 274 and 296), a desolate island on whose reefs the speaker of one of Spielhagen's sonnet sequences imagines his ship will be dashed:

> Salas y Gomez! O, jetzt weiß ich wohl,
> Weshalb so tiefes Grausen mich ergriffen,
> Trat je vor meinen Geist dein düstres Bild! (*NG*, 83).

It would be most rational to suppose that both texts go back independently to Adalbert Chamisso's widely known poem, »Salas y Gomez,«[24] especially as, at the beginning of Spielhagen's sonnet sequence, there is a specific reference to »des Weltumseglers Sang / In der Terzinen feierlichem Klang« (*NG*, 78). Indeed, an independent allusion might seem likely with such echoes as that from *Antigone*, while Spielhagen's complaint that he had been thrown »zum alten Eisen« similarly need not be a reference to Raabe's novel *Im alten Eisen*.[25] Of many it will be evident that they come independently from the cultural environment. For example, in one of Spielhagen's classis-

---

23 See my essay, »Raabe's Ravens,« in *Imagination and History: Selected Papers on Nineteenth-Century German Literature* (New York and Bern, 1988), esp. 287–97; Rosemarie Haas, »Raabe, der Rabe, ›The Raven.‹ Beobachtungen zur Intertextualität in Raabes Erzählung ›Das Odfeld,‹« *Jahrbuch der Raabe-Gesellschaft* (1992): 139–64.

24 Adelbert von Chamisso, *Sämtliche Werke*, ed. Jost Perfahl (Munich, 1975), 1: 468–76. Spielhagen had already alluded to it in *Problematische Naturen* (*AR*, 1, 1: 241), as well as later in *Mesmerismus* (*NF*, 5: 284, 309).

25 Mensch, »Erinnerungen an Friedrich Spielhagen,« 358. The phrase does, to be sure, turn up two years after Raabe's novel in *Ein neuer Pharao* (*AR*, 3, 3: 436).

tic parodies, Achilles quotes *Hamlet*, 1: 2: »Ekel, schal und unersprießlich« (*G*, 121), a phrase Raabe several times applied to his own state of mind in his private diary, which Spielhagen, of course, cannot have known.[26] This may belong generally to the category of *geflügelte Worte*, like Raabe's reference to Matthew 11: 28 in defining his role of writer as »ein guter Freund, Berather und Tröster der Mühselig-beladenen,«[27] a role Spielhagen ascribed to himself: »So kommt denn her zu mir, ihr Mühseligen und Beladenen!« (*BT*, 256) and repeated as an example to other writers: »Die mühselig ihr seid und beladen, o, kommt zu mir alle!« (*NG*, 197). In this case, however, it is interesting to see a similar concept of authorial intention. It reminds us of the large areas of agreement that we could find in the attitudes of both men.

Both men, for example, expressed irritation at the rise of Naturalism while sometimes trying to repress an intolerance that made them uncomfortable. The success of Ibsen in particular caused both to complain of foreign influences. Even in his historical novel *Hastenbeck* Raabe found occasion to complain of the Germans being hypnotized »durch nordisches Irren- und Krankenhäuslertum« as well as succumbing to »Pariser Gassenkot« (*BA*, 20: 29–30), while Spielhagen grumbled about Ibsen repeatedly and in his last book mounted a by then hoary complaint about the success of foreign literature »in dem nachahmungssüchtigen Deutschland« (*AW*, 44). Raabe was irritated by Hauptmann's *Die versunkene Glocke* (*BA*, E 4: 239) much as Spielhagen was, as I mentioned in Chapter 4. However, there were also positive points of contact. An important one is their shared opposition to the distortion of Immermann's *Münchhausen* by excising out of it the traditional rural setting as *Der Oberhof*, thus repressing its satirical dimension. Raabe wrote to Heyse: »daß das edle deutsche Volk sich den Münchhausen aus dem Münchhausen, um ihn sich mundgerecht zu machen, gestrichen hat, oder hat streichen lassen.«[28] At an early date, Spielhagen found »daß die litterarisch so instruktiven satirischen Partien in Immermanns Münchhausen mich weit mehr interessierten als die berühmte Dorfgeschichte, deren Wert mir nebenbei auch jetzt ein wenig überschätzt scheint« (*FuE*, 1: 328). This is a bit of evidence that German literary culture might well have benefited if the two writers had been more collegial.

---

[26] See Sammons, *Wilhelm Raabe*, 6, 21. The phrase appears also in *Problematische Naturen* (*AR*, 1, 1: 509).
[27] Raabe to Klara Zetkin, March 10, 1908, *BA*, E 2: 477.
[28] To Heyse, February 26, 1875, *BA*, E 2: 180.

The occasional comparisons of Raabe with Spielhagen in the past have not been very productive. There was a report that Spielhagen's biographer Hans Henning gave a lecture on the topic in 1914, in which he compared *Alte Nester* with *In Reih' und Glied.* The terms of such a comparison seem by no means obvious, especially as it juxtaposes one of Raabe's most mature novels with one of Spielhagen's least mature. The summary, with its stress on their shared rootedness in »Heimat,« makes the talk sound trite and vague.[29] In his biography Henning mentions Raabe only in a long list of personalities with whom Spielhagen is said to have been intimately acquainted, but I see no evidence of this.[30] A later essay compared the roughly contemporaneous *Hungerpastor* with *Problematische Naturen,* finding numerous similarities in character types, but otherwise disparaging Spielhagen's trivial novelistic machinery, ascribed to an inheritance from the Baroque via Ludwig Tieck, Jean Paul, Hoffmann, and the Frenchified Gutzkow, influences that Raabe left behind in a revival of German idealism and true Goethean *Humanität.* Spielhagen is said to be unreflectively confined in the spirit of Young Germany, while Raabe saw through it to »das Unbedingte der jüdischen Rasse.« Quite apart from the Nazified gibberish, a reading between the lines indicates, as usual, that the objection to Spielhagen is to his sociocritical spirit, and, particularly here, to his hostility to the aristocracy.[31]

The lack of solidarity between Raabe and Spielhagen is a product of personality differences as well as external determinants, although I think one should not ascribe too much explanatory power to notions about the »capitalist mode of literary production« or »the literary work as commodity,« because both writers had friendly and sometimes warm relations with colleagues and competitors, Spielhagen, to be sure, rather more than Raabe. The icy silence between the two of them is rather a special case. In retrospect it is to be regretted, as they were truly colleagues in substantial ways, for all that they would not acknowledge it. It has been difficult to see this

---

[29] Report of the Braunschweig-Wolfenbüttel chapter, *Mitteilungen für die Gesellschaft der Freunde Wilhelm Raabes* 4 (1914): 27. I have not found that this lecture was published.

[30] Henning, *Friedrich Spielhagen,* 135–36.

[31] Gerhard Köttgen, »Raabe und Spielhagen,« *Mitteilungen für die Gesellschaft der Freunde Wilhelm Raabes* 33, No. 1 (1943): 20–27. As an example of the quality of Köttgen's thinking, he declares »das Ideal ist, daß Adel und Bürgertum zu einer einheitlichen Gesellschaft verschmelzen, die fähig wäre, einen liberalen Staat zu tragen« and »ein Roman ohne Adel wäre ebenso unmöglich wie die Tragödie des Barock ohne Könige« (23).

because of the veil of obscurity that has been thrown over Spielhagen's career and his place in literary culture. A renewed spirit of inquiry into German literary life in the age of realism might go some way toward repairing this breach retrospectively and counterfactually.

Bibliography: Works Cited and Consulted

Albisetti, James C. *Schooling German Girls and Women: Secondary and Higher Education in the Nineteenth Century.* Princeton: Princeton UP, 1988.

Alker, Ernst. *Die deutsche Literatur im 19. Jahrhundert (1832–1914).* 3rd edn. Stuttgart: Kröner, 1969.

Allgemeine deutsche Real-Encyklopädie für die gebildeten Ständen. Conversations-Lexikon. 11th edn. Leipzig: Brockhaus, 1864–68.

Alter, Robert. *Partial Magic: The Novel as a Self-Conscious Genre.* Berkeley, Los Angeles, and London: California UP, 1975.

Anderson, Alexander Robinson. »Spielhagen's Problematical Heroes.« Diss. Brown University, 1962.

[Anonymous]. »Friedrich Spielhagen.« *Atlantic Monthly* 70 (1892): 402–07 [review of *Finder und Erfinder,* vol. 2].

– »Friedrich Spielhagen.« *The Dial* 50 (1911): 199–201.

– »Friedrich Spielhagen, A Mirror of German Life.« *American Review of Reviews* 43 (1911): 622–23.

– [Review of *Hammer and Anvil*]. *Atlantic Monthly* 26 (1870): 636–37.

– [Review of *Sturmflut*]. *Atlantic Monthly* 40 (1877): 383.

Auerbach, Berthold. *Schriften.* 2nd ser. Stuttgart: Cotta, 1871.

Auerbach, Erich. *Mimesis: The Representation of Reality in Western Literature.* Tr. Willard Trask. Garden City, New York: Doubleday, 1953.

Bachleitner, Norbert. *Der englische und französische Sozialroman des 19. Jahrhunderts und seine Rezeption in Deutschland.* Amsterdam and Atlanta: Rodopi, 1993.

– ed. *Quellen zur Rezeption des englischen und französischen Romans in Deutschland und Österreich im 19. Jahrhundert.* Tübingen: Niemeyer, 1990.

Bänsch, Dorothea. »Die Bibliothek Wilhelm Raabes nach Sachgebieten geordnet.« *Jahrbuch der Raabe-Gesellschaft* (1970): 87–165.

Bahr, Hermann. »Friedrich Spielhagen.« *Der Antisemitismus. Ein internationales Interview,* ed. Hermann Greive. Königstein: Jüdischer Verlag, 1979, 17–19.

Bahktin, M. M. *The Dialogic Imagination: Four Essays.* Ed. Michael Holquist. Austin: Texas UP, 1981.

Bartlett, John. *Familiar Quotations.* 11th edn. Ed. Christopher Morley and Louella D. Everett. Garden City, New Jersey: Garden City Publishing, 1944.

Becker, Sabina. »Literatur als ›Psychographie.‹ Entwürfe weiblicher Identität in Theodor Fontanes Romanen.« *»Realismus«? Zur deutschen Prosa-Literatur des 19. Jahrhunderts,* ed. Norbert Oellers and Hartmut Steinecke. *Zeitschrift für deutsche Philologie,* 120 (2001), Sonderheft: 90–111.

Berghahn, Klaus L. »Ein klassischer Chiasmus: Goethe und die Juden, die Juden und Goethe.« *Goethe Yearbook* 10 (2001): 203–21.

Berman, Harold. »Friedrich Spielhagen: The Novelist of Democracy.« *Twentieth Century Magazine* 4 (1911): 347–49.

Bernd, Clifford Albrecht. *Poetic Realism in Scandinavia and Central Europe 1820–1895.* Columbia, South Carolina: Camden House, 1995.

Bettelheim, Anton. *Berthold Auerbach. Der Mann – Sein Werk – Sein Nachlaß.* Stuttgart and Berlin: Cotta, 1907.

Bieber, Hugo. *Der Kampf um die Tradition. Die deutsche Dichtung im europäischen Geistesleben 1830–1880.* Stuttgart: Metzler, 1928.

Bleibtreu, Carl. *Revolution der Literatur*, ed. Johannes J. Braakenburg. Tübingen: Niemeyer, 1973.

Boyesen, Hjalmar Hjorth. *Essays on German Literature.* New York: Scribner's, 1892.

– »Literarisches Leben in den Vereinigten Staaten.« *Westermanns Monatshefte* 48 (April-September, 1880): 447–57; 50 (April-September, 1881): 383–93.

– [Review of *Ultimo*]. *North American Review* 120 (January-April, 1875): 196–200.

– *Tales from Two Hemispheres.* Boston: Osgood, 1877.

Brahm, Otto. [Review of *Uhlenhans*]. *Deutsche Rundschau* 38 (1884): 310–11.

Bramsted, Ernest K. *Aristocracy and the Middle-Classes in Germany: Social Types in German Literature 1830–1900.* Rev. edn. Chicago and London: Chicago UP, 1964.

Brecht, Bertolt. *Werke. Große kommentierte Berliner und Frankfurter Ausgabe.* Ed. Werner Hecht, Jan Knopf, Werner Mittenzwei, and Klaus-Detlef Müller. Berlin and Weimar: Aufbau; Frankfurt am Main: Suhrkamp, 1989–2000.

Brown, Frederick. *Zola: A Life.* New York: Farrar, Straus and Giroux, 1995.

Browne, Wm. Hand. »Spielhagen's Novels.« *New Eclectic Magazine* 7 (1870): 211–19.

Browning, Robert. *The Poems and Plays.* Ed. Saxe Commins. New York: Modern Library, 1934.

Büsch, Otto, ed. *Friedrich Wilhelm IV. in seiner Zeit. Beiträge eines Colloquiums.* Berlin: Colloquium, 1987.

Burrow, J. W. *The Crisis of Reason: European Thought, 1848–1914.* New Haven and London: Yale UP, 2000.

Chamisso, Adelbert von. *Sämtliche Werke.* Ed. Jost Perfahl. Munich: Winkler, 1975.

Chance, Julia. See Gordon, Julien.

Charbon, Rémy. »Der Homo œconomicus in der Literatur von 1830 bis zur Reichsgründung.« *Der literarische Homo œconomicus. Vom Märchenhelden zum Manager. Beiträge zum Ökonomieverständnis in der Literatur*, ed. Werner Wunderlich. Bern and Stuttgart: Paul, 1989, 135–52.

Coar, John Firman. *Studies in German Literature in the 19th Century.* New York: Macmillan, 1903.

Cobb, Palmer. »Edgar Allan Poe and Friedrich Spielhagen. Their Theory of the Short Story.« *Modern Language Notes* 25 (1910): 67–72.

Cosnier, Colette. *Marie Bashkirtseff. Un portrait sans retouches.* Paris: Horay, 1985.

Cruger, Julia van Rensselaer. See Gordon, Julien.

Daudet, Alphonse. *Fromont jeune et Risler aîné, mœurs parisiennes.* Paris: Charpentier, 1874.

– *Jack, mœurs contemporaines.* Paris: Dentu, 1876

Demetz, Peter. *Formen des Realismus: Theodor Fontane. Kritische Untersuchungen.* Munich: Hanser, 1964.

– *Marx, Engels and the Poets: Origins of Marxist Literary Criticism.* Tr. Jeffrey L. Sammons. Chicago and London: Chicago UP, 1967.

Doderer, Heimito von. *Grundlagen und Funktion des Romans.* Nuremberg: Glock und Lutz, 1959.

Dresch, J. *Le Roman social en Allemagne (1850–1900). Gutzkow – Freytag – Spielhagen – Fontane.* Paris: Alcan, 1913.

Drews, Axel, and Ita Gerhard. »Wissen, Kollektivsymbolik und Literatur am Beispiel von Friedrich Spielhagens ›Sturmflut.‹« *Bürgerlicher Realismus und Gründerzeit 1848–1890.* Hansers Sozialgeschichte der deutschen Literatur vom 16. Jahrhundert bis zur Gegenwart, vol. 6, ed. Edward McInnes and Gerhard Plumpe. Munich: Hanser, 1996, 708–28.

Dumas, Alexandre, fils. *Affair Clémenceau. Mémoire de l'accusé.* Paris: Calman-Lévy, [1909].

Elias, Norbert. *The Germans: Power Struggles and the Development of Habitus in the Nineteenth and Twentieth Centuries.* Ed. Michael Schröter. New York: Columbia UP, 1996.

Emerson, Ralph Waldo. *The Works of Ralph Waldo Emerson.* Philadelphia: Morris, 1906.

Engel, Eduard. »Stenographischer Bericht über die Gerichtsverhandlungen im Prozesse: ›Angela.‹ Roman von Friedrich Spielhagen.« *Magazin für die Literatur des In- und Auslandes* 50 (1881): 399–404, 413–17.

Erler, Gotthard. »Die Ardenne-Affäre bei Fontane und Spielhagen.« *Zur Entstehungs und Wirkungsgeschichte Fontanescher Romane. Fontane-Blätter,* Sonderheft (1969): 64–68.

Ermatinger, Emil. *Gottfried Kellers Leben.* Stuttgart and Berlin: Cotta, 1924.

Fehse, Wilhelm. *Wilhelm Raabe. Sein Leben und seine Werke.* Braunschweig: Vieweg, 1937.

Ferguson, Niall. *The World's Banker: The History of the House of Rothschild.* London: Weidenfeld & Nicolson, 1998.

Festausschuss der Spielhagen-Feier, ed. *Friedrich Spielhagen. Dem Meister des deutschen Romans zu seinem 70. Geburtstage von Freunden und Jüngern gewidmet.* Leipzig: Staackmann, 1899.

Feuillet, Octave. *Honneur d'artiste.* Paris: Calmann Lévy, 1890.

Fischer-Bosshardt, Andrea. *Anfänge der modernen Erzählkunst. Untersuchungen zu Friedrich Spielhagens theoretischem und literarischem Werk.* Bern, Frankfurt am Main, New York, and Paris: Peter Lang, 1988.

Fleischhack, Ernst. *Bibliographie Ferdinand Freiligrath 1829–1990.* Bielefeld: Aisthesis, 1993.

Fontane, Theodor. *Briefe.* Ed. Walter Keitel and Helmuth Nürnberger. Munich: Hanser, 1976–94.

– *Sämtliche Werke.* Ed. Edgar Gross, Kurt Schreinert, et al. Munich: Nymphenburger, 1959–75.

– *Sämtliche Werke. Aufsätze, Kritiken, Erinnerungen.* Ed. Walter Keitel and Helmuth Nürnberger. Munich: Hanser, 1968–86.

Fontane-Handbuch, ed. Christian Grawe and Helmuth Nürnberger. [Stuttgart]: Kröner, 2000.

Francke, Kuno. *Weltbürgertum in der deutschen Literatur von Herder bis Nietzsche.* Berlin: Weidmann, 1928.

Franke, Manfred. *Leben und Roman der Elisabeth von Ardenne, Fontanes »Effi Briest.«* Düsseldorf: Droste, 1994.

Franzmann, Bodo, et al., eds. *Handbuch Lesen.* Munich: Sauer, 1999.

Fredrickson, Robert S. *Hjalmar Hjorth Boyesen.* Boston: Twayne, 1980.

Freiligrath, Ferdinand. *Englische Gedichte aus neuerer Zeit.* Stuttgart and Tübingen: Cotta, 1846.

– *Sämtliche Werke in zehn Bänden.* Ed. Ludwig Schröder. Leipzig: Hesse, [1907].

Frevert, Ute. *Ehrenmänner. Das Duell in der bürgerlichen Gesellschaft.* Munich: Beck, 1991.

Frey, John R. »Author-Intrusion in the Narrative: German Theory and Some Modern Examples.« *Germanic Review* 23 (1948): 274–89.

Freytag, Gustav. *Briefe an seine Gattin.* Ed. Hermance Strakosch-Freytag and Curt L. Walter-van der Bleek. Berlin: Borngräber, 1912.

Friedemann, Käte. *Die Rolle des Erzählers in der Epik.* Berlin: Haessel, 1910; reprint Darmstadt: Wissenschaftliche Buchgesellschaft, 1965.

Frierson, William C. »The English Controversy on Realism in Fiction 1885–1895.« *Publications of the Modern Language Society of America* 43 (1928): 533–50.

[Fritsche, Emil]. »Sturmflut.« *Im Neuen Reich* 7, no. 1 (1877): 372–84.

Fuld, Werner. *Wilhelm Raabe. Eine Biographie.* Munich: Hanser, 1993.

Furst, Lilian R. *All is True: The Claims and Strategies of Realist Fiction.* Durham, North Carolina and London: Duke UP, 1995.

Gasson, Andrew. *Wilkie Collins: An Illustrated Guide.* Oxford and New York: Oxford UP, 1998.

Geissler, Rolf. »Verspielte Realitätserkenntnis. Zum Problem der objektiven Darstellung in Friedrich Spielhagens *Hammer und Amboß.*« *Deutsche Vierteljahrsschrift* 52 (1978): 496–510.

Gelber, Mark H. *Melancholy Pride: Nation, Race, and Gender in the German Literature of Cultural Zionism.* Tübingen: Niemeyer, 2000.

Geller, Martha. *Friedrich Spielhagens Theorie und Praxis des Romans.* Berlin: Grote, 1917.

Gesamtverzeichnis des deutschsprachigen Schrifttums: 1700–1910. Ed. Peter Geils and Willi Gorzny, et al. Munich, New York, London, and Paris: Saur, 1979–87.

Gheorgiu, Octavian. *Les Romans de Dumas Fils.* Paris: Presses Universitaires de France, [1935].

Glasrud, Clarence A. *Hjalmar Hjorth Boyesen.* Northfield, Minnesota: Norwegian-American Historical Association, 1963.

Goessl, Alfred F. »Die Darstellung des Adels in Prosaschriften Friedrich Spielhagens.« Diss. Tulane University, 1966.

Goethe, Johann Wolfgang von. *Romane und Novellen.* Ed. Benno von Wiese and Erich Trunz. *Schriften zur Kunst, Schriften zur Literatur, Maximen und Reflexionen.* Ed. Herbert von Einem and Hans Joachim Schrimpf. *Romane und Novellen.* Ed. Erich Trunz. *Werke* (Hamburger Ausgabe), vols. 6, 12, 7. 3rd edn. Hamburg: Wegner, 1958, 1957.

Goethes Gespräche, ed. Flodoard von Biedermann et al. Leipzig: Biedermann, 1909–11.

Göttsche, Dirk. *Zeit im Roman. Literarische Zeitreflexion und die Geschichte des Zeitromans im späten 18. und im 19. Jahrhundert.* Munich: Fink, 2001.

– *Zeitreflexion und Zeitkritik im Werk Wilhelm Raabes.* Würzburg: Königshausen & Neumann, 2000.

Gordon, Julien. *A Diplomat's Diary.* Philadelphia: Lippincott, 1890.

– *Fräulein Reseda. Ein Mann der Erfolge.* Stuttgart: Engelhorn, 1891.

– *Mademoise Réséda.* Philadelphia: Lippincott, 1891.

– »Some Letters to Julien Gordon.« *Lippincott's Monthly Magazine* 47 (January-June, 1891): 652–57.

Griswold, Rufus Wilmot. *The Poets and Poetry of America with an Historical Introduction.* Philadelphia: Carey and Hart, 1842.

Grossman, Jeffrey A. *The Discourse on Yiddish in Germany from the Enlightenment to the Second Empire.* Columbia, South Carolina: Camden House, 2000.

Grünzweig, Walter. *Constructing the German Walt Whitman.* Iowa City: Iowa UP, 1995.

Haas, Rosemarie. »Raabe, der Rabe, ›The Raven.‹ Beobachtungen zur Intertextualität in Raabes Erzählung ›Das Odfeld.‹« *Jahrbuch der Raabe-Gesellschaft* (1992): 139–64.

Hädecke, Wolfgang. *Poeten und Maschinen. Deutsche Dichter als Zeugen der Industrialisierung.* Munich and Vienna: Hanser, 1993.

Hamann, Richard, and Jost Hermand. *Deutsche Kunst und Kultur von der Gründerzeit bis zum Expressionismus.* Vol. 1: *Gründerzeit.* Berlin: Akademie, 1965.

Han, Il-Sop. »Spielhagens Ich-Roman-Theorie.« Diss. Heidelberg, 1977.

Hardin, George A., with Frank H. Willard. *History of Herkimer County New York.* Syracuse: Mason, 1893.

Harris, James F. *A Study in the Theory and Practice of German Liberalism: Eduard Lasker, 1829–1884.* Lanham, Maryland, New York, and London: UP of America, 1984.

Hart, Heinrich, and Julius. *Kritische Waffengänge.* Leipzig: Wigand, 1882–84. Reprint, ed. Mark Boulby. Classics in Germanic Literatures and Philosophy, ed. Wolfgang F. Taraba. New York and London: Johnson Reprint, 1969.

Hauff, Gustav. [Review of *In Reih' und Glied*]. *Literaturkritik. Eine Textdokumentation zur Geschichte einer literarischen Gattung,* ed. Alfred Estermann. Vol. 4, *1848–1870,* ed. Peter Uwe Hohendahl. Vaduz: Topos, 1984, 540–46.

Hebbel, Friedrich. *Sämtliche Werke.* Ed. Richard Maria Werner. Berlin: Behr, 1901–07.

Heim, Karl. »Wilhelm Raabe und das Publikum.« Diss. Tübingen, 1953.

Hein, Jürgen. *Dorfgeschichte.* Stuttgart: Metzler, 1976.

Heine, Heinrich. *Säkularausgabe.* Ed. Nationale Forschungs- und Gedenkstätten der klassischen deutschen Literatur in Weimar and Centre National de la Recherche Scientifique in Paris. Berlin and Paris: Akademie and Editions du CNRS, 1970–.

– *Sämtliche Schriften.* Ed. Klaus Briegleb et al. Munich: Hanser, 1968–76.

Hellmann, Winfried. »Objektivität, Subjektivität und Erzählkunst. Zur Romantheorie Friedrich Spielhagens.« *Deutsche Romantheorien,* ed. Reinhold Grimm. Frankfurt am Main and Bonn: Athenäum, 1968, 165–217.

Henkel, Gabriele. »Friedrich Spielhagen (1829–1911).« *Studien zur Privatbibliothek Wilhelm Raabes. Vom »wirklichen Autor,« von Zeitgenossen und »ächten Dichtern.«* Braunschweig: Stadtbibliothek, 1997, 115–22.

– »Friedrich Spielhagen, *Hammer und Amboß* (1869).« *Geräuschwelten im deutschen Zeitroman. Epische Darstellung und poetologische Bedeutung von der Romantik bis zum Naturalismus.* Wiesbaden: Harrassowitz, 1996.

Henning, Hans. *Friedrich Spielhagen.* Leipzig: Staackmann, 1910.

– »Wilhelm Raabe und Friedrich Spielhagen« [summary]. *Mitteilungen für die Gesellschaft der Freunde Wilhelm Raabes* 4 (1914): 27.

Herminghouse, Patricia B. »Schloß oder Fabrik? Zur Problematik der Adelsdarstellung im Roman des Nachmärz.« *Legitimationskrisen des deutschen Adels 1200–1900,* ed. Peter Uwe Hohendahl and Paul Michael Lützeler. Stuttgart: Metzler, 1979, 245–61.

Herzfeld, Hans. *Deutschland und das geschlagene Frankreich 1871–1873. Friedensschluß Kriegsentschädigung Besatzungszeit.* Berlin: Deutsche Verlagsgesellschaft für Politik und Geschichte, 1924.

Hettche, Walter. »Nach alter Melodie: Die Gedichte von Julius Rodenberg, Wilhelm Jensen und Paul Heyse zum 70. Geburtstag Wilhelm Raabes.« *Jahrbuch der Raabe-Gesellschaft* (1999): 144–56.

Hewett-Thayer, Harvey W. »Ferdinand Lassalle in the Novels of Spielhagen and Meredith.« *Germanic Review* 19 (1944): 186–96.

Heyse, Paul. *Gesammelte Werke.* Berlin: Hertz, 1872–1914.

Hillman, Roger. »Friedrich Spielhagen, *Problematische Naturen.*« *Zeitroman: The Novel and Society in Germany 1830–1900.* Bern, Frankfurt am Main, and New York: Peter Lang, 1983, 47–65.

Hinderer, Walter. »›Die Schornsteine müssen gestürzt werden, denn sie verpesten die Luft.‹ Diskurse über Industrialisierung und Natur im deutschen Roman des 19. Jahrhunderts.« *Literatur und Demokratie. Festschrift für Hartmut Steinecke zum 60. Geburtstag,* ed. Alo Allkemper and Norbert Otto Eke. Berlin: Erich Schmidt, 2000), 99–115.

Höppner, Wolfgang. *Das »Ererbte, Erlebte und Erlernte« im Werk Wilhelm Scherers. Ein Beitrag zur Geschichte der Germanistik.* Cologne, Weimar, and Vienna: Böhlau, 1993.

Hofmannsthal, Hugo von. *Gesammelte Werke. Reden und Aufsätze I 1891–1913.* Ed. Bernd Schoeller with Rudolf Hirsch. Frankfurt am Main: Fischer Taschenbuch Verlag, 1979.

Hoppe, Karl. »Aphorismen Raabes chronologisch geordnet.« *Jahrbuch der Raabe-Gesellschaft* (1960): 94–139.

Houben, H. H. »Spielhagen, Friedrich.« *Verbotene Literatur von der klassischen Zeit bis zur Gegenwart.* Berlin: Rowohlt, 1924, Bremen, Schünemann, 1928. Reprint Hildesheim: Olms, 1965. 1: 574–77.

Hovanec, Evelyn A. *Henry James and Germany.* Amsterdam: Rodopi, 1979.

Hughes, Arthur M. »Wilhelm von Humboldt's Influence on Spielhagen's Esthetics.« *Germanic Review* 5 (1930): 211–24.

Humboldt, Wilhelm von. *Werke in fünf Bänden.* Ed. Andreas Flitner and Klaus Giel. Stuttgart: Cotta, 1960–81.

Humphrey, Richard. »The Napoleonic Wars in the Historical Fiction of the *Gründerjahre:* Fontane and his Contemporaries in European Perspective.« *Fact and Fiction: German History and Literature 1848–1924.* ed. Gisela Brude-Firnau and Karin J. MacHardy. Tübingen: Francke, 1990, 111–22.

Immermann, Karl. *Werke in fünf Bänden.* Ed. Benno von Wiese et al. Frankfurt am Main: Athenäum, 1971–77.

Jackson, Paul. *Bürgerliche Arbeit und Romanwirklichkeit. Studien zur Berufsproblematik in Romanen des deutschen Realismus.* Frankfurt am Main: Rita G. Fischer, 1981.

James, Henry. *The Complete Tales,* ed. Leon Edel. Philadelphia and New York: Lippincott, 1963.

Jean Paul. *Werke.* Ed. Norbert Miller. Munich: Hanser, 1960–63.

Kafitz, Dieter. *Figurenkonstellation als Mittel der Wirklichkeitserfassung. Dargestellt an Romanen der zweiten Hälfte des 19. Jahrhunderts: Freytag · Spielhagen · Fontane · Raabe.* Kronberg: Athenäum, 1978.

Kapp, Friedrich. *Geschichte der deutschen Einwanderung in Amerika.* Vol. 1: *Die Deutschen im Staate New York bis zum Anfang des neunzehnten Jahrhunderts.* Leipzig: Quandt & Händel, 1868.

Karpeles, Gustav. *Friedrich Spielhagen. Ein literarischer Essay.* Leipzig: Staackmann, 1889.

Keiderling, Thomas. »Leipzig als Vermittlungs- und Produktionszentrum englischsprachiger Literatur zwischen 1815 und 1914.« *Beiträge zur Rezeption der britischen und irischen Literatur des 19. Jahrhunderts im deutschsprachigen Raum*, ed. Norbert Bachleitner. Amsterdam and Atlanta: Rodopi, 2000, 3–76.

Keiter, Heinrich, and Tony Kellen. *Der Roman. Theorie und Technik des Romans und der erzählenden Dichtung, nebst einer geschichtlichen Einleitung.* 4th edn. Essen: Fredebeul & Koenen, 1912.

Keller, Gottfried. *Briefe 1861–1890.* Ed. Emil Ermatinger. Stuttgart and Berlin: Cotta, 1925.
– *Sämtliche Werke.* Ed. Thomas Böning et al. Frankfurt am Main: Deutscher Klassiker Verlag, 1985–96.

Klatt, Gudrun, and Hans Heinrich Klatt. »Zur Romantheorie Friedrich Spielhagens.« *Zeitschrift für Germanistik* 10 (1989): 34–44.

Klatt, Hans Heinrich. »Friedrich Spielhagen. Republikaner im Herzen.« *Gestalten der Bismarckzeit*, vol. 2, ed. Gustav Seeber. Berlin: Akademie, 1986, 174–91.

Klemperer, Victor. *Curriculum Vitae. Jugend um 1900.* Berlin: Siedler, 1989.
– »Die Juden in Spielhagens Werken. (Eine Studie zu seinem achtzigsten Geburtstag.)« *Allgemeine Zeitung des Judentums* 73 (1908–09): 104–106, 116–18.
– *Die Zeitromane Friedrich Spielhagens und ihre Wurzeln.* Forschungen zur neueren Literaturgeschichte, ed. Franz Muncker, vol. 43. Weimar: Duncker, 1913.

Kloster, Elfriede. »Die Technik der Gesellschaftsszene in den Romanen Friedrich Spielhagens und Theodor Fontanes.« Diss. Frankfurt am Main, [1944].

Knodt, Manfred. *Ernst Ludwig Großherzog von Hessen und bei Rhein. Sein Leben und seine Zeit.* Darmstadt: Schlapp, 1978.

Köttgen, Gerhard. »Raabe und Spielhagen.« *Mitteilungen für die Gesellschaft der Freunde Wilhelm Raabes* 33 (1943): 20–27.

Kohl, Stephan. *Realismus. Theorie und Geschichte.* Munich: Fink, 1977.

Kolbe, Hans. *Wilhelm Raabe. Vom Entwicklungs- zum Desillusionierungsroman.* Berlin: Akademie, 1981.

Kolbe, Jürgen. *Goethes »Wahlverwandtschaften« und der Roman des 19. Jahrhunderts.* Stuttgart, Berlin, Cologne, and Mainz: Kohlhammer, 1968.

Kraus, Karl. *Literatur und Lüge.* Vienna: Verlag »Die Fackel,« 1929.

Kreyssig, Fr. *Vorlesungen über den Deutschen Roman der Gegenwart. Literar- und culturhistorische Studien.* Berlin: Nicolia, 1871.

Krumpelmann, John T. *Bayard Taylor and German Letters.* Hamburg: Cram, de Gruyter, 1959.

Kuczynski, Jürgen. »Friedrich Spielhagen.« *Gestalten und Werke. Soziologische Studien zur deutschen Literatur*, vol. 1. Berlin and Weimar: Aufbau, 1969, 194–203.

Laage, Karl Ernst. *Theodor Storm Biographie.* Heide: Boyens, 1999.

Lamers, Henrike. *Held oder Welt? Zum Romanwerk Friedrich Spielhagens.* Bonn: Bouvier, 1991.

Lees, Andrew. *Revolution and Reflection: Intellectual Change in Germany during the 1850's.* The Hague: Nijhoff, 1974.

Lensing, Leo A. »Naturalismus, Religion und Sexualität. Zur Frage der Auseinandersetzung mit Zola in Wilhelm Raabes *Unruhige Gäste*.« *Jahrbuch der Raabe-Gesellschaft* (1988): 145–67.

Link, Jürgen. *Elementare Literatur und generative Diskursanalyse.* Munich: Fink, 1983.

Löwenthal, Leo. *Erzählkunst und Gesellschaft in der deutschen Literatur des 19. Jahrhunderts. Die Gesellschaftsproblematik in der deutschen Literatur des 19. Jahrhunderts.* Neuwied and Berlin: Luchterhand, 1971.

Longfellow, Henry Wadsworth. *The Complete Poetical Works.* New York: Houghton Mifflin; Cambridge: Riverside Press, 1902.

Lubbock, Percy. *The Craft of Fiction.* New York: Viking, 1957.

Luck, Rätus. *Gottfried Keller als Literaturkritiker.* Bern and Munich: Francke, 1970.

Lundberg, E. *Strafgesetzbuch für das Deutsche Reich vom 15. Mai 1871.* Leipzig: no publ., [1880].

Mann, Thomas. *Gesammelte Werke in zwölf Bänden.* [Frankfurt am Main]: S. Fischer, 1960.

Martini, Fritz. *Deutsche Literatur im bürgerlichen Realismus 1848–1898.* 2nd edn. Stuttgart: Metzler, 1964.

Marx, Karl, and Friedrich Engels. *Werke.* Ed. Institut für Marxismus-Leninismus beim ZK der SED. Berlin: Dietz, 1956–68.

– *Über Kunst und Literatur.* Ed. Manfred Kliem. Berlin: Dietz, 1967.

Mauthner, Fritz. *Nach berühmten Mustern. Parodistische Studien.* 6th edn. Stuttgart: Spemann, [1878].

Mayer, Gerhart. *Der deutsche Bildungsroman. Von der Aufklärung bis zur Gegenwart.* Stuttgart: Metzler, 1992.

Mayer, Hans. *Von Lessing bis Thomas Mann. Wandlungen der bürgerlichen Literatur in Deutschland.* Pfullingen: Neske, 1959.

McAleer, Kevin. »Les Belles Dames Sans Merci.« *Dueling: The Cult of Honor in Fin-de-siècle Germany.* Princeton: Princeton UP, 1994, 159–81.

– »Les Belles Dames Sans Merci: Woman and the Duel in Fin-de-Siècle Germany.« *Tel Aviver Jahrbuch für deutsche Geschichte* 21 (1992): 69–97.

Mehring, Franz. »Friedrich Spielhagen.« *Beiträge zur Literaturgeschichte*, ed. Walter Heist. Berlin: Weiss, 1948, 216–17.

Mensch, Ella. »Erinnerungen an Friedrich Spielhagen.« *Westermanns Monatshefte* 110 (1911): 356–60.

– ed. *Er lebt noch immer! Ein Spielhagen-Revier.* Leipzig: Staackmann, 1929.

Merian, Hans. *Die sogenannten Jungdeutschen in unserer zeitgenössischen Litteratur. Ein Vortrag gehalten am 20. Februar 1888 in Leipzig.* Leipzig: Werther, [1889].

Meyer, Richard M. *Die deutsche Literatur des Neunzehnten Jahrhunderts.* Volksausgabe. Berlin: Bondi, 1912.

Meyer-Krentler, Eckhardt. *»Unterm Strich.« Literarischer Markt, Trivialität und Romankunst in Raabes »Der Lar.«* Paderborn, Munich, Vienna, and Zurich: Schöningh, 1986.

Meyers Großes Konversations-Lexikon. 6th edn. Leipzig and Vienna: Bibliographisches Institut, 1902–09.

Michelet, Jules. *La Mer.* 2nd edn. Paris: Hachette, 1861.

– *Œuvres complètes.* Ed. Paul Viallaneix et al. Paris: Flammarion, 1971–82.

Mielke, Hellmuth. *Der Deutsche Roman des 19. Jahrhunderts.* 3rd edn. Berlin: Schwetschke, 1898.

Mitchell, Allan. *The German Influence in France after 1870: The Formation of the French Republic.* Chapel Hill: North Carolina UP, 1979.

– *The Great Train Race: Railways and the Franco-German Rivalry, 1815–1914.* New York and Oxford: Berghahn, 2000.

Mitchell, McBurney. »Poe and Spielhagen: Novelle and Short-Story.« *Modern Language Notes* 29 (1914): 36–41.

Mojem, Hellmuth. »Literaturbetrieb und literarisches Selbstverständnis: Der Briefwechsel Wilhelm Raabes mit Eduard Engel.« *Jahrbuch der Raabe-Gesellschaft* (1995): 27–87.

Morsier, Edouard de. »Friedrich Spielhagen.« *Romanciers allemandes contemporains.* Paris: Perrin, 1890, 3–121.

Müller, Egbert, ed. *Bismarck im Urteil seiner Zeitgenossen. Hundert Gutachten von Freund und Feind.* Berlin: Verlag der Gegenwart, n. d. [ca. 1898].

Müller-Donges, Christa. *Das Novellenwerk Friedrich Spielhagens in seiner Entwicklung zwischen 1851 und 1899.* Marburg: Elwert, 1970.

National Cyclopaedia of American Biography. Clifton, New Jersey: White, 1893- .

Neuhaus, Volker. »Der Unterhaltungsroman im 19. Jahrhundert.« *Handbuch des deutschen Romans,* ed. Helmut Koopmann. Düsseldorf: Bagel, 1983, 404–17.

– »Friedrich Spielhagen – Critic of Bismarck's Empire.« *1870/71 – 1989/90: German Unifications and the Change of Literary Discourse,* ed. Walter Pape. Berlin and New York: de Gruyter, 1993, 135–43.

Neumann, Bernd. »Friedrich Spielhagen: Sturmflut (1877). Die ›Gründerjahre‹ als die ›Signatur des Jahrhunderts.‹« *Romane und Erzählungen des Bürgerlichen Realismus: Neue Interpretationen,* ed. Horst Denkler. Stuttgart: Reclam, 1980, 260–73.

Nolin, Bertil. *Den gode Europén. Studier i Georg Brandes' idéutveckling 1871–1893 med speciell hänsyn till hans förhållende till tysk, engelsk, slavisk och fransk litteratur.* [Stockholm]: Svenska Bokförlaget / Norsteds, 1965.

Offenbach, Jacques. *La Périchole.* Paris: Joubert, n. d.

Ohl, Hubert. »Spielhagens Spätwerk und das Fin de Siècle. Figuren und Motive.« *›Realismus‹? Zur deutschen Prosa-Literatur des 19. Jahrhunderts,* ed. Norbert Oellers and Hartmut Steinecke. *Zeitschrift für deutsche Philologie* 120 (2001), Sonderheft: 177–97.

Ohnet, Georges. *Serge Panine.* Paris: Ollendorff, 1881.

Oncken, Wilhelm. *Das Zeitalter des Kaisers Wilhelm. Allgemeine Geschichte in Einzeldarstellungen. Vierte Hauptabtheilung. Sechster Theil.* Berlin: Grote, 1890–92.

Orr, Linda. *Jules Michelet: Nature, History, and Language.* Ithaca and London: Cornell UP, 1976.

Ott, Ulrich, ed. *Literatur im Industriezeitalter. Eine Ausstellung des Deutschen Literaturarchivs im Schiller-Nationalmuseum.* Marbach am Neckar: Deutsche Schillergesellschaft, 1987.

Pauli, Karl. *Das Skelett im Hause. Lustspiel in 1 Akt nach Friedrich Spielhagen.* Kleines Theater. Paderborn: Kleine, 1893.

Pflanze, Otto. *Bismarck and the Development of Germany.* Princeton: Princeton UP, 1990.

Platner, S. B. »Wilhelm Scherer's Library.« *New Englander and Yale Review* 46 (1887): 383–86.

Plett, Bettina. *Problematische Naturen? Held und Heroismus im realistischen Erzählen.* Paderborn, Munich, Vienna, and Zurich: Schöningh, 2002.

Pollak, Gustav. »Friedrich Spielhagen.« *Nation* 92 (1911): 239–40.

Pompen, Gregor H. »Dichtung und Wahrheit – Spielhagen auf den Spuren Fontanes.« *Festgabe des Deutsche Instituts der Universität Nijmegen. Paul B. Wessels zum 65. Geburtstag,* ed. Hans Pörnbacher. Nijmegen: Dekker & van de Vegt, 1974, 112–30.

Prutz, Robert. [Review of *Problematische Naturen*]. *Literaturkritik. Eine Textdokumentation zur Geschichte einer literarischen Gattung,* ed. Alfred Estermann. Vol. 4, *1848–1870,* ed. Peter Uwe Hohendahl. Vaduz: Topos, 1984, 438–40.

Raabe, Wilhelm. *Sämtliche Werke.* Ed. Karl Hoppe et al. Göttingen: Vandenhoeck & Ruprecht, 1960–94.

Rarisch, Ilsedore. *Das Unternehmerbild in der deutschen Erzählliteratur der ersten Hälfte des 19. Jahrhunderts. Ein Beitrag zur Rezeption der frühen Industrialisierung in der belletristischen Literatur.* Berlin: Colloquium, 1977.

Rebing, Günter. *Der Halbbruder des Dichters. Friedrich Spielhagens Theorie des Romans.* Frankfurt am Main: Athenäum, 1972.

Restenberger, Anja. *Effi Briest: Historische Realität und literarische Fiktion in den Werken von Fontane, Spielhagen, Hochhuth, Brückner und Keuler.* Frankfurt am Main, Berlin, Bern, Brussels, New York, Oxford, and Vienna: Peter Lang, 2001.

Rhöse, Franz. *Konflikt und Versöhnung. Untersuchungen zur Theorie des Romans von Hegel bis zum Naturalismus.* Stuttgart: Metzler, 1978.

Richter, Johann Paul Friedrich. See Jean Paul.

Ridley, Hugh. »›Der Halbbruder des Vormärz‹: Friedrich Spielhagen. Reflexionen zu den Kontinuitäten seines Werkes.« *Formen der Wirklichkeitserfassung nach 1848. Deutsche Literatur und Kultur vom Nachmärz bis zur Gründerzeit in europäischer Perspektive,* I, ed. Helmut Koopmann and Michael Perraudin. Bielefeld: Aisthesis (2003), 217–31.

Rieder, Heinz. *Liberalismus als Lebensform in der deutschen Prosaepik des neunzehnten Jahrhunderts.* Germanische Studien, ed. Walter Hofstaetter, no. 212. Lübeck: Matthiesen, 1936. Reprint Nendeln: Kraus Reprint, 1967.

Rodenberg, Julius. »Briefe von Eduard Lasker. Nebst persönlichen Erinnerungen.« *Deutsche Rundschau* 38 (1884): 443–59.

Root, Winthrop H. *German Criticism of Zola 1875–1893 with Special Reference to the Rougon-Macquart Cycle and the Roman Expérimental.* New York: Columbia UP, 1931.

Roper, Katherine. »1848 in the Early Novels of Friedrich Spielhagen: The Making of a German Democrat.« *German Studies Review* 23 (2000): 427–52.

– »Friedrich Spielhagen (1829–1911).« *Dictionary of Literary Biography*, vol. 129. *Nineteenth-Century German Writers, 1841–1900*, ed. James Hardin and Siegfried Mews. Detroit and London: Gale Research, 1993, 348–60.

– *German Encounters with Modernity: Novels of Imperial Berlin.* Atlantic Highlands, New Jersey, and London: Humanities Press International, 1991.

– »Imagining the German Capital: Berlin Writers on the Two Unification Eras.« *1870/71 – 1989/90: German Unifications and the Change of Literary Discourse,* ed. Walter Pape. Berlin and New York: de Gruyter, 1993, 171–94.

Rosegger, Peter. *Mein Weltleben. Neue Folge. Erinnerungen eines siebzigjährigen.* Leipzig: Staackmann, 1914.

Sältzer, Rolf. *Entwicklungslinien der deutschen Zola-Rezeption von den Anfängen bis zum Tode des Autors.* Bern, Frankfurt am Main, New York, and Paris: Peter Lang, 1989.

Sagarra, Eda. »Spielhagen, Friedrich.« *Literatur Lexikon. Autoren und Werke deutscher Sprache.* Gütersloh and Munich: Bertelsmann Lexikon Verlag, 1988–93, 11: 106–08.

– *Tradition and Revolution: German Literature and Society 1830–1890.* London: Weidenfeld and Nicolson, 1971.

Sammons, Jeffrey L. »Friedrich Spielhagen: The Demon of Theory and the Decline of Reputation.« *A Companion to German Realism 1848–1900*, ed. Todd Kontje. Rochester: Camden House, 2002, 133–57.

– *Heinrich Heine: A Modern Biography.* Princeton: Princeton UP, 1979.

– »Raabe's Ravens.« *Imagination and History: Selected Papers on Nineteenth-Century German Literature.* New York, Bern, Frankfurt am Main, and Paris: Peter Lang, 1988, 281–300.

- [Review of Bernd, *Poetic Realism*]. *South Atlantic Review* 61, no. 3 (Summer 1996): 159–61.
- »Rückwirkende Assimilation. Betrachtungen zu den Heine-Studien von Karl Emil Franzos und Gustav Karpeles.« *Von Franzos zu Canetti: Jüdische Autoren aus Österreich. Neue Studien*, ed. Mark H. Gelber, Hans Otto Horch, and Sigurd Paul Scheichl. Tübingen: Niemeyer, 1996, 163–88.
- *Six Essays on the Young German Novel.* Chapel Hill: North Carolina UP, 1972.
- *Wilhelm Raabe: The Fiction of the Alternative Community.* Princeton: Princeton UP, 1987.
- »Wilhelm Raabe and his Reputation Among Jews and Anti-Semites.« *Identity and Ethos: A Festschrift for Sol Liptzin on the Occasion of his 85th Birthday*, ed. Mark H. Gelber. New York, Bern, and Frankfurt am Main: Peter Lang, 1986, 169–91.
- »Zu den Grundlagen des Antiamerikanismus in der deutschen Literatur.« *Alte Welten – neue Welten. Akten des IX. Kongresses der Internationalen Vereinigung für germanische Sprach- und Literaturwissenschaft*, vol. 1, *Plenarvorträge*, ed. Michael S. Batts. Tübingen: Niemeyer, 1996, 33–47.

Schafarschik, Walter. *Erläuterungen und Dokumente. Theodor Fontane. Effi Briest.* Stuttgart: Reclam, 1972.

Scherer, Wilhelm. *Geschichte der deutschen Litteratur.* Berlin: Weidmann, 1883.
- *Kleine Schriften zur neueren Litteratur, Kunst und Zeitgeschichte.* Berlin: Weidmann, 1893.
- »Zur Technik der modernen Erzählung.« *Deutsche Rundschau* 20 (1879): 151–58. Republished *Kleine Schriften*, 2: 159–70.

Scheuffelen, Thomas. *Berthold Auerbach 1812–1882. Marbacher Magazin.* Sonderheft, 36 (1985).

Schierding, Hermann. *Untersuchungen über die Romantechnik Friedrich Spielhagens (Unter Benutzung unveröffentlichter Manuskripte).* Borna-Leipzig: Noske, 1914.

Schiller, Friedrich. *Nationalausgabe.* Ed. Julius Petersen et al. Weimar: Böhlau, 1943- .

Schmidt, Julian. »Friedrich Spielhagen.« *Neue Bilder aus dem Geistigen Leben unserer Zeit.* Leipzig: Duncker & Humblot, 1873, 185–247.
- »Friedrich Spielhagen.« *Westermann's Jahrbuch der Illustrirten Deutschen Monatshefte* 29 (1870–71): 422–29

Schneider, Lothar. »Die Verabschiedung des idealistischen Realismus. Friedrich Spielhagens Romanpoetik und ihre Kritiker.« *Formen der Wirklichkeitserfassung nach 1848. Deutsche Literatur und Kultur vom Nachmärz bis zur Gründerzeit in europäischer Perspektive*, I, ed. Helmut Koopmann and Michael Perraudin. Bielefeld: Aisthesis, 2003, 233–44.

Schrader, Hans-Jürgen. »Gedichtete Dichtungstheorie im Werk Raabes. Exemplifiziert an ›Alte Nester.‹« *Jahrbuch der Raabe-Gesellschaft* (1989): 1–27.

Schröder, Rainer. »Hegels Rechtsphilosophie im realistischen Roman. Zu *Hammer und Amboß* von Friedrich Spielhagen.« *Erzählte Kriminalität. Zur Typologie und Funktion von narrativen Darstellungen in Strafrechtspflege, Publizistik und Literatur zwischen 1770 und 1920*, ed. Jörg Schönert with Konstantin Imm and Joachim Linder. Tübingen: Niemeyer, 1991, 413–28.

Schultz, Hans Martin. *Raabe-Schriften. Eine systematische Zusammenstellung.* Wolfenbüttel: Beckner, 1931.

Schumacher, Adolf. »Ferdinand Lassalle as a Novelistic Subject of Friedrich Spielhagen.« Diss. University of Pennsylvania, 1910.

Schwan, Alexander. »German Liberalism and the National Question in the Nineteenth Century.« *Nation Building in Central Europe*, ed. Hagen Schulze. Leamington Spa, Hamburg, and New York: Berg, 1987, 65–80.

Segeberg, Harro. *Literatur im technischen Zeitalter. Von der Frühzeit der deutschen Aufklärung bis zum Beginn des Ersten Weltkrieges.* Darmstadt: Wissenschaftliche Buchgesellschaft, 1997.

Seiffert, Hans Werner, with Christel Laufer. »Zeugnisse und Materialien zu Fontanes ›Effi Briest‹ und Spielhagens ›Zum Zeitvertreib.‹« *Studien zur neueren deutschen Literatur*, ed. Seiffert. Berlin: Akademie, 1964, 255–300.

Sembdner, Helmut, ed. *Heinrich von Kleists Lebensspuren. Dokumente und Berichte von Zeitgenossen.* Frankfurt am Main: Insel, 1984.

Smith, Steven B. *Spinoza, Liberalism, and the Question of Jewish Identity.* New Haven and London: Yale UP, 1997.

Spielhagen, Antonie. »Zum 80. Geburtstag Friedrich Spielhagens.« *Gartenlaube* [57] (1909): 166–69.

Spielhagen, Friedrich. *Alles fließt.* [Reclams Universal-Bibliothek, 4270.] Leipzig: Reclam, [1903].

- *Am Wege. Vermischte Schriften.* Leipzig: Staackmann, 1903.
- *Aus meinem Skizzenbuche.* Leipzig: Staackmann, 1874.
- *Aus meiner Studienmappe. Beitrage zur litterarischen Aesthetik und Kritik.* Berlin: Allgemeiner Verein für Deutsche Litteratur, 1891.
- *Ausgewählte Romane.* Leipzig: Staackmann, 1889–93.
- *Beiträge zur Theorie und Technik des Romans.* Leipzig: Staackmann, 1883. Reprint, ed. Hellmuth Himmel. Göttingen: Vandenhoeck & Ruprecht, 1967.
- »Briefe von Friedrich Spielhagen an den alten Heimgärtner.« *Roseggers Heimgarten* 35 (1911): 608–15.
- *Das Skelett im Hause*, ed. M. M. Skinner. Boston: Heath, 1913.
- *Die Dorfkokette.* Reclams Universal-Bibliothek, 4100. Leipzig: Reclam, 1900.
- *Finder und Erfinder. Erinnerungen aus meinem Leben.* Leipzig: Staackmann, 1890.
- »Friedrich Spielhagen an den Leser.« Berthold Auerbach, *Briefe an seinen Freund Jakob Auerbach. Biographisches Denkmal*, ed. Jakob Auerbach. Frankfurt am Main: Rütten & Loening, 1884.
- »Friedrich Spielhagen's Gruß an die ›New Yorker Staats-Zeitung.‹« *New Yorker Staats-Zeitung.* Sunday supplement, April 24, 1910, 3.
- [Funeral eulogy on Georg Westermann, appended to] »*In memoriam!*« *Westermanns Monatshefte* 48 (April-September 1880): 23–24.
- *Gedichte.* Leipzig: Staackmann, 1892.
- *Gerettet. Schauspiel in vier Akten.* Leipzig: Staackmann, 1884.
- *Goethe-Gallerie. Nach Original-Cartons von Wilhelm v. Kaulbach mit erläuterndem Text von Fr. Spielhagen.* Munich and Berlin: Bruckmann, n. d.
- *Goethe's Frauengestalten nach Originalzeichnungen von W. v. Kaulbach mit erläuterndem Text von Friedrich Spielhagen.* Munich: Bruckmann, n. d.
- *Hammer und Amboß.* Heyne Nostalgie Bibliothek. Munich: Heyne, 1975.
- *In eiserner Zeit. Trauerspiel in fünf Akten.* Leipzig: Staackmann, 1891.
- *Lady Clara Vere de Vere: A Story.* New York: Appleton, 1881.
- *Liebe für Liebe. Schauspiel in vier Acten.* Leipzig: Staackmann, 1875.
- *Mesmerismus. Alles fließt. Zwei Novellen.* 2nd edn. Leipzig: Staackmann, 1897.
- *Neue Beiträge zur Theorie und Technik der Epik und Dramatik.* Leipzig: Staackmann, 1898.
- *Neue Gedichte.* Leipzig: Staackmann, 1899.

- *Platt Land.* Recklinghausen: Manuscriptum, 1996.
- *Romane. Neue Folge.* Leipzig: Staackmann, 1906.
- *The Skeleton in the House.* Tr. M. J. Safford. New York: Harlan, 1881.
- *The Skeleton in the House.* The Lock and Key Library: The Most Interesting Stories of All Nations, ed. Julian Hawthorne. New York: Review of Reviews, 1915.
- *Sturmflut.* Ed. Wolfgang Gabler. Rostock: Hinstorff, 1996.
- *Vermischte Schriften.* 2 vols. Berlin: Janke, 1864–68.
- *Vermischte Schriften. Neue, vom Verfasser revidirte Ausgabe. Sämmtliche Werke,* vol. 7. Berlin: Janke, [1870].
- *Von Neapel bis Syrakus. Reiseskizzen.* Leipzig: Staackmann, 1878.
- »Vorwort.« *Frau von Staël's Corinna oder Italien.* Tr. M. Block. Leipzig: Bibliographisches Institut, n. d.
- *Was die Schwalbe sang.* Reclams Universal-Bibliothek, 4138. Leipzig: Reclam, 1900.
- *What the Swallow Sang.* Tr. Ms. New York: Holt & Williams, 1873.
- »Wie die ›Problematischen Naturen‹ entstanden.« *Die Geschichte des Erstlingswerks. Selbstbiographische Aufsätze,* ed. Karl Emil Franzos. Berlin: Concordia Deutsche Verlags-Anstalt, [1894], 33–50.
- tr. *Daphne. Nach A Diplomat's Diary von Julien Gordon, deutsch bearbeitet von Friedrich Spielhagen.* Engelhorn's allgemeine Roman-Bibliothek. Stuttgart: Engelhorn, 1891.
- tr. *Das Meer* (Jules Michelet). Leipzig: Weber, 1861.
- tr. *Die Frau* (Jules Michelet). Leipzig: Weber, 1860.
- tr. *Die Liebe* (Jules Michelet). Leipzig: Weber, 1859.
- tr. *Englische Charakteristiken* (Ralph Waldo Emerson). Hanover: Meyer, 1857.
- tr. »Glitzer-Brita« (Hjalmar Hjorth Boyesen). *Westermanns Monatshefte* 46 (April–September 1879): 673–90.
- tr. *Leben Lorenzo de' Medici genannt der Prächtige* (William Roscoe). Leipzig: Senf, 1861.
- tr. *Mademoiselle Reseda* (Julien Gordon). Michow-Bücher, vol. 16. Charlottenburg: Michow, 1898.
- tr. *Nil-Skizzen eines Howadji; oder der Amerikaner in Aegypten* (George William Curtis). Hanover: Meyer, 1856
- tr. *Novellen von Hjalmar Hjorth Boyesen. Glitzer-Brita. Einer, der seinen Namen verlor. Deutsch von Friedrich Spielhagen. Ein Ritter von Dannebrog. Deutsch von * * *.* Engelhorn's Allgemeine Romanbibliothek, erster Jahrgang, vol. 23. Stuttgart: Engelhorn, 1885.

Spiero, Heinrich. *Geschichte des deutschen Romans.* Berlin: de Gruyter, 1950.

Spuler, Richard. *»Germanistik« in America: The Reception of German Classicism, 1870–1905.* Stuttgart: Heinz, 1982.

Stahr, Adolf. *Aus Adolf Stahrs Nachlaß. Briefe von Stahr nebst Briefe an ihn.* Ed. Ludwig Geiger. Oldenburg: Schulze, 1903.

Steiner, Carl. *Karl Emil Franzos 1848–1904: Emancipator and Assimilationist.* New York, Bern, Frankfurt am Main, and Paris: Peter Lang, 1990.

Stern, Fritz. *Gold and Iron: Bismarck, Bleichröder, and the Building of the German Empire.* New York: Knopf, 1977.

Sternberger, Dolf. *Panorama oder Ansichten vom 19. Jahrhundert.* Frankfurt am Main: Suhrkamp, 1974.

Stifter, Adalbert. *Gesammelte Werke in vierzehn Bänden.* Ed. Konrad Steffen. Basel and Stuttgart: Birkhäuser, 1961–72.

Streit, Claudia. *(Re-)Konstruktion von Familie im sozialen Roman des 19. Jahrhunderts.* Frankfurt am Main, Berlin, Bern, New York, Paris, and Vienna: Peter Lang, 1997.

Strodtmann, Adolf. »Friedrich Spielhagen.« *Dichterprofile. Literaturbilder aus dem neunzehnten Jahrhundert.* Vol. 1. *Deutsche Dichtercharaktere.* Stuttgart: Abenheim, 1879, 195–212.

Swales, Martin. »Melodramen des bürgerlichen Bewußtseins (Friedrich Spielhagen).« *Epochenbuch Realismus: Romane und Erzählungen.* Berlin: Erich Schmidt, 1997, 102–07.

Tatum, John Hargrove. *The Reception of German Literature in U. S. German Texts 1864–1918.* New York, Bern, Frankfurt am Main, and Paris: Peter Lang, 1988.

Tennyson, Alfred, Lord. *The Poems of Tennyson.* Ed. Christopher Ricks. London: Longman; New York: Norton, 1969.

Turner, David. »Marginalien und Handschriftliches zum Thema: Fontane und Spielhagens Theorie der ›Objektivität.‹« *Fontane Blätter* 1 (1968–69): 265–81.

Tyrell, Thomas. »Theodor Fontanes ›Effi Briest‹ und Friedrich Spielhagens ›Zum Zeitvertreib‹: Zwei Dichtungen zu einer Wirklichkeit.« Diss. Rice University, 1986.

Viering, Jürgen. »›In welcher Welt der schauderhaften Widersprüche leben wir!‹ Überlegungen zum ›Zeitroman‹ bei Fontane und Spielhagen am Beispiel von Fontanes *Effi Briest* und Spielhagens *Zum Zeitvertreib.«* *Literatur und Sprache im historischen Prozeß. Vorträge des Deutschen Germanistentages Aachen 1982,* ed. Thomas Cramer. Tübingen: Niemeyer, 1983, 1: 329–45.

Walker, Mack. *German Home Towns: Community, State, and General Estate 1648–1871.* Ithaca and London: Cornell UP, 1971.

Walzel, Oskar. »Objektive Erzählung.« *Das Wortkunstwerk. Mittel seiner Erforschung.* Leipzig: Quelle & Meyer, 1926, 182–206.

Wehler, Hans-Ulrich. *Deutsche Gesellschaftsgeschichte.* Vol. 3: *Von der »Deutschen Doppelrevolution« bis zum Beginn des Ersten Weltkrieges 1849–1914.* Munich: Beck, 1995.

Wellek, René. *Concepts of Criticism.* Ed. Stephen G. Nichols, Jr. New Haven and London: Yale UP, 1963.

Wermuth, Paul C. *Bayard Taylor.* New York: Twayne, 1973.

Wilson, Edmund. *To the Finland Station: A Study in the Writing and Acting of History.* New York: Farrar, Straus and Giroux, 1972.

Worthmann, Joachim. *Probleme des Zeitromans. Studien zur Geschichte des deutschen Romans im 19. Jahrhundert.* Heidelberg: Winter, 1974.

Zimmern, Helen and Alice. »Spielhagen.« *Half-Hours with Foreign Novelists.* London: Remington, 1880, 189–215.

Zinken, Rosa Maria. *Der Roman als Zeitdokument. Bürgerlicher Liberalismus in Friedrich Spielhagens »Die von Hohenstein« (1863/64).* Frankfurt am Main, Bern, New York, and Paris: Peter Lang, 1991.

Zola, Emile. *Œuvres complètes.* Ed. Henri Mitterand et al. Paris: Cercle du Livre Précieux, 1966–68.

Index of Spielhagen's Works *

---

* To reduce clutter, the index is restricted to fictional, poetic, and dramatic works.

Index of Names

337